AF836631

THE UNITED KINGDOM AND THE FEDERAL IDEA

How should political power be divided within and among national peoples? Is the nineteenth-century theory of the sovereign and unitary State still fit for purpose in the twenty-first century? If not, can federalism provide a viable alternative model? This collection looks at federalism from the perspective of constitutional law. Taking the United Kingdom as a case study, Part One tracks the historical evolution of the 'Union' and explores the various expressions of federalism that emerged between the eighteenth and twentieth centuries. Part Two then assesses the experience of sovereignty-sharing with other nations in the context of international cooperation. Drawing on the expertise of the foremost commentators in their field, The United Kingdom and the Federal Idea provides a timely and reflective evaluation of how constitutional authority is being re-ordered within and beyond the United Kingdom.

The United Kingdom and the Federal Idea

Edited by
Robert Schütze and Stephen Tierney

• HART •
OXFORD • LONDON • NEW YORK • NEW DELHI • SYDNEY

HART PUBLISHING
Bloomsbury Publishing Plc
Kemp House, Chawley Park, Cumnor Hill, Oxford, OX2 9PH, UK

HART PUBLISHING, the Hart/Stag logo, BLOOMSBURY and the Diana logo are trademarks of Bloomsbury Publishing Plc

First published in Great Britain 2018

Copyright © The editors and contributors severally 2018

The editors and contributors have asserted their right under the Copyright, Designs and Patents Act 1988 to be identified as Authors of this work.

All rights reserved. No part of this publication may be reproduced or transmitted in any form or by any means, electronic or mechanical, including photocopying, recording, or any information storage or retrieval system, without prior permission in writing from the publishers.

While every care has been taken to ensure the accuracy of this work, no responsibility for loss or damage occasioned to any person acting or refraining from action as a result of any statement in it can be accepted by the authors, editors or publishers.

All UK Government legislation and other public sector information used in the work is Crown Copyright ©. All House of Lords and House of Commons information used in the work is Parliamentary Copyright ©. This information is reused under the terms of the Open Government Licence v3.0 (http://www.nationalarchives.gov.uk/doc/open-government-licence/version/3) except where otherwise stated.

All Eur-lex material used in the work is © European Union, http://eur-lex.europa.eu/, 1998–2018.

A catalogue record for this book is available from the British Library.

Library of Congress Cataloging-in-Publication data

Names: Schütze, Robert, editor. | Tierney, Stephen, editor.

Title: The United Kingdom and the federal idea / edited by Robert Schütze and Stephen Tierney.

Description: Oxford : Hart Publishing, 2018. | "This edited collection … originates in a workshop organised at Durham in late 2015, which was kindly supported by the European Research Council."—ECIP Preface. | Includes bibliographical references and index.

Identifiers: LCCN 2018000171 (print) | LCCN 2018000940 (ebook) | ISBN 9781509907168 (Epub) | ISBN 9781509907175 (hardback)

Subjects: LCSH: Federal government—Great Britain—Congresses.

Classification: LCC KD4025.A75 (ebook) | LCC KD4025.A75 U55 2017 (print) | DDC 342.41/042—dc23

LC record available at https://lccn.loc.gov/2018000171

ISBN: HB: 978-1-50990-717-5
ePDF: 978-1-50990-715-1
ePub: 978-1-50990-716-8

Typeset by Compuscript Ltd, Shannon

To find out more about our authors and books visit www.hartpublishing.co.uk. Here you will find extracts, author information, details of forthcoming events and the option to sign up for our newsletters.

EDITORS' PREFACE

How should political power be divided within and among national peoples? Can the nineteenth-century theory of the sovereign and unitary State be applied to the world of the twenty-first century? If not, what constitutional and philosophical theories can make sense of the empirical and normative world of our times? There are no convincing answers to these questions today, as contemporary constitutional and legal theory are yet to 'come to terms' with two new international and national phenomena. First, the rise of international organisations and—within Europe—the emergence of the European Union, have severely challenged the idea of the sovereign State from *outside*. And, second, at the very same time, the myth of monolithic state power has also come under attack from *within* many states where there has been a concerted move towards ever-greater political and constitutional devolution.

How can we make sense of these social and legal developments? Can we identify them with federal theory? The federal principle represents a legal structure that attempts to find 'unity in diversity'. Yet international and constitutional federalism continues to be—largely—misunderstood by mainstream legal scholarship. This edited collection wishes to fill—a part of—this theoretical gap by providing a constitutional analysis of the federal principle within and without the United Kingdom. Despite its formation as a Union of States, the United Kingdom has traditionally been understood as a unitary state, with one central parliament assuming exclusive and unlimited legislative power within an unwritten constitution. However, starting with the devolution arrangements at the end of the twentieth century and the recent Scottish referendum, a new—federal—discourse is gaining ground. A similar sense of uncertainty pertains to Britain's involvement in international or 'federal' structures. Indeed, the United Kingdom's relationship within the European Union—a federation of States—has never been easy; but can the same be said about other international organisations, such as the Council of Europe as well as the United Nations?

The debate about 'federal' Britain and Britain's future within 'federalising' international orders is now a rapidly contested one in light of proposals for radical constitutional change following the Scottish referendum and due to a dramatic reorientation of the UK's relationship with the European Union and possibly the Council of Europe. The time is therefore more than ripe for a reflective stocktaking of how constitutional authority is being reordered both within and beyond the United Kingdom. This edited collection wishes to contribute to the reflections and revaluations of these broader constitutional and conceptual problems.

It originates in a workshop organised at Durham in late 2015, which was kindly supported by the European Research Council (EU Framework Programme 2007-13: ERC Grant Agreement No 312 304). We, the editors, would like to thank Durham and Edinburgh Universities, and in particular Ms Maria Perez-Crespo for her brilliant and dedicated research and editorial assistance. With regard to Figure 1, grateful acknowledgements go to Max Galka and metrocosm.com, where a number of beautiful illustrations on the "absurdly confusing lands of the British Crown" can be found.

SUMMARY CONTENTS

DETAILED CONTENTS

Part I. Historical Evolution: From Past to Present

Part II. In Particular: The External Dimension

LIST OF CONTRIBUTORS

David Armitage is the Lloyd C Blankfein Professor of History at Harvard University.

Lorand Bartels is a Reader in International Law in the Faculty of Law and a Fellow of Trinity Hall at the University of Cambridge.

Barbara Guastaferro is Assistant Professor of Constitutional Law at the University of Naples 'Federico II'.

Alvin Jackson is Sir Richard Lodge Professor of History at the University of Edinburgh.

Roger Masterman is Professor of Law at Durham University.

Jo Eric Khushal Murkens is an Associate Professor of Law at the London School of Economics and Political Science.

Peter Oliver is Vice Dean Research and Professor of Law at the University of Ottawa.

Lucia Payero-Lopez is a Lecturer in Law at the University of Oviedo.

Robert Schütze is Professor of European Law and Co-Director of the Durham Global Policy Institute.

Sionaidh Douglas-Scott holds the Anniversary Chair in Law at Queen Mary University of London (QMUL) and is Co-director of the Centre for Law and Society in a Global Context.

Stephen Tierney is Professor of Constitutional Theory at the University of Edinburgh and Director of the Edinburgh Centre for Constitutional Law.

Adam Tomkins holds the John Millar Chair of Public Law at Glasgow University.

Nigel D White is Professor of Public International Law at the University of Nottingham and Co-Director of the Nottingham International Law and Security Centre.

TABLE OF CASES

British and Commonwealth Cases

Other Jurisdictions

Canada

European Convention on Human Rights

European Union Cases

International and WTO Cases

Italy

Spain

United States

TABLE OF LEGISLATION

British and Commonwealth Legislation

International Agreements and EU Treaties

Introduction: British 'Federalism'?

ROBERT SCHÜTZE*

I. From England to United Kingdom: Internal Structures

The United Kingdom is decidedly not a federal State. Centred on one—sovereign—Parliament, its legal structure is that of a unitary State; yet unlike classic 'unitary' States, it houses not just one but 'four nations' within its constitutional borders.[1] The United Kingdom is therefore sometimes described as a 'union';[2] or, more often, it is characterised as a 'Union State'.[3] But if the idea of a Union State is quite the same as that of a unitary State, what distinguishes it from the latter; and are there characteristics that bring it within the conceptual vicinity of a federal state or a federal union? The federal principle has remained 'alien' to British constitutional thought. According to the perhaps best-known British definition of constitutional federalism, the principle refers to 'the method of dividing powers so that the general and regional governments are each, within a sphere, coordinate and independent'.[4]

Can we find instances of such coordination and independence in the constitutional history of what has become the United Kingdom of Great Britain and Northern Ireland? And how did the 'United Kingdom' come about; what is 'Great Britain', and why is only the northern part of Ireland incorporated? The modern 'British' story begins of course with 'England', whose incorporation of Wales

* Thanks go to Katrin Flikschuh and Roger Masterman for excellent advice and helpful suggestions. Whenever this chapter refers to a piece of parliamentary legislation or an international treaty, it has tried to use the modern 'official' version available under www.legislation.gov.uk; yet for older statutes, it occasionally uses 'Pickering's Statutes at Large' which can be found here: http://statutes.org.uk/site/collections/british-and-irish/pickering-statutes-at-large/.

1 House of Lords, Select Committee on the Constitution, English Votes for English Laws (House of Lords Paper 61, 2016), para 1.

2 B Hadfield, 'Devolution, Westminster and the English Question' (2005) *Public Law* 286: '[T]he United Kingdom is both a Union and a unitary state'.

3 The notion was made popular by N MacCormick, *Questioning Sovereignty* (Oxford, OUP, 1999); and see also: N Walker, 'Beyond the Unitary Conception of the United Kingdom Constitution?' (2000) *Public Law* 384; as well as S Tierney, *Constitutional Law and National Pluralism* (Oxford, OUP, 2006).

4 K Wheare, *Federal Government* (Oxford, Oxford University Press, 1953) 11.

through conquest is formally recognised by two sixteenth-century 'Acts of Union'.[5] The association and integration of Scotland subsequently emerges as a constitutional question in the seventeenth century (Section A below). The Irish 'question' would then occupy much of the eighteenth and nineteenth centuries (Section B). Within the twentieth century, finally, the processes of incorporation were to be complemented by a reverse process of legislative devolution that has created 'regional' legislatures and governments (Section C). This first section wishes to offer a short overview of the various 'internal' structures resulting from the formation and administration of the United Kingdom. A second section explores, by contrast, the 'external' structures in the constitutional history of the British Empire-turned-Commonwealth.

A. Forming the United Kingdom I: The 'Scottish Question'

With the death of Elizabeth I, James VI of Scotland had also become the king of England; yet this 'union of the crowns' was a 'personal union'—not a political union.[6] While 'sharing' the same executive, the two kingdoms had retained their separate parliaments and therewith their distinct statehoods. For contemporaries, the 'union of the crowns' seemed to have created a political monster: a head with two distinct bodies.[7] This 'constitutional problem without precedent' demanded a solution;[8] but the search for a more 'perfect union' between the two States took some time.

After a hundred years of constitutional crises and uncertainties, no permanent solution to the Scottish problem had been found. But worse: with the English and the Scottish crown having become vacant by the end of the seventeenth century, the loose personal union between the two States became itself endangered. To settle the succession, the English Parliament therefore unilaterally decided—in 1701—to place the English Crown into the hands of its preferred new monarch.[9] The Scottish response was the Act of Security 1704, which prohibited any union of crowns unless 'there be such conditions of government settled and enacted as may secure the honour and sovereignty of this Crown and Kingdom, the freedom,

[5] The constitutional status of Wales remained vague until 1535 when Henry VIII clarified it through an 'Act of Union' which declared that the 'said country or dominion of Wales shall be, stand and continue for ever from henceforth incorporated, united and annexed to and with this realm of England'. Wales would henceforth be governed by 'the laws, ordinances and statutes of this realm of England, for ever, *and none other laws*' (ibid). This constitutional 'annexation' would become so 'absolute' that in 1747 a parliamentary statute established the simple rule 'that in acts of parliament the name England should be deemed to include Wales' (FM Maitland, *The Constitutional History of England* (Cambridge, Cambridge University Press, 1908) 330).

[6] The distinction builds on the notion of dual majesty. On the theory of the king's two bodies, see the magisterial study by E Kantorowicz, *The King's Two Bodies: A Study in Mediaeval Political Theology* (Princeton, Princeton University Press, 1998).

[7] BP Levack, *The Formation of the British State: England, Scotland and the Union, 1603–1707* (Oxford, Clarendon Press, 1987) 7.

[8] PP Scott, *1707: The Union of Scotland and England* (Edinburgh, Saltire Society, 1979) 4.

[9] See 1701 Act of Settlement.

frequency and power of parliaments, the religion, liberty and trade of the nation from English or any foreign influence'.[10] This Scottish retaliation prompted the English Parliament to adopt the 'Alien Act 1705',[11] which—despite its threatening message—nevertheless proposed to solve the constitutional problem of the succession through a treaty of union between the two States.

What legal possibilities to 'consolidate' the union between England and Scotland were known at the end of the seventeenth century? While the idea of a political 'union' did not have a single meaning,[12] the debate on what kind of union could be established quickly produced two rival categories: the 'incorporating union' and the 'federal union'. They were characterised as follows:

> The Title of an Incorporating Union denotes that Kind, whereby distinct and independent Kingdoms and Dominions parting with their Distinction, and Independency do so unite themselves with another Kingdom, as to be embodied with it, and to become a particular Part, Province, or District of the Kingdom with which they do so Unite, being subject to the Laws and Government thereof. … A Confederate or Federal Union is that, whereby Distinct, Free, and Independent Kingdoms, Dominions or States, do unite their separate Interests into one common Interest, for the mutual benefit of both, so far as relates to certain Conditions and Articles agreed upon betwixt them, retaining in the mean time their several Independencies, National Distinctions, and the different Laws, Customs, and Government of each.[13]

The distinction between 'incorporating union' and 'federal union' here mapped onto the distinction between a 'united' State and 'separate' States. Various political bodies could, by means of incorporation, subject themselves to *one* (new) government and henceforth form one state; whereas States in a federal union would retain their different governments and therefore 'their several independencies'. Scotland generally favoured a 'federal' union with two independent parliaments,[14] while the federal idea was deeply irritating to England. For not only had seventeenth-century English constitutional theory come to insist that sovereignty could not be divided;[15] in political practice, there was no English appetite to 'share' power on equal terms. The sole constitutional and political option consequently seemed the creation of an incorporating union.

[10] Quoted in Scott, above n 8, 14.

[11] The Alien Act deprived Scottish denizens of their rights under *Calvin's Case* (and imposed an economic embargo on Scottish products). For a copy of the case, see: http://oll.libertyfund.org/titles/coke-selected-writings-of-sir-edward-coke-vol-i--5.

[12] Cf BP Levack, 'English Law, Scots Law and the Union, 1603–1707' in A Harding (ed), *Law-making and law-makers in British history* (London, Royal Historical Society, 1980) 105.

[13] J Hodges, *The Rights and Interests of the Two British Monarchies* (Caledonia Coffee-House, 1703) 2–4.

[14] ibid, 8. This support for a federal union also came from Andrew Fletcher of Saltoun—perhaps 'the' Scottish political thinker of the period. In his *State of the Controversy betwixt United and Separate Parliaments* (1706—reprinted for the Saltire Society by Blackwood Publishing, 1982), we find a passionate plea against an 'incorporating union', which he thought bedevilled by 'many insuperable Difficulties' (ibid, 29).

[15] For a discussion of the long path to this discovery, see: JR Tanner, *English Constitutional Conflicts of the Seventeenth Century, 1693–1689* (Cambridge, Cambridge University Press, 1962).

What was the legal nature of this incorporating union? The Union of England and Scotland was to be based on an 'international' treaty—the 'Articles of Union' that had to be ratified by both States.[16] Once this happened, the two kingdoms of England and Scotland would be 'united into *one* kingdom': the United Kingdom of Great Britain.[17] This was a new State whose constitutional structure was spelled out in Articles II and III of the Union Treaty. Here, the crown was permanently united,[18] while the new 'Great Britain' would 'be represented by one and the same Parliament': the British Parliament.[19] The new Union was therefore more than an 'executive' union; it was a 'legislative' Union.[20]

But was this legislative union a 'national' union that also united the two nations of Scotland and England into one 'British' people? Article IV of the Treaty of Union spoke of 'the subjects *of the United Kingdom of Great Britain*' but it only guaranteed the 'communication of all other rights, privileges, and advantages which do or may belong to the subjects of either kingdom'. This principle of 'mutual recognition' signalled that the 'incorporating union' was only 'the union of the two states—not the union of two peoples'.[21]

B. Forming the United Kingdom II: The 'Irish Question'

The status of Ireland within English constitutional law had long remained ambivalent. It was partly clarified in 1542 when Ireland became a 'kingdom' whose

[16] Parliamentary ratification was the traditional route for both States. The idea of holding a referendum, albeit broached by the Scottish advocates of federal union, was rejected in the Scottish Parliament, see: W Ferguson, *Scotland's Relations with England* (Edinburgh, John Donald Publishers, 1977) 257.

[17] 1707 Union Treaty, Art I (emphasis added). Importantly, and unlike Wales, Scotland was not 'incorporated' into England, but both England and Scotland were equally incorporated into the new state. However, for many this formal equality masked a marked political asymmetry, see only: AI Macinnes, *Union and Empire: The Making of the United Kingdom* (Cambridge, Cambridge University Press, 2007) esp 5 as well as 316: 'Scottish representation was less than that for the counties of Devon and Cornwall, a tangible indication that the Union marked the culmination of England's intrusive hegemony throughout the seventeenth century.'

[18] 1707 Union Treaty, Art II.

[19] 1707 Union Treaty, Art III. This 'new' parliament would be composed of English and Scottish commoners and peers. The English numbers would remain the same, while Scotland was entitled to forty-five commoners and sixteen peers (ibid, Art XXII). When compared to the English representation, Scottish representation within the Westminster Parliament here followed a ratio of 12:1—a ratio that significantly overrepresented the English over the Scottish population (ratio 5:1).

[20] As regard the judicial function, by contrast, Scotland had insisted on the continuance of Scottish law. With the exception of laws concerning regulation of trade, customs and excises 'all other laws in use within the kingdom of Scotland do, after the Union, and notwithstanding thereof, remain in the same force as before (except such as are contrary to or inconsistent with this Treaty)' (ibid, Art XVIII). Scottish laws that did not violate the Union Treaty retained their legal validity (ibid, Art XXV); yet, they would generally be 'alterable by the Parliament of Great Britain' and thus be subject to the supremacy of the Westminster Parliament. The interpretation of Scottish laws was moreover left in the hands of the Scottish judiciary, for the autonomy of the Scottish judiciary was principally guaranteed (ibid, Art XIX).

[21] Levack, above n 7, 198.

monarch would formally coincide with the king of England.[22] This union was however more than a personal union. For under English constitutional law, Ireland had been conquered and annexed to England.[23] But did its conquered status imply its subordination to the English Parliament? According to *Calvin's Case*, this was indeed so;[24] yet doubts remained until the English Civil War; and after the 'Glorious Revolution', the Irish question gained new momentum.

i. British Parliamentary Sovereignty: From Colony to Incorporation

Following the Glorious Revolution, Ireland began to contest its 'colonial' status under the English Constitution. Pointing to its 'own' legislative and judicial institutions, one popular argument here asserted that Ireland was solely connected to England via an (executive) royal 'union'.[25] This view compared Ireland to Scotland before the 1707 Union Treaty; and this view was endorsed by the Irish House of Lords.[26]

This interpretation was firmly opposed by the British Parliament which responded with the 1719 Declaratory Act.[27] The latter declared that the British Parliament 'had, hath and of right ought to have full power and authority to make laws and statutes of sufficient force and validity, to bind the kingdom and the people of Ireland'.[28] Under British constitutional law, Ireland was '*a distinct kingdom*, though a dependent subordinate kingdom'; and this meant, with regard to Westminster parliamentary sovereignty, that 'where Ireland is particularly named, or is included under general words, they are bound by such acts of parliament'.[29] This British right to 'superiority' was seen to derive from 'the right of conquest: a right allowed by the law of nations, if not by that of nature'.[30]

This 'Westminster' view was however dropped in the aftermath of American independence. The Declaratory Act was repealed in 1782; and only a year later the British Parliament would recognise that Ireland should be *exclusively* governed

[22] See Crown of Ireland Act 1542.

[23] This was confirmed after the Glorious Revolution, see only: P Kelly, 'Ireland and the Glorious Revolution: From Kingdom to Colony' in R Beddard (ed), *The Revolutions of 1688* (Oxford, Clarendon Press, 1991) 163.

[24] For a copy of the case, see above n 11. The case distinguished between kingdoms by 'descent' and kingdoms by 'conquest'; and while Scotland was considered to belong to the former class, Ireland fell into the latter category.

[25] The famous pamphlet here is W Molyneux's 'The Case of Ireland being bound by Acts of Parliament in England, Stated' (Dublin, 1698), which can be found under: http://oll.libertyfund.org/titles/molyneux-the-case-of-ireland-being-bound-by-acts-of-parliament-in-england-stated.

[26] For an extensive discussion of this point, see: MS Flaherty, 'The Empire Strikes Back: *Annesley v Sherlock* and the Triumph of Imperial Parliamentary Supremacy' (1987) 87 *Columbia Law Review* 593.

[27] For a copy of the Act, see: http://statutes.org.uk/site/the-statutes/eighteenth-century/1719-6-george-1-5-irish-dependency-act/.

[28] ibid.

[29] W Blackstone, *Commentaries on the Laws of England* (1765) (editor: TM Cooley, Callaghan, 1899) 89–90.

[30] ibid, 92.

by the *Irish* Parliament.[31] This British 'cession' transformed Ireland into an 'independent' and 'coordinate' kingdom. Yet this independence was not to last too long: after a proposal for a commercial Union between Ireland and Britain had failed,[32] Britain quickly pushed for an Anglo-Irish 'Union Treaty' that was modelled on the 1707 Union Treaty with Scotland.[33] And in 1800, the British and the Irish Parliament indeed 'severally agreed' to adopt their respective Acts of Union which would see Great Britain and Ireland 'incorporated' into a new third State: the United Kingdom of *Great Britain and Ireland*.[34]

ii. The Quest for Irish 'Home Rule': Independence and Devolution

After the Union with Great Britain, the constitutional status of Ireland was akin to that of Scotland; yet in some important respects it also retained a unique position within the (new) United Kingdom.[35]

This unique status came to the fore in the nineteenth century, especially the second half of that century, when 'Great Britain' and 'Ireland' entered a lasting and severe political crisis. Ireland had long pressed for 'Home Rule'—an early form of devolution.[36] Yet the 'Home Rule' question remained unresolved until the outbreak of the First World War; and after the Great War, the Government of Ireland Act 1920 aimed to solve the problem once and for all. It thereby took the dramatic step of—administratively—partitioning Ireland into 'Northern Ireland' and 'Southern Ireland' with both parts granted 'home rule' through their respective regional parliaments.

These devolution arrangements however came too late for Southern Ireland. Wishing to break free from British rule altogether, a War of Independence led to the 1921 Anglo-Irish Peace Treaty that created the 'Irish Free State'. Irish independence meant 'legislative' independence—though it at first accepted 'dominion' status within the British Empire.[37] Independence had thereby been offered to all

[31] In 1782, the Irish Parliament repealed Poynings' law; and to remove all doubts that the 'Declaratory Act' had been repealed, the Westminster Parliament also adopted, in 1783, the Irish Appeals Act (Renunciation Act), whose first section stated: 'That the said right claimed by the people of Ireland, to be bound only by laws enacted by his Majesty and the parliament of that kingdom, in all cases whatever, and to have all actions and suits at law or in equity, which may be instituted in that kingdom, decided in his Majesty's courts therein finally, and without appeal from thence, shall be, and is hereby declared to be established and ascertained for ever, and shall at no time hereafter be questioned or questionable.'

[32] For a discussion of this point, see: J Livesey, 'Free Trade and Empire in the Anglo-Irish Commercial Propositions of 1785' (2013) 52 *Journal of British Studies* 103.

[33] J Kelly, 'The origins of the Act of Union: an examination of unionist opinion in Britain and Ireland, 1650–1800' (1987) 25 *Irish Historical Studies* 236 at 259.

[34] Union with Ireland Act 1800, Art I. That new state was represented by 'one and the same Parliament, to be stiled the Parliament of the United Kingdom of Great Britain and Ireland' (ibid, Art III).

[35] Maitland, above n 5, 336.

[36] For an excellent historical account here, see: A O'Day, *Irish Home Rule 1867–1921* (Manchester, Manchester University Press, 1998). See also A Jackson's chapter in this volume.

[37] 1921 Anglo-Irish Peace Treaty, Art 1: 'Ireland shall have the same constitutional status in the Community of Nations known as the British Empire as the Dominion of Canada, the Commonwealth of Australia, the Dominion of New Zealand, and the Union of South Africa, with a Parliament having powers to make laws for the peace, order and good government of Ireland and an Executive responsible to that parliament, and shall be styled and known as the Irish Free State.'.

of Ireland; yet in light of the political differences between the northern and the southern parts, the 1921 Treaty envisaged the possibility of a Northern Irish 'opt-out';[38] and since this opt-out was requested, 'Northern Ireland' remained a region within the United Kingdom.

What was the status of Northern Ireland under the Government of Ireland Act 1920? The latter created a 'Parliament' for Northern Ireland that was endowed with 'legislative powers'.[39] The 'Stormont' Parliament was however a subordinate legislature;[40] and according to section 75 of the Act, 'the supreme authority of the Parliament of the United Kingdom' had remained 'unaffected and undiminished' over all of Northern Ireland.[41] This devolution-like system was only suspended, 50 years later, when a conflict between a 'Unionist' majority and a 'nationalist' minority escalated; and the Northern Ireland Constitution Act 1973 replaced 'home rule' with 'direct rule'. Under this arrangement, a Northern Irish 'Assembly' continued to exercise legislative powers,[42] but the executive power would be 'directly' held in the hands of the British cabinet.[43]

C. Devolving the United Kingdom: The 'English Question'

The constitutional arrangements among its component 'nations' had—with the exception of the Irish question—hardly been an issue within British political debates until the 1970s.[44] Thereafter, devolution questions gradually emerged. Discovering a degree of over-centralisation within the United Kingdom, the 1973 Report of the 'Royal Commission on the Constitution' (Kilbrandon Report) suggested the establishment of representative institutions within Scotland and Wales.[45] Yet despite the passing of the 1978 Scotland and Wales Acts, the legislatively required devolution referendums within Scotland and Wales were lost and devolution would thus have to wait for another 20 years.

In the wake of 'New Labour''s constitutional agenda and following two successful referendums in 1997, the Westminster Parliament finally adopted a Scotland Act

[38] ibid, Art 12.

[39] Section 4 of the Government of Ireland Act 1920 gave the Parliament of Northern Ireland the 'power to make laws for the peace, order, and good government' within its territorial jurisdiction, while this power was expressly excluded for certain enumerated 'reserved' matters.

[40] ibid, s 6(2) of the 1920 Act stated: 'Where any Act of the Parliament of Southern Ireland or the Parliament of Northern Ireland deals with any matter with respect to which that Parliament has power to make laws which is dealt with by any Act of the Parliament of the United Kingdom passed after the appointed day and extending to the part of Ireland within its jurisdiction, the Act of the Parliament of Southern Ireland or the Parliament of Northern Ireland shall be read subject to the Act of the Parliament of the United Kingdom, and so far as it is repugnant to that Act, but no further, shall be void.'

[41] ibid, s 75.

[42] Northern Ireland Constitution Act 1973, s 4(1).

[43] ibid, s 7(2).

[44] See only: V Bogdanor, *Devolution in the United Kingdom* (Oxford, Oxford University Press, 1998) 166: 'After the settlement of the Irish problem in 1920–1, devolution disappeared from the British political agenda.'

[45] For a brief academic discussion of the Report, see: T Daintith, 'Kilbrandon: The Ship that launched a Thousand Faces' (1974) 37 *Modern Law Review* 544.

and a Government of Wales Act in 1998. They were—after the conclusion of the 'Good Friday Agreement'—joined by a third act: the Northern Ireland Act 1998.

Originally, the three 'devolution' acts were quite different.[46] These differences have however largely disappeared with subsequent amendments.[47] Focusing on the Scottish devolution model, four core principles can today be identified. First, all devolution acts (re)create representative assemblies or parliaments that are endowed with 'legislative' powers.[48] Second, all devolved legislative powers are limited powers with certain matters 'reserved' and within the exclusive competences of the Westminster Parliament.[49] Third, while devolved powers were formally conceived as shared powers (allowing the Westminster Parliament to act within them),[50] a constitutional convention immediately developed according to which Westminster 'will not normally legislate with regard to devolved matters' without the consent of the regional parliament.[51] Fourth, and last, the Queen remains—of course—the formal head of the devolved executive 'government'.[52]

Today, three of the four nations within the United Kingdom are consequently governed by two parliaments—a central and a regional parliament. But what about the 'English' nation? This question has become famous as the 'West Lothian question',[53] or simply: the 'English question'.[54] It essentially asks to what extent the largest nation within the United Kingdom should also enjoy the benefits of regional representation. For in the absence of an 'English Parliament', the English nation is exclusively represented by the (British) Westminster Parliament.

In order to mitigate this democratic deficit, the British government has recently introduced the idea of 'English votes for English laws' (EVEL). This very 'British'

46 Writing in 2000, N Burrows, *Devolution* (London, Sweet & Maxwell, 2000) 3 has noted that '[t]he most striking feature of the three Acts of Parliament enacted in 1998 is the extent of the differences between the devolution settlements for Scotland, Wales and Northern Ireland'.

47 The devolution arrangement for Wales in particular was originally very different. According to R Brazier, 'The Constitution of the United Kingdom' (1999) 58 *Cambridge Law Journal* 96 at 111 'the Welsh Assembly represent[ed] an extension to Wales of local democracy at the expense of the Government and Parliament in London, but not so as to affect the place of Wales in the United Kingdom'. This has changed dramatically after the Wales Act 2006 and especially after the Wales Act 2017. For a discussion of the latter as well as the Scotland Act 2016, see S Tierney in this volume.

48 Scotland Act 1998, s 1(1): 'There shall be a Scottish Parliament.'

49 ibid, s 29(1): 'An Act of the Scottish Parliament is not law so far as any provision of the Act is outside the legislative competence of the Parliament.' S 29(2) specifies the situations in which the Parliament will act ultra vires, and here in particular clarifies the existence of 'reserved matters' (subsection (b)), which are themselves defined in Schedule 5 of the Scotland Act 1998.

50 ibid, s 28(7): 'This section does not affect the power of the Parliament of the United Kingdom to make laws for Scotland.' This formulation has been taken to confirm—like s 75 of the Government of Ireland Act 1920—the supremacy of the Westminster Parliament (Brazier, above n 47).

51 This so-called Sewel Convention can—following the Scotland Act 2016—now be found in s 28(8) of the Scotland Act 1998.

52 Scotland Act 1998, s 45 (1): 'The First Minister shall be appointed by Her Majesty from among the members of the Parliament and shall hold office at Her Majesty's pleasure.'

53 The name derives from the constituency (subsequently renamed) of the Member of Parliament that asked the question in 1977.

54 House of Lords, English Votes for English Laws House of Lords (above n 1) para 5.

reform involved a change to the Standing Orders of the House of Commons in 2015. This—devilishly—complex non-legislative solution represents an uneasy compromise,[55] which tries to balance the need for a distinct English voice with the desire to *not* create distinctions among Westminster parliamentarians.[56] The compromise found lies in granting a negative 'veto' power to English MPs, yet it has stopped short of granting the English nation a positive power of legislative agenda-setting. In thus denying 'devolution all round' through the creation of an 'English Parliament' led by an 'English executive',[57] the English question continues to be unresolved.

II. From British Empire to Commonwealth: External Structures

What was (and is) the constitutional structure of the British Empire and the (British) Commonwealth? When English colonists settled outside England, one constitutional doctrine travelled with them: as English subjects, they carried with them their 'common law' rights under English law.[58] And once English colonies gradually formed overseas, elective assemblies soon emerged; and after the end of the seventeenth-century, these 'regional' 'parliaments' were 'recognised as a normal constituent part of the organisation of a British colony'.[59]

The sovereignty of the British Parliament over the colonies was however less clear. A vision of Westminster supremacy had emerged with the 'Commonwealth Act' during the English Civil War;[60] and after the restoration period,[61] the colonies gradually came to be seen as an integral part of the British State. This—unitary—legal structure of the (first) British Empire was challenged by the end of the

[55] ibid, para 124.

[56] ibid, para 68.

[57] For the recent rejection of an English Parliament as an option, see only: House of Lords, Select Committee on the Constitution, The Union and Devolution (HL Paper 149), para 376: 'Given the relative size of England within the UK, the creation of an English Parliament would introduce a destabilizing asymmetry of power to the Union.' See also MacCormick, above n 3, 194: 'This solution, looking to make England one state of a redesigned and fully federal United Kingdom, is in fact the least workable of all.'

[58] JH Kettner, *The Development of American Citizenship, 1608–1870* (Chapel Hill, University of North Carolina Press, 1978) 65: 'The same common law principles that made subjects of the Scottish *postnati* applied equally well to persons born in America.'

[59] F Madden and D Fieldhouse, *The Classic Period of the First British Empire, 1689–1783* (Westport CT, Greenwood Press, 1985) xxvii.

[60] In 1649 the English Parliament adopted the 'Commonwealth Act', in which it declared that 'the people of England, *and of all the dominions and territories thereto belonging*, are and shall be, and are hereby constituted, made, established, and confirmed to be a Commonwealth and Free-State, by the supreme authority of this nation, the representatives of the people in Parliament' (emphasis added).

[61] The 1696 Navigation Act was clearly built on the idea of parliamentary supremacy. According to Madden and Fieldhouse (above n 59, 9), the Act contained the first codification of the principle of imperial supremacy over colonial law.

eighteenth century (Section A below). The American Revolution and independence ultimately led to a serious re-conceptualisation of the 'external' constitutional structures of the United Kingdom and finally led to the idea of the British Commonwealth (Section B). The latter would, in the twentieth century, compete with alternative forms of international organisation, and here in particular: the European Union (Section C).

A. The Fall of the First Empire: The 'American Question'

According to the classic conception of Westminster sovereignty, the British Parliament could legislate for all matters within the colonies—including their internal affairs. This view became increasingly contested in the course of the eighteenth century. In the eyes of many colonists, the competence of the British Parliament was legally limited to external affairs and therefore should not cover internal matters. This 'federal' vision came into conflict with the unitary vision, adopted in London, after the Seven Years' War. In an attempt to raise revenue from the colonies, the Empire had adopted a series of Acts that shock the colonies into resistance;[62] and which led to the articulation of a distinctly 'American' interpretation of the imperial constitution.[63]

In the ensuing constitutional conflict, the British Parliament unconditionally confirmed the principle of absolute parliamentary sovereignty. Not only was the distinction between 'internal' and 'external' taxes found to be unconvincing; the idea of 'home rule' was rejected as having no place within the constitutional structure of the Empire. The 1766 Declaratory Act—modelled on its 1719 Irish predecessor—thus confirmed that 'the said Colonies and Plantations in America, have been, are, and of right ought to be, *subordinate unto, and dependent upon, the Imperial Crown and Parliament of Great Britain*' and that the British Parliament 'had, hath, and of right ought to have, *full power and authority to make laws and statutes if sufficient force and validity to bind the Colonies and the People of America, subjects of the Crown of Great Britain, in all cases whatsoever*'.[64] The idea of parliamentary sovereignty, given its first orthodox expression by Blackstone in the year of the Stamp Act,[65] here blocked any federal compromise.[66] And

[62] The most famous of these parliamentary statutes were: the Sugar Act (1764) and the Stamp Act (1765).

[63] The 'Stamp Act Congress', while confirming its allegiance to the King, put forward the constitutional principle of 'no taxation without representation'.

[64] 1766 Declaratory Act (emphasis added).

[65] Blackstone, above n 29, 82: 'Because the legislature, being in truth the sovereign power, is always of equal, always of absolute authority; it acknowledges no superior upon earth, which the prior legislature must have been, if its ordinances could bind a subsequent parliament.'

[66] In the strong judgment of AC McLaughlin, 'The Background of American Federalism' (1918) 12 *American Political Science Review* 215 at 221: 'Men that could not comprehend federalism, who denied the possibility of its existence, were incapable of dealing with a crisis of an imperial system in which federalism already existed.'

without a theoretical compromise that the Empire could offer, the American colonists soon moved from the narrower constitutional claim of 'no taxation without representation' to the—dangerous—constitutional question of the locus of imperial sovereignty.[67]

This clash between the 'British' and the 'American' interpretation of imperial sovereignty derived from 'a collision of the older interpretation of the English constitution, continuing in America, but superseded after 1689, if not 1649, in England, with the post-revolutionary interpretation as held in England.'[68] Britain compared the American colonies to Ireland (before the Union) and considered their status to be one of constitutional subordination. The American colonies, on the other hand, aspired to the constitutional status of Scotland (before the Union) and argued for constitutional coordination under a single monarch.[69] The Empire was here seen not as a unitary State but as a quasi-federal Union 'in which the King was the executive head of many *co-equal* legislatures in as many *co-equal* political communities'.[70] This 'Scottish' solution was still espoused during the First Continental Congress,[71] whose Article 4 perhaps best represents the colonial idea of a 'federal' British Empire. It stated:

> That the foundation of English liberty, and of all free government, is a right in the people to participate in their legislative council: and as the English colonists are not represented, and from their local and other circumstances, cannot properly be represented in the British parliament, they are entitled to a free and exclusive power of legislation in their several provincial legislatures, where their right of representation can alone be preserved, in all cases of taxation and internal polity, subject only to the negative of their sovereign, in such manner as has been heretofore used and accustomed: But, from the necessity of the case, and a regard to the mutual interest of both countries, we cheerfully consent to the operation of such acts of the British parliament, as are bona fide, restrained to the regulation of our external commerce, for the purpose of securing the commercial advantages of the whole empire to the mother country, and the commercial benefits of its respective members; excluding every idea of taxation internal or external, for raising a revenue on the subjects, in America, without their consent.

The 'American' interpretation of the constitutional structure of the British Empire is here characterised by four important elements. First, British colonies could not

[67] On sovereignty becoming the central problem, see only: B Bailyn, *The Ideological Origins of the American Revolution* (Cambridge MA, Harvard University Press, 1967) 219.

[68] CH McIlwain, *The American Revolution: A Constitutional Interpretation* (Clark NJ, The Lawbook Exchange, 2005) 11.

[69] In the words of McIlwain (ibid, 80): 'If Ireland was the closest constitutional parallel to colonial America, Scotland was its constitutional ideal[.]'

[70] RG Adams, *Political Ideas of the American Revolution: Britannic-American Contribution to the Problem of Imperial Organisation* (London, Trinity College Press, 1922) 56 (emphasis added).

[71] Following the Declaration Act, the British Parliament adopted a number of trade measures. One of these measures—the 'Tea Act'—inspired open rebellion: the Boston Tea Party. Parliament's reply were the 'Intolerable Acts' of 1774— a response that inspired the colonies to coordinate their future behaviour in what was to become the 'First Continental Congress'.

be represented in the British Parliament—a claim that put an end to the idea of an 'incorporating union' with the colonies. They would therefore—secondly—have to be entitled to 'a free and *exclusive* power of legislation' over their internal affairs, while each colonial legislature would of course—thirdly—acknowledge 'the negative of their sovereign'. Fourthly, the colonies would submit to imperial legislation that dealt with '*external* commerce', yet, taxation—whether internal or external—was out of the question.

None of the 'American' constitutional demands were accepted; and when the Continental Congress met a second time, the War of Independence had already started. The Second Congress now recommended the total suppression of royal authority within the colonies and issued 'The Unanimous Declaration of the Thirteen United States of America': the Declaration of Independence.[72]

B. The British Commonwealth: The 'Dominion Question'

If the American question had been a test for 'the capacity of the British constitution to fulfil an imperial as well as a national function',[73] it had spectacularly failed.

The lessons of this imperial failure were not immediately learnt.[74] Only after the publication of the Durham Report did a new—liberal—spirit gradually enter imperial government.[75] The Report had famously recommended 'responsible government' for the remaining North-American British colonies. Starting to take hold after 1848, the new principle insisted that the 'regional' government within each colony should be 'responsible' to an existing regional parliament.[76] Akin to 'Home Rule', this principle became 'the political cornerstone of the British Commonwealth'.[77] Yet responsible government was hardly legislative independence;

[72] In the famous words of the Declaration, the colonists henceforth considered 'that these United Colonies are, and of right ought to be, free and independent States; that they are *absolved from all allegiance to the British crown and that all political connection between them and the state of Great Britain is, and ought to be, totally dissolved*' (emphasis added). For an analysis of how federalism is developed and conceived in the United States after independence, see: R Schütze, 'Federalism as Constitutional Pluralism: "Letter from America"' in M Avbelj and J Komárek (eds), *Constitutional Pluralism in the European Union and Beyond* (Oxford, Hart, 2012), 185; as well as A Tomkins in this volume.

[73] J Ewing, 'The Constitution and the Empire: From Bacon to Blackstone' in J Holland Rose et al (eds), *The Cambridge History of the British Empire—Volume I: The Old Empire* (Cambridge, Cambridge University Press, 1929) 603 at 631.

[74] On the contrary, according to R Livingston Schuyler, *Parliament and the British Empire* (New York, Columbia University Press, 1929) 198, as a response to American independence, 'British colonial administration became [even] more restrictive', as 'Great Britain was afraid that a liberal colonial policy would result in further secessions from the Empire'.

[75] Earl of Durham, Report on the Affairs of British North America (House of Commons, 1839).

[76] For a monumental historical analysis here, see: AB Keith, *Responsible Government in the Dominions* (Oxford, Oxford University Press, 1928).

[77] Livingston Schuyler, above n 74, 201.

indeed: the Colonial Laws Validity Act 1865 unquestionably confirmed the supremacy of imperial legislation adopted by the Westminster Parliament.[78]

A second principle of British 'imperial' organisation gradually emerged alongside the idea of 'responsible government': federalism. Beginning with the British North America Act 1867, the British Parliament began to adopt various 'Union Acts' that 'federally united' distinct colonies into one 'dominion' under the Crown.[79] The term 'federal' had been deliberately chosen to underline the similarities with the US American Constitution.[80] For as regards the legislative function, the powers of the (central) Canadian Parliament and the powers of the (regional) provincial legislatures were divided into mutually exclusive spheres.[81]

Yet despite its willingness to 'export' federalism into its 'dominions', a 'federal' British Empire had—long debates notwithstanding—not emerged.[82] A major imperial re-conceptualisation took however place after the end of the First World War. The 1926 Imperial Conference adopted, after pressure from Ireland, the 'Balfour Declaration'; and the latter ultimately led to the most important piece of imperial reform of the twentieth century: the 1931 Statute of Westminster. The 1931 Statute determined the position of the British 'dominions' as autonomous communities that formed a 'free association' with the United Kingdom under the name of 'the British Commonwealth of Nations'.[83] While 'united by a common allegiance to the Crown',[84] all legislative matters were henceforth within the 'internal' sovereignty of each dominion.[85] The Colonial Laws Validity Act 1865

[78] Colonial Laws Validity Act 1865, Art 2: 'Any colonial law which is or shall be in any respect repugnant to the provisions of any Act of Parliament extending to the colony to which such law may relate, or repugnant to any order or regulation made under authority of such Act of Parliament, or having in the colony the force and effect of such Act, shall be read subject to such Act, order, or regulation, and shall, to the extent of such repugnancy, but not otherwise, be and remain absolutely void and inoperative.'

[79] See for example: the British North America Act 1867, Preamble. For a discussion of this point, see P Oliver in this volume.

[80] I Jennings, *Constitutional Laws of the Commonwealth* (Oxford, Clarendon Press, 1952) 187.

[81] British North America Act 1867, ss 91 and 92.

[82] M Burgess, *The British Tradition of Federalism* (Madison NJ, Dickson University Press, 1995) Chs 2 and 3.

[83] 1931 Statute of Westminster, Preamble. According to s 1, the term 'dominion' referred to the Dominion of Canada, The Commonwealth of Australia, the Dominion of New Zealand, the Union of South Africa, the Irish Free State and Newfoundland; and following s 11, the term 'colony' could henceforth no longer be used to describe these 'dominions'.

[84] ibid, Preamble.

[85] Two qualifications must nonetheless be made. First, many dominions continued to require royal consent by the 'British' monarchy; and secondly and more importantly: 'constitutional' autonomy had not yet been given. The two federations—Canada and Australia—consequently insisted that the newly granted legislative supremacy should not be allowed to affect their 'constitutional' charters, which were after all, framed in the form of an act of the British Parliament (see ss 7 and 8 of the 1931 Westminster Statute). The Canadian Constitution was only 'repatriated' in 1982 via the (British) Canada Act 1982, whose second section stated: 'No Act of the Parliament of the United Kingdom passed after the Constitution Act 1982 comes into force shall extend to Canada as part of its law.'

was repealed and the principle of legislative supremacy was inverted.[86] With the supremacy of 'dominion' legislation established, Westminster legislation constituted henceforth only subsidiary and subordinate legislation. The Westminster Parliament had 'ceded' its 'supremacy'.[87]

What is the constitutional structure of the 'Commonwealth' today? After a process of 'decolonisation', British constitutional law today distinguishes between 'Commonwealth Countries',[88] 'British Crown Dependencies',[89] and 'British Overseas Territories'.[90] Crown dependencies are self-governing possessions of the Crown, which do formally not constitute a part of the United Kingdom. British overseas territories are, as an 'imperial' heritage, under the sovereignty and within the jurisdiction of the United Kingdom. Commonwealth countries, finally, are independent States that, together with the United Kingdom, form the 'Commonwealth of Nations'. This 'new' Commonwealth is an international organisation that constitutes 'a voluntary association of independent and equal sovereign states, each responsible for its own policies'.[91] And having dropped the obligatory adherence to the British monarchy as a distinctive qualifying element,[92] its central connecting factor is a shared—imperial—history and common interests; even if vestiges of the imperial architecture remain in the jurisdiction of the Judicial Committee of the Privy Council.

C. British Commonwealth or European Union: The 'European Question'

While it might have been viable for States to isolate themselves from international politics in the nineteenth century,[93] the 'globalisation' of warfare and the economic

[86] 1931 Statute of Westminster, s 2(2).

[87] For a die-hard Diceyan interpretation of the 1931 Westminster Statute, see however AB Keith, *The Governments of the British Empire* (London, Macmillan, 1936) 34–35: 'Under the statute no attempt is made to renounce the legislative supremacy of the United Kingdom Parliament ... It must be noted that the restriction of authority thus laid down as a constitutional principle, though it could not operate as a renunciation of legislative power, would be effective as a rule of interpretation.'

[88] There are currently 52 Commonwealth Countries.

[89] These are today: the Isle of Man and the Channel Islands.

[90] The 14 British Overseas Territories are: Akrotiri and Dhekelia; Anguilla; Bermuda; British Antarctic Territory; British Indian Ocean Territory; British Virgin Islands; Cayman Islands; Falkland Islands; Gibraltar; Montserrat; Pitcairn Islands; Saint Helena, Ascension and Tristan da Cunha; South Georgia and the South Sandwich Islands; Turks and Caicos Islands.

[91] See Charter of the Commonwealth (http://thecommonwealth.org/our-charter), Preamble—Second Indent.

[92] Following the 1931 Westminster Statute, a Republic could not be part of the British Commonwealth; yet ever since the 1949 (London) Commonwealth Declaration allowed India to remain within the Commonwealth, an allegiance to the Crown is no longer required.

[93] On the US American policy of isolationism until World War I, see: GC Herring, *From Colony to Superpower: US Foreign Relations since 1776* (Oxford, Oxford University Press, 2011).

crisis in the first half of the twentieth century had shown this to be impossible—even for the British Empire. The post-1945 world was an *international* world—a world of *collective* security systems and *collective* trade agreements.

Two alternative approaches to the problem of international 'cooperation' thereby developed: universal cooperation and regional integration. The 'universal' approach—seen at work in the creation of the 1945 United Nations and the 1947 GATT—was based on the belief that 'security' and 'trade' had become global problems; yet formally, both international organisations continued to acknowledge the 'sovereign equality' of its Member States.[94] A second—European—approach, by contrast, tried to go further. Post-war Europe thus saw the establishment of the 'Council of Europe' and the conclusion of the European Convention on Human Rights (ECHR), whose 'supranational' adjudicatory system would allow individuals to directly apply to a European Court.[95]

However, the main illustration of European 'supranationalism' would be the European Union. From the very start, the European Union differed from ordinary international coordination in two essential ways.[96] Not only could the Union adopt secondary law that was to be 'directly applicable' in the national legal orders; it also envisaged that this adoption could go against the sovereign veto of a single Member State. The European Union would indeed have 'real powers stemming from a limitation of sovereignty or a transfer of powers from the States'.[97]

The British relationship to this—federal—European Union was 'awkward' from the start.[98] For even if a distinguished British hero had commended the 'United States of Europe',[99] when it came to joining the first supranational project the British simply would not have it. British thinking still followed a 'three circles' logic in which Europe simply ranked last; and when it thus came to choosing between the British Commonwealth and the 1957 European Economic Community, the British favoured the former over the latter.[100] To nevertheless contain the

[94] For this point see Art 2(1) UN Charter: 'The Organization is based on the principle of the sovereign equality of all its Members.' For an analysis of the UN and the place of the United Kingdom within the organisation, see the chapter by N White in this volume.

[95] For a discussion of this point, see the chapter by R Masterman in this volume.

[96] P Pescatore, *The Law of Integration: Emergence of a new Phenomenon in International Relations, based on the Experience of the European Communities* (Leiden, Sijthoff, 1974).

[97] Case 6/64, *Costa v ENEL* (1964) ECR 585 at 593.

[98] For an excellent general account, see: S George, *An Awkward Partner: Britain in the European Community* (Oxford, Oxford University Press, 1994) Ch 1. See also especially the chapters by J Murkens and S Douglas-Scott in this volume.

[99] This had been done by Sir Winston Churchill in Zurich on 19 September 1946. The speech can be listened to here: https://www.youtube.com/watch?v=Ln4SRnt4VE0.

[100] For the classical analyses, see G St J Barclay, *Commonwealth or Europe* (Brisbane, University of Queensland Press, 1970); as well as: M Camps, *Britain and the European Community: 1955–1963* (Princeton, Princeton University Press, 1964) esp 48: 'It was generally accepted uncritically and as an article of faith that the United Kingdom should not join a supranational organization and could not join a customs union, partly because of its arrangements with the Commonwealth and partly because the British, like the Six, were always very conscious of the pressure towards political union inherent in a customs union.'

consequences of this choice against the 'common market', the British government swiftly suggested the creation of a 'European Free Trade Association (EFTA). The 1960 Stockholm Convention created EFTA, which—unlike the Community common market—would allow Britain to retain its imperial preference system.[101] But in an extraordinary act of pragmatic re-orientation, British membership in the European common market nevertheless became a priority in the 1960s; and in 1972, the British Accession Treaty was concluded.

Ever since, the relationship between the United Kingdom and the European Union has remained complex. Fundamentally opposed to the idea of a 'federal' Europe, the United Kingdom has consistently favoured an ever-wider over an ever-deeper European Union; and while the British government has traditionally supported the liberalisation of the common market, it has been deeply critical towards European market *regulation*. Its critical attitude towards transfers of legislative powers to the European Union has found numerous expressions in a wide range of 'opt-outs' and the persistent blocking of all efforts to move towards a closer political union.

This 'British' unease to be part of a federal union of European states was given its strongest expression in 2016, when a British referendum on Union membership opted to withdraw from the European Union altogether.[102] Triggering the 'secession' procedure via Article 50 of the Treaty on European Union (TEU), the reason for leaving the Union, offered by the British Prime Minister, was the wish of the British people to restore 'national self-determination' and to again become a fully sovereign State in the international sphere.[103]

III. Sovereignty and Federalism: Uneasy Relationships

How to best characterise the constitutional structures within and without the United Kingdom? First and foremost, one is forced to admit this: while based on the—seemingly—simple idea of parliamentary sovereignty, nothing is simple in the legal relationships between the four nations within the United Kingdom; nor are the external relationships between the United Kingdom and its crown dependencies and overseas territories much easier to understand (Figure 1). Far from being a regular nation State, the United Kingdom constitutes an 'irregular body resembling a monster'.[104]

[101] The creation of EFTA may have also followed more sinister motives. For it was secretly hoped to dissolve the (supranational) common market in an (intergovernmental) free trade area 'like a lump of sugar in an English cup of tea'. I am grateful to Anne Deighton for having pointed me to this 'British' treasure.

[102] European Union (Notification of Withdrawal) Act 2017.

[103] The official Art 50 letter can be found under: https://www.gov.uk/government/publications/prime-ministers-letter-to-donald-tusk-triggering-article-50.

[104] I am of course paraphrasing the famous Pufendorf characterisation for the old 'German Empire'.

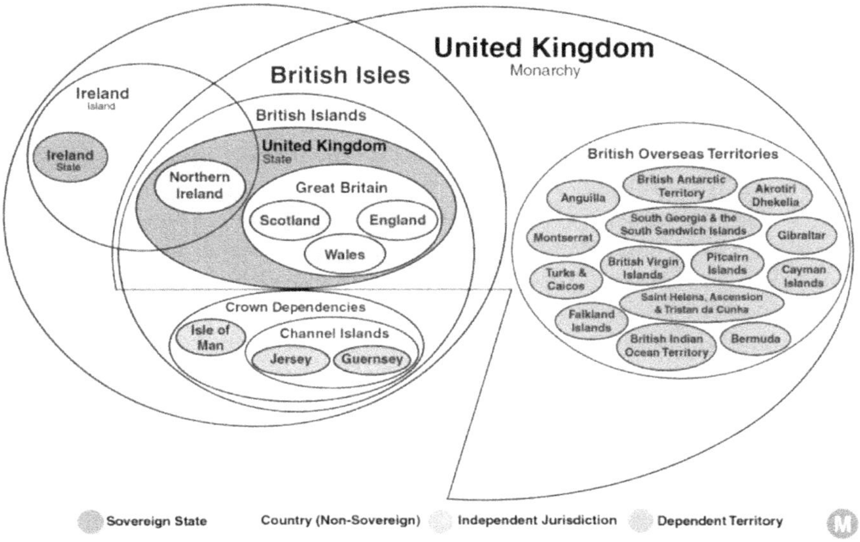

Figure 1: British (Inter)national Relations

Secondly, despite the co-existence of diverse political communities, the idea of a federal union has been persistently rejected—both in the internal and the external sphere. The reason for the categorical suppression of federal thought lies in 'the most durable and damaging concept' of British legal and political thought: the concept of sovereignty.[105] The obsession with sovereignty—parliamentary sovereignty—has indeed blocked the development of all 'normative' constitutional concepts within the United Kingdom, including that of constitutional federalism. Proud not to impose any legal limits on Parliament, the latter is revered as an 'absolutely sovereign legislature' that has 'the right to make or unmake any law whatever; and, further, that no person or body is recognised by the law of England [!] as having the right to override or set aside the legislation of Parliament'.[106]

This absolutist conception of—legal—parliamentary power simply cannot envisage a constitutional division of powers 'so that the general and regional governments are each, within a sphere, coordinate and independent'.[107] The absolute supremacy of the Westminster Parliament, as a legal doctrine, leaves no room for 'federal' limitations on the competence of the British Parliament, whether they derive from the 1707 Union Treaty or the 1957 Rome Treaty. All law—whether internal or external—must be subordinate to the will of the British Parliament; and this final section takes a closer look at the legal and political dimension of this view before introducing the various contributions to this volume.

[105] Burgess, above n 82, 186.

[106] AV Dicey, *Introduction to the Study of the Law of the Constitution* (Carmel IN, Liberty Fund, 1982) 3.

[107] K Wheare, *Federal Government* (Oxford, Oxford University Press, 1953) 11.

A. Parliamentary Sovereignty and Federalism I: The Legal Dimension

i. De-constitutionalising the Union I: The 1707 Union Treaty

How could a 'Union State' that was formed on the basis of two 'Union Treaties' come to see its 'constituting' treaties as 'ordinary' legislation?

An excellent illustration of this process of 'de-constitutionalisation' is the evolution of the 1707 Union Treaty between England and Scotland. The Treaty, it will be recalled, 'incorporated' England and Scotland into a new kingdom; and while leaving the English and Scottish legal orders generally intact, it established the supremacy of the newly established Westminster Parliament.[108] And yet: the 1707 Union Treaty had made an express distinction between alterable and unalterable rights and decreed 'that the Laws which concern publick Right, Policy, and Civil Government, maybe made the same throughout the whole United Kingdom; *but that no Alteration be made in Laws which concern private Right, except for evident Utility of the Subjects within Scotland*.'[109] What was the status of this entrenchment? For Daniel Dafoe, the answer was clear:

> Since, as nothing is more plain than that the articles of the treaty, and consequently the great heads mentioned in the above address, cannot be touched by the Parliament of Britain; and that the moment they attempt it, they dissolve their own Constitution; so it is a Union upon no other terms, and is expressly stipulated what shall, and what shall not be alterable by the subsequent Parliaments. *And as the Parliaments of Britain are founded, not upon the original right of the people, as the separate Parliaments of England and Scotland were before, but upon the treaty which is prior to the said Parliament, and consequently superior; so, for that reason it cannot have power to alter its own foundation, or act against the power which formed it, since all constituted power is subordinate, and inferior to the power constituting.*[110]

Traces of this 'constitutional' interpretation could still be found, 50 years later, in the writings of Blackstone. The great English legal commentator also generally accepted that infringements of a 'fundamental and essential condition of the union' would dissolve the Union,[111] yet a major qualification was already added:

> It may justly be doubted whether even such an infringement (though a manifest breach of good faith, unless done upon the most pressing necessity) would of itself dissolve

[108] 1707 Union Treaty, Art XXV: 'That all Laws and Statutes in either Kingdom, so far as they are contrary to, or inconsistent with the Terms of these Articles, or any of them, shall, from and after the Union cease and become void and shall be so declared to be, by the respective Parliaments of the said Kingdoms.'

[109] ibid, Art XVIII (emphasis added).

[110] D Defoe, *History of the Union between England and Scotland* (Stockdale, 1786) 246 (emphasis added).

[111] Blackstone, above n 29, 88: 'That the two kingdoms are now so inseparably united, that nothing can ever disunite them again, except the mutual consent of both, or the successful resistance of either, upon apprehending an infringement of those points which, when they were separate and independent nations, it was mutually stipulated should be 'fundamental and essential conditions of the union.'

> the union: for the bare idea of a state, without a power somewhere vested to alter every part of its laws, is the height of political absurdity. The truth seems to be, that in such an incorporate union (which is well distinguished by a very learned prelate from a foederate alliance, where such an infringement would certainly rescind the compact) the two contracting states are totally annihilated, without any power of a revival; and a third arises from their conjunction, in which all the rights of sovereignty, and particularly that of legislation, must of necessity reside.[112]

120 years later, the Blackstonian doubt had become a Diceyan certainty. For in the most influential textbook of twentieth century British constitutional law, we now read as follows:

> That Parliaments have more than once intended and endeavoured to pass Acts which should tie the hands of their successors is certain, but the endeavour has always ended in failure. Of statutes intended to arrest the possible course of future legislation, the most noteworthy are the Acts which embody the treaties of Union with Scotland and Ireland. The legislators who passed these Acts assuredly intended to give to certain portions of them more than the ordinary effect of statutes. Yet the history of legislation in respect of these very Acts affords the strongest proof of the futility inherent in every attempt of one sovereign legislature to restrain the action of another equally sovereign body ... The one fundamental dogma of English [!] constitutional law is the absolute legislative sovereignty or despotism of the King in Parliament. But this dogma is incompatible with the existence of a fundamental compact, the provisions of which control every authority existing under the constitution.[113]

The legal foundation of the Union between England and Scotland is here seen in the (English) Act of Union that—as Dicey famously claims—has the same legal status as the (British) 'Dentists Act, 1878'.[114] This argument however simply assumed that the British Parliament was built on the English (!) constitutional ideal of a sovereign parliament.[115] This was not a matter of logic; but only a few decades later, the Diceyan experience had become 'the established doctrine'.[116] This 'English' conception of 'British' constitutional law has been—weakly—challenged by a 'Scottish' conception within the second half of the twentieth century;[117] yet no

[112] ibid, 88.

[113] Dicey, above n 106, 21–22 and 78.

[114] ibid.

[115] TB Smith, 'The Union of 1707 as Fundamental law' (1957) *Public Law* 110.

[116] Maitland, above n 5, 332.

[117] *MacCormick v Lord Advocate*, 1953 SC 396 at 411: 'The principle of the unlimited sovereignty of Parliament is a distinctively English principle which has no counterpart in Scottish constitutional law. It derives its origin from Coke and Blackstone, and was widely popularised during the nineteenth century by Bagehot and Dicey, the latter having stated the doctrine in its classic form in his Law of the Constitution. Considering that the Union legislation extinguished the Parliaments of Scotland and England and replaced them by a new Parliament, I have difficulty in seeing why it should have been supposed that the new Parliament of Great Britain must inherit all the peculiar characteristics of the English Parliament but none of the Scottish Parliament, as if all that happened in 1707 was that Scottish representatives were admitted to the Parliament of England. That is not what was done.' For excellent academic discussions of this Scottish perspective, see especially Smith, above n 115; as well as JDB Mitchell, 'Sovereignty of Parliament—Yet Again' (1963) 79 *Law Quarterly Review* 196; and much later: E Wicks, 'A New Constitution for a New State? The 1707 Union of England and Scotland' (2001) 117 *Law Quarterly Review* 109.

legal revisionism has ever taken hold of Scotland's normative outlook and the better view now holds that she has tacitly 'consented' to the organic dis-entrenchment of the 1707 Union Treaty.[118]

ii. De-constitutionalising the Union II: The European Union

The British denial of any 'internal' legal limitations imposed on the British Parliament is complemented by the rejection of all 'external' limitations imposed on the United Kingdom. The most extreme illustration of this 'sovereignism' surfaced in the context of the European Union. For despite the 'federal' doctrines of direct effect and supremacy—already well-established in European Union law when the United Kingdom joined the European Union,[119] the traditional position of the British Parliament has always been that it is the British Parliament that stands supreme behind every European norm. The European Communities Act 1972 thus stated:

> All such rights, powers, liabilities, obligations and restrictions from time to time created or arising by or under the Treaties, and all such remedies and procedures from time to time provided for by or under the Treaties, as in accordance with the Treaties are without further enactment to be given legal effect or used in the United Kingdom shall be recognised and available in law, and be enforced, allowed and followed accordingly[.][120]

Instead of conceiving European law as an 'autonomous' legal order that directly applied within the United Kingdom *qua* membership of the European Union, the 1972 Act established the view that European law was derivative and subordinate to British legislation. The provision was consequently seen as 'a missed opportunity to declare positively the fundamental nature of the constitutional change wrought by the Act';[121] and the 'national' view was subsequently reinforced by the (British) European Union Act 2011 that unambiguously states:

> Directly applicable or directly effective EU law (that is, the rights, powers, liabilities, obligations, restrictions, remedies and procedures referred to in section 2(1) of the European Communities Act 1972) falls to be recognised and available in law in the United Kingdom only by virtue of that Act or where it is required to be recognised and available in law by virtue of any other Act.[122]

[118] Ironically, the Scotland Act 1998 itself recognised the dis-entrenched nature of the 1707 Union in its s 37, which states (emphasis added): 'The Union with Scotland Act 1706 and the Union with England Act 1707 have effect *subject to this Act*.'

[119] R Schütze, *European Union Law* (Cambridge, Cambridge University Press, 2015) Chs 3 and 4.

[120] 1972 European Communities Act, s 2(1). For special provisions with regard to the Northern Ireland Parliament, see s 2(5), and with regard to a 'law passed by the legislature of any of the Channel Islands or of the Isle of Man, or a colonial law (within the 1865 c. 63 meaning of the Colonial Laws Validity Act 1865) passed or made for Gibraltar', see s 2(6) of the Act.

[121] E Wicks, *The Evolution of a Constitution: Eight Key Moments in British Constitutional History* (Oxford, Hart, 2006) 145.

[122] European Union Act 2011, s 18.

This national 'sovereignist' perspective has, in the past, led to enormous judicial acrobatics—some have called it 'judicial hypocrisy'—to explain away Supreme Court judgments that simply contradict the Diceyan view that an earlier Parliament could not bind its successors.[123] The high mark of this concerted effort 'to preserve the formal veneer of Diceyan orthodoxy while undermining its substance' is *Factortame No 2*.[124] The (then) House of Lords here impliedly repealed the doctrine of implied repeal; but instead of embracing the federal idea that parliamentary sovereignty had been limited *qua* EU membership,[125] the official view continued to insist that absolute—British—supremacy remains untouched. For instead of locating the supremacy of (earlier) European law over (later) Westminster legislation in the European legal order, the British view came to locate it in the (English) common law by introducing a distinction between 'ordinary' and 'constitutional' statutes.[126] This clearly un-Diceyan approach formally preserves the supremacy of British over European law by paying homage to the sovereignty of the Westminster Parliament.[127]

B. Parliamentary Sovereignty and Federalism II: The Political Dimension

The British conception of legal sovereignty as belonging to the legislature contrasts with the American and 'European' conception according to which legal sovereignty cannot pertain to a constituted power. The British conflation between what is 'constituent' and what is 'constituted' has thereby blocked all normative conceptions of constitutional law as 'prior' or 'above' ordinary government and

[123] J Murkens, *Contested constitutional concepts: state, constitution, sovereignty in Germany and the United Kingdom, and the European challenge* (unpublished EUI thesis), 293 (with reference to *Macarthys v Smith* (1979) 3 All ER 325).

[124] P Craig, 'Sovereignty of the United Kingdom Parliament after Factortame' (1991) 11 *YEL* 221 at 251.

[125] For the view that *Factortame* represented a legal revolution, see: HWR Wade, 'Sovereignty—Revolution or Evolution?' (1996) 112 *Law Quarterly Review* 568. For a specifically 'federal' interpretation, see A Tomkins, *Public Law* (Oxford, Oxford University Press, 2003) 118: 'Since 1 January 1973 there have been two legal systems operating in this country, not one, and the doctrine of the legislative supremacy of statute is a doctrine known to only one of these two systems.'

[126] *Thoburn v Sunderland City Council* (2003) QB 151; as well as *R (HS2 Action Alliance Ltd) v Secretary of State for Transport* (2914) UKSC 3. Especially on the latter decision, see: P Craig, 'Constitutionalising Constitutional Law: HS2' (2014) *Public Law* 373. In *R (on the application of Miller and another) (Respondents) v Secretary of State for Exiting the European Union (Appellant)*, (2017) UKSC 5, the Supreme Court has now—ironically at the moment of leaving the European Union—come to accept the 'autonomous' and 'independent' nature of European Union law.

[127] For a recent invocation of Dicey, see: *Miller* (above n 126), esp para 43: 'Parliamentary sovereignty is a fundamental principle of the UK constitution … It was famously summarised by Professor Dicey as meaning that Parliament has "the right to make or unmake any law whatsoever; and further, no person or body is recognised by the law as having a right to override or set aside the legislation of Parliament".'

in which the power of the legislature is 'constitutionally' limited. And without a legal or normative conception of a 'constitution', there simply cannot be any legal conception of federalism as a system of 'constitutionally' limited government.[128]

Yet what about the political dimension of federalism? After all, such a conception might well align itself to the British idea of a *political* constitution; and the distinction between legal and political sovereignty is indeed equally well known in British constitutional thought. The distinction contrasts legal theory with political reality and accepts that, politically, the Westminster Parliament is 'nothing like an omnipotent body'. Not only are powers 'practically limited in more ways than one', but as Dicey further explains:

> A sovereign may wish to do many things which he either cannot do at all or can do only at great risk of serious resistance, and it is on many accounts worth observation that the exact point at which the *external limitation begins to operate*, that is, the point at which subjects will offer serious or insuperable resistance to the commands of a ruler whom they generally obey, is never fixed with precision. It would be rash of the Imperial [!] Parliament to abolish the Scotch Law Courts, and assimilate the law of Scotland to that of England. But no one can feel sure at what point Scotch resistance to such a change would become serious.[129]

The Scottish 'resistance' to any formal or substantive amendment to the 1707 Union Treaty had, as we saw above, been minimal; yet the idea that there are political *limitations* imposed on Westminster sovereignty—strongly—resurfaced in the aftermath of British devolution. A sociological perspective here criticises legal theory for ignoring a *political* reality in which the (re-)creation of the Scottish Parliament marks a new 'constitutional' beginning.[130] Devolution, seen in this light, represents 'the start of a new song' in which 'the United Kingdom is becoming a union of nations, each with its own identity and institutions'.[131] And even if the Scottish Parliament is deemed legally subordinate, politically 'it will be anything but subordinate'.[132] For if the British Parliament were ever to try to abolish the Scottish Parliament, the chance of political resistance would be 'real';[133] and this political reality has now been legally recognised in the Scotland Act 2016.[134]

[128] For Wheare's legal definition of federalism, see text to above n 4.

[129] Dicey, above n 106, 33.

[130] For the classic 'legalist' perspective, see only: K Bradley and K Ewing, *Constitutional and Administrative Law* (London, Longman, 2010) 40–41 (emphasis added)): 'Devolution is *not* a term of art in constitutional law. *Unlike* federalism, its nature within the United Kingdom depends not on a written constitution, but on the legislation authorizing devolution, and on the practice that develops through new structures of decision-making.'

[131] V Bogdanor, *Devolution in the United Kingdom* (Oxford, Oxford University Press, 1998) 287.

[132] ibid, 288.

[133] Burrows, above n 46, 182: 'It is probably true to say that the Scottish Parliament, in whatever form it may take in the future, is now a permanent feature of the Scottish constitutional landscape. It is unthinkable that there will not be a Scottish Parliament.'

[134] The latter has introduced a new s 63 A, which states: 'The Scottish Parliament and the Scottish Government are a permanent part of the United Kingdom's constitutional arrangements. … In view of that commitment it is declared that the Scottish Parliament and the Scottish Government are not to be abolished except on the basis of a decision of the people of Scotland voting in a referendum.'

By allowing for distinct parliamentary representation, devolution has indeed reinforced the national identity of (at least) two nations within the United Kingdom. The political loyalty of British citizens, who are subject to two legislatures, may thus gradually be divided; and to quote Dicey one last time:

> True of course it is that if in one State two persons, or two bodies, each are considered to be in a strict sense sovereign, i.e. each to have power of legislating on every topic whatever, a logical contradiction may lead to constant conflict. But the further dogma of Austinian jurists that in very State there must of necessity exist some absolutely sovereign power is not in fact true. If, as may often happen, the citizens of one State habitually obey one sovereign (e.g. the Pope) on one class of matters, e.g. matters of religious doctrine, but also habitually obey another person (e.g. the King) on another class of matters, e.g. political matters, there may well exist for an infinite time a system which may properly be called one of divided sovereignty. Such was in fact the state of things in Scotland under the Constitution of 1603[.][135]

This socio-psychological understanding of the relationship between 'sovereign' and 'subject' was, half a century later, developed by HLA Hart.[136] Yet the best conceptualisation of this divided loyalty, and its identification with compound—federal—orders, has come from the pen of C Schmitt.[137] Writing against the backdrop of the German Empire and the (federal) Weimar Republic, Schmitt identified the essence of a federal order with the co-existence of 'two kinds of *political* bodies' that 'must remain *coordinate* in order for the federal union to remain alive'.[138] Unlike unitary states, every citizen within a compound union will thus 'feel' part of two political orders simultaneously; and the divided loyalty engendered will translate into an 'existential' equilibrium in which political sovereignty is 'suspended'.[139]

Following this line of thought, a federal union is best identified—to use a physics metaphor—as a political 'molecule'. Combining various 'atoms of sovereignty' into a broader structure, federal unions coordinate diverse political units into a political entity within which the units are sharing common institutions and in which the question of internal 'sovereignty' has no longer any meaningful solution. (And while a federal union may, like any molecule, eventually fuse into a single unit or disintegrate into many, this will only happen in the exceptional situation of an 'existential' crisis. Sovereignty theories are concerned with these crisis exceptions, whereas federal theories concentrate on the normative rule.) Political federalism here means the—normal—political co-existence of two legislatures and the ordinary co-obedience of citizens to two political bodies within a union.

[135] AV Dicey and RS Rait, *Thoughts on the Union between England and Scotland* (London, Macmillan, 1920) 100.

[136] HLA Hart, *The Concept of Law* (Oxford, Clarendon Press, 1997), esp Ch 4: 'Sovereign and Subject'.

[137] C Schmitt, *Verfassungslehre* (Berlin, Duncker and Humblot, 2003) Part IV.

[138] ibid, 371 (emphasis added).

[139] ibid, 372.

C. Sharing Sovereignty within and without Great Britain: Our Contributions

A political understanding of federalism may portray the United Kingdom as a federation 'in normal times', while—still—a unitary state 'in crisis times'.[140] And indeed, from a 'political' point of view, many of the 'legal' phenomena within the history of the United Kingdom can fruitfully be seen through a federal lens. Political federalism may thus be found behind the descriptive term 'devolution', while Britain's 'imperial' relationships also assume a federal colour. This broader—sociological—definition of federalism prioritises 'political' practice over 'legal' theory in that it accepts that a State 'may possess a unitary set of institutions and employ them as though they were federal in nature'.[141]

However, even from a legal perspective some relationships within and without the United Kingdom are potentially 'federal' in nature. For while there is no political body inside the United Kingdom that formally contests the absolute legal authority of the Westminster Parliament,[142] the European Union has certainly challenged the idea of national supremacy from without. In the words of the European Court of Justice:

> By contrast with ordinary international treaties, the E[U] Treaty has created its own legal system which, on the entry into force of the Treaty, became an integral part of the legal systems of the Member States and which their courts are bound to apply … *The integration into the laws of each Member State of provisions which derive from the [Union], and more generally the terms and the spirit of the Treaty, make it impossible for the States, as a corollary, to accord precedence to a unilateral and subsequent measure over a legal system accepted by them on a basis of reciprocity. Such a measure cannot therefore be inconsistent with that legal system. The executive force of [European] law cannot vary from one State to another in deference to subsequent domestic laws, without jeopardising the attainment of the objectives of the Treaty* … It follows from all these observations that the law stemming from the Treaty, an independent source of law, could not, because of its special and original nature, be overridden by domestic legal provisions, however framed, without being deprived of its character as [European] law and without the legal basis of the [Union] itself being called into question.[143]

Here indeed co-exist two legal supremacy claims; and this can easily be identified with constitutional federalism.[144]

[140] Bogdanor, above n 131, 291: 'It is in constitutional theory alone that the supremacy of Parliament is preserved. For power devolved, far from being power retained, will be power transferred; and it will not be possible to recover that power except under pathological circumstances, such as those of Northern Ireland after 1968. Thus the relationship between Westminster and Edinburgh will be quasi-federal in normal times and unitary in crisis times.'

[141] W Livingston, *Federalism and Constitutional Change* (Oxford, Clarendon Press, 1956) 1–2.

[142] A starting point may well be a future 'Scottish' decision to hold a second independence referendum without (!) the permission of the Westminster Parliament.

[143] Case 6/64, *Costa v ENEL*, above n 97, 593–94 (emphasis added).

[144] Schütze, above n 119, 127 et seq.

The chapters within this edited collection wish to bring both the political and the legal dimension of the federal idea to the internal and external structures of the United Kingdom. The book is thereby divided into two parts. Part I further explores the historical evolution of quasi-federal arrangements within (and without) the United Kingdom; whereas Part II concentrates on the contemporary 'external' relationships that the United Kingdom entertains with the 'outside' world.

Many of the historical themes within Part I have been—lightly—touched in earlier sections of this 'Introduction'. Chapter 1, written by Alvin Jackson, revisits the failures of British and Irish federalism from 1800–1950. A 'colonial' or 'commonwealth' perspective is added by Peter Oliver in Chapter 2 where he explores the intellectual climate in which the Canadian and Australian federations were created. In Chapter 3, Adam Tomkins contrasts the Scottish devolution arrangements with US American federal doctrines and the Commonwealth lessons as regards 'the constitutional law of shared rule', while Stephen Tierney explores the 'drifting' towards a more 'federal' British constitution caused by the latest Scotland and Wales Acts in Chapter 4. Chapter 5 finally brings an external perspective to the British discussion by exploring two devolved unitary States: Italy (Barbara Guastaferro) and Spain (Lucía Payero).

What are the thematic choices behind Part II? The United Kingdom is (currently) a member of four major supranational and international organisations. Ranging from the most 'regional' to the most 'universal', they are: the European Union, the Council of Europe, the World Trade Organization and the United Nations. Having joined the European Union in 1973, the uneasy relationship between British constitutional law and the European Union will be extensively explored by Jo Murkens in Chapter 6; a theme that is continued by Sionaidh Douglas-Scott, who also specifically analyses the constitutional situation following the British decision to withdraw from the European Union in Chapter 7.[145] Chapter 8, written by Roger Masterman, turns to a second regional European organisation: the Council of Europe and its European Convention on Human Rights. Chapters 9 and 10 finally explore the World Trade Organization and the United Nations albeit from two different perspectives. In Chapter 9, Lorand Bartels concentrates on the consequences Brexit will have for the status of the United Kingdom within the World Trade Organization;[146] whereas Nigel White explores the British relations to the

[145] This chapter includes a brief discussion of the relationship between Brexit and British devolution. The most complex question here is undoubtedly the status of Northern Ireland and its relationship to the Republic of Ireland. Our book cannot discuss these questions in much detail and for a more extensive analysis of the devolution aspects of Brexit, see: House of Lords—European Union Committee, 'Brexit: UK-Irish Relations' (HL Paper 76); as well as M Dougan, 'The "Brexit" Threat to the Northern Irish Border: Clarifying the Constitutional Framework' in M Dougan (ed), *The UK After Brexit: Legal and Policy Challenges* (Cambridge, Intersentia, 2017) 53.

[146] Both the European Union and the United Kingdom are formally members of the WTO—an arrangement that is the result of what is called a 'mixed agreement' (on this idea, see R Schütze, *Foreign Affairs and the EU Constitution* (Cambridge, Cambridge University Press, 2014) ch 5). With Brexit,

United Nations as an international organisation in which the United Kingdom has traditionally held a privileged position.

An overall *Conclusion* is offered by David Armitage. It returns to the broader historical contingencies by masterfully applying a *longue durée* perspective on federalism and sovereignty within and without the United Kingdom. There are three 'legal' afterthoughts that I wish to add to his wonderfully synthetic lines. First, the British rejection of a 'constitutionally' fixed division of vertical (and horizontal) powers has had, since the second half of the twentieth century, not a stabilising but a destabilising effect on governing contemporary Britain.[147] Second, to characterise the federal solution as legalistic and overly complex has lost all of its bite within the twenty-first century British context. For the pragmatic and simple 'unitary' solution that may have existed in the nineteenth century has given way to terrifyingly complex and detailed devolution arrangements that hardly anyone can understand.[148] Third, and most importantly: all constitutional law must reflect constitutional practice; yet a constitutional law whose classic vocabulary was coined in the era of the 'sovereign' state must fail to properly reflect a socio-economic reality in which the United Kingdom simply is no longer 'an empire entire unto itself'. This Diceyan world has passed and to understand the new one, a new constitutional vocabulary needs to be found.[149] For constitutional law is not just about the 'grammar' of politics,[150] it offers (or suppresses) the concepts and options in which we can think of the present and imagine the future.

the central question to be answered here is whether the British withdrawal from the European Union affects its formal status or the substantive concessions that it received when still a Member State of the European Union; and this is the question that Bartels's chapter explores.

[147] The great promise of the unitary state is a 'strong' legislature, which however only translates into a 'strong' and 'stable' government if the overall 'constitutional' framework in which the polity works is seen as a given—a premise which no longer seems to be the case within the United Kingdom.

[148] Anyone who has read the EVEL Standing Order Procedure, the Scotland Act 2016 and the Wales Act 2017 will realise that devolution is not for the legally faint-hearted.

[149] For this argument in the context of (internal) devolution, see: Burrows, above n 46, 192: 'a new constitutional language and new constitutional concepts are required to attempt to describe and develop the process of devolution'.

[150] H Laski, *A Grammar of Politics* (Crows Nest, Allan and Unwin, 1938).

Part I

Historical Evolution: From Past to Present

1

The Failure of British and Irish Federalism, circa 1800–1950

ALVIN JACKSON

I. Introduction: Groundhog Day?

On 19 April 2015, in the prelude to the United Kingdom general election, the then Prime Minister David Cameron told the presenter and historian Andrew Marr that—if the election produced a hung parliament with a minority Labour government and a substantial Scottish nationalist presence—SNP control over any Miliband administration would be the 'first time in our history' that nationalists had ever exercised an influence over a British government.

Mr Cameron had forgotten his political history. Many others have been struck by the similarities between our current constitutional debates and the last great crisis of the British state, almost exactly a century ago, over Home Rule and Irish independence—when (contrary to Mr Cameron's assertions) nationalists did in fact exercise considerable influence over HH Asquith's Liberal government. Nor did Mr Cameron choose to recall the influence wielded by Irish and Ulster Unionists over the Conservative leadership at this time—an issue which would decisively reemerge after his own departure from office. As the Irish Times journalist, Paul Gillespie, has said, commenting on the 2014 debate on the Scots referendum—'it is all uncannily reminiscent of the Home Rule dynamic that preoccupied British politics from the 1880s through to the First World War'.[1]

A key part of that dynamic, and a key part of the ways in which Home Rule was addressed within British politics, was through the proposed federalist reform of the British constitution—or at any rate by what was then consistently defined as 'federalist' reform of the constitution. Thus, in 1914 a group of young unionist and imperialist ideologues pitched such a reform as a way of breaking the

[1] P Gillespie, *Scotland's Vote on Independence: the Implications for Ireland* (Dublin, Institute of International and European Affairs, 2014) 9. Thomas Mohr has extended this idea by looking to analogies between the debates on Brexit and those on imperial federation: see his 'Imperial Federation, 1900–39: a precedent for British legal relations with the European Union?' (2016) 4(2) *Comparative Legal History* 131–61.

impasse over the third Home Rule bill. And since 2014 several prominent unionists, impressed by the strength of Scottish nationalism, have moved to a tentative advocacy of federalism: these include the members of the cross-party Constitution Reform Group at Westminster (Lords Salisbury and Menzies Campbell), the ex-Prime Minister, Gordon Brown, and the prominent Welsh Conservative, David Melding, a former Deputy Presiding Officer of the National Assembly for Wales.[2]

Current debates on federalist reform are thus intimately connected with the lengthy historical roots of the issue—even though some within the political elite clearly have little sense of these antecedents. Just as the federal idea still touches British politics at both the national and transnational levels (in terms of Scotland and Europe), so in the nineteenth century federalism was a central part of debates on the British constitution (given Irish Home Rule), and on Britain's wider relationships, in particular the governance of the empire.

While each of these nineteenth century debates illuminates its later counterparts, the emphasis in this essay is largely upon the United Kingdom, since the analogies here between past and present are particularly close. In essence, British federalism in the nineteenth century was characterised by vigorous advocacy and eloquence, a mixture of ideological conviction and conceptual ambiguity, and some conservative and elite interest together with (at best) popular and nationalist indifference. Much, though not all, of this pathology remains in place in the early twenty-first century.

II. Definitions

Though the terms 'federalism', 'federal home rule' and 'home rule' were (and are) deployed frequently, their meaning and use were much less exact than contemporary political scientists or indeed lawyers would now find useful. This is not the place to revisit lengthy and essentialist debates about the ultimate meaning of federalism, and on the whole attitudes towards definition are more relaxed than formerly (a key authority, Michael Burgess, refers to the now 'tired' debates on definition).[3] However, it is all-too-rarely grasped that nineteenth and early twentieth century advocates of federalism were both clearly aware of the ambiguities of their faith, and to some extent were more concerned with earnest evangelism than with rigorous theology. It is also worth noting that, while political scientists and others have long since achieved precision, or at any rate equanimity, with this issue, the tradition of ambiguity in discussing federalist constitutional reform is deep-seated, and has a continuing relevance in contemporary debates,

[2] G Brown, *My Scotland, Our Britain: A Future Worth Sharing* (London, Simon & Schuster UK, 2014); D Melding, *Will Britain Survive Beyond 2020?* (Cardiff, Institute of Welsh Affairs, 2009); D Torrance, *Britain Rebooted: Scotland in a Federal Union* (Edinburgh, Luath Press Limited, 2014).

[3] M Burgess, *Comparative Federalism: Theory and Practice* (London, Routledge, 2006) 9.

when federalist, devolutionist and Home Rule vocabularies are still readily mixed (even for example by Gordon Brown).

Isaac Butt, the Irish nationalist leader of the 1870s, and one of the patriarchs of federalist debate in the United Kingdom, pointed out in 1870 that 'it is not worthwhile to consider whether the word "federalism" *in its proper sense* be the most appropriate here to express what is proposed'.[4] Equally, one of the foremost Edwardian advocates of a federal reconstruction of the British constitution—the Scots polemicist and businessman, Frederick Scott Oliver—in propounding the cause admitted that 'there are ... considerable difficulties at the outset; for, although the [federalist] idea has sprung up very vigorously in a great variety of quarters during the past few months, it is impossible to discover any authoritative explanation of the true doctrine'.[5] Oliver also admitted later, in 1914, that

> 'federalism' may possibly not be the best word to describe what is in the minds of some of us; but in any case, I am not responsible for it. I did not invent it, or dig it up ... the term 'federal' is a loose designation, and is not to be subjected to fine academic tests. We can know roughly what it means and that is quite enough for any practical end.[6]

Oliver and his contemporaries (like the other great Edwardian federalist, Lionel Curtis) inherited some of these difficulties in terminology from the debates on the American constitution: indeed Oliver was an influential celebrant of Alexander Hamilton, one of the architects of the US constitution of 1787, and a leading 'federalist' at a time when of course the term implied support for a strong central executive at the expense of state powers.[7] An admirer of the US constitution, Oliver was more impressed by the nation-building that occurred than in the autonomy of the component American states—and his advocacy of a federalist reform of the British constitution was driven by the desire to consolidate the unity of the government of the British empire as well as to sustain a unified and efficient United Kingdom government—rather than through any wish to compromise the sovereignty of Westminster.

There is no doubt, however, that, despite this awareness, ambiguities in terminology caused difficulty, partly because of different notions of what constituted federalism—and partly because at the end of the nineteenth and early twentieth centuries federalism was entwined within two concurrent but discrete debates (on the reformed governance both of the wider empire and of the United Kingdom). The practice of 'federation' throughout the empire was so varied that colonial analogies to the United Kingdom tended to compound the confusion (for example the Union of South Africa (1910) was clearly a much more centralised polity

[4] Emphasis added. I Butt, *Home Government for Ireland: Irish Federalism! Its Meaning, its Objects and its Hopes* (Dublin, John Falconer, 1870) 21, 29.

[5] FS Oliver ['Pacificus'], *Federalism and Home Rule* (London, John Murray, 1910) 50.

[6] FS Oliver, *What Federalism is Not* (London, John Murray, 1914) viii.

[7] FS Oliver, *Alexander Hamilton: an Essay on American Union* (London, Archibald Constable, 1906). For Lionel Curtis see D Lavin, *From Empire to International Commonwealth: a Biography of Lionel Curtis* (Oxford, Clarendon Press, 1996).

than Canada (1867) or Australia (1901)). Moreover, comparing Ireland (or Scotland) with Canada begged the question of whether Ireland constituted the federation as a whole, or was merely one of the component states of a federated United Kingdom. Oliver himself wrote in 1917:

> It is hardly necessary to say that I entirely agree ... about the false analogy between Ireland and a Dominion. For seven years at least I have been trying to get this into the heads of Unionists and Liberals alike, but it is extraordinarily difficult to do so ... we may drift into some kind of position where we shall find that we are pledged to give dominion status to Ireland or to all Ireland except the Six Counties instead of 'state' status. You can't possibly in my opinion give any kind of control over customs without landing yourself in Dominion status sooner or later.[8]

A key irony here was that contemporary federalists pushed imperial analogies, hoping that Ireland would emerge as a Quebec or even as an Ontario. In fact, Ireland emerged from British rule in 1921 as a Canada.

III. The Drivers of Federalism?

There were in essence three key determinants of the centrality (or otherwise) of federalism in nineteenth and early twentieth century British politics: the challenges of closer and more efficient imperial governance, the seriousness of nationalist challenge in Ireland, and the apparently demonstrable success of federalism in other national contexts. A fourth aspect—the European or global federal ambitions of internationalists like Lord Lothian in the 1930s—was swiftly overwhelmed by war in 1939, and was anyway often characterised by the 'shaky' thinking that vitiated so much federalist advocacy (and thus cannot be regarded as a 'key' driver of the issue).[9] Taken together, and viewed over the longue durée, these first three themes constitute what has been described (by Michael Burgess) as 'the British tradition of federalism'.[10] However, lest this discussion appear overly eschatological, the existence of an intellectually vigorous, and indeed often dominant, British tradition of opposition to federalism should be immediately flagged (and will be discussed shortly).

Taking first the challenge of empire, Britain's external relationships constituted one set of roots for the federalist debate in the late nineteenth century (as, indeed, in the twenty-first). The successful federal unification of several major polities both inside and outwith the empire—the USA, Canada, Germany—provided an exemplar to British politicians and ideologues who, writing in the last three

[8] Public Record Office of Northern Ireland, Edward Carson Papers, D.1507/A/22/20: Oliver to Carson, 30 March 1917.

[9] See J Kendle, *Federal Britain: a History* (London, Routledge, 1997) 163.

[10] M Burgess, *The British Tradition of Federalism* (Leicester, Leicester University Press, 1995).

decades of the nineteenth century, were ever more concerned with the threat of imperial disintegration. Such apprehensions, and their federal remedies, were reflected in the writings of John Seeley,[11] Charles Dilke, and other, lesser, ideologues such as Francis de Labilliere and Thomas Spalding.[12] But the key agency for the their evangelising, the Imperial Federation League (1884–92), ultimately failed, partly because the complex and largely ad hoc structure of the British empire was simultaneously a stimulus to reformers, as well as a major obstacle in the way of any coherent reform. Furthermore, unlike a later generation of British federalists in the years between 1910 and 1920, those within the League largely failed to connect their cause with the preeminent constitutional question of the day—Irish Home Rule. Ultimately, then, a combination of the intractability of the core issues, the dominance of other—Irish—questions, as well as popular (and some elite) apathy, derailed the first comprehensive effort to apply federal principles to the governance of the empire.

A second, though sometimes entangled strand of federalist thought, was stimulated by the challenge of Irish nationalism, which in turn was related to both contemporary critiques of the Scottish union, as well as (ultimately) its continuing problems in the twenty-first century. Certainly in the mid-late nineteenth century Irish protest on national rights and on specific issues such as land reform informed Scottish protest. The pulses of federalist intellectual and political activity coincided with periods of successful mobilisation of Irish nationalist opinion. Indeed, this highlighted a fundamental part of the problem with federalist advocacy in the nineteenth century: it often looked like (and indeed was) a conservative and propertied reaction to the challenge of more radical constitutional proposals.

Federalism, in other words, has frequently appeared to be both a reactive as well as an instrumentalist strategy rather than an ideal. Thus, federalism won an early and important airing in the context of the popular campaign for the repeal of the Act of Union (1801), which developed from the 1830s, and flourished in the early and mid-1840s under the leadership of Daniel O'Connell. The federal idea was briefly and unsuccessfully promoted by conservative constitutional nationalists in Ireland in the 1870s partly as a device to soften British and unionist opposition to an Irish parliament. And it was widely promoted by young Tory and imperialist intellectuals in the Edwardian era as a means of addressing several key problems of empire—but especially the challenges of Irish nationalism after 1910.

Third, while 'home rule' was (as AV Dicey memorably alleged, adapting Lord Derby on parliamentary reform) 'a leap in the dark', and was thus readily

[11] JR Seeley, *The Expansion of England: Two Courses of Lectures* (London, Macmillan, 1883). See D Bell, *Reordering the World: Essays on Liberalism and Empire* (Princeton NJ, Princeton University Press, 2016), 265–96.

[12] F De Labilliere, *British Federalism: its Rise and Progress* (London, Royal Colonial Institute, 1893); TA Spalding, *Federation and Empire: a Study in Politics* (London, Henry & Co., 1896). For an excellent recent reappraisal of the failure of successive schemes of imperial federation see Mohr, above n.1. See also D Bell, *The Idea of Greater Britain: Empire and the Future of World Order, 1860–1900*, paperback edition (Princeton NJ, Princeton University Press, 2011).

susceptible to the catastrophising of Edwardian unionists (the 'project fear' of the time), British and Irish federalists could point to a range of successful new or reformed federal—or confederal—states as inspiration. The US constitution of 1787 was a fundamental underlying influence. Both Irish nationalists and British unionists (with some exceptions) looked favourably on the American constitution, and both British and Irish federalist thinkers referred to its success. For Irish Catholics, with a strong migrant presence in the USA, American models were attractive—and both Daniel O'Connell and other lesser lights (such as the Irish Catholic priest and political thinker, Father Thaddeus O'Malley) looked to the American federal model.[13] The success of the federal or union cause in the American civil war tended to be interpreted as an international victory for the federal ideal. Edwardian English imperialists were interested in a range of federal models; but (as has been noted) perhaps the most well-connected and influential of these ideologues, FS Oliver, was also deeply interested in the origins of the American federal constitution.

Equally, the Canadian constitutions of 1840 and 1867 had an impact in terms of the British-Irish relationship—particularly through the British North America Act (1867) and its creation of a federal government overlying the three provinces of Canada, New Brunswick and Nova Scotia. This was a perceptible influence on Irish nationalist promotion of federalism in 1870 as a model for the Irish-British relationship. Isaac Butt argued in 1870 (following EA Freeman) that there were different layers of precedent for his federalist proposals—ancient (the Achaean League), medieval (the Swiss cantons) and more modern—the United States, but also preeminently Canada:

> [P]erhaps the most remarkable tribute to the principle of Federalism is to be found in the course taken by the British parliament in the year 1867 when it was thought to incorporate into one dominion all the north American provinces of the British crown.[14]

The apparently successful creation of a strongly centralised Union state in South Africa (by 1910) bringing together Cape Colony, Natal, Transvaal and the Orange Free State supplied an even more direct model to Conservative constitutional reformers in Britain, since the Union operated on a devolved rather than federal principle. Moreover, the idea of converting Boer insurgents into loyal citizens of a new British dominion was a strong influence on those English imperialists who actively sought to bring Irish insurgents into a loyal constitutional relationship with the British crown.

Other continental European examples provided models: the Swiss Confederation (1848), the United Kingdom of Norway and Sweden (created under the

[13] eg T O'Malley, *Home Rule on the Basis of Federalism* (London, William Ridgeway, 1873).

[14] Butt, above n 4, 23. See C Reid, '"An Experiment in Constructive Unionism": Isaac Butt, Home Rule and Federalist Political Thought during the 1870s' (2014) 129(537) *English Historical Review* 348, for Butt on Canada. See also JJ Golden's excellent 'The Protestant Influence on the Origins of Irish Home Rule, 1861–1871' (2013) 128(535) *English Historical Review* 1502.

Treaty of Kiel, 1814), Germany (with its federal constitution of 1870)—all of these were referenced in Irish and British federalist apologetics from the 1870s onwards. Equally, even failed states offered federalist lessons—such as the United Kingdom of Denmark-Norway (1536–1814), and especially the United Kingdom of the Netherlands (1815–30). The United Kingdom of Norway-Sweden (1814–1905) ultimately proved an embarrassment to federalists, in so far as it was originally hailed as a success story, but by the 1890s was less obviously so (a point made ironically by AV Dicey in commenting that 'the goodwill generated by a system of Home Rule is bringing these countries to the brink of civil war').[15]

For its British and Irish proponents in the nineteenth and early twentieth centuries, federalism was a constitutional wonder-drug: Thaddeus O'Malley called it 'the acme of the science of government; it is the eclecticism of political philosophy'.[16] Brand new polities had been made possible by federalism: nationalist federalists in Ireland like O'Malley pointed to the substantial success of the USA, temporarily disrupted (it was true) by civil war, but delivering an enormously wealthy and lasting federal union out of unpromising materials.[17] German economic and social advances had been secured similarly by confederation and federalism ('we see the young German Empire, by this same federalism, springing up in a bound, into a gigantic colossus overshadowing and overawing all Europe').[18]

For these true 'believers', old polities had been restored either by federalism or a reform of their federal constitutions: Switzerland had been refreshed in this way, and even the antique Habsburg empire had evidently been given (through the *Ausgleich* of 1867, which established a dual monarchy and shared foreign, finance and defence ministries) 'a fresh lease of power'.[19]

IV. Federalist Programmes?

British, Irish and American political elites from the end of the eighteenth century onwards were effectively engaged in a political dialogue about the merits of federation: indeed to some extent the federalism of the American constitution was defined and defended in relation to the perceived strengths and weaknesses of the British constitution. In the fifth Federalist Paper, published in November 1787, John Jay argued that America could learn from the problems encountered by

[15] AV Dicey, *A Leap into the Dark: a Criticism of the Principles of Home Rule as Illustrated by the Bill of 1893* (London, John Murray, 1911) 154.

[16] O'Malley, above n 13, 32.

[17] ibid, 33–34, 77.

[18] ibid, 33.

[19] ibid, 33; cf RW Seton-Watson [Scotus viator], *Racial Problems in Hungary* (London, Constable, 1908); RW Seton-Watson, *The Southern Slav Question and the Habsburg Empire* (London, Constable, 1911).

the British before the Union of 1707: 'the history of Great Britain is the one with which we are in general the best acquainted, and it gives us many useful lessons', Jay wrote:

> [W]e may profit by their experience without paying the price which it cost them. Although it seems obvious to common sense that the people of such an island should be but one nation, yet we find that they were for ages divided into three, and that those three were almost constantly embroiled in quarrels and wars with one another.

In fact Linda Colley has been able to point out that a key aspect of the British response to the American federal constitution of 1787 was an emphasis upon those aspects which seemed essentially British; and she has also commented upon the interconnections (perceived by Thomas Paine and others) between that constitution and the British tradition of legal charters.[20]

The growth (in the 1830s and afterwards) of a popular movement in Ireland in favour of repeal of the Act of Union (1801) helped to stimulate a debate about the range of constitutional alternatives available at that juncture—and in particular both the American constitution of 1787 and the new Canadian Act of Union (1840) were identified as possible influences which might be examined at Westminster. The intellectual protagonists of this debate in Ireland were (again) Thaddeus O'Malley as well as the County Down landowner, William Sharman Crawford, and John Grey Vesey Porter, the son of a County Fermanagh landowner.

Sharman Crawford in February 1833 sought a constitutional *via media* in asking whether there was 'no intermediate course (between the existing union and its complete repeal) by which, at least, an attempt could be made to secure in some degree the benefits of local legislation without throwing off the beneficial control of imperial legislation in imperial concerns?'.[21] In October 1839 he argued that the repeal of the Union would create a parliament in Dublin which would be as powerless in contest with London as had the lately suppressed parliament of Lower Canada: in each case there was a need for a federal connection with Great Britain.[22]

The development of the repeal movement into a thoroughly popular mobilisation after 1841 brought with it increased interest in a federalist compromise, and in August 1843 Crawford enlarged upon his previous ideas, advocating parliaments not only for Ireland, but also for Scotland and England, each with powers of 'local' taxation. John Kendle has rightly complained that 'Crawford's scheme was more devolutionary than federal in nature. There was no clear-cut division of sovereignty; the imperial parliament retained veto powers in crucial areas'.[23] But in

[20] L Colley, 'Empires of Writing: Britain, America and constitutions, 1776–1848' (2014) 32 (2) *Law & History Review* 237–66, 243, 247.

[21] HA Cronne, TW Moody and DB Quinn (eds), *Essays in British and Irish history in Honour of James Eadie Todd* (London, Frederick Müller, 1949) 238.

[22] ibid, 241.

[23] J Kendle, *Ireland and the Federal solution: the Debate over the United Kingdom Constitution, 1870–1921* (Kingston and Montreal, McGill-Queen's University Press, 1989) 9–10.

fact Crawford's intellectual leadership stimulated others both within and beyond the repeal movement.

John Grey Vesey Porter, outside the movement at this time, published two influential pamphlets in 1843–44, the first praising the confederal United Kingdom of Norway-Sweden, created in 1814 out of the old and heavily centralised union of Denmark-Norway, and with Norway and Sweden each united only by foreign policy concerns and a shared monarchy (much else—legislatures, administrations, state churches, and armed forces—was separated): '[until 1814] Norway was' he declared, 'a miserable backward out-farm; now a very flourishing kingdom'.[24] Porter's later work lauded the American constitution, and proposed similar arrangements in the British Isles: he called for a British and Irish parliament, each exercising sovereignty over its domestic affairs, and with an overarching imperial parliament with responsibility for external affairs.[25] He summarised his pitch in these terms:

> [N]ow a federal union between Great Britain and Ireland, each island under one and the same king or queen, sovereign at home in its own affairs, over its own land, with an imperial congress or assembly or parliament (no matter what the name may be) of so many members for each island to settle all their common foreign and colonial affairs, is the only fair kind of union between them.[26]

His argument was that 'free trade does not depend in any degree on a union of parliaments but on a union of the two nations which I hope and am sure will always continue between us'.[27]

Even Daniel O'Connell was momentarily persuaded, announcing in October 1844 through his Derrynane Manifesto his 'preference for the federative plan'.[28] But in essence, while federalism appealed to pragmatists like O'Connell, it cut little ice with more fundamentalist nationalists—and this would emerge as a key feature of the political pathology of federalist debate over the next 150 years. Federalism was frequently posited as a compromise formula, which centrists and pragmatists could only accept at the risk of isolation and rejection from more extremist forces; and indeed this remains the case in the early twenty-first century.

The federal idea reemerged in the 1870s, again pitched as a compromise which would deliver an Irish parliament, while retaining an imperial or metropolitan connection. The international contexts here were the reconstruction of the federal government of the United States after the civil war—and also the Canadian constitution of 1867: the national contexts were the failed Irish Republican Brotherhood (separatist) uprising of 1867, the mobilisation of subsequent popular sympathy for the imprisoned or executed insurgents—and also the alienation of some Irish

[24] JGV Porter, *Some Agricultural and Political Irish Questions Calmly Discussed* (London, Ridgway, nd [1843]) 82.

[25] JGV Porter, *Ireland* (Dublin, 1844); Cronne and others, above n 21, 247.

[26] Porter, ibid, vii.

[27] ibid, 70.

[28] Cronne and others, above n 21, 248.

conservatives from the reformist strategies of the Liberal government in London. In addition federalism drew upon a tradition of nationally minded conservative and unionist thought in Ireland.

This set of influences delivered a proposal for Irish self-government, articulated through a body called the Home Government Association (1870), and led by Isaac Butt: Butt believed in federalism, but he also saw pragmatically that it might unite nationalists and conservatives within the one national cause. He called both for an Irish parliament with domestic autonomy and for a federated United Kingdom that would respect local needs while preserving the 'one great imperial state'. He fleshed out his ideas in the pamphlet *Home Government for Ireland* (1870), where he directly proposed Canada as a model for the constitutional relationship between Ireland and Britain. He envisioned an imperial parliament which would retain English, Scots and Irish MPs and which would continue to legislate on military matters and foreign and imperial affairs (the latter to include relevant taxation).[29] The Irish parliament, by contrast, was to have complete control over Irish matters and was to comprise a House of Commons with some 250 members as well as a House of Lords.

However, Butt was wary of supplying too much detail for fear of diverting attention away from the main thrust of his scheme and into the minutiae—and there are aspects of his federalist vision that are at best hazy. Butt did not tightly define the relationship between the proposed imperial and Irish parliaments, and he did not trouble to enlarge upon the crucial issue of customs and excise. In so far as Butt seems to have had in mind a division of sovereignty between the two assemblies, Irish and imperial, and in so far as the Irish parliament was to have had 'supreme control' over Irish affairs unless specifically reserved to London, it seems likely that he favoured local control of customs and thus a loose confederation. But the evidence is ultimately unclear—in part because Butt wanted it that way.[30] In any event, and even though he led the Irish nationalist grouping at Westminster, his federalist pitch won little traction either in Ireland or in the House of Commons, where it was debated in June 1874 and again in 1876.

For Isaac Butt's contemporary and ally, Thaddeus O'Malley, the 'best exemplar' of federalism remained unquestionably the United States.[31] And in essence O'Malley's own proposal for a federated United Kingdom was a direct adaptation of the US constitution, with both the Scots and the Irish sharing the same case for state parliaments, and with the real possibility of adapting the model of the Supreme Court and other federal institutions for British and Irish use.[32]

Gladstone, as Liberal leader and Prime Minister, sought to address the challenge of Irish national sentiment—looking (in August 1885) at the Austro-Hungarian

[29] Butt, above n 4, 42–54. The most recent exploration of Butt's federalist thought is Reid, above n.14, 332–61.

[30] See A Jackson, *Home Rule: an Irish History*, paperback edition (London, Phoenix, 2004) 32–33.

[31] O'Malley, above n 13, 34.

[32] ibid, 77, 85.

model of the *Ausgleich*, and (in October) at the two key constitutional acts governing Canada (those of 1840 and 1867). His two Home Rule Bills (1886, 1893) drew in particular upon the latter settlement, though it was also thought that the form of Home Rule (however unsatisfactorily) bestowed by Hungary upon Croatia through the *nagodba* of 1868 had been an influence. Gladstone's successor as Liberal leader and Prime Minister, HH Asquith, essentially built upon the two earlier bills in launching his own Home Rule legislation in April 1912. None of these measures was strictly federal, but each had federal influences or (arguably) federal trajectories: AV Dicey certainly complained that the 1893 Home Rule Bill 'is at bottom a federalist or semi-federalist constitution; it introduces into English institutions many of the forms of federalism and still more of its spirit'.[33]

The 1886 Bill provided (*inter alia*) for a unicameral Irish legislature, the abolition of Irish representation at Westminster, and wide-ranging powers for the Irish legislature over domestic issues. Westminster was to retain reserved (and residual) powers, control over domestic taxation—but not customs duties. The 1893 Bill provided for the *explicit* supremacy of Westminster, an executive committee of the Irish Privy Council as a form of cabinet, a bicameral parliament, and (originally) the retention of Irish MPs on an 'in and out' basis—they would be excluded from specifically British debates and divisions, but admitted to all others.[34] The 'in and out'—a precursor of subsequent devices such as 'English votes for English laws' (2015–16)—was a feature of Croatian Home Rule, but was abandoned here because of criticism of its evident impracticality. In 1886 and 1893 it was proposed that Ireland pay an 'imperial contribution' to London as a first charge on its revenue—this 'first charge' being ultimately equated with the yield from Ireland's customs duties.

Asquith's third Home Rule bill of 1912 also affirmed the supremacy of Westminster; and it provided for the retention of Irish members, albeit in much smaller numbers than proposed in 1893. As in 1893, there was to be a bicameral Irish legislature. As in the past, most domestic matters were ascribed to the proposed Irish parliament, but there remained a range of such matters (and imperial concerns) reserved to Westminster (eg land purchase, pensions, national insurance, tax collection, the Royal Irish Constabulary).[35] The financial arrangements were complex—but in essence allowed for the transfer of all Irish revenue into the imperial exchequer which would then pay out the operating costs of those areas of administration under Irish control with an additional amount to provide a margin of error (this combined payment was the 'transferred sum'). The Irish government could levy new taxes, but not any that conflicted with imperial taxation. It could not levy customs duties. The Irish could raise existing taxes but not by more than 10 per cent.

[33] Dicey, above n 15, 13.
[34] Jackson, above n 30, 94.
[35] ibid, 127.

Between 1910 and 1918 a group of imperialist unionists, but particularly FS Oliver and Lionel Curtis acting alongside the second Earl of Selborne, agitated to put a federalist reform of the British constitution at the centre of the debate on Irish Home Rule. They were essentially elite activists, and they looked to high-level conferencing and intricate published manifestos rather than mass mobilisation. The Liberal Home Rule measures were, for them, imperfectly federal, not so much because of the issue of indivisible sovereignty, but because they did not embrace the other constituent nations of the United Kingdom. They dismissed the alternatives to federalism—a centralised union and independent dominion status. FS Oliver defined his version of federalism in 1914 in saying that:

> [W]hatever its [legislative] form, its effect should be to grant to Ireland powers of local government substantially similar to those exercised by local assemblies in Canada, Australia, and South Africa, while reserving to the Westminster parliament powers not substantially less than those reserved to the central governments of those three great self-governing dominions.[36]

England, Ireland and Scotland instead would get a legislature and responsible executive for their national concerns, while the common needs of the three kingdoms (and of the empire) would be treated within a supreme parliament. Each of these national parliaments would have wide powers, but the supreme authority would lie with the central power, which would also control customs and excise. Un-allotted powers should be retained by the central parliament. The detailed shape of the national legislatures would be left to separate national conventions: in a premonition of the 'asymmetric' devolution of the twenty-first century, Oliver decreed that it was 'not necessary that there should be uniformity in these constitutions. Their variety will not impair the unity, not threaten the security of the United Kingdom'.[37]

In so far as these federalist activists had any direct legislative legacy, then it lay with the last of the Home Rule measures, the Government of Ireland Act (1920). The legislation which created the partition settlement, a separate Northern Ireland, and a parliament and executive in Belfast, was a product of the Home Rule and federalist debates in British politics. The Government of Ireland Act did not create a strictly federal constitution: Westminster remained sovereign in all the circumstances envisioned by the 1920 Act. However the measure did create two bicameral parliaments in Ireland, in Belfast and Dublin, and created as well a Council of Ireland as a means of communication and cooperation between the two. While Westminster remained sovereign, the Act did envision the possibility that authority over customs and excise might be granted to the Council of Ireland by agreement and in the future. More generally, because the convention was swiftly established at Westminster that the Northern Ireland parliament had autonomy within its own statutory areas of jurisdiction, an approximation of shared sovereignty was effectively put in place.

[36] Oliver, above n 6, vii.
[37] See Jackson, above n 30, 219.

The Act therefore embodied a settlement which, while nominally devolutionist, came very close to being federal in practice. Certainly, before the fluid devolution settlements of 1998 and after, the Government of Ireland Act was the nearest federal-style encroachment that the British parliament was prepared to countenance. While later parliamentarians and administrators were prepared to countenance elaborate federalist reforms for Malaya (1948–63), Rhodesia and Nyasaland (1953–63) the West Indies (1958–62) and Nigeria (1960–63), Northern Ireland was as close as it was allowed to threaten Britain itself.[38] Even then its unhappy denouement between 1969 and 1972, when the Stormont parliament was finally prorogued, served to reinforce the British tradition of opposition to federalism.

V. The British Tradition of Opposition to Federalism

Michael Burgess, writing in the mid-1990s, eloquently defined a British tradition of federalism, dating from the 1870s and surviving through to the end of the twentieth century.[39] Others, such as John Kendle, have defined a 'federal Britain' with an even greater longevity, spanning from the first theorising at the time of the union of the English and Scottish crowns in 1603 through to the debates upon the British role within an evidently developing federal Europe.[40] But in some ways a no less influential and striking tradition has been British opposition to federalism—those, often unionist, thinkers who have elaborated detailed critiques of the federalist idea, and whose arguments continue to present a challenge to federalist advocates. Paradoxically, these intellectuals have often found themselves in a tacit but effective alliance with radical nationalists, for whom federalism has always constituted a dangerous diversion from the true faith.

One of the key opponents of the application of federalist reform within a British and Irish context (as distinct from the federalist principle) was the historian and Gladstonian, EA Freeman (from 1884 Regius Professor of Modern History at Oxford). Writing in his epic but uncompleted *History of Federal Government in Greece and Italy* (1863) Freeman claimed that replacing the unions with a federated United Kingdom would be a poor substitution: 'no one could wish to cut up our United Kingdom into a Federation, to invest English counties with the same rights as American states, or even to restore Scotland and Ireland to the quasi-federal position which they held before their respective Unions'.[41] Subsequently,

[38] Kendle, above n 9, 128, 136, 143, 146. Mohr, above n 1, has elaborated Kendle's emphasis on some British elite resistance to federalism.

[39] Burgess, above n 10.

[40] Kendle, above n 9, 2–3.

[41] EA Freeman, *History of Federal Government in Greece and Italy*, second edition (London, Macmillan, 1893) 76. For Freeman see (for example) GA Bremner and J Conlin (eds), *Making History: Edward Augustus Freeman and Victorian Cultural Politics* (Oxford, Oxford University Press, 2015). For Freeman and imperial federation see Bell, above n 12, 327–33. See also Reid, above n 14, 357. Reid notes that, while John Stuart Mill also opposed a federal reconstitution of the United Kingdom, he did not engage with Irish reformers in the same comprehensive manner as Freeman and later Dicey.

in the context of Isaac Butt's advocacy of federal reform for Ireland, Freeman argued—in the *Fortnightly Review* of July 1874—that a federal system was to be supported if it tended to greater union, but not if it were a step towards separation: 'I am inclined to think that total separation would be a lesser evil than such a scheme of federation, or whatever it is to be called, as is now proposed'.[42] Kendle has suggested that the apogee of Freeman's assaults came in April 1885, when 'the most punishing criticism of imperial federation' was supplied by him in an essay published in the April edition of *Macmillan's Magazine*.[43]

AV Dicey built upon this foundation, arguing, like Freeman, that if 'the strict enforcement of ordinary law and strict protection for legal rights' was unworkable, 'then, tho' with the greatest regret, I should advocate separation'.[44] Dicey, Vinerian Professor of English Law at Oxford (1882–1909), and the most distinguished jurist of the age, was in fact the key critic of federalism—with his arguments first aired in a *Contemporary Review* essay in 1882, and later elaborated in his *Law of the Constitution* (1885) and in subsequent publications. Federalism, he wrote in 1882, 'revolutionises the whole constitution of the United Kingdom; by undermining the parliamentary sovereignty, it deprives English institutions of their elasticity, their strength, and their life; it weakens the Executive at home and lessens the power of the county to resist foreign attack'.[45] Moreover, this would be a fundamentally unnecessary revolution: it

> holds out no hope of conciliation with Ireland. An attempt, in short, to impose on England and Scotland a constitution which they do not want, and which is quite unsuited to the historical traditions and to the genius of Great Britain, offers to Ireland a constitution which Ireland is certain to dislike which had none of the real or imaginary charms of independence, and ensures none of the solid benefits to be hoped for from a genuine union with England.[46]

Dicey's great critique of Gladstone's Home Rule Bill was embodied in his *England's Case against Home Rule*, published in November 1886, wherein he argued famously that Home Rule would destroy parliamentary sovereignty and weaken Britain and its empire. John Kendle's crisp analysis of Dicey's 1886 case is worth quoting at length:

> For Dicey the disadvantages of federalism were three fold: first, the sovereignty of parliament would be destroyed and all constitutional arrangements would be dislocated; second, the power of great Britain would be diminished; and third, the chance of further disagreement with Ireland would be increased rather than lessened. As far as Dicey was concerned, parliamentary sovereignty provided the United Kingdom with more flexibility than would an American-style constitution. From the moment the United Kingdom

[42] Quoted in Kendle, above n 23, 18.
[43] Kendle, above n 9, 50.
[44] Kendle, above n 23, 23.
[45] See also the discussion of Dicey and sovereignty by Oliver and Tomkins in this book.
[46] Quoted in Kendle, above n 23, 22–23.

> became a federation the omnipotence of parliament would be gone, and the authority of central and local parliaments would be limited by articles of the constitution and by the Federal Court.[47]

Dicey's critique was further elaborated in his assault on the later iterations of Gladstonian Home Rule, published as *A Leap in the Dark* in 1893, and tweaked again in 1911. Federalism, he repeated, would not satisfy Irish nationalists: it would mean a division of powers which would undermine the strength of the country. It would mean government by the courts rather than parliament (Thomas Mohr has commented on this illusory but remarkably hardy British self-image of minimal legal and constitutional regulation); and yet at the same time the rule of law would be subverted—because state authorities would not always enact imperial judgements. While Dicey is sometimes accused of racist insensitivity, the example that he chose to illustrate this subversion of the rule of law was the flouting of federal protection of the rights of African Americans in the southern, ex-confederate, states.[48]

Dicey also saw the practical political problems facing any federal reform as overwhelming. There was still no substantial desire for federalisation in Wales and Scotland. The exclusion of Irish MPs from the federal (or rather) imperial parliament (as in the 1886 Home Rule Bill) was tantamount to 'taxation without representation'. On the other hand, the 'in and out' arrangement for Irish MPs (as in the first draft of the 1893 Home Rule Bill) was wholly impractical. Nor would the unity of the Empire be augmented by the disunity of the United Kingdom: federalism in fact would produce divided loyalties between state and centre. The international successes that federalists cited were inapplicable: 'all the conditions which make a federal constitution work successfully in the United States, in Switzerland, and possibly in Germany, are wanting in England and Ireland'. He pointedly denied the applicability of other analogies commonly deployed ('of Hungary and its relation to the Empire of which it forms a part, nothing at all will be said. There is nothing in that relation analogous to Irish Home Rule').[49]

Aspects of Dicey's critiques are unpalatable to a modern readership: his extreme unionist partisanship, especially in 1912–14, allied with his crude characterisation and easy dismissal of Irish nationalism. His identification of an indivisible parliamentary sovereignty is now commonly questioned. His occasionally patronising and combative tones grate against modern susceptibilities. But at the same time his elaborate arguments have not always produced reasoned rebuttals; and indeed he is sometimes rebuffed, even by scholars, using the same polemical register which he himself increasingly adopted. Thus his influence—which was commanding during his lifetime—still resonates a century after his death.[50]

[47] ibid. 55.

[48] Dicey, above n 15, 158. Mohr, above n.1, 159.

[49] ibid, 154; cf Seton-Watson (1911), above n 19.

[50] Burgess, above n 10, 21; Kendle, above n 9, 56–57, 172; I McLean, *What's Wrong with the British Constitution?* (Oxford, Oxford University Press, 2010) 313.

One aspect of this resonance has become clear for the first time with the opening of the John Murray archive in the National Library of Scotland. While it has long been recognized that federalist advocates like FS Oliver and Lionel Curtis were tireless and skilful publicists, it is now evident from the Murray archives that Dicey invested a great deal of care in tailoring his publications for the marketplace.[51] In other words, the considerable influence of his *England's Case Against Home Rule* (1886), which contained his core anti-federalist critique, was not accidental, but reflected considerable tactical thought and skill. It was Dicey who wrote to Murray in June 1886 proposing the work and recognising the need to produce it quickly before the public's interest in Home Rule waned: it was Dicey who urged a cheaper price and second edition, since he wanted his arguments to circulate widely 'even at the cost of pecuniary sacrifice'.[52] Again, it was Dicey who was the driving force behind an abridged version of the volume.[53] Dicey selected Murray to produce his key anti-federal statements, including also *A Leap in the Dark* (1893)—but this was a carefully calibrated decision since he also used rival publishing houses such as Cassell for lesser tracts and pamphlets and Macmillan for more learned lecture and monographic material. In brief, Dicey was not only the most respected constitutional lawyer of his time, but also an extremely shrewd communicator. This combination of learning and strategy would help to create momentum for a lasting Diceyan tradition of unionist and anti-federal argument within British politics.

VI. Failure and its Legacies

There clearly was no federalist reform of the British constitution in the nineteenth century, or in the first decades of the twentieth century, and the obvious concluding questions arise: why not—and what have been the legacies of this failure?

Federalism was almost always in effect a compromise. Imperial federalists were seeking to reverse what they saw as a dangerous drift in empire, and to balance colonial autonomy with a central imperial structure and vision. The patriarchs of Irish federation, influenced by north American analogies, were consciously seeking to find a middle way between the restoration of a wholly autonomous Irish parliament under the crown—in effect Irish legislative independence—and the Union settlement of 1800. Sharman Crawford and his supporters were seeking a balance between O'Connellite repeal and the status quo in the 1840s: Isaac Butt in the 1870s was proposing a moderate form of self-government which would unite different forms of Irish supporter, including Tories (even though he claimed that

[51] National Library of Scotland, John Murray Papers, Ms.40331.
[52] Murray Papers, Ms.40331, f.27: Dicey to Murray, 20 Nov 1886.
[53] Murray Papers, Ms.40331, f.70: Dicey to Murray, 21 March 1887.

'federal home rule was for him no mere tactical second-best; it was at once the thought-out expression of his own emotional view of the relationship between the two islands, and an offer of partnership to Irish protestantism').[54] Federalists in the Edwardian era were seeking to cut through Irish nationalist concerns and to provide a more efficient imperial parliament.

In each of these cases federalism exercised a brief popularity, but failed partly because it did not ultimately satisfy deep-seated nationalist sentiment. Federalism in the 1840s, while interesting to O'Connell, did not appeal to the Young Ireland movement. Federalism in the 1870s, while securing a fragile alliance between disenchanted Irish Tories and some nationalists, ultimately did not appeal to militants or indeed hardline constitutionalists led by Parnell. Federalism in the era of Home Rule, while attracting John Redmond, was of no interest to those who rose in 1916 to fight for an independent Irish republic.

Federalism, accordingly, was often seen in effect as a constitutionally conservative or unionist pitch. Even the Home Ruler Isaac Butt, originally a Tory and an Orangeman, argued that:

> [T]here is no people on earth less disposed to democracy than the Irish. The real danger of democratic or revolutionary violence is far more with the English people. The time may not be far distant when a separate Irish parliament might be in the best sense the Conservative element in the British constitution … I am not sure that one of the effects of a Federal Constitution would not be in many respects to strengthen the royal prerogatives out of the abeyance in which the system of governing by party has placed them. For myself I would not regret this …[55]

The key advocates of British federalism after 1910 were, however, usually conservative unionists motivated partly by wider ideas of imperial federation. Edward Carson, the militant leader of Ulster Unionism, wrote in 1918 that (aside from Home Rule and partition):

> [T]he only other possible solution seems to me to lie in a system of federalism for the whole United Kingdom. Averse as I am from any change in the present constitution with its single parliament for all purposes, I do not deny that Union which I regard as the keystone of the British Commonwealth may nevertheless be preserved upon the principle of a true federation.[56]

But this identification of the federalist ideal with what was seen as hardline Ulster Unionism was ultimately toxic so far as the possibilities of alluring Irish nationalism were concerned.

These federalist advocates were generally educationally or socially privileged and were characterised by a tendency to promote their cause *de haut en bas.*

[54] D Thornley, *Isaac Butt and Home Rule* (London, MacGibbon & Key, 1964) 20.
[55] Butt, above n 4, 64. Reid, above n 14, endorses the idea (frequently advocated by Butt's opponents) that there were many continuities between his Tory and Orange careers and his subsequent development. See also Jackson, above n 30, 29.
[56] Carson Papers, D.1507/A/26/42: Carson to unidentified, 14 Feb 1918.

Federalist ideals were propagated uniformly by learned and elaborate essays and pamphlets, as distinct from mass campaigns. On this FS Oliver lamented in 1918,

> I have found ... that the role of one who writes but does not talk in Parliament is necessarily limited. He finds the gate shut in his face at a certain point, a notice up that only practical statesmen are admitted beyond the barrier.[57]

While federalism had in fact colonised a substantial part of the House of Commons by the end of the First World War (there was an inconclusive Speaker's Conference on the theme in 1919–20), it never succeeded in gaining popular support.[58] The varieties and complexities of federalism proved harder to market than ostensibly simpler formulae such as 'union' or 'independence'—or even the somewhat more nebulous, but carefully packaged 'Home Rule'. Indeed, it would seem that some of these difficulties in communication have lingered even in 2016–17, in so far as much popular debate over Britain's complex relationship with a federalising Europe has ultimately crystallised around the ostensibly unambiguous notions of 'remain' and 'leave' (or 'taking back control').

The federal idea suffered, therefore, because it was characterised by lack of definition, by lack of conceptual clarity, and by division amongst its advocates. Federalism in the nineteenth and twentieth centuries was used to designate a wide range of potential United Kingdom constitutions—from in effect loose confederal arrangements, echoing the United Kingdom of Norway and Sweden, favoured by 'nationalist unionists' like Butt, through to centralised devolutionist proposals offered by imperialist unionists like FS Oliver. Linked with this—it was being asked to carry too much political and conceptual weight. Irish nationalists saw federalism as (at best) a loosening of union, while imperialist federalists saw the reform as a means of attaining a more united United Kingdom, and indeed a more united Empire.

Moreover, federalism was countered by a robust tradition of unitary unionism which (while its main features have sometimes been delineated) has never been comprehensively evaluated. The ideas of Freeman and Dicey dominated discussion of federalism in the era of Irish Home Rule and independence—and long afterwards; and while aspects of this dual critique were challenged, and while the polemical tones of Dicey increasingly grated, many features of the case remained standing. In addition, Dicey's skills in terms of marketing his arguments and ideas have only recently become apparent.[59]

[57] Jackson, above n 30, 224. See also DG Boyce and J Stubbs' important article, 'F S Oliver, Lord Selborne and Federalism', (1976) 5 (1) *Journal of Imperial and Commonwealth History* 53–81.

[58] For a reappraisal of the Speaker's Conference (1919–20) see the work of A Evans: '"Too old a country ... too long accustomed to regard her life as one and indivisible": England and the Speaker's Conference on Devolution' (2017) 31(3), *Contemporary British History* 366–83. Also A Evans, '"A Lingering Diminuendo?": The Conference on Devolution, 1920' (2016) 35(3) *Parliamentary History* 315–35.

[59] Murray Papers, Ms 40331.

Federalism, in the end, became an export product—a set of concepts which by 1950 were well-understood within important sections of the British political and administrative elite, which were freely adapted for colonial purposes, but which were not judged to be politically expedient for United Kingdom consumption.[60] In a sense the issue for federalist advocates has not been the sustained resistance of truculent elites, or indeed the deeply-entrenched cult of the 'unwritten' British constitution. The British elite has in fact flirted with federalist ideas for over a century, while the lengthy experience of decolonisation (including federalist experiments in the West Indies, Malaya, Rhodesia and Nyasaland) as well as of Home Rule and devolution endowed some British politicians and civil servants with a considerable experience of producing written constitutions. The issue, in the end, has been partly one of popular apathy and incomprehension.[61]

In essence, federalism was often too much of a compromise, and too suspiciously conservative in origin and design: it was too elitist, too literary—and too slowly reactive to nationalism, in particular Irish nationalism. Whether federalism has now re-emerged too late in the day to engage Scots nationalists, and thus to provide a reform mechanism for the United Kingdom constitution, remains to be seen. But here, as elsewhere, there are clear symmetries between the British state's last great constitutional crisis, arising from Irish Home Rule, and the current storms over Brexit and Scottish independence.

[60] Kendle, above n 9, 149. Mohr, above n 1.

[61] Jackson, above n 30, 225–26.

2

Parliamentary Sovereignty, Federalism and the Commonwealth

PETER C OLIVER

I. Introduction

Given interest in recent years regarding how the British tradition of parliamentary sovereignty might or might not fit with some of the federal models that are sometimes proposed in order to accommodate Scotland, Northern Ireland and Wales within a contemporary version of the United Kingdom, it seems appropriate to go back and look at how that same tradition of parliamentary sovereignty was understood in the context of transition to other federal constitutional systems, as occurred in the creation of the Canadian and Australian federations, for example. This chapter will begin by looking at how parliamentary sovereignty was understood in the nineteenth century before looking at how, if at all, that understanding accounted for Canadian and Australian independence and Canadian and Australia federalism. The chapter will conclude with some reflections on how understandings of sovereignty evolve, and the extent to which that evolution is a product of constitutional principle, Canadian and Australian contexts, or both.

II. Parliamentary Sovereignty in the Nineteenth Century

During the nineteenth century, parliamentary sovereignty was the dominant rule of the British Constitution. Those who have read Jeffrey Goldsworthy's masterful history of parliamentary sovereignty will know that this doctrine was understood in absolute terms:[1] Parliament could enact any law whatever, and the courts would

[1] Jeffrey Goldsworthy, *Sovereignty of Parliament: History and Philosophy* (Oxford, Oxford University Press, 2001).

not stand in Parliament's way where that will was expressed clearly. That is to say that, unlike in the United States of America, there was no judicial review of legislation.

By the end of the nineteenth century, parliamentary sovereignty would take its best-known form, in the writings of Professor AV Dicey.[2] Dicey repeated the well-known and well-understood formulation regarding Parliament's ability to enact any law whatever and the courts' corresponding duty to put those laws into effect, but he added an important corollary. Given that Parliament's sovereignty was by definition absolute, it stood to reason that there must be one thing that a parliament could not do: that is, it could not bind a future parliament, for if it could do so successfully then Parliament would cease to be sovereign in the absolute sense that Dicey and others assumed to be the case.[3]

III. Canadian and Australian Autonomy and Parliamentary Sovereignty

Three British North American colonies came together to form the Dominion of Canada in 1867, creating a new country with four original provinces: New Brunswick, Nova Scotia, Ontario and Quebec. The constitutional terms had been negotiated at conferences in Quebec City and Charlottetown in the years preceding 1867 and were finalised in London. The Constitution Act, 1867, which set out the written part of the new Canadian Constitution (the rest consisting of the unwritten customs, conventions and principles of the British Constitution), was an Act of the Imperial Parliament at Westminster.

One might have expected for issues to arise immediately regarding the incompatibility of Canada's status as a new polity and the doctrine of the Westminster Parliament's absolute sovereignty, and this with respect to Canada as much as anywhere else in the United Kingdom and Empire. Furthermore, it might be thought odd that Canada was created in 1867 only two years after the Westminster Parliament had confirmed, by means of the Colonial Laws Validity Act 1865, its power to legislate with paramount force for the Empire.

In fact there was little or no concern of this nature, and this for a variety of reasons. First, Canada was proclaiming itself a new polity not rejecting its ongoing role and subordinate position in the Empire (at least where the Mother Country was concerned). The new Constitution contemplated, for instance, that Britain

[2] AV Dicey, *Lectures Introductory to the Study of the Law of the Constitution* (London, Macmillan, 1885). In this chapter, unless otherwise indicated, references to Dicey will be taken from the more widely available AV Dicey, *An Introduction to the Study of the Law of the Constitution*, 10th edn by ECS Wade (London, Macmillan, 1959).

[3] Dicey (1959), ibid, 68n. See also the discussion of Dicey by Jackson in this volume.

would continue to exercise foreign policy on Canada's behalf.[4] Second, Canadians could see the value in having an Imperial legislator, especially where there was a need to create a level playing field across the Empire, regarding merchant shipping or copyright, for example. Third, the Canadian Constitution did not have a domestic amending formula. What would now be seen as a serious oversight was seldom discussed in the pre-Confederation debates. Those who did speak to the issue pointed out what seems to have been obvious to all: that the Westminster Parliament would continue to exercise its power to amend the Constitution Act, 1867, a document which it had after all enacted.[5] So Westminster's ongoing sovereignty was vital to the management of Canada's constitutional text. In case this sounds excessively colonial to contemporary ears, one should remember that constitutional conventions soon emerged which moderated the strict legal position. That is, the Westminster Parliament would only enact laws for Canada on the basis of a request from Canadian authorities, usually a joint resolution of the House of Commons and Senate of Canada.[6]

Many of the same points were true for Australia whose Constitution was enacted by the Westminster Parliament in 1900. Australia was a new country but one which for the time being accepted its subordinate status in the Empire. Like Canada, it recognised the advantages of being part of the political, economic and military network of the British Empire. Unlike Canada, the new Australian Constitution contained a domestic amending formula. This made it less likely that Australia would have to call on the Westminster Parliament to amend the document that it had enacted, but no one prior to the Statute of Westminster denied its power to do so.[7]

So 1867 and 1900 put Canada and Australia on the road to independence by increasing their autonomy, but it seems that, early on at least, this did not destabilize the structure of British thinking on parliamentary sovereignty. As we have seen, Dicey set out the so-called logical impossibility of a sovereign Westminster Parliament binding future Westminster parliaments regarding the subject matter of legislation, whether that subject matter was regarding domestic United Kingdom issues or Canadian-Australian matters, constitutional or other. As Dicey's friend, James Bryce, would explain to his fellow parliamentarians regarding the prospect of Irish Home Rule:

> We shall retain as a matter of pure right the power to legislate for Ireland, for all purposes whatsoever, for the simple reason that we cannot divest ourselves of it. There is no principle more universally admitted by constitutional jurists than the absolute omnipotence of Parliament. This omnipotence exists because there is nothing beyond Parliament,

[4] As contemplated by Constitution Act, 1867, s 132.

[5] For further discussion, see Peter C Oliver, 'Canada, Quebec and Constitutional Amendment' (1999) 49 *University of Toronto Law Journal* 526–31.

[6] ibid.

[7] For discussion see Peter C Oliver, *The Constitution of Independence: The Development of Constitutional Theory in Australia, Canada and New Zealand* (Oxford, Oxford University Press, 2005) chs 9–10.

> or behind Parliament. … There is one limitation and one only upon our omnicompetence and that is that we cannot bind our successors. If we pass a statute purporting to extinguish our right to legislate on any given subject, or over any given district, it may be repudiated and repealed by any following Parliament—aye even by this present Parliament on any later day.[8]

Dicey himself set out the relevant basics of parliamentary sovereignty in his 1893 publication regarding Irish Home Rule, *A Leap in the Dark*: 'As a matter of legal theory Parliament has the right to legislate for any part of the Crown's dominions. Parliament may lawfully impose income tax upon the inhabitants of New South Wales; it may lawfully abolish the Constitution of the Canadian Dominion.'[9]

We will see that, unlike Dicey, Bryce had less rigid ideas regarding how sovereignty and federalism might fit together. We will now consider how Canadians in the late-nineteenth and early-twentieth century understood the compatibility of federalism and parliamentary sovereignty. We will then look at the creative writings of James Bryce on these points, writings which proved popular in discussions regarding a possible Australian Commonwealth Constitution.

IV. Canadian and Australian Federalism and Parliamentary Sovereignty

Thus far, we have been considering the interaction between Imperial parliamentary sovereignty and the emerging autonomy of countries such as Canada and Australia.[10] As stated at the outset, I have chosen Canada and Australia because they are federations, so it is now appropriate to consider how parliamentary sovereignty squared, if at all, with federalism, according to contemporary observers.

Beginning with Canada, it is important to set the scene by noting that the preamble to the Constitution Act, 1867 sets out both that the British North American colonies wished to be 'federally united' and that they proposed to do so under 'a Constitution similar in principle to that of the United Kingdom'. Early constitutional writing in Canada had little difficulty reconciling sovereignty and federalism. However, this early flexible attitude began to shift in a more rigid and orthodox direction after the publication of Dicey's influential treatise.

[8] Parliamentary Debates (10 May 1886), quoted in G Marshall, *Parliamentary Sovereignty and the Commonwealth* (Oxford, Clarendon Press, 1957) 65–66.

[9] AV Dicey, *A Leap in the Dark: A Criticism of the Principles of Home Rule as Illustrated by the Bill of Rights 1893* (1st edn, 1893; 2nd edn, London, John Murray, 1911) which was dedicated to the Irish Unionists. Admittedly, here Dicey was making the point that Parliament's power was theoretical not real in the Dominions, whereas in Ireland its power was at that point still real and effective.

[10] The following discussion of early Canadian and Australian constitutional understandings reworks and revises parts of Oliver, above n 7, especially chs 2 and 5.

A. Early Canadian Writing on the Compatibility between Sovereignty and Federalism

The first detailed legal analysis of the Canadian Constitution, DA O'Sullivan's *A Manual of Government in Canada* was published in 1879.[11] A second edition appeared in 1887.[12] O'Sullivan, a Toronto practitioner,[13] was in some ways quite independent spirited, though it is hard to gauge the extent to which he was aware of being so. He showed sympathy for the view that 'exclusive authority' in section 91 of the 1867 Act pre-empted even the Imperial Parliament from (ever)[14] legislating under the powers listed there, apparently in opposition to the idea that the Westminster was *incapable* of binding itself. In the first and second editions, O'Sullivan regularly referred to the way in which sovereignty in Canada was divided between Imperial, Canadian and provincial authorities. These were 'separate and distinct sovereignties acting separately and independently of each other within their respective spheres'.[15] This way of speaking about sovereignty contradicted the traditional absolutist view associated with Austin. During the interval between O'Sullivan's first and second editions, Dicey's *Law of the Constitution* appeared reaffirming the absolutist version in a new, more legal guise.[16] O'Sullivan had clearly read Dicey's famous book, but the Canadian was not willing to abandon his 'heretical' views on sovereignty in the second edition. He persisted in referring to 'a *three-fold division* of sovereignty', 'separate and distinct'.[17] However, a certain amount of uncertainty or schizophrenia crept into his analysis.

The problem was that the preamble to the 1867 Act made clear that Canada's was 'a Constitution similar in principle to that of the United Kingdom', and yet its federal structure made it seem more similar to the United States of America. O'Sullivan, like other Canadian constitutional writers after him,[18] rebuked Dicey for implying that the 1867 Act was more American than British in inspiration, and for describing the preamble statement as 'official mendacity'.[19] And yet O'Sullivan's

[11] DA O'Sullivan, *A Manual of Government in Canada; or, The Principles and Institutions of our Federal and Provincial Constitutions* (Toronto, JC Stuart, 1879).

[12] DA O'Sullivan, *Government in Canada: The Principles and Institutions of our Federal and Provincial Constitutions: The BNA Act 1867 Compared with the United States Constitution, With a Sketch of the Constitutional History of Canada*, 2nd edn (Toronto, Carswell, 1887).

[13] RCB Risk, 'Constitutional Scholarship in the Late Nineteenth Century: Making Federalism Work' (1996) 46 *University of Toronto Law Journal* 427.

[14] O'Sullivan, above n 12, 98, added the word 'ever' to the relevant passage from the first edition: 'in regard to these [powers listed in section 91] the English legislature has no concern, and have deprived themselves of the right of *ever* interfering' (emphasis added).

[15] O'Sullivan, above n 11, 59.

[16] Dicey (1885), above n 2.

[17] O'Sullivan, above n 12, 20 (emphasis added).

[18] See, eg, Clement (1892), below n 30, 3; Lefroy (1897–8), below n 31, xliii–iv.

[19] Dicey (1885) above n 2, 151–53. Dicey later watered down his accusation of 'official mendacity' to 'diplomatic inaccuracy'. AV Dicey, *An Introduction to the Study of the Law of the Constitution* 4th edn (London, Macmillan, 1893) 156. See Mark D Walters, 'The British Legal Tradition in Canadian Constitutional Law' in P. Oliver, P. Macklem & N Des Rosiers (eds), *The Oxford Handbook of the Canadian Constitution* (Oxford, Oxford University Press, 2017) ch. 3.

federalist and relativistic usage of the term 'sovereignty' could have been said to vindicate Dicey's criticism.[20] O'Sullivan made up for his equivocation on 'sovereignty' by reasserting in true Dicey fashion the absolute sovereignty of the Westminster Parliament: 'The British legislature has no division of powers, it legislates on all classes of subjects and there is no limit to its powers ... it is omnipotent.'[21] Furthermore, the Canadian legislatures, federal and provincial, 'deriv[ed] their power from the same sovereign authority'.[22] O'Sullivan was clearly torn between his American and British influences, as further on in the text he expanded on this idea of derivation to include an element of popular sovereignty: 'Both [the federal and the provincial] powers were derived from the will of the people of Canada, acting under British authority, and these powers cannot be altered but by that same will and authority.'[23] We will see more of popular sovereignty in the discussion of the Australian Constitution.

The unapologetic way in which passages originally written for O'Sullivan's first edition referred to federal and provincial 'sovereignty' was followed by more tentative writing in the second edition, in which new worries appeared. For example in elaborating on the distribution of powers, O'Sullivan stated that 'the parliament of Canada stands midway between the sovereignty of the British parliament and *what is sometimes called* the sovereignty of the local legislatures', commenting at the same time that 'the accepted meaning of the term sovereignty as used by constitutional lawyers in England is not readily adjusted to the jurisprudence of any country governed under a purely federal system'.[24]

O'Sullivan's intellectual anguish was evident elsewhere. 'All the American constitutional writers speak of divided sovereignty', he noted in a footnote, 'while the English writers from Austin down regard this as a contradiction in terms.'[25] In the end O'Sullivan was inclined to downplay the power of Westminster as 'nominal'[26] and to emphasise the powers of Canadian authorities, the latter having 'complete, absolute and supreme' powers 'within their respective limits'.[27]

Canadian constitutional writers following O'Sullivan persisted in using the term 'sovereignty' more flexibly than Austinian or Diceyan usage would recommend in order to make room for Canadian autonomy and Canadian federalism. However, O'Sullivan had begun to take matters even further, suggesting perhaps that Westminster had 'deprived itself of the right of *ever* interfering'[28] with matters

[20] O'Sullivan, above n 12, 3n.
[21] ibid, 12.
[22] ibid, 7.
[23] ibid, 22.
[24] ibid, 96 (emphasis added). See also ibid, 97: '[C]entral and state governments are each sovereign within their own limits,—a description, however, which falls short of the English theory of sovereign power, inasmuch as it is limited.'
[25] ibid, 9n.
[26] ibid, 99.
[27] ibid, 107.
[28] ibid, 98.

of federal and provincial competence, and exploring a sense of constitutional derivation linked to 'the will of the people of Canada'.[29] These early green shoots of a new view of sovereignty theory did not take hold, though they would reappear later in the twentieth century.

For the moment, Canadian constitutional theory remained fairly bound in an orthodox, Dicey-inspired frame. Strong evidence of the orthodox theory having taken hold can be found in the two textbook writers who followed on O'Sullivan's early efforts. WHP Clement, another Toronto legal practitioner (and later British Columbia judge), published three editions of *The Law of the Canadian Constitution* between 1892 and 1916.[30] AHF Lefroy, also a Toronto practitioner, was Oxford educated, and as of 1900 a professor of law at the University of Toronto. Between 1897 and 1920, roughly the period in which Clement was writing, Lefroy published four textbooks on Canadian constitutional law.[31]

Unlike O'Sullivan who was inclined to emphasise the unconventional aspects of Canada's constitutional arrangements, Clement was intent on reasserting Diceyan orthodoxy, especially in the first two editions of *The Law of the Canadian Constitution*. Whereas O'Sullivan showed sympathy for the view that the Imperial Parliament had forever renounced legislative competence in areas granted to the federal Canadian legislature in the 1867 Act, Clement removed the doubt:

> We have spoken of the want of legal limit to the power of the 'national' government under the British Imperial system. The expression is perhaps hardly accurate—the want which really exists is the want of legal limit to the legislative power of the British Parliament. ... No judge within the Empire can legally limit the British Parliament as a legislative body, or treat its enactments as ultra vires ...[32]

Clement continued: 'The "sphere of authority" of the British Parliament, as a law-making body for the Empire, is legally unlimited, and within that unlimited sphere it may exercise its law-making powers in whatever fashion may appear proper to it.'[33] Dicey could not object to any of this. Clement was also clear on the supposed corollary to Parliament's absolute sovereignty: 'No power, even its own, can tie the

[29] ibid, 22.

[30] WHP Clement, *The Law of the Canadian Constitution* (Toronto, Carswell, 1892; 2nd edn, 1904; 3rd edn, 1916). See Risk above n 13, 429.

[31] *The Law of Legislative Power in Canada* (Toronto, Toronto Law Book and Publishing, 1897–98); *Canada's Federal System* (Toronto, Carswell, 1913); *Leading Cases in Canadian Constitutional Law* (Toronto, Carswell, 1914; 2nd edn, 1920); and *A Short Treatise on Canadian Constitutional Law* (Toronto, Carswell, 1918). See RCB Risk, 'A.H.F. Lefroy: Common Law Thought in Late Nineteenth-Century Canada: On Burying One's Grandfather' (1991) 41 *University of Toronto Law Journal* 307 and RCB Risk, 'The Scholars and the Constitution: P.O.G.G. and the Privy Council' (1996) 2 *Manitoba Law Review* 496.

[32] Clement (1892), above n 30, 11, and similarly 55–56: 'For the whole British Empire, legislative sovereignty resides in the Imperial Parliament, and when that body undertakes to legislate for the colonies generally, or for any one of them in particular, its enactments are a law unto such a colony, binding its inhabitants, and peremptorily requiring recognition by the judges in its courts; and no colonial legislature has power, directly or by side wind, to alter, in one jot or tittle, any such Imperial enactment.' See also Clement (1904), above n 30, 25 for a more compact statement of the same.

[33] Clement (1892), above n 30, 12.

hands of the Imperial Parliament; and the boundaries set to colonial freedom of action in one session of that parliament may be enlarged in the next, and again restricted in a third.'[34]

Clement kept to essentially the same line on these points in the second edition. His third edition began similarly:

> In the study of the Canadian Constitution the first fact which challenges attention is that the Dominion of Canada is a British colony; ... It was no part of the scheme of Confederation to alter in any essential respect the colonial relationship ...; and there is nothing in the Act to indicate a surrender in any degree by the British Parliament of that cardinal principle of the Constitution, the supreme legislative authority of the British Parliament over and throughout the Empire.[35]

This was as orthodox a statement of constitutional theory as one might find. However, in the third edition, Clement pursued two paths of inquiry which promised something in the way of a new theory.

First, Clement referred to the United Kingdom Parliament as a 'constituent assembly',[36] and as 'the constitution-maker for the colonies'.[37] Perhaps there were things that the United Kingdom Parliament could do as a constituent assembly that were different from that which it could do (or not do) as a mere Parliament. Pointing himself down a path which might lead to constitutional independence, he asked '[t]o what extent have constituent powers been bestowed upon the Canadian legislatures'.[38] Sadly, from a Canadian perspective, he had little to provide by way of reply.

Secondly, Clement in his third edition discussed the force of Imperial legislation from two perspectives, a 'British View' and a 'Colonial View'.[39] The 'British View' simply involved 'legislative supremacy over the colonies', a principle 'now thoroughly established in the constitutional law of the Empire'.[40] However, the 'Colonial View' was more varied. 'Remarkable' as it was, he observed 'that at each step in Canada's constitutional progress it has been contended that the Imperial Parliament in legalising such a step had surrendered, so far as related to Canada, some portion of its paramount authority'.[41] Clement left no doubt, however, that there was 'ample' recognition for the 'British View' in the Colonies, and this was clearly his view as well, at least in so far as the Canadian colony was concerned.

Clement's contemporary, AHF Lefroy, wrote widely in matters of Canadian constitutional law, but he was less forthcoming as to the theoretical assumptions underpinning his work. The most authoritative commentator on Lefroy's legacy

[34] ibid, 56, citing Dicey's *Law of the Constitution*. See also Clement (1904), above n 30, 25.
[35] Clement (1916), above n 30, 1.
[36] ibid, 3, 29.
[37] ibid, 32.
[38] ibid, 3.
[39] ibid, ch VI.
[40] ibid, 52.
[41] ibid, 60.

notes that he 'never speculated in any rigorous and abstract way about questions of sovereignty, although the general structure of this thought and his jurisprudence courses suggest that he accepted without question that there always must be a sovereign power'.[42] Lefroy's *The Law of Legislative Power in Canada* was made up of a series of Propositions, the twelfth of these being that '[t]he powers of legislation conferred upon the Dominion Parliament and the Provincial Legislatures, respectively, by the British North America Act, are conferred subject to the sovereign authority of the Imperial Parliament'.[43] Lefroy adopted freely Dicey's vocabulary of sovereignty and subordination where the Imperial Parliament and the Canadian legislatures were concerned.[44] His only criticism of Dicey was to join others in affirming that Canada could be both federal *and* 'similar in principle' to the United Kingdom. Lefroy's criticism of Dicey was apt and thorough in this regard, but Lefroy nonetheless felt obliged to begin the paragraph following the criticism in somewhat contrite fashion, referring deferentially to 'the last two editions of [Dicey's] brilliant lectures on the *Law of the Constitution*'.[45]

In a recent study of the British influence on Canadian constitutional law, Mark Walters points to a possible reconciliation between claims to Westminster sovereignty and the reality of federalism. He notes that there was 'a connection between federalism in Canada and the older idea of legal pluralism within the empire'.[46] Walters states that Clement believed that 'Dicey, in claiming that Canada's constitution was more American than British because of its federal character, overlooked "the presence of the federal principle in the British constitution"'.[47] As Walters summarises, 'the "federal idea" of "reconcil[ing] national unity with the right of local self-government" was, Clement said, part of British imperial constitutional law long before American federalism was established'.[48]

B. Bryce on Sovereignty and Federalism

In between the founding of Canada in 1867 and the founding of the Commonwealth of Australia in 1900, we have seen that Dicey produced the first few editions of his highly influential *The Study of the Law and the Constitution*. Dicey had much to say about sovereignty but less to say about federalism.[49] Regarding both

[42] Risk (1991), above n 31, 323.
[43] Lefroy (1897–98), above n 31, 208. This appears as Proposition 13 in Lefroy (1913), above n 31, 51.
[44] Lefroy (1897–98), above n 31, 248.
[45] ibid, xliv.
[46] Walters, above n 19.
[47] Walters, ibid, quoting Clement (1892), n 18, 10.
[48] Walters, ibid, quoting Clement (1892), ibid 5, 8–9.
[49] An important exception is AV Dicey, 'Federal Government' (1885) 1 *Law Quarterly Review* 80 which discussed federalism principally in the context of proposals for Irish Home Rule. Dicey shows his cards early on, referring to 'faith in federalism' as 'faith without knowledge'. ibid, 1. It is in this article, that Dicey first described as 'official mendacity' the Canadian preamble's reference to 'federally united' alongside 'a constitution similar in principle to that of the United Kingdom'. ibid, 93.

sovereignty and federalism, but more expansive regarding the latter, we should look to the writings of Dicey's friend and colleague, James Bryce.

It is worth reiterating that Bryce had a particularly strong influence in Australia, where his *The American Commonwealth*[50] had been required reading for participants in the Conventions of the 1890s which drafted the Australian Constitution. Accordingly it may be relevant to look at Bryce before we move on to look at the moment of Australia's founding.

As we have already seen, James Bryce the politician took an orthodox line regarding Home Rule for Ireland. While a grant of constitutional protection for Ireland (or it would seem for any self-governing Dominion or colony) was ruled out by Bryce, he was more creative when it came to then-popular proposals to create a sort of federal Imperial scheme or Confederation of Empire:

> If this idea were ever to take practical shape, it would probably be carried out by a statute establishing a new Constitution for the desired Confederation, and United Kingdom, and (being expressed to be operative over the whole Empire) would have full legal effect for the Colonies as well as for the mother country. Now if such a statute assigned to the Federal Assembly certain specified matters, … taking them away from the present and future Parliament as well as from the parliaments of the several Colonies (or perhaps of the Federal Assembly itself), it is clear that the now unlimited powers of the British Parliament would have to be reduced. … Parliament would not be fully sovereign; and if either the British or Colonial Parliament passed laws inconsistent with statutes passed by the Federal Assembly in matters assigned to the latter, the Courts would have to hold the transgressing laws invalid.[51]

This scheme appeared to allow for the sort of limited sovereignty and judicial review of Westminster legislation that Dicey had excluded. In fact, Bryce too was quick to reassert the Dicey orthodoxy in a footnote:

> It may of course be observed … that the British Parliament, while it continues to be elected as now, may be unable to divest itself of its general power of legislating for the whole Empire, and might therefore repeal the Act by which it had resigned certain legislative matters to the Federal Assembly and resume them for itself.[52]

This was the Irish Home Rule issue reappearing in another context, and the response was the same as before. Any protection for Ireland or for the Empire under a federal scheme would have to be political—'no Parliament can be supposed capable of the breach of faith which such a repeal would involve'—rather than legal. If legal protection were required, a much more elaborate constitutional transition would have to take place, seemingly inspired by Dicey's ideas on the abdication or transfer of sovereignty.

[50] James Bryce, *The American Commonwealth* (London, Macmillan, 1888).

[51] James Bryce, *Studies in History and Jurisprudence*, Vol I (Oxford, Oxford University Press, 1901) 246.

[52] ibid, 246n.

Bryce however applied his ingenuity not to reconsidering the nature of Parliament's sovereignty but to the sort of more elaborate scheme which his orthodox views deemed essential:

> Upon the general question whether Parliament could so enact any new Constitution for the United Kingdom as to debar itself from subsequently repealing the Constitution, it may be suggested, for the consideration of those who relish technicalities, that Parliament could, if so disposed, divest itself of its present authority by a sort of suicide, ie, by repealing all the statutes under which it is now summoned, and abolishing the common law right of the Crown to summon it, and thereupon causing itself forthwith to be dissolved, having of course first provided means for summoning such an assembly, or assemblies, as the new Constitution created. There would then be no legal means of summoning another Parliament of the old kind, and the new Constitution, whatever it was, would therefore not be liable to be altered save in such a manner as its own terms provided.[53]

Sovereignty here appeared to be such a powerful and resilient beast that nothing could be left to chance in making sure that it was well and truly dead before creating something new in its place.

While Bryce was in the main true to Dicey's orthodox standards where the Westminster parliament was concerned, Bryce showed some flexibility in his more general writing on sovereignty. Like Dicey he agreed that 'the Imperial Parliament has an unquestioned right to legislate for every part of the British Dominions so as to override all local legislation'.[54] And we have just seen how difficult it would be, in Bryce's view, for the Imperial Parliament ever to end this sovereignty. However, unlike Dicey and other orthodox writers on sovereignty, Bryce placed less emphasis on the absolute or untrammelled nature of that sovereignty, preferring the ability to have the last word (though not necessarily on all matters) as the true indicator of sovereignty.[55] Accordingly, unlike Dicey, Bryce found it possible, without contradiction, to speak of 'limited sovereignty' or, as he termed it 'partial sovereignty':

> In every country the legal Sovereign is to be found in the authority, be it a Person or a Body, whose expressed will binds others, and whose will is not liable to be overruled by the expressed will of any one placed above him or it. The law may, in giving this supremacy, limit it to certain departments, and may divide the whole field of legislative

[53] ibid, 207n. Bryce develops the same idea further on when discussing a possible Federation of the United Kingdom, ibid 248: 'If such a scheme provided, as it probably would provide, for an exclusive assignment to the local legislatures of local affairs, so as to debar the Imperial Parliament from interfering therewith, it would destroy the present Flexible British Constitution and substitute a Rigid one for it. Care would have to be taken to use proper legal means of extinguishing the general sovereign authority of the present Parliament, as for instance by directing the election for the new Federal Legislature to be held in such a way as to effect a breach of continuity between it and the old Imperial Parliament, so that the latter should absolutely cease and determine when the new Constitution came into force. Upon this scheme also it would be for Local Legislatures had exceeded its powers.'

[54] ibid, 525–26.

[55] It should be noted that once it is acknowledged that absoluteness is not an essential attribute of sovereignty, then Dicey's logical objections to limiting that sovereignty fall by the way side. On sovereignty as having the last word, see P Oliver, 'Sovereignty in the Twenty-First Century' (2003) 14 *King's College Law Journal* 137.

> or executive command between two or more authorities. The sovereignty of each of these authorities will then be, to the lawyer's mind, *a partial sovereignty. But it will none the less be a true Sovereignty, sufficient for the purposes of the lawyers.* He may sometimes find it troublesome to determine in any particular instance the range of action allotted to each of the several Sovereign authorities. But so also is it sometimes troublesome to decide how far a confessedly inferior authority has kept within the limits of authority conferred upon it by the supreme authority.[56]

Dicey would have regarded this a nonsense, whereas Bryce's prior in-depth study of the American Constitution would have made it seem uncontroversial. Bryce went even further. He could even conceive of some part of the totality of sovereignty being excluded altogether from legislative hands:

> We have already seen that Legal Sovereignty may be limited or divided. But it is further to be noted that the totality of possible legal sovereignty may, in a given State, not be vested either in one sovereign or in all the sovereign bodies and persons taken together. In other words, there may be some things in which by the constitution of the State no authority is competent to do, because those things have been placed altogether out of the reach of legislation. ... And we may imagine a case in which a Constitution has been enacted with no provision for any legal method of amending it.[57]

With Bryce, therefore, limited sovereignty (which characterises, inter alia, federalism) was conceivable in theory. However, for him, the fully sovereign Westminster Parliament could only achieve a state of limited sovereignty with great disruption to the existing Constitution, and with considerable practical trouble. We will return to this issue later in this chapter.

C. Early Australian Writing on the Compatibility between Sovereignty and Federalism

In discussing sovereignty (and its relationship to federalism) in Australia, one needs first to determine whether one is speaking of parliamentary sovereignty or popular sovereignty. In terms of constitutional theory, many Australians now take seriously the possibility that their Constitution is grounded, politically *and* legally, in the sovereignty of the Australian people. There is ample support for this interpretation in terms of the way in which the Constitution was prepared and adopted.[58] It is also reflected in the preamble to the Commonwealth of Australia

[56] James Bryce, *Studies in History and Jurisprudence*, Vol II (Oxford, Oxford University Press, 1901), 54 (emphasis added).

[57] ibid, 58.

[58] J Brown, 'The Australian Commonwealth Bill' (1900) 61 *LQR* 24, 31–32 set out a striking selection of quotations from leading politicians regarding the importance of popular participation:

> '"I welcome the constitution as the most magnificent institution into which the chosen representatives of a free and enlightened people have ever breathed the spirit of popular sentiment and of national hope."—Mr Kingston.

Constitution Act which states that 'the people of New South Wales, Victoria, South Australia, Queensland, and Tasmania, humbly relying on the blessing of Almighty God, have agreed to unite in one indissoluble Federal Commonwealth'.

What of the alternative explanation, whereby the ultimate legal validity of the Australian federation was provided by the Imperial Parliament at Westminster? The Framers of the Australian Constitution were well aware of the American model of revolutionary constitutional beginnings based in popular sovereignty, but they had no appetite for it. As Helen Irving relates, 1900 was more of a marriage[59] between the various colonies rather than an attempt to become independent. The vast majority of Australians still felt a genuine attachment to Britain and the monarchy.[60] Their preference was for legality and constitutional continuity. The Australian colonies had obtained their powers of government from the Imperial Parliament at Westminster, and they naturally assumed that they would have to go there again in order to obtain authorisation for the new federal Constitution.

In strict legal terms, the final version of the Commonwealth of Australia Constitution Act 1900 could only be the product of the Imperial Parliament. However, to understand it exclusively in strict legal terms would be to ignore 10 years of popular political commitment to the Constitution by the people and political institutions of Australia.

Even if the Constitution of the Commonwealth of Australia Act 1900 owed its legality to the Imperial Parliament, the people and political institutions could claim ownership of the Constitution by virtue of section 128, according to which that same Constitution was 'not to be altered except' as therein provided. Section 128 required approval of the alteration by each House of Parliament (or, in special circumstances, one House) and by the Australian people voting in state referendums (approval of the alteration by a majority of electors voting in a majority of States and by a majority of electors overall). 'Not to be altered except' seemed to exclude even the Imperial Parliament. However, that conclusion seemed to contradict the supposed sovereignty of the latter Parliament. According to the orthodox Diceyan understanding, whatever the Australian Constitution might say, the Act of 1900 could not bind a future Westminster Parliament, and the Australian legislatures, including the section 128 amendment procedure, could only be considered 'subordinate legislatures'.

The Commonwealth of Australia Constitution Act 1900 had created a Constitution for the new federation. However, in terms of constitutional arrangements for the original Australian colonies, the new Constitution basically left the States

"Nothing can be done under the constitution which is contrary to the will of the people."—Sir Edward Braddon.

"It is a constitution framed for a free people."—Mr Barton.

"If ever there was a people's constitution it is this one."—Mr Holder.'

59 H Irving, To Constitute a Nation: A Cultural History of Australia's Constitution (Cambridge, Cambridge University Press, 1999) 211.

60 ibid, 205.

as they were, in contrast to the Canadian Constitution Act, 1867, which incorporated the four founding colonies into the new constitutional arrangements. The Australian colonies, now States, had their Constitutions recognised in section 106 of the 1900 Act: 'The Constitution of each State of the Commonwealth shall, subject to this Constitution, continue as at the establishment of the Commonwealth … until altered in accordance with the Constitution of the State.' Amendment of State Constitutions was governed by those Constitutions rather than by section 128 of the Commonwealth Constitution.[61] The details of these constitutional arrangements would be especially important at the time of the enactment and adoption of the Statute of Westminster and just prior to the enactment of the Australia Acts 1986 (Cth and UK).

It may now be appropriate to consider, as was done regarding Canada, how local constitutional commentators viewed the new federal constitutional arrangements.

Alongside Quick and Garran, perhaps the most influential commentator on the Australian Constitution in the early years after 1900 was Harrison Moore, Dean of the Faculty of Law at the University of Melbourne and author of *The Constitution of the Commonwealth of Australia*.[62] The first edition of this work was published in 1902, only a year after the Australian Constitution had come into force, and too early for Australian courts to have added anything but a trickle of interpretation. Much of the work was therefore historical. He discussed the sources of Australian law, including the rules regarding settled colonies. Moore concluded this account with a firm statement of the importance of popular input into the new federal Constitution of Australia:

> The Federation of Australia was a popular act, an expression of the free will of the people of every part of it, and therein, as in some other respects, it differs in a striking manner from the federation of the United States, of Canada, and of Germany.[63]

One might then have anticipated references to the foundation of the Australian Constitution in popular sovereignty, but this would have been not only to ignore the constraints of Moore's legal education and the constitutional understandings of the time, but also to treat the events of 1900 as more about independence than federation. '*Federation*' not 'independence' was 'a popular act', according to the statement by Moore just quoted. In terms of the relationship between Australia and the Imperial Parliament, however, Moore was seemingly orthodox, an adherent of what in the consideration of the development of Canadian constitutional theory was termed the orthodox theory.

61 Because a State Constitution could be amended in accordance with s 106 of the Australian Constitution, strictly speaking, s 106 and therefore State Constitutions, could be amended in accordance with s 128.

62 W Harrison Moore, *Constitution of the Commonwealth of Australia* (London, John Murray, 1902); W Harrison Moore, *Constitution of the Commonwealth of Australia* 2nd edn (Melbourne, Charles F Maxwell, 1910) (reprinted by Legal Books, 1997, with an Introduction by George Winterton).

63 Moore (1902) ibid, 61.

In a chapter entitled 'The relation of the legislative authorities (the Imperial Parliament, the Commonwealth Parliament, the State Parliaments) and the Validity of Laws'[64] Moore was clear that they formed a 'hierarchy' with the Imperial Parliament at the apex:[65] 'The Imperial Parliament remains paramount, and is capable now, as at all times previously, of legislating for this as for all parts of the dominions of the Crown.' He then addressed a Canadian unorthodoxy that Dicey had criticised, and Moore showed no sympathy for egregious errors of this type:

> The view that obtained some currency in Canada, that the 'exclusive' powers conferred by the British North America Act, 1867, meant exclusive of the Imperial Parliament, is now so far discredited that it is unnecessary to discuss the grounds upon which it is based ...[66]

In the chapter on 'The Alteration of the Constitution' Moore was equally orthodox in his assertions. He noted that

> all constitutional alteration ... must be 'for the Commonwealth [of Australia]', and no alteration of the Constitution may be repugnant to any Imperial Act in operation in the Commonwealth, unless, expressly, or by implication, power over such an Act has been given by the Imperial Parliament.[67]

One such Imperial Act, over which the Commonwealth had no power according to Moore, was the Constitution of the Commonwealth of Australia Act, as opposed to the Australian Constitution itself. The latter owed its existence and validity to Covering Clause IX which stated: 'The Constitution of the Commonwealth shall be as follows.' In Moore's words, 'the Commonwealth is established in virtue of this part of the Act, and it would appear to be dissoluble only by Imperial Act'.[68]

Regarding the Constitution itself, however, 'no part ... [was] withdrawn from the power of the Commonwealth'.[69] There was 'no doubt, that the whole Constitution could be repealed under section 128, and that without any provision being made to substitute anything for it'.[70] Moore justified his confidence here by citing Dicey:

> It seems an irresistible conclusion, that, as Professor Dicey (Law of the Constitution, 5th edition, p. 65) says, 'The impossibility of placing a limit on the exercise of sovereignty does not in any way prohibit, either logically, or in matter of fact, the abdication of sovereignty.'[71]

Moore's comments here relate only to Australian powers under section 128, but one wonders whether he was already asking questions regarding how the Imperial Parliament might eventually grant full constitutional independence to the

[64] ibid, ch X.
[65] ibid, 167.
[66] ibid, 167.
[67] ibid, 320–21.
[68] ibid, 321.
[69] ibid, 321.
[70] ibid, 321.
[71] ibid, 321–22.

Australian federation. Moore's other writing at the time indicated that eventual constitutional independence was within his contemplation, but that he was inclined to close doors leading in that direction rather than open them, assuming, that is, that we can take what he says at face value.

Moore had anticipated his more in-depth study by producing a short article on the Constitution Bill in the January 1900 issue of *The Law Quarterly Review*.[72] In the main, it was a familiar tour through the Bill pointing out its main features. There is little in this article which helps us determine Moore's theoretical assumptions. However, there are occasional glimpses. One such passage was also noteworthy because of its prophetic nature. Moore here identified the power which was eventually employed to enact the Commonwealth version of the Australia Act 1986:

> There is one power conferred upon the Commonwealth Parliament ... which seems to me more far-reaching and perhaps more dangerous than those which are merely concerned with external affairs. The 38th article [the present section 51(xxxviii)] of legislation includes the power to 'exercise within the Commonwealth at the request or with the concurrence of the Parliaments of all the States concerned, any power which can at the establishment of this Constitution be exercised only by the Parliament of the United Kingdom. ...' This article may lead to serious trouble. Claims to legislative independence have been founded on lighter grounds than this; and ... the theoretical power of the Imperial Parliament to recall constitutional powers is not one of great practical value. Under this article it would seem that the Commonwealth Parliament might, at the request of a State Parliament, repeal any Act of the Imperial Parliament applicable in the colony; in other words, the Commonwealth and State parliaments, acting together, might nullify Imperial legislation. Here, if anywhere, the Imperial Parliament may in future be said to have intended to divest itself of authority. It is not enough that we may be able to show by abstract reasoning that this is not or could not be the case.[73]

This is a surprising and ambiguous passage. If Moore really believed in the theoretical, but formal legal power of the Imperial Parliament to 'recall' Australian constitutional powers and if 'abstract reasoning', presumably of the Diceyan variety, could demonstrate that a subordinate legislature cannot (without express or implied power) nullify Imperial legislation, then presumably he should have been confident that the courts would view the matter similarly—unless, that is, Moore was more interested in 'claims to legislative independence' and the 'serious trouble' that they represented than he was willing here to admit.

[72] W Harrison Moore, 'The Commonwealth of Australia Bill' (1900) 16 *LQR* 35. This article was in fact a reply to a series of articles on the Constitution Bill by the Canadian constitutional writer AHF Lefroy: 'The Commonwealth of Australia Bill' (1st Article) (1899) 58 *LQR* 155; (Second Article) (1899) 59 *LQR* 281. In the same series, Brown, above n 58 24: '[t]he Australian Commonwealth Bill embodies the political ideals of a Constitutional Assembly, convened in the closing years of the nineteenth century, and favoured by conditions which afforded a unique opportunity for the achievement of grand constitutional results. All history for precedent! All the world-wide literature of political science as a guide!'

[73] Moore, ibid, 39–40.

If that had been the case, one might have expected such independent-minded statements to unfold in the second edition of *The Constitution of the Commonwealth of Australia*, but that was not to be the case. That work was stoutly Diceyan, perhaps even to a greater extent than the first edition. Moore was by then able, for example, to dismiss any 'doubt or speculation as to the theoretical origin or legal foundation of the Commonwealth and the Constitution'.[74]

Part IV of the second edition, 'The Powers of the Commonwealth Government', was full of references to subordinate legislatures and contrasts between the US sovereignty of the people model and the British/Australian alternative.[75] However, Moore's writing often seemed to pose hidden questions for readers willing to make links. For instance, his discussion of the Imperial Parliament's constituent powers followed by an account of constituent powers under section 128 raised questions, unvoiced by Moore, about whether and when the former might give way to the latter. A closer look at these passages may assist here.

Moore began by noting that 'the real nature of the power' exercised by the Imperial Parliament was obscured by the fact that its sovereign power 'to make paramount laws on all subjects whatever' involved 'uniformity in the mode of exercising' that power.[76] Despite the uniformity of procedure, the Imperial Parliament was exercising very different powers: 'legislative' for the most part, but in establishing a colonial Constitution by Act of Parliament, 'constituent'.[77] The important legal principle which followed from this distinction was that the colonial legislature created by such constituent powers possessed sovereign powers of self-government (subject to control by the Imperial government in the form of disallowance) not merely powers delegated to it by the Imperial Parliament in its legislative mode.[78] Colonial legislatures such as those in Australia had 'plenary powers' with limitations only in 'certain definite restrictions'.[79] Plenary powers would not '*per se*' carry a power to alter the Constitution itself, but such a power had been conferred in the case of the Australian Commonwealth:

> The power to amend the Constitution of the Colony … exists as a distinct power from the ordinary power of legislation. … [I]t seems that the 'constituent power' is so far distinct from the 'legislative', that ordinary acts of legislation are controlled by the Constitution until is has been amended.[80]

Putting the two constituent legislatures together, one cannot help but wonder whether the Imperial Parliament in its constituent role could hand over any residual powers regarding Australia to the relevant Australian institutions, or whether the constituent powers in section 128 could remove any such residual limitations

[74] Moore (1910), above n 62, 66–67, quoted in A Dillon, 'A Turtle By Any Other Name: The Legal Basis of the Australian Constitution' (2001) 29 *Federal Law Review* 241, 244.
[75] Ibid, 243–47.
[76] ibid, 249.
[77] ibid, 249.
[78] ibid, 249–50.
[79] ibid, 255.
[80] ibid, 256.

by its own action. Moore did not develop the point other than to note, as he did in the first edition, that, according to Dicey, abdication of sovereignty was possible.[81]

Another highly influential text in the early period of the Australian Constitution was Quick and Garran's *Annotated Constitution of the Australian Commonwealth*.[82] As the title suggests, this weighty tome was designed to explain the various provisions of the new Constitution rather than to speculate on theoretical issues. However, it is possible to identify a relatively small number of instances where the authors' fundamental assumptions begin to emerge. For instance, Quick and Garran referred to the Constitution as 'founded on the will of the people who it is designed to unite and govern'.[83] The most revealing passages in Quick and Garran appear in the section dealing with section 128, the constitutional amendment provisions. Here, Quick and Garran sounded much like Clement in Canada, emphasising the colonial and subordinate nature of the Australian Commonwealth in the spirit of Imperial theory:

> If … the Commonwealth were a sovereign and independent State, no amendment, duly passed in the prescribed form [following s. 128], would be beyond its powers; the amending power would have no limits. But the Commonwealth is only quasi-sovereign, and *the amending power*, though above the State Governments and above the Federal Government, *is below the Imperial Parliament. The Commonwealth is a dependency of the Empire; and the amending power—the highest legislature of the Commonwealth—is a colonial legislature.* It can therefore pass no law which is repugnant to any Act of the British Parliament extending to the Commonwealth, or repugnant to any order or regulation founded upon such Act; and on the other hand no law passed by the amending power will be void on the ground of repugnancy to the law of England unless it is repugnant to the provisions of some such Act, order, or regulation. (Colonial Laws Validity Act, 1865).[84]

One of the surprising, though logically comprehensible, consequences of this constitutional hierarchy was that the covering clauses of the Constitution, that is sections 1 to 9 of the Commonwealth of Australia Act 1900 (Imp), could be altered only by the Imperial Parliament.[85] As Quick and Garran put the matter, 'the amending power can amend the Constitution, but the Constitution Act is above its reach'.[86] Quick and Garran acknowledged that the Imperial Parliament was an *alternative* method of amending the Constitution, especially where the section 128 procedure was blocked for whatever reason. However, they warned that 'such a radical and drastic method of settling a deadlock, unsolvable by the Constitution itself, could only be justified by the gravest considerations of a most serious emergency'.[87]

[81] ibid, Part X.

[82] R. Quick and R. Garran, The Annotated Constitution of the Australian Commonwealth (reprint of 1901 edition) (Sydney, Legal Books, 1976).

[83] ibid, quoted in L Zines, 'The Sovereignty of the People' in M Coper and G Williams (eds), *Power, Parliament and the People* (Annandale, Federation Press, 1997) 94.

[84] ibid, 994 (emphasis added).

[85] ibid, 989.

[86] ibid, 989.

[87] ibid, 991.

V. The Canadian and Australian Federations and the End of the Sovereignty of the Westminster Parliament

A sovereign Westminster Parliament had clearly successfully created two federations, in 1867 in Canada and in 1900 in Australia. However, as we have seen, for most constitutional commentators at the time, this left the Westminster Parliament in its hierarchically superior position as sovereign legislator. It was hard to see how that situation might end, especially given Dicey's reminder that no Parliament may bind a future Parliament.

A first opportunity to visit this question arose in the years between the 1926 Balfour Declaration and the enactment of the Statute of Westminster. The Balfour Declaration effectively announced that Dominions such as Canada and Australia would acquire what the American colonies had sought a century and a half earlier: equality with the United Kingdom under the Crown. This was easy to say politically but much harder to achieve, legally and constitutionally. Given contemporary understandings of Westminster's sovereignty it was not thought possible simply and straightforwardly to limit that sovereignty. Instead, the Statute of Westminster declared in section 4 that

> No Act of Parliament of the United Kingdom passed after the commencement of this Act shall extend, or be deemed to extend, to a Dominion as part of the law of that Dominion, unless it is expressly declared in that Act that that Dominion has requested, and consented to, the enactment thereof.

This statement could be and was interpreted in quite a variety of ways. At one extreme, in South Africa and Ireland, it was widely understood to do that which orthodox understandings of parliamentary sovereignty excluded: that is, it was understood to limit the powers of the Westminster Parliament fully and finally where South Africa and Ireland were concerned. At the other extreme, constitutional lawyers educated according to the Dicey way of looking at things noted that, strictly speaking, the Westminster Parliament could still legislate for the Dominions as it pleased, by first repealing section 4, by declaring Dominion request and consent whether that had been received or not, or by some other means which emphasised the ongoing sovereignty of that Parliament. In between, a compromise position developed whereby Parliament was still said to be sovereign, but bound in the exercise of the sovereignty to a certain 'manner and form'. The weak version of this has already been mentioned: Parliament would at least have to state in its legislation for the Dominions that Dominion request and consent had been received. The strong version was that Dominion legislatures had effectively been added to the body which constituted 'Parliament', and that only that elaborate Parliament could exercise its sovereign will regarding the Dominions.

In any event, Canada and Australia did not immediately benefit from section 4 of the Statute of Westminster. Canadians could not agree on a domestic amending formula in 1931, so section 7 of the Statute made clear that section 4 would not apply to the amendment of the Constitution of Canada. In other words, the status quo ante would still prevail, whereby the Westminster Parliament would enact amendments to the Constitution Act, 1867. By convention, as before, it would do so only on receipt of a resolution of the House of Commons and Senate of Canada. These fundamental rules would not change until 1982.

Australia opted not to adopt the Statute of Westminster until the 1940s. However, many Australians nonetheless view 1931 as the moment when Australia acquired independence, given that from that moment on it had all the legal tools in its own hands to fashion its constitutional system according to its own will.[88] Despite Australia's constitutional origins based, at least in part, in popular sovereignty, there was remarkably little discussion regarding popular participation in the final, somewhat technical acts of independence.

In 1982 in Canada and in 1986 in Australia (in a United Kingdom and in a Commonwealth enactment, out of abundance of caution in the latter case), it was enacted that:

> No Act of the Parliament of the United Kingdom passed after the Constitution Act, 1982 comes into force shall extend to Canada as part of its law.[89]

> No Act of the Parliament of the United Kingdom passed after the commencement of this Act shall extend, or be deemed to extend, to the Commonwealth, to a State or to a Territory, as part of the law of the Commonwealth, or of the State, or of the Territory.[90]

While some United Kingdom courts and commentators may adhere to the traditional position to the effect that the Westminster Parliament could still legislate for Canada and Australia, the Supreme Court of Canada and the High Court of Australia take the opposite view. This was most clearly stated by the Supreme Court of Canada in *Reference re Objection to a Resolution to Amend the Constitution*, commonly known as the *Quebec Veto Reference*, which was decided just months after the Constitution Act, 1982 had been proclaimed: 'The Constitution Act, 1982 is in force. *Its legality is neither challenged nor assailable.* It contains a new procedure for amending the Constitution of Canada which *entirely replaces* the old one in its legal as well as its conventional aspects.'[91]

Australian courts and commentators generally regard the Australia version of the Australia Act 1986 as capable of completing the process of constitutional independence. They go further in substituting the sovereignty of the Australian people for the sovereignty of the Westminster Parliament as the foundational principle of their Constitution. But even those who insist that the UK Parliament version of the Australia Act 1986 was essential to terminate that Parliament's powers over Australia view that termination as effective.[92]

88 WJ Hudson and MP Sharp, *Australian Independence: Colony to Reluctant Kingdom* (Melbourne, Melbourne University Press, 1988).
89 Canada Act 1982 (UK), s 2.
90 Australia Act 1986 (UK) and (Aus), s 1.
91 [1982] 2 SCR 793 (emphasis added).
92 See Oliver, above n 7, chs 11 and 13.

None of this is very surprising when one recalls that the Westminster Parliament has been enacting independence legislation since the middle of the twentieth century. In his *Parliamentary Sovereignty and the Commonwealth* published in 1957 Geoffrey Marshall pointed out that even if the intricate legal and logical aspects of permanently limiting Westminster Parliament sovereignty were not understood, all the relevant actors in the United Kingdom and in the newly independent states assumed that this irreversible action was possible by means of a final Independence Act.[93] And in many cases—India, Nigeria, Canada, Australia, etc—these independent states were federations.

VI. Evolving Sovereignty, Emerging Federalism

If there were sufficient space to tell this story in greater detail what would emerge is that Westminster's sovereignty has never been as clear and absolute as is often made out. That is a descriptive claim. But even if conceptions of sovereignty can be set out as much more of a spectrum than as a fixed point, those who believe that the United Kingdom Parliament's sovereignty is at the most expansive or absolute end of the spectrum may feel disinclined to see any change in that state of affairs. Is there, then, any normative pull away from the absolute version of sovereignty? This is an important question, because it is only by disengaging from that absolute version of sovereignty that one arrives, by constitutional means, at federalism and the divided sovereignty which characterises it.

I have developed more detailed arguments on many of these points elsewhere. Here I will simply try to set out a number of propositions that may fuel discussion.

1. If we view sovereignty as the ultimate, actual or real power of the state ('power to' rather than 'power over'), along the lines of Martin Loughlin's recent work,[94] then it is not clear whether absolute legal sovereignty or limited legal sovereignty is more conducive to that power. Clearly, going back to the period in which Hobbes and others were writing, there was emphasis on the practical need for absolute legal sovereignty in order to ensure conditions in which citizens could flourish and prosper. However, even in Hobbes' times, as James Tully and others have convincingly pointed out, notions of limited sovereignty were prevalent.[95] Whatever were the dominant understandings

[93] G Marshall, *Parliamentary Sovereignty and the Commonwealth* (Oxford, Oxford University Press, 1957) 101–02. See also G Marshall, *Constitutional Conventions* (Oxford, Oxford University Press, 1984) 205.

[94] M Loughlin, *The Foundations of Public Law* (Oxford: Oxford University Press, 2010) generally, and regarding 'power to' at 69.

[95] See James Tully, *Strange Multiplicity: Constitutionalism in an Age of Diversity* (Cambridge, Cambridge University Press, 1995) for an account of competing theories of sovereignty around the time when Hobbes was writing. See also E Fox-Decent, *Sovereignty's Promise: The State as Fiduciary* (Oxford, Oxford University Press, 2012) for a re-reading of Hobbes in which sovereignty emerges as necessarily limited.

of sovereignty in Hobbes's time, it is striking that contemporary understandings of the state assume that some level of self-limitation rather than absolute power is optimal and most conducive to the state exercising effective power, perhaps because such limitations increase citizens' willingness to trust the state with that power. Typical contemporary limitations include human rights and federalism.[96]

2. Even if we accept Jeffrey Goldsworthy's (and others') well-documented historical finding regarding the prevalence of an absolute version of parliamentary sovereignty—'Parliament may enact any law whatever'—we can at the same time acknowledge that a separate assertion has far less pedigree: that is, the assertion that no Parliament may bind a future Parliament. Much of the force of Dicey's assertions along these lines was grounded in our acceptance of his starting point: that a sovereign's powers must be absolute, as if that were the only possible understanding of 'sovereignty'. We have seen that Tully and others would strenuously dispute that point. If sovereignty must be absolute, then Dicey must be right that a sovereign Parliament cannot bind a future Parliament for to do so would be to constrain that supposed absolute power. If, however, sovereignty can be limited, much as we see it in federalism, human rights law and international law, then the logic of Dicey's prohibition falls apart. And as I have written elsewhere, it turns out that Dicey's 'no Parliament may bind a future Parliament' was based on a very limited amount of very weak authority.[97] While it is clearly true that United Kingdom courts are very reluctant to interpret the United Kingdom Parliament as having intended to bind a future Parliament, a separate, highly relevant question relates to what courts will do when the United Kingdom Parliament expresses a clear intention to limit itself. The United Kingdom courts have so far accepted the partial limitation represented by the European Communities Act 1972, though this is of course currently at issue. What is striking about United Kingdom independence legislation is that, from the United Kingdom perspective, it may be seen in strict law as partial and reversible; however, from the local Canadian, Australian or other perspective, the previous sovereign lawmaker's self-limitation is entire and irreversible. It is that which locks in both constitutional independence and the federal structure that goes with that independence. Is this sort of locked-in federal transition possible for the United Kingdom?
3. It is easy to see why the sort of self-limitation that accompanies Westminster-enacted independence is appropriate for countries such as Canada and Australia. If the question regarding Parliament's ability to limit itself was a 'hard question', then followers of Dworkin might want to point out that the democratic principle and the principles of constitutionalism and the rule of law dictate a conclusion in favour of such self-limitation. In a recent article,

[96] See Tully, ibid.
[97] Oliver, above n 7, 70.

I use a counter-factual regarding New Zealand to point out that principles such as democracy, constitutionalism and the rule of law can dictate a range of logically acceptable conclusions, one version which makes sense in the counter-factual of New Zealand political development in the context of Commonwealth Economic Union, and an opposite version which makes sense according to the course that New Zealand actually travelled.[98] The point is that, regarding the seldom-considered, finer aspects of parliamentary sovereignty, the rightness or wrongness of settling for a particular point on the spectrum of sovereignty possibilities is more a matter of judgement, wisdom or statecraft than of clearly identifiable law or principle, whatever proponents of one or the other position might like to say.

4. Assuming that federalism is right for the United Kingdom at the present moment—and that admittedly is a separate, difficult question—how could the Westminster Parliament ensure that the legal rules regarding this new federation were properly enacted and secured? What follows is based on the collective wisdom of constitutional writers[99] with whom I am familiar who have considered the question regarding how ultimate rules in a legal system change.[100] Neil MacCormick believed that the traditional rule regarding Westminster's sovereignty—usually termed 'continuing' sovereignty—could change, that the Westminster Parliament itself operated a rule or power of change which could direct that 'continuing' sovereignty be reinterpreted so as to allow for parliamentary self-limitation. Given the change from past understandings, Parliament would have to express itself in the clearest of terms, as occurred with independence enactments and indeed the European Communities Act, 1972. For those who believe that 'continuing sovereignty' is the United Kingdom rule of recognition, and not subject to any rule or power of change, MacCormick's approach would not work. However, those who take the latter view, such as Jeffrey Goldsworthy, nonetheless see change in the rule of recognition as possible, provided that officials change their view as to what is the rule of recognition. From a Goldsworthy-inspired perspective it would be possible to imagine a wide-ranging consultation process regarding the path to federation, accompanied by White Papers and a referendum, which would reassure officials that the change in rule of recognition was appropriate.[101] And while I have expressed the view that principles (and political morality) point to a range of possible constitutional results, and for that reason cannot

[98] P Oliver, 'Change in the Ultimate Rule of a Legal System: Uncertainty, Hard Cases, Commonwealth Precedents and the Importance of Context' (2015) 26 *King's Law Journal* 281.

[99] I have excluded from the list HWR Wade who viewed the changes that I am describing as a 'disguised revolution', a view which, though widely cited, strikes me as unnecessary and, because unnecessary, inappropriate, especially for constitutional lawyers.

[100] For more detailed discussion, see Oliver, above n 7.

[101] See Goldsworthy, above n 1.

be said to dictate right answers, it seems reasonable nonetheless to say that the process and the new federal arrangements themselves should be guided by our long experience of working out how constitutionalism, the rule of law and democracy can best be actualised.[102]

VII. Conclusion

In this chapter, I began by discussing the late nineteenth-century and early twentieth-century constitutional climate in which the Canadian and Australian federations were created. At that time, legal thinking regarding sovereignty was dominated by the absolutist version favoured by Austin and, later, Dicey. According to this version, the Westminster Parliament could certainly constitute a federation in Canada and later Australia; but anything that the Westminster Parliament enacted could, in strict law, be altered or undone at a later time. The period from the Balfour Declaration and Statute of Westminster 1931 to the 1980s saw considerable evolution in understandings of sovereignty, to the point where it was assumed, at least by Canadian and Australian courts and commentators, that the Westminster Parliament could limit itself entirely, where their legal systems were concerned, and that such limitations were permanent, that is, irreversible. So viewed from a Canadian and Australian perspective, the Westminster Parliament not only created federal Constitutions but also put them beyond the reach of that so-called sovereign Parliament.

I then consider in the form of a series of propositions whether that which the Westminster Parliament created for Canada, Australia and other Commonwealth federations could be created for the United Kingdom itself. I conclude that it is possible, and were it to happen, it should involve legislation by Parliament indicating a clear intention to limit itself in the creation of a federation, together with a process—widespread consultation, a referendum and conspicuous respect for the best-learned lessons regarding principles such as constitutionalism, the rule of law and democracy—which would reassure officials that the change in the ultimate rule of the legal system was right and proper and appropriate.

[102] And here the various writings of Trevor Allan, most recently, *The Sovereignty of Law* (Oxford, Oxford University Press, 2013), are relevant.

3

Shared Rule: What the UK Could Learn from Federalism

ADAM TOMKINS*

I. Introduction

The United Kingdom is not about to become a federal country. Equally unrealistic, however, is the notion that the United Kingdom Parliament remains sovereign in the full Diceyan sense—ie, that Westminster may 'make or unmake any law whatsoever'.[1] This may remain true as a matter of high legal theory but, perfectly plainly, there are all sorts of political constraints on the United Kingdom Parliament. Among them are those created by, or arising as a result of, devolution. Unless it first seeks and obtains Holyrood's consent to do so, the United Kingdom Parliament may not normally legislate for Scotland on matters that are devolved to Edinburgh, for example.

If the UK is not a fully federal state, then neither does the unitary model of 'one Parliament to rule us all' hold any longer. The UK is somewhere in between these models and, moreover, its direction of travel is clear. We are moving further away from Dicey's orthodoxy towards something resembling federalism. Even if the pace of travel slows in the years ahead, it is difficult to see that there will be any reversal or retreat. Devolution is here to stay and, whether one looks to Scotland, to Wales or to the city regions of northern England, it seems set not merely to stay, but to deepen and grow.

* Adam Tomkins has held the John Millar Chair in Public Law at the University of Glasgow since 2003. In 2016 he was elected a Member of the Scottish Parliament. This essay is written in a personal capacity and is not a statement of party policy. This essay draws on Adam Tomkins, *Shared Rule: What Scotland Needs to Learn from Federalism*, published by Reform Scotland in April 2016. Research for this essay was undertaken with the support of the ESRC, under the auspices of Policy Scotland at the University of Glasgow. A debt of thanks is owed to Des McNulty, Duncan Maclennan and Ken Gibb. This chapter was written before the EU Referendum of 23 June 2016 and does not take account of developments since that date.

[1] AV Dicey, *The Law of the Constitution* (London, Macmillan, 1885). See also Jackson and Oliver in this book.

This chapter is not a call for a federal Britain. Rather, it seeks to illuminate something of the territorial Constitution that the UK has now and, in particular, it attempts to recast the way we see devolved power and how we understand its relation to reserved power. Thus far in the short history of devolution in Britain, we have done as if a power is *either* devolved *or* reserved. If it's devolved, it is for the Scottish Ministers to exercise, accountable as they are to the Scottish Parliament in Holyrood. And if it's reserved, it is for Ministers of the Crown to exercise, accountable to the United Kingdom Parliament in Westminster. On this understanding there is no meeting point, no middle ground, no power that is partly devolved and partly reserved, no power that is shared. Even if this limited understanding of devolution has been sufficient to make sense of devolution as it has operated since 1999, it will soon prove inadequate. The Smith Commission Agreement and the legislation it has spawned—the Scotland Act 2016—require us to see devolution in a more sophisticated way than the simple binary divide of devolved/reserved allows. There will, of course, continue to be both devolved and reserved powers. But, in addition to these, a new category of power will also come to the fore—shared powers. This may be new for the United Kingdom, but it is routine in federal countries.

How will it work in the United Kingdom? What sort of institutional architecture is needed to operate shared powers? What sort of legal framework should underpin a regime of shared rule? What can Britain learn from federal experience overseas about the strengths and limitations, the opportunities and drawbacks of shared powers? These are the questions addressed in this chapter.

II. Shared Rule

A. Why Shared Rule Matters

First, we need to understand why the Smith Commission Agreement and the Scotland Act 2016 mean that we should start taking shared rule seriously. When devolution first came to Scotland under the Scotland Act 1998, the decision as to what to devolve and what to reserve to Westminster was based largely on what the old Scottish Office had done in the era before devolution. The health service in Scotland had never been run by Whitehall's Department of Health (who ran the health service in England). Likewise, Scotland's schools had never fallen within the remit of the Department for Education. Rather, both health and education in Scotland were overseen by the Scottish Office, as was the justice system in Scotland. Crudely, if a matter was the responsibility of the Scottish Office before 1999 the presumption was that it would be devolved to the new Scottish Parliament, but if a matter was overseen for Scotland by another department of state in Whitehall, the presumption was that it would remain reserved. Thus, social security, almost all taxation, defence and foreign affairs all remained reserved. This was no arbitrary division imposed by the Blair Government: it was what the Scottish Constitutional Convention had understood by 'home rule', and it is what the long campaign for Scottish devolution had always been about.

This model delivered home rule—or 'self-rule'—for Scotland, but it did so by dividing powers into two types—devolved and reserved—and making a different government responsible for each type. Daniel Elazar, an American political scientist who devoted much of his career to the study of federalism, wrote in his book *Exploring Federalism* that federalism is 'self-rule plus shared rule'.[2] This has become a widely cited definition in discussions in Scotland about devolution and federalism. If the first iteration of Scottish devolution delivered the 'self-rule' part of Elazar's equation, the 'shared rule' element was yet to be accounted for.

B. The Smith Commission

The Smith Commission met in the immediate aftermath of the 2014 Scottish independence referendum. Its task was to find common ground among the five parties represented in the Scottish Parliament—those who had campaigned in favour of independence as well as those who had campaigned in favour of the Union—as to how devolution should be enhanced beyond the 1998 model.[3] Clearly, Smith had to move substantially beyond the devolution of tasks that had formerly been undertaken by the Scottish Office. Of the domestic functions of government[4] two became the prime candidates for fresh devolution: welfare and taxation. An important constraint on the Smith Commission, however, was that a majority of those voting in the independence referendum had elected to preserve Scotland's status within a United Kingdom that, as the rhetoric of the Better Together campaign had repeatedly put it, 'pools and shares risks and resources'. The full devolution of either taxation powers or welfare powers would cut against this and, it was felt, would risk undermining the 18 September 'No' vote. Yet, at the same time, too great a resistance to the devolution of tax or welfare powers would result in an agreement that would not satisfy those—quite possibly a very large majority of Scots—who wanted to see much greater devolution than the 1998 model had delivered. A compromise was reached, both on tax and welfare. In other words, once the Smith Commission's recommendations come fully into force through the Scotland Act 2016, tax and welfare in Scotland will become the shared responsibilities of both the United Kingdom Government and the Scottish Ministers.

[2] Daniel Elazar, *Exploring Federalism* (Tuscaloosa, University of Alabama Press, 1987) 12.

[3] The present author was a member of the Smith Commission.

[4] There was no prospect that the Smith Commission would recommend the devolution of the external or international functions of government, such as defence, immigration and foreign affairs.

In outline, the deal on taxation results in the following split: taxes on land and local government taxation are generally devolved;[5] taxes on wealth[6] and profits[7] are generally reserved; and taxes on income are shared. Whilst the details vary from country to country, this basic division reflects the practice of federal jurisdictions such as the USA, Canada and Australia. For our purposes it is the last category that is most interesting. Smith agreed that national insurance contributions would remain reserved to Westminster and that income tax would be divided as follows: Westminster should determine the definition of 'income' for the purposes of the Taxes Acts, should continue to control income tax on savings and dividends, and should continue to set the personal allowance (ie the point at which earnings become liable to income tax); beyond that the Scottish Ministers should be responsible for determining all the rates and bands of income tax in Scotland on earned income.

The welfare deal likewise sees a basic three-way split. First, it was decided that the state pension should remain the responsibility of the UK Parliament across the whole of the United Kingdom. Working-age benefits actually do two quite different things. First, they assist those on very low incomes; second, they assist those with additional needs. Most of the first category are being rolled up into a single benefit—Universal Credit. It was agreed that this should remain under the overall responsibility of the United Kingdom Government, but that Scottish Ministers should have the power to adjust certain aspects of the way Universal Credit operates in Scotland. Most of the benefits in the 'additional needs' category, by contrast, are to be devolved under Smith (Carer's Allowance, Attendance Allowance, Disability Living Allowance, Personal Independence Payments, and Cold Weather and Winter Fuel Payments). The only major benefit in this category that remains reserved to Westminster is Child Benefit. As with taxation, then, so too with welfare we see a mix of powers for London, powers for Edinburgh, and powers to be shared between them.

That the Smith Commission and the Scotland Act 2016 have introduced into the British constitutional landscape a new category of shared powers has been recognised both by Ministers and by parliamentary committees that scrutinised the Scotland Bill during its passage through Parliament. Giving evidence to the Scottish Parliament's Devolution (Further Powers) Committee in June 2015, Secretary of State for Scotland David Mundell talked, for example, of 'the environment that Smith envisaged, *which involves having shared responsibilities and which must be based on a different type of relationship*' between governments within the United Kingdom. Likewise, in its report on the Scotland Bill the House of Lords Constitution Committee noted that it is 'a feature' of the legislation that

[5] Stamp Duty (Land and Buildings Transaction Tax), Non Domestic Rates and Council Tax were already devolved in Scotland before Smith. Smith added Air Passenger Duty to the list of fully devolved taxes in Scotland.

[6] eg Capital Gains Tax and Inheritance Tax.

[7] eg Corporation Tax.

its provisions 'will require co-operation between UK and Scottish Governments across a range of new areas'.[8] In the Committee's analysis, such cooperation will take a variety of forms, from the existence of concurrent powers, to duties of consultation, requirements to obtain consent, information-sharing and the management of cross-border bodies. Of these, it is the new arrival of concurrent powers that is the most important. 'The hitherto fairly straightforward demarcation between reserved powers and those devolved to the Scottish Parliament', the Committee said, 'will become considerably less clear'.[9] The Committee noted that, among other matters, this would make the United Kingdom's inter-governmental relations 'both more complex and more important'.[10]

III. A Constitutional Law of Shared Rule: Learning from the United States

A. Federalism in the United States

Federalism as we understand it today was invented by the Founding Fathers in eighteenth-century America. They inherited an older idea and converted it in two ways. The older idea was confederation and it applied to relations between states.[11] Countries had formed alliances, groups or leagues since ancient times—the Achæan League and the Lycian Confederacy, for example—and in early-modern Europe the experiment was repeated in such forms as the Hanseatic League and the United Provinces of the Netherlands. The Articles of Confederation, under which the 13 American colonies had formed a loose association since 1781, was based on this idea.

The United States Constitution took this idea of confederation, tightened it so that a much greater degree of sovereignty would be pooled at the centre, and applied it not to the relations between countries but to relations within a single country. Thus was the single American nation born by the 'more perfect Union' of the 13 colonies—now States. The Federalists knew that they would face resistance in several of the States, nine of which needed to ratify the new Constitution before it could take effect, so they launched a remarkable campaign to persuade the States that it was in their interests, as well as in the interests of the newborn American nation as a whole, to embrace this change. The crowning glory of this campaign is *The Federalist*, a series of 85 papers published between October 1787

[8] House of Lords Constitution Committee, *6th report of 2015–16*, para 17.

[9] ibid, para 18.

[10] ibid, para 19. See also the chapter by Tierney in this book.

[11] The European Union is a confederation. Even under the failed Constitutional Treaty of 2005 this would have remained the case. That Treaty would not have turned the EU into a federal entity.

and May 1788 written principally by James Madison and Alexander Hamilton to persuade the State of New York to ratify. *The Federalist* is one of the great works of constitutional theory published in the English language, as well as an unrivalled practical guide to the US Constitution.

American federalism is based on the fundamental principle that the federal government has only those powers that are ascribed to it in the Constitution. In the words of the Tenth Amendment, 'the powers not delegated to the United States by the Constitution ... are reserved to the States respectively'. *Federalist* Nos 41–44 take the reader through the various powers the Constitution confers on the federal government, arguing why each one needs to be exercised at that level and not reserved to the States. *Federalist* No 45 then examines how the relationship between the federal government and the States will work. Madison notes how the balance between them is not designed to be equal, but is intended to benefit the States at the expense of the national government. Federal government is dependent on the States in ways that are not reciprocated, Madison notes (the President, for example, is elected by a College comprising delegates from each State, whereas the federal government has no similar role in electing State governments). The States will retain a greater degree of popular support than will the federal government. They will have more power to disrupt federal activity than the federal government will have to interfere with State activities, Madison claims (we shall return to this point below). And, despite the fact that the Constitution clearly empowers the centre to a far greater degree than had the Articles of Confederation,[12] it remains the case even under the Constitution, Madison argued, that the powers vested in the States outweigh those conferred on the federal government. Madison's conclusion was famously expressed: 'The powers delegated by the proposed Constitution to the Federal Government, are few and defined. Those which are to remain in the State Governments are numerous and indefinite'.[13]

The intervening two centuries of American government have not been kind to this appraisal. In modern-day America Madison was wrong on both counts. The national government has grown so much that it would be completely unrecognisable to the Founders, and the States have withered by comparison. It has been remarked that, if the United Kingdom is moving from Dicey's unitary Constitution towards something resembling a quasi-federal model, the United States has moved in the opposite direction. This has been particularly the case since the 1930s, and President Franklin D Roosevelt's New Deal 'reconstruction' of the American economy after the Great Depression. It was in this period that a truly national economy developed in the United States, with Congress legislating on nationwide labour standards and employment conditions in order to try to reboot the economy after the disaster of 1929. At first resisted on States' rights grounds by the US Supreme Court, after threats of Court packing, there was a decisive change

[12] Under the Articles of Confederation, Congress had no powers over taxation, for example.
[13] James Madison, *Federalist No 45* (1787).

in the direction of the Court's jurisprudence, as the constitutional constraints on Congressional power came to be understood much more loosely, and the constitutional protections formerly afforded to State sovereignty diminished.

There is an important lesson here for Scotland and the United Kingdom. No matter what the original intent, language used to seek to delimit the differences between reserved and devolved powers (or, in the American case, between federal and State powers) is always open to judicial interpretation, with courts able to construe it more or less generously depending on the needs of the times. Take the famous Commerce Clause of the US Constitution, for example. This provides that 'Congress shall have Power ... to regulate Commerce with foreign Nations, and among the several States ...'.[14] Perfectly plainly, this means that Congress has the power to legislate on *international* trade ('Commerce with foreign Nations') and on trade *between* the various States of the USA ('among the several States') but not to legislate on trade *within* States. Under the Tenth Amendment, the power to regulate *intra-State* trade is reserved to the States themselves. This was the constitutional hurdle at which Roosevelt's New Deal legislation fell—at least, to start with. But, in a series of landmark decisions between 1937 and 1942 the Supreme Court changed course, and significantly relaxed its interpretation of the Commerce Clause. The Clause itself has never been amended, but its meaning has changed considerably so as to accommodate within the US constitutional order a far greater degree of national economic regulation than the Founders could ever have contemplated.

The post-war period saw an acceleration of this trend. Defence of States' rights became associated with support for Jim Crow segregation as it was the federal government and the Supreme Court—and not the States—that transformed America in fields such as civil rights and abortion, as well as in national economic terms. It was not until President Ronald Reagan arrived at the White House in 1980 that any official encouragement was given to the idea that the pendulum may have swung too far. Reagan's first two appointees to the Court—Justices Sandra Day O'Connor and Antonin Scalia—began, with Chief Justice Rehnquist, the task of resetting the federalist balance.[15]

B. Enumerated Powers

Part of this was about seeking to revive what had become known as the 'dormant' Commerce Clause. The breakthrough finally came in a case called *United States v Lopez*, in 1995.[16] Federal legislation made it an offence to possess a firearm at or near a school. By a five-to-four majority the Supreme Court struck the legislation

[14] US Constitution, Art I, s 8, clause 3.

[15] Rehnquist had been appointed to the Court in 1972; Reagan elevated him to Chief Justice in 1986 when Warren Burger retired.

[16] *United States v Lopez* 514 US 549 (1995).

down as exceeding Congressional power under the Commerce Clause. This was the first time in 65 years that the Court had invalidated a provision of federal legislation on this ground. A second example followed in 2000, when the same five-to-four majority struck down certain provisions of the Violence Against Women Act.[17] Congress had enacted that legislation on the basis that violent crimes against women could have a number of adverse effects on interstate commerce. The Court ruled, however, that these effects were too remote and indirect to bring the legislation within the scope of the Commerce Clause.

Whilst interesting in their own right, and whilst they are central to the contemporary law of federalism in the United States, these cases do not tell us anything very much about shared rule. All systems of multi-level government must have ways of distinguishing those powers exercisable at the centre from those exercisable by states, provinces or regions. European Union law has such a system. So do Canada and Australia. And so too does the United Kingdom. In all of these places the limits of legislative competence are a matter of law for the courts to rule on, in the event of any dispute. The Scottish Parliament may not legislate on the powers the Scotland Act 1998 reserves to the United Kingdom. The Welsh Assembly may legislate only within the powers that are conferred upon it by the Government of Wales Act 2006. Courts in the United Kingdom can and do enforce these limits.[18] There is little difference between what the UK courts do in such cases and what the US Supreme Court was doing in *Lopez*. The judicial enforcement of the limits of legislative competence is a key part of federal constitutional law, but it has little to do with shared rule.

Cases such as *Lopez* rely on an understanding of federalism known as 'dual sovereignty'. This is familiar to us in the UK. Some powers are for this government (Scotland, or the US States); other powers are for that government (the United Kingdom, or the US federal government). On this understanding, powers are for one government or another: they are not shared. The job of a Constitution is to delimit the powers, identifying which powers are for which level of government. And the constitutional job of the courts is to rule on disputes, determining whether (for example) gun control falls within or outwith the regulation of 'commerce … among the several States'—or whether, to take a Scottish example, legislation limiting tobacco sales is related to the devolved subject-matter of public health or to the reserved subject-matters of consumer protection and product safety.[19]

Cases such as *Lopez*, strategies of federalism such as enumerated powers, and the model of dual sovereignty may tell us quite a lot about how much 'self-rule' is afforded to the States or provinces or regions that make up a country, but they

[17] *United States v Morrison* 529 US 598 (2000).

[18] For an account of the key UK Supreme Court cases, see Bingham Centre for the Rule of Law, *A Constitutional Crossroads: Ways For the United Kingdom* (London, 2015) 59–66.

[19] See *Imperial Tobacco v Lord Advocate* [2012] UKSC 61, in which the UK Supreme Court ruled that the Tobacco and Primary Medical Services (Scotland) Act 2010 was within the legislative competence of the Scottish Parliament.

are only one element of the federal picture. They are generally the place to start but, on their own, they do not take us very far. A court that was able to enforce or protect federalism only by ensuring that constitutional lists of enumerated powers were adhered to would not be a court with many tools in its box. It is a thin and, experience would show, weak form of federalism that relies only or even mainly on this strategy. Of course, delimiting the powers of central government and regional government is a necessary component of federal and quasi-federal orders but, on its own, it is far from sufficient.

This was recognised in the United States more than half a century ago. Two sets of cases can be used to illustrate what, in addition to a jurisprudence of enumerated powers, is needed to append an understanding of shared rule to the basic building-blocks of self-rule. These cases concern the spending power and the doctrine of pre-emption.

C. The Spending Power and the Anti-commandeering Rule

For our purposes, much more interesting than the revival of the Commerce Clause is the second main prong of the Reagan appointees' approach to federalism: to curb the reach of Congress' spending power. The US Constitution authorises Congress to 'provide for the … general welfare of the United States'. Congress has the power to tax and, under this clause, it also has the power to spend. Congress' power to spend is far wider than its power to legislate. It may legislate only in relation to the powers conferred upon it by the Constitution, but it may spend to provide for the *general* welfare. Congress may spend money even in areas over which it has no legislative competence.

The case of *South Dakota v Dole* illustrates both the breadth of Congress' spending power, and its direct relevance to shared rule.[20] In South Dakota the minimum drinking age for alcoholic drinks was 19 years. Congress directed the federal government to withhold a percentage of federal highway funds allocated to States where the State in question had a minimum drinking age of less than 21 years. South Dakota challenged this as being, among other matters, in excess of Congress' spending power. The State's challenge was unsuccessful. It has long been accepted that, under its spending power, Congress may attach conditions to the receipt of federal funds (including conditions designed to further broad policy objectives preferred by the federal government). The Supreme Court ruled as long ago as 1936 that such conditions were not limited by and did not have to match Congress's enumerated legislative powers.[21] That is to say, Congress could seek to achieve through conditional funding what it could not require by positive legislation.

[20] *South Dakota v Dole* 483 US 203 (1987).
[21] *United States v Butler* 297 US 1 (1936).

This does not mean that there are no constitutional limits to the conditions that Congress may attach when allocating federal funding to the States but, 'in considering whether a particular expenditure is intended to serve general public purposes, courts should defer substantially to the judgment of Congress',[22] the Supreme Court ruled. Conditions attached to federal funding must be unambiguous, so that States may exercise their choices knowingly. And conditions must be 'reasonably related to the purpose of the expenditure'.[23] In *South Dakota v Dole* the Court ruled that these requirements were amply met. 'The condition imposed by Congress is directly related to one of the main purposes for which highway funds are expended—safe interstate travel',[24] the Court ruled. Justice O'Connor dissented. She agreed with the Court's elaboration of the basic principles, but found that in this instance the condition attached to the funding (that the State should raise its minimum drinking age from 19 to 21) was not sufficiently related to the purpose of that funding (the construction of interstate highways).

In the 1990s the Court sharpened the limits to Congress' spending power, just as it gave fresh bite to the Commerce Clause. In *New York v United States* the State of New York challenged certain provisions of federal legislation that incentivised States to encourage them to comply with Congressional policy about the disposal of low-level radioactive waste.[25] The Court ruled that a number of the incentives fell within Congress' spending power but that one of them went too far: namely, a requirement that a State unable to provide for the disposal of the waste had to take possession of the waste and had thereby to assume associated liabilities in relation to that waste (the 'take title' provision). Justice O'Connor gave the Opinion of the Court. She saw the case as being about the extent to which Congress could direct the States to regulate in a particular field or in a particular way. She ruled that Congress may not 'commandeer' the States by 'directly compelling them to enact and enforce a federal regulatory program'. She added: 'While Congress has substantial powers to govern the Nation directly, including in areas of intimate concern to the States, the Constitution has never been understood to confer upon Congress the ability to require the States to govern according to Congress' instructions'.

As is evident from the earlier case of *South Dakota v Dole*, this does not mean that Congress lacks the ability to encourage States to regulate in a particular way; nor does it mean that Congress may not offer incentives to seek to influence a State's policy choices. But 'outright coercion', as Justice O'Connor put it, is forbidden. Justice O'Connor referred to the Clean Water Act as an example of what she said had been termed 'co-operative federalism'. Legislation such as the Clean Water Act 'anticipates a partnership between the State and the federal government, animated by a shared objective'. Such a scheme is perfectly compatible with the Constitution, but when cooperation becomes coercion—or commandeering—a line is crossed

[22] *South Dakota v Dole*, above n 20, 207.
[23] ibid.
[24] ibid, 208.
[25] *New York v United States* 505 US 144 (1992).

into territory the Court will rule to be unconstitutional. This is because 'States are not mere political subdivisions of the United States. State governments are neither regional offices nor administrative agencies of the federal government'. States must be free to choose whether to cooperate with federal programmes (such as in the area of environmental protection). The 'take title' provision, by requiring States to take possession of certain radioactive waste, crossed the line from cooperation to coercion and was, for that reason, unlawful. We return to cooperative federalism below.

The anti-commandeering rule in *New York v United States* was taken further in *Printz v United States*, a decision of the US Supreme Court in 1997 in which the Opinion of the Court was written by Justice Scalia.[26] *Printz* concerned federal legislation that required State officers to carry out background checks on prospective purchasers of handguns. Unlike in *New York* there was no question in *Printz* that the federal legislation required a State to adopt any particular *policy*. State officers were simply required to assist in the *administration* of federal gun controls. None the less, in another five-to-four decision the Supreme Court read across from *New York* to hold that, just as Congress could not commandeer a State's legislative processes, neither could a State officer be pressed into federal service: 'the federal government', Justice Scalia wrote, 'may not compel the State to implement, by legislation or by executive action, federal regulatory programs'.

The same point arose in the more recent court challenges to President Obama's Affordable Care Act—informally known as Obamacare. One of the key elements of Obamacare is what Chief Justice Roberts described as a 'dramatic increase' in State obligations under Medicaid.[27] Medicaid is a federal programme that requires States to cover certain medical needs of particular groups of people (pregnant women, children, poorer families, the blind, the elderly and the disabled). The Affordable Care Act significantly extended the categories of people covered by Medicaid. Some 90 per cent of this increased coverage would be paid for by federal funds. However, if States did not extend Medicaid's coverage, not only would they be denied the additional federal funding, but Congress threatened to withdraw *all* Medicaid funding from such States. (To put this in context, Medicaid spending accounts for more than 20 per cent of the average State's total budget, with federal funding covering between 50 per cent and 83 per cent of those costs.) Thus, between 10 per cent and 18 per cent of the average State's *total* budget was at risk if States did not comply with the Affordable Care Act's extension of Medicaid.

Clearly, this raises the same issue as was determined in Congress' favour in *South Dakota v Dole*: namely, are the conditions attached to federal funding so coercive that they pass the point at which 'pressure turns into compulsion'? A seven-to-two majority of the Court distinguished *South Dakota v Dole*. In that case the federal funds at stake constituted less than 0.5 per cent of South Dakota's budget.

[26] *Printz v United States* 521 US 898 (1997).

[27] *NFIB v Sebelius* 567 US __ (2012).

By contrast, Chief Justice Roberts ruled that 'the financial "inducement" Congress has chosen [in the Affordable Care Act] is much more than relatively mild encouragement—it is a gun to the head'.[28] The Court did not invalidate those aspects of Obamacare concerned with Medicaid expansion. Congress remained free to attach lawful conditions to its increased Medicaid funding, but it was prohibited from threatening to withhold the entirety of a State's Medicaid funds if that State sought to resist expanding its Medicaid coverage.

These cases illustrate an element of multi-level government that remains almost entirely unexplored in Scotland and the United Kingdom. Hitherto, we have understood devolution in terms of devolved and reserved legislative and executive *powers*; we have not yet come to understand it in terms of *money*. In part this is because the fiscal relationship between the UK and Scottish Governments is not one in which conditional funding features. The block grant is transferred from HM Treasury to the Scottish Ministers with no strings attached. When this is explained to American (or Canadian) colleagues, their reaction is astonishment: how could the United Kingdom Government have set up powerful devolved institutions without seeking to influence them through conditional funding? It is an aspect of devolution that has never received the attention it merits.

Despite the unconditional nature of the UK's block grant funding, there are two valuable lessons to learn from the American spending power and anti-commandeering case law. The first is to recall that, as well as having legislative powers over reserved matters, UK institutions also retain spending powers in Scotland. There is nothing to stop the UK spending money in Scotland, even where the UK Parliament would not be able to legislate (without Holyrood's consent). As in the USA, so too in the United Kingdom: there is no reason to think that spending powers and law-making powers have to match and mirror each other. The second lesson is that, even if the block grant is transferred free of conditions, other Scottish public expenditure emanating from the Treasury can and does come with conditionalities attached. The lead examples are the City Deals signed with Glasgow and the Clyde Valley in 2014 and with Aberdeen and Aberdeenshire in 2016.[29]

In Glasgow's case, the UK Government has undertaken to invest £500 million in the Glasgow city region over the coming years for the purpose of assisting the city region with boosting its local economy, raising productivity and creating jobs. That financial commitment was matched by the Scottish Government, making Glasgow's city deal the richest in the United Kingdom (at the time it was signed), and marking another example, it is to be noted, of shared rule. Glasgow City Council, its neighbouring local authorities, the Scottish Government and the United Kingdom Government are jointly responsible for cooperating in the delivery of the city deal. Westminster could not legislate on local authority law

[28] ibid, Opinion of Roberts CJ, 51.

[29] In November 2016 the UK Government announced that, in due course, every city in Scotland would have a City Deal.

in Scotland without Holyrood's consent, as the matter is devolved; but this rule does not inhibit UK Ministers from dealing directly with local authorities in Scotland, using their spending powers rather than their law-making powers. There is ample opportunity here for UK Ministers to seek directly to influence the shape of public policy in Scotland, even in areas that are devolved. Thinking about shared rule through the prism of spending, rather than of powers, lends a quite different complexion to it.

D. Pre-emption

The US Constitution provides that federal law is 'the supreme law of the land'.[30] Thus, in the event of a clash between State law and federal law, the latter prevails over the former (as long as it is otherwise compatible with the Constitution). Further, where State law 'stands as an obstacle to the accomplishment and execution of the full purposes and objectives of Congress', the Courts will set the State law aside. This is known as pre-emption. States are also precluded from regulating conduct in a field that Congress, acting within its proper authority, has determined must be regulated by federal law exclusively. The intent to displace State law can be inferred from a framework of regulation 'so pervasive that Congress has left no room for the States to supplement it'. This is known as 'field pre-emption'.[31]

The 2012 case of *Arizona v United States* concerned the validity of various provisions of immigration law that Arizona had enacted. The authority of the federal government over matters of immigration and naturalisation is well settled in the United States. As the Court expressed it in *Arizona*,

> federal governance of immigration and alien status is extensive and complex. Congress has specified categories of aliens who may not be admitted ... Unlawful entry and unlawful re-entry into the United States are federal offences ... Once here, aliens are required to register with the federal government and to carry proof of status on their person ...

and so on. But, as the Court also noted, the 'pervasiveness of federal regulation does not diminish the importance of immigration policy to the States'. Hundreds of thousands of deportable aliens are apprehended in Arizona every year (Arizona has a long land border with Mexico). It has been estimated that unauthorised aliens comprise as much as six percent of the State's population. In 2010 Arizona enacted a controversial law that sought to supplement federal immigration law in a number of ways. Several provisions of the Arizona statute were challenged by the US Government on grounds of pre-emption.

The first was a provision that made it a State offence for an alien wilfully to fail to complete or carry an alien registration document. This was already a federal offence. The federal offence could be punished by fine, imprisonment or a term

[30] US Constitution, Art VI, cl. 2.
[31] See *Arizona v United States* 567 US __ (2012).

of probation. Under the Arizona law the only punishments available in respect of the offence were a fine or imprisonment. Arizona argued that its law should be upheld because it had the same aim as federal law and used the same standards, but the Supreme Court ruled that the provision was pre-empted by federal law. The Court held that Arizona's law created a framework of sanctions that conflicted with Congress' plan and, moreover, that 'the federal government has occupied the field of alien registration'.[32]

The second provision the United States challenged made it a State offence for an unauthorised alien knowingly to apply for work. Federal law makes it an offence for employers knowingly to hire, recruit or continue to employ unauthorised workers. While federal law may impose some civil sanctions on unauthorised aliens who seek work in the United States, it does not criminalise them—rather, it imposes criminal sanctions on the employer side. The Court held that 'Congress made a deliberate choice not to impose criminal penalties on aliens who seek, or engage in, unauthorised employment' and that the Arizona law was an obstacle to the regulatory system Congress had chosen. It was therefore pre-empted.

A further provision of the Arizona law successfully challenged by the United States in this case concerned powers of arrest. Again, the State sought to increase the powers of arrest already provided for by federal law. And, again, the Court ruled these extensions to be pre-empted.

Three Justices dissented from these rulings. Among them was Justice Scalia, who saw the case as going to the very core of State sovereignty. The power of States to exclude requires that Congress has unequivocally expressed its intention to abrogate, he ruled: 'implicit field pre-emption will not do'.[33] Seen in this light, the Arizona law should be upheld unless it conflicted with federal law (which it did not, in Justice Scalia's judgment). Arizona, he ruled, 'is entitled to have its own immigration policy—including a more rigorous enforcement policy—so long as that does not conflict with federal law'.[34] Arizona was seeking to act not to contradict or reverse any provision of federal immigration law, but solely to enforce federal immigration law more effectively.

In contrast to the case law on the spending power, the doctrine of pre-emption is decidedly unhelpful from a shared rule point of view. *Arizona v United States* is a good example of the sort of direction that UK case law on devolution should not take (and is extremely unlikely to take). The structure of powers over tax, welfare and employment in the Smith Commission Agreement and in the Scotland Act 2016 is based on a very different approach to shared rule from that preferred in the US doctrine of pre-emption. The power of the Scottish Parliament to top-up welfare benefits, for example, could not operate at all were the United Kingdom courts to hold that Westminster had so comprehensively legislated in the field of social security as to pre-empt Holyrood from adding to or reinforcing that law. Whatever the rights and wrongs of Arizona's uncompromising stance on immigration—and

[32] ibid, Opinion of the Court, 9.
[33] ibid, Opinion of Scalia J, 8.
[34] ibid, 12.

no comment is made on that here—from a shared rule point of view, the judgment of the US Supreme Court in *Arizona v United States* is to be regretted. A shared rule perspective would suggest that States should be encouraged to act, not prohibited from acting, to supplement federal law in areas where they share responsibility with the federal government.

E. From Dual Sovereignty to Cooperative Federalism

The spending power cases and the *Arizona* case on pre-emption are all, in their different ways, about the possibilities and the limits of shared rule. To what extent may Congress use federal funds to encourage States to behave in a particular way? To what extent may Congress rely on the States to implement federal policy? And to what extent may States seek to enhance—or, indeed, to resist—federal rule-making? These are all questions of shared rule or, as the academic literature in the United States would have it, of 'cooperative federalism'.

As we saw above, the old model of federalism was that a federal country has two layers of government, each with its own set of powers: if Congress has 'sovereignty' over foreign relations and national security, the States have 'sovereignty' over everything not enumerated in the Constitution as one of Congress' legislative powers. (Likewise in Scotland and the UK: if Westminster controls immigration law and the state pension, Holyrood controls the health service in Scotland and the Scottish education system.) Commentators in the United States have long since recognised that this older model of federalism, which was referred to above as the 'dual sovereignty' model, fails to describe the reality of modern American government. In so many areas of public policy, both law-making and administration are shared between the States and the federal government, rather than owned exclusively by one or the other. Lawyers call this 'concurrent jurisdiction'. In the United States it is very much the norm, not the exception. Think of the broad array of contexts the cases we have considered represent: environmental law (*New York v US*), criminal law (*Lopez* and *Printz*), health care (the Obamacare case) and immigration (*Arizona*). Each of these areas, like so many more, are examples of concurrent jurisdiction, cooperative federalism, or shared rule.

That is to say, there is 'a sharing of regulatory authority between the federal government and the states that allows states to regulate within a framework delineated by federal law'.[35] This is a style of government that developed in the US from the late 1960s. If, under Roosevelt's New Deal programme, national bureaucracies tended to regulate directly, since the late 1960s the trend has been much more for federal government to seek to regulate through the agency of the States. Environmental regulation is often regarded as the place where this started in the US. The Clean Air Act, for example, provided for certain 'uniform federal standards, but

[35] Philip J Weiser, 'Towards a Constitutional Architecture for Co-operative Federalism' (2001) 79 *North Carolina Law Review* 664, at 665.

left the States with considerable flexibility in addressing the statute's objectives'.[36] In the UK context this is completely familiar, not because of devolution but because of the European Union. The description just given of the Clean Air Act in the United States is precisely what an EU directive does. Brussels sets the standards with which—for example—Member States' data protection legislation must comply, but leaves to each Member State 'the choice of form and methods' by which those standards are implemented into national law.

The federal Environmental Protection Agency (EPA) works closely with States in administering legislation such as the Clean Air Act and the Clean Water Act. The EPA will *negotiate* with State counterparts in prioritising and implementing enforcement actions. Indeed, federal legislation now requires the EPA to follow States' lists of priority pollution clean-up projects, rather than imposing its own priorities on States. Decisions as to which treatment facilities are built where and when are the result of negotiations between the EPA and the relevant State.[37] Such practices of negotiation make for what has been described as 'an iterative process of joint decision-making' encompassing 'political haggling', collaborative policy-making and a variety of 'signalling processes'.[38]

Practices such as this—shared rule in action—are not limited to the environmental field. One academic who has researched this matter reports that 'collaborative state-federal programmes have been especially popular to combat gang violence'.[39] The Project Safe Neighbourhoods programme, for example, partnered regional US Attorney's offices with corresponding State Attorney General's offices, the FBI, State and local police, and State probation and parole officers 'to co-ordinate the deterrence, investigation, and prosecution of gun violence in metropolitan areas'.[40] Another example comes from energy policy. State actors were instrumental in the making of the federal Energy Independence and Security Act in 2007 which, among other matters, authorised the transfer of federal funds to States to encourage the use of clean energy.

> Thanks to State leadership in the design of the programme, federal grants … offer funds to State … and municipal governments in exchange for their development and implementation of community-based projects to improve energy efficiency, reduce energy use, and reduce carbon emissions.[41]

F. Cooperation and Uncooperation

If cooperative federalism were only about the assistance that States can give in the implementation of federal policy it would not be a very attractive model

[36] ibid, at 670.
[37] See Erin Ryan, 'Negotiating Federalism' (2011) 52 *Boston College Law Review* 1, 33.
[38] ibid, 5.
[39] ibid, 32.
[40] ibid.
[41] ibid, 39.

to those who consider federalism to be a check on—rather than a mere means of—national law-making. But if States can choose to cooperate with federal policy-makers, they may also be able to choose not to. Further, they may be able to seek to resist federal policy—to be uncooperative, rather than cooperative. To this end, a new school of 'uncooperative federalism' has recently emerged in American legal thinking.[42] Three brief examples will illustrate the argument: on immigration, national security and drugs control. We saw above that Arizona's attempts to strengthen immigration law enforcement were met with stiff resistance in the US Supreme Court. A number of States (and, indeed, a number of municipalities within States) have sought to go the other way, and to resist the enforcement of aspects of federal immigration law.

Federal immigration law makes it designedly difficult for illegal migrants to integrate into American society. But most of the institutions that migrants need in order to integrate are controlled not by the federal government but by States or by localities within States—schools, civic associations, the workplace, public health and safety institutions, and the like.[43] Cristina Rodriguez has documented how municipalities across America have, for example, established Day Labour Centres at which (typically) immigrant men can register to seek employment, thus 'regularising and even formalising a labour market that operates in the shadow of federal law'.[44] Additionally, local 'sanctuary laws'—more accurately, resolutions or executive orders—may limit the authority and ability of State and local officers to cooperate with federal officials in the enforcement of federal laws. Going yet further, by 2007 at least 10 States had passed laws permitting unauthorised students to pay in-state tuition at public colleges, despite this being contrary to federal law.[45] Congress can legislate to outlaw all of these practices. The United States can take legal action to have the federal courts declare them unlawful. But all this takes time and, in the meantime, States can seek to use public opinion to support their efforts either to go beyond, or to undermine, federal immigration law.

In the US there are about 10 State or local law-enforcement officers for every federal one. One estimate has it that there are as many as 17,000 State and local law-enforcement agencies, comprising about 700,000 officers. The FBI, by contrast, has 12,000 agents.[46] In the immediate aftermath of 9/11 Congress passed the Patriot Act and the Bush Administration established a new federal Department of Homeland Security. Much as these measures increased the reach of the federal government's counter-terrorism operations, great reliance continued to be made

[42] Jessica Pulman-Rozen and Heather K Gerken 'Unco-operative Federalism' (2009) 118 *Yale Law Journal* 1256.

[43] See Cristina M Rodriguez, 'The Significance of the Local in Immigration Regulation' (2008) 106 *Michigan Law Review* 567, 581.

[44] ibid, 598.

[45] ibid, 605.

[46] Matthew C Waxman, 'National Security Federalism in the Age of Terror' (2012) 64 *Stanford Law Review* 289, 306.

on cooperation with local and State law enforcement. But when the Justice Department requested assistance from local police agencies in locating and questioning men holding visas from countries where al Qaeda operated, many declined to participate in the questioning, not wanting to jeopardise carefully developed relationships with immigrant communities.[47] If States' rights and support for federalism had long been the preferred terrain of the political right in America, post 9/11 law enforcement saw the tables turned, as more liberal States (and, indeed, cities) sought refuge in 'uncooperative federalism' as means of resisting what they considered to be the illiberal and authoritarian reaction of the Bush Administration.[48]

Our final example is similar. In November 2012 two States—Colorado and Washington—legalised recreational marijuana use despite the fact that this is in contravention of federal law and policy. Federal law classifies marijuana as a Schedule 1 drug under the Controlled Substances Act; its manufacture, distribution and possession are thereby prohibited categorically.[49] Ernie Young's analysis of the Colorado and Washington position is compelling:

> if State non co-operation undermines federal enforcement ... then one might think federal authorities would have a strong argument that State marijuana laws are pre-empted. After all, surely they 'stand as an obstacle to the accomplishment and execution of the full purposes and objects of Congress'. But the anti-commandeering cases have established that States have no obligation to implement or enforce federal law unless they voluntarily agree to do so. It follows that States have no obligation to criminalise conduct simply because federal law does ...[50]

Given that some 99 per cent of arrests in the US for marijuana are made by State officials,[51] even if the federal government were to take legal action to have the Colorado and Washington laws declared unconstitutional on pre-emption grounds, the anti-commandeering doctrine suggests that there is little either the President or the US Congress can do to require State officials to enforce federal law.

G. Conclusions

As Ernie Young says in his essay on Colorado and Washington's marijuana laws, 'the scholarly literature on federalism [in the United States] is only just beginning to explore the full implications of co-operative federalism for inter-governmental relations and the constitutional balance of power'.[52] Even now, it is a model of

[47] ibid, 316.
[48] See Ernest A Young, 'Welcome to the Dark Side: Liberals Rediscover Federalism in the Wake of the War on Terror' (2004) 69 *Brooklyn Law Review* 1277.
[49] Ernest A Young, 'Modern-Day Nullification: Marijuana and the Persistence of Federalism in an Age of Overlapping Regulatory Jurisdiction' (2015) 65 *Case Western Reserve Law Review* 769, 774.
[50] ibid, 776.
[51] See Jessica Bulman-Pozen, 'Unbundling Federalism: Colorado's Legalisation of Marijuana and Federalism's Many Forms' (2014) 85 *University of Colorado Law Review* 1067, 1083.
[52] Young, above n 49, 778.

federalism which finds much more support in American law schools than it does in the US Supreme Court. Justice Scalia's dissent in *Arizona v United States* was firmly based on what he considered to be the 'sovereign' power of the States to exclude—this is the language of dual sovereignty, not of cooperative federalism (or self-rule, rather than shared). In a Supreme Court case decided in 2013 Justice Scalia went so far as to condemn cooperative federalism as 'faux-federalism'.[53] The academic commentary on federalism in America is some way ahead of the Court's case law, it seems.

What this survey of American case law and commentary on federalism tells us is the following:

— focusing on enumerated powers—on the division between reserved and devolved power—is a limited and ultimately not very useful way of thinking about multi-level governance;
— at least as much thought should be given to spending powers, and to the ways in which the United Kingdom could seek to influence and shape public policy in Scotland, Wales and Northern Ireland—even in devolved areas—by means of public expenditure rather than law-making;
— thinking about cooperation between governments may be a more productive way forward than focusing only on the 'sovereignty' or autonomy of different levels of government;
— where governments have the chance to cooperate, however, they may also have opportunities to leverage power by being uncooperative; whether this should be encouraged or constrained by a constitutional architecture of shared rule may be open to question. US case law on this point is under-developed but, as we shall see in the next section, there are valuable insights to be gained on this front by considering experience in Canada and South Africa.

IV. A Constitutional Law of Shared Rule: Learning from the Commonwealth

A. Canada

Federalism is as important an animating principle of the Canadian Constitution as it is in the United States but, as we shall see, it has taken a different shape from its southern neighbour. The Canadian Constitution is nearly a century younger than the American, with the constitutional text dating from 1867 rather than 1787.[54] And, unlike the USA but like the United Kingdom, Canada has had to deal

[53] *Arlington v FCC* 569 US __ (2013) (Slip Opinion, p 14.)
[54] See also the chapters by Schutze and Oliver in this book.

with a powerful secessionist movement, with two secession referendums having been held in Quebec, in 1980 and 1995.

The starting point is sections 91 and 92 of the Constitution Act 1867. Section 92 lists the 'exclusive powers of the provincial legislatures'. Section 91 provides that the Canadian Parliament has legislative competence over 'the peace, order and good governance' of Canada, subject to the exclusive competences of the provincial legislatures. And, 'for greater certainty', section 91 then lists a number of powers that fall within the rubric of 'peace, order and good governance'.

Until the middle of the twentieth century judicial decisions approached sections 91 and 92 as if each provided a list of mutually exclusive competences. They were 'watertight compartments', the judges said. Except they never really were. The main test that the Canadian courts use to determine whether a matter is properly for the Provinces or for the federal government is the 'pith and substance' doctrine. If the pith and substance of the impugned legislation can be related to a matter that falls within the jurisdiction of the legislature that enacted it, the courts will declare it *intra vires*. To assess this, courts will look both at the purpose of the legislation and at its legal effects. The courts are concerned to identify the dominant purpose and effects of the legislation: as long as they are within the powers of the legislature in question, the law will be upheld as constitutionally valid even if it has secondary objectives or incidental effects that would be beyond the powers of that legislature. Recognition that legislation may have secondary or incidental effects on areas beyond a parliament's competence shows that we are not talking about 'watertight compartments'. As the Supreme Court of Canada put it in one of its leading cases on federalism:

> [T]he 'pith and substance' doctrine is founded on the recognition that it is in practice impossible for a legislature to exercise its jurisdiction over a matter effectively without incidentally affecting matters within the jurisdiction of another level of government. For example … it would be impossible for Parliament [in Ottawa] to make effective laws in relation to copyright without affecting property and civil rights [which under section 92 are for the Provinces] …[55]

The Supreme Court went on to note in the same case that 'some matters are by their very nature impossible to categorise under a single head of power: they may have both provincial and federal aspects'. Thus, 'the fact that a matter may for one purpose and in one aspect fall within federal jurisdiction does not mean that it cannot, for another purpose and in another aspect, fall within provincial competence'.[56] An example is dangerous driving: Ottawa may make laws in relation to the public order aspect, and provincial legislatures in relation to its property and civil rights aspect. This 'double aspect' doctrine ensures that the policies of elected legislators of both levels of government are respected.

This is a modern approach to federalism, much championed by Chief Justice Brian Dickson, who was Chief Justice of Canada from 1984–90. It emphasises what

[55] *Canadian Western Bank v Alberta* [2007] 2 SCR 3, para 29.
[56] ibid, para 30.

the Court has described as 'the legitimate interplay between federal and provincial powers'.[57] As Dickson CJ wrote, Canadian constitutional law allows for 'a fair amount of interplay and indeed overlap between federal and provincial powers'.[58] Overlapping powers are 'inevitable', the Court has said, and this requires a 'flexible federalism'.[59]

The Supreme Court of Canada, unlike its US counterpart, regularly uses the language of 'cooperative federalism' to describe its approach. In a 2011 case, for example, the Court wrote that

> in the spirit of co-operative federalism, courts should avoid blocking the application of measures which are taken to be enacted in furtherance of the public interest ... Where possible, courts should allow both levels of government to jointly regulate areas that fall within their jurisdiction ...[60]

This is a live-and-let-live approach to multi-level government; it is quite starkly at odds with the old dual sovereignty model on which American federalism was formerly said to be based. Under the Canadian approach, cooperation is *expected*. Government in silos is discouraged as policy fields are understood to engage the legitimate attention of both federal and provincial authorities.

Accordingly, the Supreme Court tries to uphold legislation against federalism-based challenges where it can. It will hold legislation to be unconstitutional not where it merely affects the jurisdiction of the other layer of government but only where it impairs that jurisdiction. *Impairment* is a higher standard than *affects*: it suggests that the courts should intervene to quash provincial legislation, for example, only when it 'seriously or significantly trammels ... federal power'.[61] The 2010 case of *Quebec v COPA* illustrates this nicely. The case concerned an aerodrome that was built by two private citizens on land zoned by Quebec as agricultural. Quebec wanted the aerodrome to be dismantled, but this was disputed on the basis that it is the federal government, and not the Provinces, that has jurisdiction over air travel. As the Supreme Court put it, 'the question posed in this appeal is which level of government has the final say on where airfields and aerodromes may be located'.[62] The Court answered the question by ruling that, whilst the Quebec law limiting the non-agricultural uses that may be made of designated agricultural land was valid, applying that law in a manner that impaired federal jurisdiction over aeronautics was invalid. Thus, Quebec's legislation was upheld, but the scope of its application was limited to the extent necessary to protect federal jurisdiction.[63]

[57] ibid, para 36.
[58] *OPSEU v Ontario* [1987] 2 SCR 2, 17.
[59] *Canadian Western Bank*, above n 55, para 42.
[60] *Attorney General (Canada) v PHS Community Services Society* [2011] 3 SCR 134, para 63.
[61] *Quebec v COPA* [2010] 2 SCR 536, para 45.
[62] ibid, para 1.
[63] Two Justices dissented on the ground that Quebec's requirement that the aerodrome be dismantled did not interfere with the core of Canada's jurisdiction over aeronautics and ought therefore to be upheld as a lawful exercise of provincial authority over land-use.

That this is a two-way street, and not an approach that will always allow federal interests to restrict provincial concerns, is illustrated by another decision from 2011, the *Securities Act Reference*.[64] The Canadian Parliament enacted the Securities Act and the Supreme Court was asked whether the legislation fell within federal law-making powers. The Act sought comprehensively to regulate the securities market in Canada. The Court ruled that aspects of the Act over-reached what it called 'genuine national concerns'. The case is reminiscent of US cases on the Commerce Clause. Here, Canada sought to rely on the provision in section 91 of the Constitution Act 1867 that Ottawa has power over the regulation of trade and commerce. Supreme Court case law has established that, to fall within this head of legislative power, 'legislation must engage the national interest in a manner that is qualitatively different from provincial concerns'.[65] In order to establish whether this test is met or not, courts will ask, for example, whether the law in question is part of a general regulatory scheme, whether the law is concerned with trade as a whole or with a particular industry, whether the law is such that the Provinces acting alone could not have enacted it, etc. Aspects of the Securities Act failed these tests, in the Court's judgment: 'while the economic importance and pervasive character of the securities market may, in principle, support federal intervention … they do not justify a wholesale takeover of the regulation of the securities industry'.[66] Investor protection, ensuring the fairness of capital markets, and other such matters included within the scope of the Act 'have long been considered local concerns subject to provincial legislative competence over property and civil rights', the Court ruled.[67]

The Court noted that a more cooperative alternative was available: 'a co-operative approach that permits a scheme recognising the essentially provincial nature of securities regulation while allowing Parliament to deal with genuinely national concerns remains available and is supported by Canadian constitutional principles', the Court said.[68] The problem with the over-reach of the Securities Act was that it 'effectively eviscerate[d]' provincial powers to regulate in the field. 'Federalism', said the Court, 'demands that a balance be struck'.[69] In other words, federalism, in this field, demands cooperation between the federal government and the Provinces.

B. Cooperative Federalism and its Limits

This is a striking judicial dictum: federalism 'demands' balance. It suggests that, where there are opportunities for shared rule, those opportunities should be taken

64 *Securities Act Reference* [2011] 3 SCR 837.
65 See, eg, ibid, para 124.
66 ibid, para 128.
67 ibid, para 6.
68 ibid, para 130.
69 ibid, para 7.

and, indeed, that where they are not taken this may be unlawful. Unfortunately, however, in its subsequent case law the Supreme Court of Canada has not always carried this dictum through. An opportunity arose in 2015 for it to do so but the Court, by the narrowest of margins, squandered it. This was a case that had the makings of a new and potentially very significant jurisprudence of shared rule, or of cooperative federalism, but, despite a very strong dissent from four Justices, the Court turned in another direction. The case—*Attorney General (Quebec) v Attorney General (Canada)*[70]—concerned the decision of the federal government to relax aspects of its gun control laws. A federal firearms registry had been in existence for some years; in 2012 the legislation governing it was amended to remove the requirement that long guns be registered (and to decriminalise possession of an unregistered long gun). Quebec wished to maintain a registry for long guns and asked the federal registry for its data pertaining to the registration of long guns in Quebec. The federal registry refused to share the data with Quebec.

Quebec argued that the courts should recognise that 'the principle of co-operative federalism prevents Canada and the Provinces from acting or legislating in a way that would hinder co-operation between both orders of government'.[71] This a five-to-four majority of the Supreme Court refused to do. 'Quebec's position has no foundation in our constitutional law', the majority ruled.[72] Cooperative federalism has its limits, the majority opined, and 'it cannot be seen as imposing limits on the otherwise valid exercise of legislative competence'.[73] In particular, the principle of cooperative federalism cannot be relied upon to 'impose a positive obligation to facilitate co-operation where the constitutional division of powers authorises unilateral action'.[74]

The four dissenting Justices, whose judgment is much more impressive than the cursory reasoning offered by the majority, upheld the constitutionality of the federal legislation relaxing federal gun controls: there was nothing unlawful about Ottawa deciding to exclude long guns from its registration requirements under the Firearms Act. But the decision that all data pertaining to long guns should be destroyed (and not shared with Provinces that wished to maintain controls over long guns) was not necessary to the achievement of Ottawa's legislative purposes and should, for that reason, have been declared invalid. Importantly, the dissenting Justices would have ruled that there was no legal basis upon which Quebec could *require* the federal government to transfer data pertaining to long guns—this was for the governments to figure out, not for the courts to rule on.[75] This is what the dissenting Justices had to say about cooperative federalism:

> [C]o-operative federalism reflects the realities of an increasingly complex society that requires the enactment of co-ordinated federal and provincial legislative schemes

[70] *Attorney General (Quebec) v Attorney General (Canada)* 2015 SCC 14.
[71] ibid, para 15.
[72] ibid, para 16.
[73] ibid, para 19.
[74] ibid, para 20.
[75] ibid, paras 51–52.

> to better deal with the local needs of unity and diversity ... The federal-provincial partnership with regard to firearms control is consistent with the spirit of co-operative federalism. This partnership has enabled the federal and provincial governments to work together, rather than in isolation, to achieve both federal (criminal law) and provincial (public safety and administration of justice) purposes ... In our opinion, our courts must protect such schemes both when they are implemented and when they are dismantled ... Thus, Parliament or a provincial legislature cannot adopt legislation to terminate such a partnership without taking into account the reasonably foreseeable consequences of the decision for the other partner ... In other words, a co-operative scheme from which both the federal and provincial governments benefit cannot be dismantled unilaterally by one of the parties without taking the impact of such a decision on its partner's heads of power into account.[76]

This is a verdict which, from the point of view of shared rule, has much to commend it. It has echoes of the 'respect agenda' that informs the Memorandum of Understanding on inter-governmental relations in the United Kingdom. Indeed, the dissenting Justices quoted from the judgment of the Supreme Court in the *Securities Act Reference*, in which the Court had said that 'the backbone of these [cooperative] schemes is the respect that each level of government has for each other's own sphere of jurisdiction'.[77] In the United Kingdom that respect agenda is a matter of political agreement between governments, rather than of strict constitutional law. The Supreme Court of Canada had the chance to turn it into a matter of constitutional law in *Attorney General (Quebec) v Attorney General (Canada)*. That the opportunity was seized by only a minority of the Court is regrettable. None the less, the dissenting judgment in that case offers a number of signposts as to what a constitutional law of shared rule should look like.

It ought to be the case in Canada and the UK alike that, in sharing power, governments may not act unilaterally without taking into account the impact of their actions on the other level of government. To adopt this as a legal principle in the United Kingdom would be a welcome addition to our public law.

C. South Africa

The South African Constitution dates from 1996 and was written, of course, as South Africa emerged from the era of apartheid. In many ways it is an exercise in nation-building. It is designed to assist in the consolidation of the country's transition to democracy. The inclusion within its Bill of Rights of judicially-enforceable social and economic rights is a well-known component of this. In a country more ravaged than most by the evils of inequality the jurisprudence of the South African Constitutional Court on rights to housing and to the healthcare has been of

[76] ibid, paras 148–54.

[77] *Securities Act Reference*, above n 64, para 133.

cardinal importance.[78] Less well known, at least internationally, is what the South African Constitution says about federalism and shared rule. The South African Constitution establishes three 'spheres' of government: local, provincial and national. Section 41 of the Constitution, 'principles of co-operative government and intergovernmental relations', provides that all spheres of government must

> preserve the peace, national unity and indivisibility of the Republic; ... be loyal to the Constitution, the Republic and its people; respect the constitutional status, institutions, powers and functions of government in the other spheres; ... exercise their powers and perform their functions in a manner that does not encroach on the ... integrity of government in another sphere; and co-operate with one another in mutual trust and good faith.

This is perhaps the fullest articulation of the principle of cooperative federalism in any of the world's English-language Constitutions. Yet it is more than that. Section 41 clearly incorporates principles of cooperative federalism, but it goes further, extending to a constitutional principle of federal loyalty. This is an idea which has more to do with German traditions of federalism than with American or Canadian traditions. In Germany, however, federal loyalty—*Bundestreue*—is concerned principally with fiscal federalism: that is to say, with the way in which public money is transferred from wealthier Länder to poorer ones. In South Africa, by contrast, the constitutional principle of federal loyalty is more general: there is nothing in section 41 to suggest that it pertains only to fiscal matters.

Section 41 and the principle of federal loyalty have not featured prominently in the case law of the South African Constitutional Court in the 20 years since the Constitution came into force. In part this is because the principles enshrined in section 41 are intended to be protected politically. Section 41(3) provides that governments 'must make every reasonable effort to settle' any dispute politically before turning to the courts. If a court is not satisfied that this has been the case, the court may decline to rule on the matter, referring it back to the political process (section 41(4)). A leading commentary on the constitutional law of South Africa states that the Constitutional Court's case law on section 41 'can appear a bit soft' and is 'highly qualified', reflecting the fact that section 41 is 'designed to facilitate political solutions'. The Court has 'shied away' from using section 41 to impose judicial solutions, the commentary says.[79]

The most significant case on section 41 was decided only a few years after the Constitution came into force: *Premier of Western Cape v President of South Africa*.[80] The Province of the Western Cape challenged aspects of an Act of the national legislature which was aimed at the structural transformation of the public service. The legislation required various institutions of provincial government to be structured in a certain way, and the Western Cape argued that this infringed the

[78] Theunis Roux, *The Politics of Principle: The First South African Constitutional Court, 1995–2005* (Cambridge, Cambridge University Press, 2013).

[79] S Woolman, T Roux and B Bekink, *Constitutional Law of South Africa* (Cape Town, Juta and Co, 2008) Ch 14.3.

[80] Case CCT 26/98, *Premier of Western Cape v President of South Africa.*

constitutional autonomy of the Provinces. The Constitutional Court sought to understand the legislation in the light of the principles of cooperative federalism and federal loyalty set out in section 41. It noted that the three spheres of government in South Africa are 'distinctive, inter-dependent and inter-related' and it observed that 'the inter-dependence and inter-relatedness flow the founding provision that South Africa is one sovereign, democratic state'.[81] The Court noted that the Constitution sets out which powers are to be exercised by which sphere of government, and that these constitutional provisions vest 'concurrent legislative competences' in various of the spheres.[82] Both national and provincial legislatures have competences in respect of the structuring of local government and for overseeing its functioning, for example. Cooperation, the Court said, is 'of particular importance in the field of concurrent law-making'.[83]

This is all well and good, but it does not seem to have made any material difference to the way the Court decided the case. The Court's comments on section 41 are scene-setting, giving the context within which South African federalism is to be construed, rather than laying down actual rules of construction. When it came to *determining* which provisions of the legislation on the restructuring of the public service were within the national parliament's competence and which were not, the Court relied principally not on section 41 but on what the Constitution says about the executive power that is allocated to the Provinces (section 125 of the Constitution). Indeed, the Court stated that 'the circumstances in which [section 41] can be invoked to defeat the exercise of a lawful power are not entirely clear'.[84] In the event, most of the provisions of the national legislation in question were found to be compatible with the Constitution; only one provision was found to be unconstitutional.

Despite the fact that the South African Constitutional Court has not made very much of section 41, the values enshrined in that provision nonetheless point to a further way in which constitutional law can articulate and protect principles of shared rule. A legally enforceable principle of constitutional fidelity could be used to help structure practices of shared rule, not least as regards the fair resolution of disputes that arise between governments.

V. Conclusion

In none of the federal jurisdictions surveyed in this essay is there anything resembling a constitutional law of shared rule that the UK could copy-and-paste as it learns to understand and develop its new territorial Constitution. But from each of them discrete lessons may be learned. That we should think of devolution

[81] ibid, para 50.
[82] ibid.
[83] ibid, para 55.
[84] ibid, para 58.

and federalism in terms of spending powers as well as law-making competences. That shared rule can empower governments both through cooperation and non-cooperation. That principles of mutual respect and recognition can be given judicial expression and do not have to be mere platitudes. And that shared rule can be pushed yet further to embrace formal ideas of federal loyalty. All of these—and no doubt many more—are ways in which the idea of shared rule could be given constitutional shape as the UK's ongoing devolution journey unfolds and progresses.

4

Drifting Towards Federalism? Appraising the Constitution in Light of the Scotland Act 2016 and Wales Act 2017

STEPHEN TIERNEY

I. Introduction

The UK appears to be set upon a federal trajectory, although the implications of Brexit make the constitutional future somewhat uncertain. The Scotland Act, with the extensive new powers it gives to the Scottish Parliament, the constitutional guarantee of the permanency of the devolved institutions, and the implicit need for more formalised intergovernmentalism are the main drivers of change in a federal direction. Nonetheless, we wait to see how the UK will relate externally to the EU's own federalising telos, whether through a 'hard' Brexit of dissociation, a 'soft' Brexit of ongoing close market cooperation, or some version of variegated Brexit, giving the devolved territories an asymmetrical relationship with the EU, different from that of the central UK state. This issue is unknowable, but what is clear is that Brexit will arrive at a time when the internal territorial Constitution of the UK is itself rapidly changing. This chapter seeks to explain the evolving nature of the UK's devolution arrangements since it is these very arrangements which look set to complicate the process of Brexit itself.

II. Federalism and the United Kingdom: Constitutionally Impossible?

What we have seen over two decades is the gradual dispersal of powers to the devolved territories. Despite this, the United Kingdom tends not to be discussed in federal terms; a categorical distinction between federalism and devolution remaining the norm in descriptions of the UK as a state. For the first two decades of devolution it has also been rare to find any suggestions that the UK ought to become federal. However, in light of constitutional changes since the Scottish independence referendum of 2014 it now appears that the federal question can no longer be avoided. The Scotland Act 2016 brings with it extensive new powers for the Scottish Parliament, the Cities and Local Government Devolution Act 2016 introduces potentially radical changes to the system of local, city and even regional government in England; the Wales Act 2017 promises the most fundamental reform of Welsh devolution since 1998, while further tax powers have been devolved to the Northern Ireland Assembly.[1] The hollowing-out of the United Kingdom has occurred without any sense of coherent planning, and the extensive new powers for the Scottish Parliament in particular brings to light the danger of a form of decentralisation without direction.[2]

It is now apparent to Parliament that devolution continues to be extended with no vision of the state as a union of peoples.[3] The direction is also entirely one way, with no concentration upon the central institutions of the state and their role in binding the union together, as a counterbalance to the way in which more and more autonomy for the devolved territories loosens the bonds of the state. The Scotland Act 2016 is focused only upon the grant of more powers to Scotland, including extensive tax powers. It does not address how these powers will work in terms of establishing a clear framework for cooperation and dispute resolution between the UK and Scottish governments, nor does it say anything about the need to realign intergovernmental relations to manage the diversification of fiscal regimes within the UK. The lop-sidedness of devolution is such that radical solutions seem to be needed, and at last we find parliamentary committees which are beginning to address the issue of federalism as a possible destination for the UK's territorial Constitution.[4]

There are very good reasons why federalism has hitherto been considered an impossibility for the UK. Federal systems elsewhere in the world are all founded upon the basis of a written Constitution. How could a federal system emerge in

[1] Corporation Tax (Northern Ireland) Act 2015. See also, Northern Ireland Office, 'The Stormont House Agreement and The Stormont House Agreement—Financial Annex', December 2014.

[2] House of Lords Constitution Committee, 'Inquiry into The Union and Devolution 2015–16' http://www.parliament.uk/union-and-devolution; Bingham Centre for the Rule of Law, 'A Constitutional Crossroads: Ways Forward for the United Kingdom' (BICCL, May 2015).

[3] The House of Commons Political and Constitutional Reform Committee concluded in a report that in the post-referendum proposals for further devolution for Scotland, Wales and Northern Ireland there was a 'devolution mind-set' but that a 'new Union mind-set' was difficult to perceive. House of Commons Political and Constitutional Reform Committee, 'The future of devolution after the Scottish referendum' (11th Report, Session 2014–15, HC Paper 700) 46. See also: 'Our future union—a perspective from Wales', speech by the Rt Hon Carwyn Jones AM, Minister of Wales, Institute for Government, October 2014.

[4] House of Lords Constitution Committee, 'Inter-governmental relations in the United Kingdom' (11th Report, Session 2014–15, HL Paper 146); House of Commons Political and Constitutional Reform Committee, 'The future of devolution after the Scottish referendum' ibid.

the UK without such a document? Another trope of federalism is the division of ultimate constitutional authority between the centre and the regions. The British constitutional principle of parliamentary sovereignty would seem prima facie to make the protection of self-rule for the regions impossible in the face of Parliament's ultimate power. Another issue is the deep asymmetry of the UK territorial Constitution. England has never been the subject of any devolution. It is also argued that the size of England compared to the other territories of the UK makes federalism impossible. Only regional government for England could create territories comparable to the size of the already devolved territories[5] and there is no appetite for this. Another feature is the lack of any formalisation of the shared rule dimension of the UK territorial Constitution, and a general lack of any encompassing vision of the union as a system with a federal mentality or spirit.[6]

In this chapter we will explore whether these obstacles to federalism remain as salient as they once appeared. It will be argued that in fact many of these objections to federalism are declining in significance, and that the gradual emergence of a federal UK is increasingly feasible. Before making this case however, we will address two scene-setting issues. The first is a comment on the Scotland Act 2016 (and to a lesser extent, the Wales Act 2017) which will illustrate how far the United Kingdom is going in devolving self-rule; the second is a short account of what is meant by 'federalism'. This is a much contested term, but it will be argued that federalism is a much more flexible option for territorial government than it is often thought to be.

III. After the Independence Referendum: The Scotland Act 2016

The Scotland Act 2016 contains a number of provisions of the highest constitutional importance. It affirms the permanence of the Scottish Parliament and Scottish Government and declares that they are not to be abolished except following a referendum in Scotland;[7] in a related way it gives statutory recognition to the Sewel convention.[8] The Scottish Parliament acquires control of its own composition and electoral system.[9] At the same time the Bill devolves significant tax powers, particularly in relation to the rates and bands of income tax and allocates a significant share of VAT receipts to the Scottish Government.[10] Powers in relation

[5] Alan Trench, 'UKIP digs itself into another hole over an English Parliament', 11 Sept 2011, http://devolutionmatters.wordpress.com/2011/09/11/ukip-dig-themselves-into-another-hole/#comment-2619.

[6] Michael Burgess, *In Search of the Federal Spirit* (Oxford, OUP, 2012).

[7] s 1.

[8] s 2.

[9] ss 3–10.

[10] ss 13–19.

to welfare benefits are devolved for the first time;[11] the Scottish Parliament and Government acquire new powers in policy areas such as employment, transport, energy efficiency, fuel poverty, and onshore oil and gas extraction, and authority in relation to a range of public bodies, hitherto reserved,[12] plus many other public functions;[13] while abortion policy[14] and almost all Tribunals will be devolved.[15]

Scotland is already more heavily devolved than many federal sub-units in other states, and the Scotland Act will make it one of the most devolved territories anywhere in Europe.[16] It is notable however that this Act, emerging as it did from the Smith Commission[17] process, is the result of a hasty attempt to live up to the Vow[18] given by the unionist parties in the lead up to the referendum, does not attempt to contextualise the new powers for Scotland within a broader consideration of their implications for the other devolved territories or for the British Constitution as a whole.[19] The House of Lords Constitution Committee in its review of the Draft Clauses which preceded the publication of the Scotland Bill, questioned how any process that did not consider the future of the Union 'could provide for an "enduring" settlement'.[20]

The Scotland Act is, therefore, yet another instalment of a process of radical reorganisation of territorial authority carried out on the hoof. The system of devolution since 1998 can be characterised as ad hoc, reactive and incremental. Indeed, the Scotland Act was passed shortly before the introduction to Parliament of the Wales Bill, which as the Wales Act 2017 has brought about a complete reorientation of the nature of Welsh devolution (towards a reserved powers model), and the extension of further significant powers to the National Assembly of Wales. It is notable that there was no serious attempt to link these two processes.

[11] ss 22–31.

[12] Part 4 of the Act.

[13] Part 4 of the Act.

[14] s 53.

[15] Clause 39.

[16] David Bell, 'Scotland's Fiscal Future', Centre on Constitutional Change blog, 22 September 2014, http://scotfes.com/2014/09/22/scotlands-fiscal-future/.

[17] The Smith Commission, 'Report of the Smith Commission for further devolution of powers to the Scottish Parliament', 27 November 2014: http://www.smith-commission.scot/wp-content/uploads/2014/11/The_Smith_Commission_Report-1.pdf.

[18] 'David Cameron, Ed Miliband and Nick Clegg sign joint historic promise which guarantees more devolved powers for Scotland and protection of NHS if we vote No', *Daily Record*, 15 September 2014 [and 16 September print edition]: http://www.dailyrecord.co.uk/news/politics/david-cameron-ed-miliband-nick4265992.

[19] The House of Lords Constitution Committee has expressed concern that the UK Government had simply transformed the Smith Commission proposals into draft legislation without addressing their implications for the United Kingdom as a whole. House of Lords Constitution Committee, 'Proposals for the Devolution of Further Powers to Scotland' (10th Report, Session 2014–15, HL Paper 145), para 13.

[20] House of Lords Constitution Committee, 'Proposals for the Devolution of Further Powers to Scotland', ibid, para 23.

Another consequence of the lack of joined-up thinking is that the focus since 1997 has been almost exclusively upon autonomy and not on the role of the devolved territories at the centre. Scottish representation in the House of Commons was reduced (from 73 to 59 seats), but there was no realignment of working practices in response to the 'West Lothian question'. The composition of the House of Lords was reformed[21] but not in any attempt to make it a territorial second chamber along the lines of federal systems such as Germany or the USA. At the executive level there was the early promise of a detailed system of intergovernmentalism. A Joint Ministerial Committee (JMC) established a format for co-operation between ministers in London and their counterparts in Edinburgh and the other devolved administrations.[22] But its operations vary between the quasi-formal and the entirely informal,[23] and without legislation to set out its parameters the system has continued to operate largely at the discretion of the UK government through a unified home civil service. There was even a break it its operations from 2002–07.[24]

In current debates about imbalances in the system much of the focus of course is upon the English question, and rightly so. From this perspective there is clearly an 'autonomy deficit'; England has no devolved legislature and laws passed which, as a consequence of devolution elsewhere, apply only to England still involve MPs from other parts of the UK. But from another perspective it is possible also to identify what we might call a 'representation deficit' affecting the devolved territories; a minimal role for the devolved territories in central decision-making within a system driven only by the imperative of autonomy.

This imbalance seems to be increasingly destabilising. More and more autonomy coupled with a lack of shared rule will increasingly make the UK state seem, respectively, irrelevant and unreachable to the devolved territories. The question with which we are now faced is clear: can further powers simply be piled one on top of another, making Scotland one of the most devolved territories in the world, while also taking Welsh devolution in a radical new direction, without reworking the institutional infrastructure at the centre and arriving at a viable set of principles with which to undergird the union as a cohesive project?

[21] House of Lords Act 1999.

[22] The JMC was established under the Memorandum of Understanding, Cm 4806, July 2000. Generally it operates through meetings between officials or in direct relationships between one London department and its devolved equivalent. Its remit is to deal with reserved matters insofar as they might affect devolved territories, and devolved matters where they impact upon the rest of the UK. Flowing from this arrangement are a series of Memoranda of Understanding, and Supplementary Agreements known as 'concordats'. Richard Rawlings, *Concordats of the Constitution* (2000) 116 *Law Quarterly Review* 257.

[23] For an overview see House of Lords Constitution Committee, 'Inter-governmental relations in the United Kingdom', above n 4, paras 21–29.

[24] ibid, paras 23–24.

IV. Federalism: How Does it Fit?

The second scene-setting issue concerns the nature of federalism itself. Federalism has rarely been taken seriously as a realistic prospect for the UK state. Although Vernon Bogdanor has described the UK as quasi-federal,[25] others observe that the in-built hostility towards federalism within the British political psyche has led to a broader reticence even to recognise just how federal the devolved arrangements are, and continue to become.[26] David Marquand in fact has gone so far as to describe the British aversion to federalism 'neurotic', concluding that 'misconceptions and myths blind British political elites to its potential benefits.'[27]

My key contention is that federalism is a more flexible device than it is often taken to be in British debates. But it is also a subject about which detailed constitutional theory is lacking.[28] My starting point is to consider federalism primarily as an *idea* rather than as a prescribed set of *institutional arrangements*. I believe that in this way we can come closer to the reality of federalism as a variable template for different, but related, forms of political practice; a reality which has manifested itself in highly diverse forms of federalism around the world.

Most work on federalism has been conducted by political scientists addressing either particular federations or engaging in broader comparative study. There is a strong emphasis upon empirical institutional analysis, attempting to assess what defines a federal state, the political and constitutional structures of particular states, often from a comparative perspective, and assessing how federal relations play out in practice in terms of party politics and political attitudes and identities. This work has served greatly to illuminate the practice of federalism, and in particular the tensions and strains which attend it. But, in light of this scholarship, and of federalism's proliferation as a form of government, it remains something of a surprise that federalism has not been the subject of more widespread theoretical analysis by political and constitutional theorists.[29] Michael Burgess for example has recently argued that as yet there is 'no fully fledged theory of federalism.'[30]

[25] V Bogdanor, *Devolution in the UK* (Oxford, Oxford University Press, 2001); V Bogdanor 'Asymmetric devolution: toward a quasi-federal constitution' in P Dunleavy et al (eds), *Developments in British Politics* (London, Palgrave Macmillan, 2003) 7.

[26] A Gamble, 'The Constitutional Revolution in the United Kingdom' (2006) 36 *Publius* 19–35; M Flinders, 'Constitutional Anomie' (2010) 44 *Government and Opposition* 383–409; S Tierney, 'Federalism in a Unitary State: A Paradox too Far?' (2009) *Regional and Federal Studies* 237–54.

[27] D Marquand, 'Federalism and the British: Anatomy of a Neurosis' (2006) 77 *The Political Quarterly* 175–83.

[28] Anna Gamper, 'A "Global Theory of Federalism": The Nature and Challenges of a Federal State' (2005) 6(10) *German Law Journal* 1297–1318, 1299.

[29] Eg D Karmis and W Norman (eds), *Theories of Federalism* (New York, Palgrave-Macmillan Publishing, 2005).

[30] He continues: 'At best there is partial theory based upon rigorous conceptional analysis and the pursuit of terminological precision. At worst there is crass empiricism rooted in the failure to develop concepts and define the key terms.' M. Burgess, *Comparative Federalism: Theory and Practice* (London, Routledge, 2006) 1.

Kyle Scott in another recent book contends that federal theory lacks a 'normative theory that is prior to policy making and implementation.'[31] Indeed he goes so far as to say 'there is no theory of federalism'.[32]

The issue which scholars such as Burgess and Scott identify is the lack of analysis of the underlying purposes behind federalism as the genus of a particular constitutional system. This deficit becomes more noticeable as we see the expansion of federalism in new and different practices, including normative structures beyond the state, most notably of course in Europe.[33] One area in which federal scholarship has become bogged down is in a debate over terminology, with the words federal, federation and federalism subjected to detailed and fiercely contested structural scrutiny. This has had the consequence that commentators disagree even about the number of federal states that exist. For example, in 1994 Daniel Elazar estimated that of the world's 180 states, over half were federal or had some kind of federal arrangement.[34] In 1996, using a narrower definition, Ronald Watts estimated there were merely 23 federations in the world.[35] This is a stark contrast of course, but in fact it is a figure with which in some sense Elazar agreed depending upon what definition is used.[36]

In reality the term 'federation' is being used in a very precise way to define a particular set of institutional arrangements which meet what we might call the 'classical test' of federalism. This is associated with KC Wheare who described the federal principle as 'the method of dividing powers so that the general and regional governments are each within a sphere co-ordinate and independent.'[37] To this definition he added considerable detail, seeking to confine federalism within a very precise set of institutional parameters. Wheare's approach however has in recent decades lost traction, being described, for example, as a 'somewhat static and legalistic interpretation'.[38] It is in this way that scholars like Elazar, Burgess and others seek to release 'federalism' from the narrow constraints of 'federation'.

[31] Kyle Scott, *Federalism: A Normative Theory and its Practical Relevance* (New York, Continuum, 2011) preface vii.

[32] ibid, 1. See also M Feeley and E Rubin, *On Federalism: Political Identity and Tragic Compromise* (Ann Arbor MI, University of Michigan Press, 2008).

[33] As Burgess comments: 'Since the end of the Cold War we find most of the classic theories of federal state formation and their subsequent maintenance simply redundant.' M Burgess, 'Opening Pandora's Box: Process and Paradox in the Federalism of Political Identity' in Alberto López-Basaguren and Leire Escajedo San Epifanio (eds), *The Ways of Federalism in Western Countries and the Horizons of Territorial Autonomy in Spain* (Berlin, Springer, 2013) 3–14, 11.

[34] D Elazar, *Federal Systems of the World: A Handbook of Federal, Confederal and Autonomy Arrangements* 2nd edn (Harlow, Longman, 1994) xvi–xvii.

[35] R Watts, *Comparing Federal Systems* 2nd edn (Montreal/Kingston, McGill-Queens University Press, 1999).

[36] Notably, Elazar also arrived at this number using the more narrow species of 'formally federal systems in the world today'. Elazar, above n 34, xvii.

[37] KC Wheare, *Federal Government* 4th edn (Oxford, Oxford University Press, 1963) 11.

[38] Michael Burgess, 'Federalism and Federation' in Michael Burgess and Alain-G Gagnon (eds), *Comparative Federalism and Federation: Competing Traditions and Future Directions* (Hemel Hempstead UK, Harvester Wheatsheaf, 1993) 3–14, 4.

This is indeed the starting point from which to try to tease out the kernel of the federal idea; a task which is also illuminating as we explore the current British constitutional trajectory.

A key contention of the Elazar/Burgess school is that we are mistaken if we define federalism in purely institutional terms. Such an approach leads one to generalise from the specific, and it is inevitable that in doing so the purported genus will in fact be informed by a particular model or tradition of federal practice; Wheare's purportedly objective account of federalism was in fact heavily reliant upon the American federal model. Instead, a more open approach to definitions releases us from the tight constraints of a fixed vision of federal practice. A particularly useful intervention is by Elazar. For him federalism can be characterised as a balance between autonomy for sub-state territories to run their own affairs, and representation of these territories in the central organs of the state: what he calls the 'self-rule' and 'shared rule'[39] dimensions of federalism. These two components are needed to give the state balance, coherence and the mutual or multiple interdependence upon which the very idea of union rests.

When we think of federalism therefore not as a firmly circumscribed institutional model, but as a balance between self-rule and shared rule, we move from an either/or proposition to the more nuanced question: how federal is the UK? Where does the UK sit on Elazar's scale, combining the two aspects which he considers to be central for stable multi-level government?

V. Further Devolution: Widening or Narrowing the Federal Gap?

Although Brexit hangs over the constitutional future of the UK, making it impossible to predict how things will develop, I will now return to six key issues which seem set to determine whether a more, or possibly less, coherent relationship between self-rule and shared rule is likely to emerge within the UK's territorial Constitution in the next few years:

- constitutionalising self-rule for the devolved territories;
- making the system more (or less) symmetrical;
- England's lack of 'self-rule';
- second chamber reform/regional government for England;
- intergovernmental relations and the 'representation deficit' for the devolved territories; and
- attempts to articulate principles of 'union'.

[39] D Elazar, *Exploring Federalism* (Tuscaloosa AL, University of Alabama Press, 1987) 12.

A. Constitutionalising Self-rule for the Devolved Territories

In light of the Scotland Act, one question is, can the Scottish Parliament (and in due course the National Assembly of Wales) become so autonomous without also formalising their status and making firmer the competence limits between these regional legislatures and Westminster? An objection to the feasibility of federalism for the UK is of course that the very notion of formalisation runs up against the doctrine of parliamentary supremacy, explained by Dicey as the principle that Parliament can make or unmake any law which no other body can over-ride;[40] in the face of such a power the competence of a devolved parliament and even its very existence lie at the whim of Parliament's legislative will.

A potentially seminal development, therefore, is Section 1 of the Scotland Act 2016 which seeks to confirm the permanence of the Scottish Parliament. This clause was dramatically amended at Report Stage in the House of Commons. The enacted provision inserts a new section 63A(1) into the Scotland Act 1998, as follows: 'The Scottish Parliament and the Scottish Government are a permanent part of the United Kingdom's constitutional arrangements.' Two further subsections follow:

> (2) The purpose of this section is, with due regard to the other provisions of this Act, to signify the commitment of the Parliament and Government of the United Kingdom to the Scottish Parliament and the Scottish Government.
>
> (3) In view of that commitment it is declared that the Scottish Parliament and the Scottish Government are not to be abolished except on the basis of a decision of the people of Scotland voting in a referendum.

This replaces the clause contained in the originally drafted Bill which provided that section 1(1) of the 1998 Act, which states that 'There shall be a Scottish Parliament' would be followed by the statement: 'A Scottish Parliament is recognised as a permanent part of the United Kingdom's constitutional arrangements.' A similar provision would also have recognised 'a' Scottish Government as permanent on the same terms.

The enacted provision seems to be a considerably stronger protection, introducing as it does a form of contingent entrenchment. Unlike the original draft, Section 1 does not say that the Scottish Parliament and Government are 'recognised' as permanent, but states boldly that they *are* permanent. For those who gave evidence on the Draft Clauses to the House of Lords Constitution Committee[41]

[40] 'The principle of Parliamentary sovereignty means neither more nor less than this, namely that Parliament thus defined has, under the English constitution, the right to make or unmake any law whatever: and, further, that no person or body is recognised by the law of England as having a right to override or set aside the legislation of Parliament.' AV Dicey, *Introduction to the Study of the Law of the Constitution* (London, MacMillan and Co, 1885).

[41] House of Lords Constitution Committee, 'Proposals for the Devolution of Further Powers to Scotland', above n 19, Appendix 2, Q9.

and to the House of Commons Political and Constitutional Reform Committee, the term 'recognised' was significant in arguments that Parliament's sovereignty was not affected by the original clause 1.[42]

Secondly, sub-section 1(2) signifies the commitment of the Parliament and Government of the United Kingdom to the Scottish Parliament and the Scottish Government. Certainly it can be argued that 'signifying' a commitment is not the same as guaranteeing that there can be no retreat from that commitment,[43] but another reading, and the one seemingly more consistent with the overall thrust of the new section, seen in the light of the Vow, the Smith Commission etc, is that this is indeed an explicit attempt by Parliament to make clear what is intended by the section as a whole; sub-section 2 is in effect an aid to interpretation that affirms Parliament's commitment to the permanence of the Scottish institutions.

Of course it can be argued that Parliament could later change its mind and abolish the Scottish Parliament in any event.[44] But even to those who considered the original version of Clause (Section) 1 to be no constraint on Parliament's legal power, this scenario was thought to be in political terms, highly implausible, if not absurd.[45] The enacted provision seems to offer a stronger argument that, even in legal terms, such a move might be interpreted by the courts as no longer valid. The most significant provision is Section 1(3). This introduces a step by which Parliament appears to make its own legislative competence contingent upon an intervening stage, namely a referendum result in Scotland in favour of abolition of the Scottish Parliament. This provision may be seen as something of a half-way house; a contingent rather than an absolute form of self-limitation. It is not that Parliament cannot abolish the Scottish Parliament, but that it has circumscribed the conditions under which it may do so by creating the referendum requirement.

There is some disagreement as to whether or not the courts would recognise such a contingent self-limitation, but it is at least arguable that they would.[46] Parliament has legislated previously to alter the process by which legislation is to be made.[47] The Parliament Acts created only *internal* procedural changes to the

[42] See Prof Mark Elliott's evidence to the PCRC. House of Commons Political and Constitutional Reform Committee, 'Constitutional implications of the Government's draft Scotland clauses' (10th Report, Session 2014–15, HC 1022), para 9: 'by including the word "recognised", Clause 1 might be taken to be merely declaratory of the supposed fact of the Scottish Parliament and Government's permanence.' See also 'Constitutional implications of the Government's draft Scotland clauses', ibid, para 24, and M Elliott, 'The Draft Scotland Bill and the sovereignty of the UK Parliament', Public Law for Everyone blog, 22 Jan 2015 http://publiclawforeveryone.com/2015/01/22/the-draft-scotland-bill-and-the-sovereignty-of-the-uk-parliament/.

[43] I am grateful to Mark Elliott for discussion on this point.

[44] Dr Mike Gordon in evidence to the PCRC expressed the view that even if the word 'recognised' had been omitted, Parliament's sovereignty would remain unaffected. 'Constitutional implications of the Government's draft Scotland clauses', above n 42, para 29.

[45] House of Lords Constitution Committee, 'Scotland Bill Report' (6th Report, Session 2015–16, HL Paper 59) para 32.

[46] *Jackson v Attorney General* [2006] 1AC 262.

[47] Parliament Acts 1911 and 1949.

mode of passage of legislation, but a closer analogy to Section 1 of the Scotland Act is the European Union Act 2011 section 2 which, in a similar way, seeks to introduce an *external* procedural step, by providing that a treaty amending the European treaties is not to be ratified unless certain conditions are met, including a referendum approving the change.

Despite the terms of Section 1 it is still arguable that Parliament's supremacy remains unaffected. The 'Member's explanatory statement' which accompanied the final version of Clause 1 tabled at Report stage in the Commons explains that the Scottish Parliament and Government '*are not* to be abolished except on the basis of a decision of the people of Scotland in a referendum.'[48] Noticeably this does not say *cannot be*, and can therefore be read as seeking to maintain the possibility that Parliament could over-ride this provision. However, the Explanatory Notes which accompanied the Bill's introduction to the House of Lords do in fact say that the Scottish Parliament and Government '*cannot* be abolished except on the basis of a decision of the people of Scotland in a referendum.'.[49] As the House of Lords Constitution Committee commented in a report on the Scotland Bill: 'There is now a strong argument that Parliament is seeking to limit its own competence in a way that the courts may seek to uphold in future given that it rests on a requirement for popular consent.'[50]

The Government's intention therefore seems clear, and there is a point at which theoretical possibility becomes fanciful. In Section 1 Parliament is seeking explicitly to limit its own competence by way of an external procedural limitation (a referendum in Scotland). In any event, since Parliament is extremely unlikely ever to attempt to repeal the provision without a preceding referendum, this may also serve to consolidate its constitutional significance.

Section 2 is also significant. This recognises that the Parliament of the United Kingdom will not normally legislate with regard to devolved matters without the consent of the Scottish Parliament. This is simply recognition of a convention. But it is a seemingly expansive convention, the reach of which is not clear.[51]

[48] Emphasis added. House of Commons, Consideration of Bill (Report Stage), Scotland Bill as amended, HC Deb vol 602 col 50 (9 November 2015).

[49] Emphasis added. House of Lords, Scotland Bill Explanatory Notes, HL Bill 73, 10 November 2015 http://www.publications.parliament.uk/pa/bills/lbill/2015-2016/0073/en/15073en.pdf.

[50] House of Lords Constitution Committee, 'Scotland Bill Report', above n 45, para 36.

[51] It is notable that the Sewel convention is set out here in relation to 'devolved matters'. This is a more narrow definition than that recognised by the UK Government in Devolution Guidance Note 10, which suggests that the convention covers a proposed bill which: 'contains provisions applying to Scotland and which are for devolved purposes, or which alter the legislative competence of the Parliament or the executive competence of the Scottish Ministers.' *Devolution Guidance Note 10*, Department for Constitutional Affairs, November 2005. The UK Government seems to have accepted that the convention covers bills that will change the legislative competence of the Scottish Parliament either restrictively or in an empowering way. The Scottish Government also takes an expansive view of the convention. The Scottish Government, *The Sewel Convention: Key Features* http://www.gov.scot/About/Government/Sewel/KeyFacts. These differences in understanding could be a source of future disagreement and potentially of legal dispute.

It could also be the case that Section 1 will impact upon the interpretation given to Section 2. A legislature that is recognised as permanent and in relation to whose existence Parliament has sought to limit its own competence will, in the eyes of many, acquire an even stronger constitutional status than that which it currently enjoys.[52] It might be argued that the powers of such a parliament ought similarly to be considered to be beyond the reach of Westminster's unilateral interference. These speculations have however been somewhat unsettled by the *Miller* case in which applicants to the High Court sought to contest the power of the UK Government to give notification of the intention to leave the European Union under TEU Article 50 by way of the royal prerogative. When the case reached the Supreme Court the issue of devolution was also in play. The Court, asked whether the Sewel convention would require the consent of the Scottish Parliament for any legislation used to trigger Article 50, took a very narrow view of the convention, holding that it operates only as 'a political constraint on the activity of the UK Parliament', and that while it plays an important role in the operation of the UK Constitution, 'the policing of its scope and operation is not within the constitutional remit of the courts'.[53] The fact that the courts would not enforce it is not in the end at all surprising, although their failure to acknowledge its constitutional salience perhaps was. Nonetheless, as devolved powers expand, and the institutions of devolution are given stronger legislative recognition, its political force is still likely to grow.

One of the key features of a federal system is that the constitutional powers of the constituent units are protected beyond the unilateral competence of the central legislature. The combination of Sections 1 and 2 would appear, in effect, to have created the near complete protection for the 'self-rule' of the Scottish Parliament.

Given the nature of the political commitments made since the Vow, the terms of section 1 itself, and the Government's stated purpose in bringing forward the amended clause,[54] there is a now strong argument that, for the first time, Parliament has passed into law a provision which the courts will seek to uphold even against the later, express intention of Parliament. The federalising potential of this is clear. In its report in March 2015 the Constitution Committee of the House

[52] There have already been moves by the courts to recognise the constitutional status of the Scottish Parliament and the Welsh Assembly as well as the significance of their legislation: *AXA General Insurance v Lord Advocate* [2011] UKSC 46, per L Hope, para 46; Recovery of Medical Costs for Asbestos Diseases (Wales) Bill [2015] UKSC 3 per Lord Thomas.

[53] *R (on the application of Miller and another) v Secretary of State for Exiting the European Union* [2017] UKSC 5, para 151.

[54] In debate at Report Stage the Secretary of State explained: 'The new clause removes the words "recognised as" and makes it clear beyond question that the Scottish Parliament and the Scottish Government are permanent institutions, and that it would take a vote by the people of Scotland in a referendum to ever abolish them. The amendment puts it beyond doubt that, as the Prime Minister has said, "Scottish devolution is woven into the very fabric of our United Kingdom."' HC Deb 9 Nov 2015, col 5.

of Lords observed that Section 1 (even in its weaker form as contained in the Draft Clauses) appeared 'to be moving the United Kingdom in a federal direction, attempting to crystallise by way of statute, if not a written Constitution, the status and powers of the devolved institutions in a way that has hitherto not been the case.'[55]

B. Making the System More or Less Symmetrical

Not all federal systems are, or even aim to be, symmetrical, but regional government in the United Kingdom is uniquely diverse. The systems of devolution among Scotland, Wales and Northern Ireland vary not only in terms of the range of powers devolved, with the Scottish Parliament having the most extensive range of competences, followed by Northern Ireland and then Wales, but also in terms of the structure of the system in each: a reserved powers model in Scotland, a consociational arrangement in Northern Ireland, and a shared powers model in Wales.

Although the Scotland Act 2016 extends significantly the range of powers of the Scottish Parliament, the Wales Act 2017 brings about a realignment of Welsh devolution that may in some respects reduce the high degree of variance between the two models. In addition to extensive tax powers and competence over a range of welfare benefits, the Scottish Parliament is gaining control over its own composition: how it operates, its size and the electoral system. The Wales Act was been influenced by the power grab in Scotland since the 2014 referendum.[56] In substantive terms, the Act provides the National Assembly with a range of powers similar to those either currently held by, or granted to, Scotland in the Scotland Act 2016, including competence over energy policy and transport.[57] The Wales Act also contains further tax powers which can be transferred to the National Assembly without the need for a referendum.[58] The National Assembly will, like the Scottish Parliament, also gain control over its own composition and possibly also of the voting age for elections to the Assembly.[59] It will even have the power to change its name, paving the way for it possibly also to adopt the moniker 'parliament'. It also guarantees the permanence of the Welsh institutions on the same terms as the

[55] House of Lords Constitution Committee, 'Proposals for the devolution of further powers to Scotland', above n 19, para 77.

[56] The First Minister of Wales, Rt Hon Carwyn Jones AM, told the Commons PCRC that he saw 'no reason why the Smith Commission offer in Scotland should not be made to Wales'. House of Commons Political and Constitutional Reform Committee, 'The future of devolution after the Scottish referendum Eleventh', above n 3, para 29, Evidence Q366.

[57] Wales Act 2017, ss 23–28. This was proposed by the Richard Commission (Commission on the Powers and Electoral Arrangements of the National Assembly for Wales, 2004) and by the Silk Commission II ('Empowerment and Responsibility: Legislative Powers to Strengthen Wales, 2014).

[58] Wales Act 2017, s 17.

[59] Wales Act 2017, s 5.

Scottish Parliament and provides statutory recognition of the application of the Sewel convention to Wales.[60]

The story of Welsh devolution has been one of attempted catch-up with the Scottish system,[61] and the way is paved for this to continue. The most dramatic change brought about by the Wales Act is a reorientation of Welsh devolution in the direction of a reserved powers model similar to that of Scotland. There are likely to be considerable teething problems in such a switch. One of the reasons why the reserved powers model for Scotland has worked smoothly is the distinctive legal system which has meant that the Scottish Parliament has had considerable leeway in implementing its powers. The Wales Act, in seeking to preserve the integrity of the common England/Wales legal system, builds in a complex array of checks on the exercise of the powers which it proposes to devolve. This poses potential problems in terms of complexity and the potential for dispute between the National Assembly and central government in the medium term.[62] The broader direction of travel however is towards a model of Welsh devolution that is ever more similar in structure, design and substantive powers to that of Scotland.

Northern Ireland does, however, remain an outlier here. The range of devolved powers of the Northern Ireland Assembly is not dissimilar to those of the Scottish Parliament, and there has been a move towards further tax devolution,[63] and every possibility that both unionist and nationalist parties would welcome further control over revenue and spending. Northern Ireland is however likely to remain structurally very different from that of Scotland and Wales. The consociational system is a response to the underlying inter-communal tensions in Northern Ireland. The continuation of a power-sharing system is likely to remain essential to the future of devolve government in Northern Ireland.

It is also significant that devolution in Northern Ireland is seen by many nationalists as a contingent and temporary solution. The Northern Ireland Act 1998 section 1 leaves open the issue of a possible reunification of the island of Ireland.[64] In light of this, there is no prospect that an equivalent to Section 1 of the Scotland Act 2016 or Wales Act 2017, declaring the Northern Ireland Assembly as permanent, would be acceptable to Irish nationalists. A more general extension of a Section 2-type commitment, giving statutory recognition to the existence of the Sewel convention in relation to Northern Ireland, would be less controversial, although it could restrict the default power of the UK Parliament temporarily to suspend Northern Ireland devolution which it has found necessary in the past.

[60] Wales Act 2017, ss 1 and 2 respectively. See also: 'The UK Government agrees that the Assembly should be formally recognised as permanent and that the Assembly and Welsh Government are permanent parts of the United Kingdom's constitutional arrangements. This should be enshrined in legislation.' 'Powers for a purpose: Towards a lasting devolution settlement for Wales', Wales Office, 27 Feb 2015, 2.2.4.

[61] Government of Wales Acts 2006, 2010.

[62] House of Lords Constitution Committee, Wales Bill (5th Report, Session 2016–17, HL Paper 59).

[63] Corporation Tax (Northern Ireland) Act 2015.

[64] 'It is hereby declared that Northern Ireland in its entirety remains part of the United Kingdom and shall not cease to be so without the consent of a majority of the people of Northern Ireland voting in a poll'. Northern Ireland Act s1(1).

Northern Ireland has its own system and for historical reasons this will retain its own distinctiveness. At the same time we are likely to see the closer alignment of the devolved models of Scotland and Wales which should pave the way for a better coordination of devolution, at least in the mainland of Britain. This should help overcome the objections of those who consider deep asymmetry to be incompatible with federalism. But it is also important to bear in mind that the flexibility of federalism as an idea means that asymmetry is no impediment to a feasible system, provided that the elements of self-rule and shared rule, however they may be manifested, are properly coordinated.

C. England's Lack of Self-rule

Despite this conclusion, with the endless roll-out of devolution another problem is being exacerbated. Symmetry may be achieved through devolving more and more powers to Scotland and Wales, but this does nothing to address England's lack of self-rule or to shore up the lack of shared rule within the system as a whole and deal with the larger picture of intergovernmental relations. I will now address the first of these issues, returning to the second below.

The additional layer of asymmetry within the UK system, and for many the most odd, is that the constitutional position of England did not change despite the dramatic developments of 1998. England continued to be governed from Westminster with no realignment of how Parliament operated to take account of the anomaly best known as the West Lothian question. This situation is at last changing. The Scottish independence referendum brought England's constitutional position to a head both constitutionally and politically. The day after the vote the Prime Minister announced on the steps of 10 Downing Street: 'the question of English votes for English laws—the so-called West Lothian question—requires a decisive answer.' In his view new powers for Scotland would require to be mirrored by a concomitant recalibration of the influence of Scottish MPs at Westminster.

The issue of English Votes for English Laws (EVEL) was a manifesto commitment of the Conservative Party ahead of the 2015 general election. The proposal was taken forward by the new Government and already an experimental system is in place. There are some difficulties with the system. One is how the Speaker is able to identify an England-only bill. Another is that important decisions taken for England can, given the size of England, have knock-on consequences for other parts of the UK. The current model is being trialled, and may be modified, but it seems certain that an 'England only' stage for English legislation (and 'England and Wales' only where appropriate), giving an effective veto to the MPs concerned is set to become a fixture of the legislative process.[65]

[65] M Elliott and S Tierney, 'House of Lords Constitution Committee Reports on Wales Bill', UK Constitutional Law Association Blog (28 Oct 2016) (available at https://ukconstitutionallaw.org/).

This development has the potential further to institutionalise the federal dynamic of devolution. The new procedures represent arguably the first, and certainly the most significant, adjustment to the central law-making process that takes account of the reality of devolution. And in this way, a more formalised categorisation of state-wide legislation on the one hand and 'devolved' or sub-state legislation on the other—a distinction common to most federal systems—will become part of the UK's constitutional architecture.

D. Second Chamber Reform/Regional Government for England

Another feature of many federal systems is a second chamber representing the federal regions such as the American Senate or German Bundesrat. The notion that Parliament's composition, at least insofar as law-making is concerned, should be adjusted in recognition of devolution, may also lead to a debate about the composition and role of the House of Lords, a debate which has never taken on a territorial dimension. It is testament to the compartmentalisation of constitutional change in the UK that House of Lords reform, brought about by the House of Lords Act in 1999—passed in the same period in which devolution was being implemented—was seen by the Labour Government as an entirely separate issue, with the focus upon removal of most hereditary peers from the House. Similarly, reform inquiries and proposals which have been advanced since then have focused upon the balance between an elected and unelected element in the House's composition[66] and not upon whether it should be remodelled as a 'territorial chamber', reflecting the realities of a devolved UK. This started to change again in light of the proposals of the Smith Commission and a belief in some quarters that these would require to be reflected in changes at the centre. For example, the Labour Party manifesto for the 2015 General Election proposed an 'elected Senate of the Nations and Regions to replace the House of Lords'.

However, the major impediment in the way of 'territorialising' the UK's second chamber, apart from a lack of political will, is the absence of regional government in England. England itself, with approximately 85 per cent of the UK population, seems too big to be one of four regional subunits for such a chamber: in no other multi-level state is one 'region' such a huge part of the state. Notably, the House of Commons Political and Constitutional Reform (PCR) Committee, heard evidence that tied the EVEL issue to English devolution to regions and cities, with some commentators considering the former no substitute for the latter, and the latter in any case a more important issue.[67]

[66] '"The Greatest Quango of them All", "a rival Chamber" or "a hybrid nonsense"? Solving the Second Chamber Paradox' [2004] *Public Law* 352–79.

[67] House of Commons Political and Constitutional Reform Committee, 'The future of devolution after the Scottish referendum', above n 3, paras 96–97.

Proposals for English regional government of course stalled under the Blair government. But the new Cities and Local Government (Devolution) Act 2016 promises a potentially radical reform of local government. The Act implements the Government's plans for more powers for cities and regions, creating the opportunity for a 'combined authority' and directly elected Mayor to be created for the areas which seek these powers. The range of competences over which the Government might seek to devolve powers is potentially extensive judging by a speech given by the Chancellor of the Exchequer on 14 May in which he said the Bill would 'pave the way for ... cities ... to take greater control and responsibility over all the key things that make a city work, from transport and housing to skills, and key public services like health and social care'.[68] There have also been proposals for a draft code which would set out the broad principles which should govern the relationship between central and local government in England, these principles to include that local government should be independent of central government and have a secure financial base.[69] The Government rejected the idea of codifying the relationship between local and central government within the Act, but it is still a potentially radical measure.

That said, there is certainly a considerable distance between these proposals and the levels of devolution enjoyed by Scotland, Wales and Northern Ireland. Indeed, before the election the PCR Committee was sceptical of these proposals, which they felt did not promise 'the genuine transfer of power from the centre to localities which many are seeking.'[70] Therefore they recommended a

> Convention for England, held over the term of the next Parliament, with broad popular representation from the public and civil society, could examine the relationship between England and the United Kingdom and develop a process for further agreed devolution from the centre to regions and localities.[71]

No such process is in the offing and we must wait to see how cities and other localities attempt to use the new powers and how much local control they actually offer.

It is a long way from local government reform in England to a second chamber designed to represent a multi-national and regionalised UK, thereby addressing the 'representation deficit' of devolution. But the move towards local government in England, which may lead to extensive economic powers being transferred from London, could be the first step in such a process. Again the flexibility of federalism should be borne in mind. As the Canadian experience shows, an effective second 'territorial' chamber is certainly not an essential component of an effective federal system.

[68] Rt Hon George Osborne, 'Chancellor on building a Northern Powerhouse', Victoria Warehouse, Manchester, 14 May 2015 https://www.gov.uk/government/speeches/chancellor-on-building-a-northern-powerhouse.

[69] Political and Constitutional Reform Committee, 'Prospects for codifying the relationship between central and local government', Third Report of Session 2012–13, HC 656-I, Summary.

[70] ibid, para 75.

[71] ibid, para 79.

E. Intergovernmental Relations and the 'Representation Deficit' for the Devolved Territories

There is a broader and more fundamental question which emerges in the context of the radical new powers brought about by the Scotland Act 2016 and Wales Act 2017: can the Scottish and Welsh Governments, enjoying such an accretion of new powers, continue to interact with Whitehall on the basis of informal and discretionary intergovernmental arrangements?

The current system works on the basis of a Memorandum of Understanding (MOU) among the four administrations. The original MOU was published in 1999.[72] Since 2009 it has been reviewed and amended regularly, most recently in 2013.[73] In addition, a number of concordats in specific areas were signed. This system has established a quadrilateral forum comprised of representatives of the UK Government and the three devolved territories: the Joint Ministerial Committee (JMC). But beyond this semi-formal structure, which in any case was in abeyance for several years, the system in reality works mainly on a bilateral basis.[74]

The House of Lords Constitution Committee conducted an inquiry into inter-governmental relations (IGR) in 2015 and found that 'in the eyes of the devolved administrations at least the way the JMC system works at present is not satisfactory'.[75] A key recommendation of the Committee was that consideration be given as to whether IGR should be given a statutory basis, replacing the quasi-formality of the Memorandum of Understanding and concordat system.[76] The Committee also recommended that the Government consider whether 'more formal structures are needed at a civil service level to manage these increasingly complex inter-governmental relations'.[77]

Institutional architecture is one thing, another is how the system works. A general concern for the Committee was that the informality of the system had left the devolved territories playing a subordinate role. In addition to further formalisation, the Committee recommended the better coordination of IGR[78] and that opportunities should exist for policy initiatives to come from the devolved administrations, as well as from the UK Government.[79] Concordats should be

[72] Lord Chancellor, *Memorandum of understanding and supplementary agreements between the United Kingdom Government, Scottish Ministers and the Cabinet of the National Assembly for Wales*, Cm 4444, October 1999.

[73] Cabinet Office, *Devolution: Memorandum of Understanding and Supplementary Agreements between the United Kingdom Government, the Scottish Ministers, the Welsh Ministers, and the Northern Ireland Executive Committee*, October 2013 (hereafter Memorandum of Understanding): https://www.gov.uk/government/uploads/system/uploads/attachment_data/file/316157/MoU_between_the_UK_and_the_Devolved_Administrations.pdf.

[74] House of Lords Constitution Committee, 'Inter-governmental relations in the United Kingdom', above n 4, para 19.

[75] ibid, para 50.

[76] ibid, para 86.

[77] ibid, para 147.

[78] ibid, paras 62 and 70.

[79] ibid, para 70.

reviewed at least once during each Parliament[80] and 'should set out clearly how the devolved administrations should be consulted on, and alerted to, forthcoming changes to UK Government policy that might have an effect on the devolved administrations'.[81] Another issue is how disputes are resolved. A new system was put in place in 2012 and so far it has not been fully tested. The view that emerged from evidence to the Lords inquiry however was that the UK Government has significant control over the outcome of disagreements; therefore, another recommendation of the Committee was that the four governments consider 'how the process of dispute resolution might be made more independent of the UK Government.'[82]

One of the interesting features of the Scotland Bill is that it has so little to say about intergovernmental relations, despite the fact that it will devolve extensive tax and welfare powers, creating significant areas of shared and overlapping competences between the Scottish Parliament and Westminster.[83] In the Command Paper with which the UK Government published the draft clauses, it indicated acceptance of the recommendation of a change to intergovernmental working practices, and committed itself to working with the devolved administrations on a revised Memorandum of Understanding. This work was commissioned at the Joint Ministerial Committee meeting on 15 December 2014.[84] No new MOU has yet been agreed between the UK Government and the devolved territories. We wait to see whether this will take account of the Constitution Committee's recommendations. It is notable however that two House of Lords committees called for passage of the Scotland Bill to be delayed until two crucial aspects of IGR—a new fiscal framework and a new Memorandum of Understanding—are finalised.[85]

Although there are no current plans to move any part of the system onto a statutory basis, it would be wrong to be too prescriptive here. The federal model is a broad one, and IGR systems vary between countries: some operate largely on a bilateral basis, others are more multilateral; some are heavily formalised, others operate in a more idiomatic way. As the UK seems set to move towards a more systematic approach, and in particular one that gives guarantees of a more significant role to the devolved territories in central decision-making, this will help to redress the representation deficit; it will also strengthen the shared rule dimension of the state, which is in the eyes of many a key feature of a nascent federal system. Brexit is however set to test IGR to the limit, and it will be interesting to observe just what influence the devolved administrations are able to exert upon Whitehall in the course of negotiations.

80 ibid, para 162.

81 ibid, para 163.

82 ibid, para 76.

83 House of Lords Constitution Committee, 'Scotland Bill Report', above n 45, para 8.

84 'Scotland in the United Kingdom: An enduring settlement', Scotland Office, Cm 8990, January 2015, paras 9.2.2 and 9.2.3.

85 Respectively: House of Lords Select Committee on Economic Affairs, 'A Fracturing Union? The Implications of Financial Devolution to Scotland' (1st Report, Session 2015–16, HL 55) para 4; House of Lords Constitution Committee, 'Scotland Bill Report', above n 45, para 21.

F. A Move Towards 'Union' or 'Federal' Principles?

A number of federal systems have principles of 'good federal conduct' or 'federal loyalty' which require branches of government to act in a cooperative way with one another; an approach seen for example in Germany, Belgium, South Africa and Switzerland. We also see a form of this in the European Union. One of the side effects of devolution in the UK being effected in an ad hoc and case by case way, is that there has never been a clear articulation of the overall purpose of devolution. Once again the proposals for radical change for Scotland and Wales draw attention to this deficit. As the House of Commons PCR Committee observed: 'As the devolution settlement matures, the implications for the operation of the Union as a whole of each transfer of powers must be fully taken into account.'[86] This issue was also addressed by the HL Constitution Committee Report into the Draft Clauses which stated: 'The UK Government and the major UK-wide political parties need urgently to devise and articulate a coherent vision for the shape and structure of the United Kingdom, without which there cannot be constitutional stability.'[87] Similarly in its report into IGR it stated:

> [T]he Government, and the major UK-wide parties, need to devise and articulate a vision for the future of the state and its devolution settlements. An overarching vision for the future shape of the United Kingdom should be a stabilising force in its own right and would also allow for inter-governmental arrangements to be organised on a more stable basis.[88]

Proposals for a more coherent conception of the Union are starting to appear. The Conservative Party has talked about a 'Statute of the Union' to enshrine and reinforce the constitutional arrangements for each part of the Union, and 'to assist in achieving a stable, long-term settlement across the United Kingdom.'[89]

The deficit in this area also led to the launch of a major inquiry by the House of Lords Constitution Committee on The Union and Devolution. The focus of the inquiry was 'to try and identify what binds the constituent parts of the UK together in a single Union, and to consider ways in which that Union might be strengthened and reinforced.'[90] And in doing so

> to identify and articulate the principles that should underlie the existence and governance of the Union and how power is exercised both by Westminster and by the devolved

[86] House of Commons Political and Constitutional Reform Committee, 'The future of devolution after the Scottish referendum', above n 3, para 35.

[87] House of Lords Constitution Committee, 'Proposals for the Devolution of Further Powers to Scotland', above n 19, para 24.

[88] House of Lords Constitution Committee, 'Inter-governmental relations in the United Kingdom', above n 4, para 211.

[89] 'The Implications of Devolution for England', Office of the Leader of the House of Commons, Cm 8969, December 2014, 27.

[90] House of Lords Constitution Committee, 'Inquiry into The Union and Devolution' 2015–16, *Scope of the inquiry*, http://www.parliament.uk/union-and-devolution.

> nations … [and to] consider what practical steps can be taken to stabilise and strengthen the Union in line with those underlying principles.[91]

There is a considerable challenge here. Current devolution processes have already reached an advanced stage without the benefit of a wider consideration of their impact upon the UK Constitution and the union or unions upon which it is founded. It will be no easy task to build in principles after the event as it were.

VI. Conclusions

The diversity of federal models around the world demonstrates that the federal idea is an open canvas that is accommodating of a range of institutional possibilities. It is also dynamic and is as much about becoming as it is about arriving. It seems in fact that the UK has been on a federal trajectory since 1998. It has been feeling its way without relying upon any detailed roadmap. The Scotland Act 2016 and Wales Act 2017 together seem likely to push this process further. We can see various ways in which a more federal complexion is being added to the Constitution: the entrenchment of self-rule seems to be all but complete. At the same time the systems of Scottish and Welsh devolution are set to become more symmetrical while the position of England is at last being taken into account. We also await what is likely to be a more formalised system of intergovernmental relations which will perhaps relieve the 'representation deficit' for the devolved territories and in doing so strengthen shared rule within the system. But other challenges remain: devolution within England is not really on the horizon, nor is a territorial second chamber. But arguably, given the flexibility of federal models, neither are essential elements of the federal idea.

The biggest challenge will be Brexit. How the UK leaves the EU could well determine if there will be pressure for referendums on Scottish independence and Irish reunification. So the prospects for a federal state are of course contingent upon the state remaining whole. But, leaving this aside and assuming an outcome to EU withdrawal that does not lead to a break-up of the UK, federalisation is in a state of becoming, but the very flexibility in the term suggests that a federal Britain may well emerge without a full blown written Constitution, without a fully formalised symmetry of powers involving a model of regional government for England in any way comparable to Scottish devolution, and also with only a modest tampering with Parliament's supremacy or its institutional architecture. In fact, from certain angles it probably will continue to look not very federal at all.

[91] ibid.

5

Devolution and Secession in Comparative Perspective: The Case of Spain and Italy

BARBARA GUASTAFERRO AND LUCÍA PAYERO*

I. Introduction

A regional state is a unitary state in which some powers have been decentralised to sub-national territories. In this sense, it could be described as a half-way category between a unitary and a federal state. Regional states possess some features which are typical from unitary-centralised states, whereas some other characteristics are shared with federal states.

This chapter analyses two regional states in Europe: Spain and Italy. Both the Spanish and the Italian Constitutions guarantee the unity of the whole country; thus, secession of sub-national regions is forbidden. At the same time, some kind of territorial autonomy is constitutionally recognised. Accordingly, power is distributed between the central state and the regions, and the Constitutional Court plays the role of a referee that resolves disputes on competences. However, on many occasions the Constitutional Court takes the central state's side to the detriment of the territories.

Slight differences can also be observed when Spain and Italy are compared. First of all, although the principle of unity is sanctioned in both constitutional texts, the Spanish one refers to the unity of the 'Spanish Nation' (Article 2), while the Italian Constitution alludes to the unity of the 'Republic' (Article 5). The term 'Republic' can be understood as a synonym for state; this is not the case with the expression 'Spanish Nation': within the Spanish state, other territorial subunits claim to be nations, but the Constitution makes clear they are 'nationalities' and hence different from the Spanish nation (eg Catalonia and the Basque Country).

* Grateful acknowledgments are due to the European Research Council (FP/2007–2013–ERC Grant Agreement n 312304). The co-authors are listed in alphabetical order, since the chapter is the result of joint effort: in particular Barbara Guastaferro is the author of paragraphs V, VI, VII, and Lucía Payero is the author of paragraphs I, II, III, IV, VIII.

Second, the autonomic design differs. The 1978 Spanish Constitution establishes a symmetrical system of autonomy by which all the Autonomous Communities can assume the same number of competences (*café para todos*). On the contrary, the Italian Constitution, taking as a model the 1931 Spanish Constitution (the Republican Constitution), shaped a highly asymmetrical regional state in which five peripheral territories enjoy a special statute.

Third, the Senate performs different functions in each country. In Spain, the Constitution establishes that the Senate is a territorial chamber; nonetheless, it only acts as a House for the second reading of bills. Italy has hitherto embodied the archetype of perfect bicameralism (deputies and senators are directly elected, and both the House of Deputies and the Senate exercise the same powers); however, a reform of the Constitution has been initiated. The constitutional bill creates a Senate that will represent territories, as in many federations.

In line with this reform of the Italian Constitution, a fourth difference can be pointed out: Spanish politicians are very reluctant to amend the Constitution. In 40 years, only two articles of the Spanish Constitution have been modified, neither of them related to the territorial organisation of the state. In contrast, social movements, new political parties and a growing number of citizens want a deep constitutional reform, or even a new constituent process.

Finally, the different approach to constitutional revision may partially explain the divergent political momentum independence has in each country. In Spain the central government flatly refuses to negotiate a new territorial arrangement which could satisfy sub-state entities with a strong national identity. This refusal also includes the possibility of reforming the Constitution. That is the reason why independence support has been exponentially growing in Catalonia during the last few years leading to the attempted declaration of independence on 27 October 2017. In Italy, there is no fear to change the territorial Constitution, either in a centripetal or a centrifugal sense. First in 2001 and then in 2014, two major reforms have affected the vertical division of powers and the representation of territorial autonomies at the central level.

Be that as it may, similarities between Spain and Italy weigh more than disparities. Both states represent good examples of regionalism, so it is interesting to analyse them in order to understand the gap that separates regional and federal states. Moreover, as well as explaining why Spain and Italy are not federations—some scholars have called them de facto federal states—the possibilities of the federal idea to solve territorial problems in these two countries will be assessed.

The chapter wants to cast light upon the historical developments and the current challenges of the territorial Constitution in both Italy and Spain. To this end, the structure of the chapter has been arranged in a way that, for each of the two countries first, the territorial organisation as envisaged by the Constitution and as eventually amended is explained; second, the differences between these two states and federations are put forward; finally, a comparative analysis between the UK and these states is made. In the section on Spain, stress is put on whether federalism could serve as an antidote for secession. Additionally, in light of the experiences of the 2014 referendums held in Scotland and Catalonia, some lessons will be drawn for Spain. The section on Italy is centred on the process of devolution and the power that unitarian dogmas have both in Italy and the UK, thus explaining the limited appeal of the federal idea there.

II. Spain's Territorial Organisation

Spain is not a federal state.[1] This is true when talking from either a formal perspective or a material one. From a formal point of view, the Spanish Constitution does not mention federalism as the principle which informs the territorial organisation of the state. From a material perspective, the State of the Autonomies is a system of devolution in which key federal principles and institutions are absent. Indeed, the federal idea is alien to the constitutional tradition in Spain: the Spanish state only adopted a federal form during the First Republic (1873–74), and the experience was so ephemeral and turbulent that it cannot be said to have set a strong precedent. Moreover, in the Spanish social imaginary the First Republic is associated with notions of violence and political instability,[2] an additional reason for rejecting federalism.

However, some politicians have recently proposed a federal evolution of the State of the Autonomies as a good remedy against secessionism. Even intellectuals from divergent political tendencies are currently waving the federal flag.

[1] Scholars and politicians disagree on this issue. Among the academics who argue for the federal or quasi-federal character of Spain, R Blanco, '¿No es ya España un Estado federal?' (2012) 226 *Claves de Razón Práctica*; G Sala, 'Federalism without Adjectives in Spain' (2014) 44 *Publius: The Journal of Federalism*; and A Arroyo, 'Alemania y España: el aprendizaje federal' in J Cagiao and V Martin (dirs), *Federalismo, autonomía y secesión en el debate territorial español. El caso catalán* (Paris, Le Manuscript, 2015) can be cited. V Navarro, cited in S Baiges, '"Quien controla la bandera, controla el país" (interview to Vicenç Navarro)' *El Diario* (Madrid, 7 September 2014) www.eldiario.es/catalunya/Vicenc-Navarro-controla-bandera-pais_0_300620217.html; J Cagiao, 'El federalismo ante la consulta catalana. Una lectura federal del derecho a decidir' in J Cagiao and V Martin (dirs), *Federalismo, autonomía y secesión en el debate territorial español. El caso catalán* (Paris, Le Manuscript, 2015); and M Sanjaume, 'Federalismo, pluralismo nacional y autodeterminación: la acomodación de Cataluña y Quebec' in ibid, on the contrary, defend the position that Spain is not a federation.

However, it is interesting to notice than even some authors who hold that Spain is a federal state argue that a 'resymmetrization of the federal structure (by putting all the Autonomous Communities on an equal footing) and [a] recentralization of powers' have taken place in the last few years. 'Roughly, the state is responsible for core legislation (the codes of civil, labour, commercial, penal, administrative and process law); for economic and fiscal policy; for internal and external security (although some Autonomous Communities already have their own police forces, and the possibility of their creation is included in almost all the Statute reforms currently in progress); for communication structures involving more than one Autonomous Community; for social security; for the guiding principles of education and health policy; and for support and reinforcement of the basic rights of the citizens'; R Máiz et al, 'The Hidden Counterpoint of Spanish Federalism: Recentralization and Resymmetrization in Spain (1978–2008)' (2010) 20 *Regional and Federal Studies* 63, 79–80.

[2] JJ García-Escribano, 'Federalismo: el caso español' (2002) 27 *Daimon: Revista de Filosofía* 55, 58.

The federal idea is therefore gaining in strength in the context of the debate on Catalan independence.

This section will be divided in three parts. In the first one, the territorial structure of Spain, according to the Constitution and the Constitutional Court, will be explained. Once the State of the Autonomies has been described, the differences between the Spanish State of the Autonomies and federalism will be better understood. Finally, the current momentum of the federal idea in Spain will be connected with the independence movement in Catalonia.

A. The Constitution of 1978

According to the Constitution, territorial organisation in Spain adopts a monist or unitary character. Article 2 reads:

> The Constitution is based on the indissoluble unity of the Spanish Nation, the common and indivisible homeland of all Spaniards; it recognises and guarantees the right to self-government of the nationalities and regions of which it is composed and the solidarity among them all.

This provision should be connected with Article 1.2, which states: 'National sovereignty belongs to the Spanish people, from whom all State powers emanate.' The Constitution establishes that in Spain a single nation exists, and under no circumstance can the nation be divided. Moreover, the Constitution is founded on the indissoluble unity of the Spanish Nation (in capitals), and not the other way round. Thus, Spain is a nation-state where the borders of the nation match those of the state. The use of the same name, Spain, to refer to both the nation and the state helps to encapsulate such Jacobin homogenisation.

Alongside the Spanish nation, there are also nationalities and regions. The Constitution remains silent on what territorial entities are included in each of these two categories, but the use of the term *nationality* to refer to Catalonia seems unproblematic. However, nationalities do not enjoy the official status of nations and, therefore, they are not sovereign. Sovereignty is a feature that only characterises the Spanish nation. Nationalities are simply entitled to the right of autonomy,[3] but not to self-determination. This right is conferred on the Spanish nation exclusively. In this sense, the Constitution does not keep quiet (it would be a possible option); rather it explicitly prohibits nationalities' self-determination. It is interesting to notice that the 'indissoluble unity of the Spanish Nation' prevents the existence of other national communities within the same territory: while the unity of the state allows national plurality, the unity of the nation renders it impossible.[4]

[3] The right to 'self-government' that Art 2 confers on nationalities and regions means autonomy. The right to autonomy implies that Autonomous Communities can exercise legislative and executive powers within the framework of the Constitution. However, autonomy is not sovereignty; thus the unity of the Spanish Nation cannot be called into question.

[4] It is interesting to know that the first draft of the Constitution, which was leaked to the press in November 1977, did not contain the current interdiction on nationalities' self-determination. The original article read: 'The Constitution recognises and the Monarchy guarantees the right to

B. The Exegesis of the Constitutional Court

The Constitutional Court, the supreme interpreter of the Constitution, offers a particularly narrow exegesis on national matters. In the judgment that ruled out several articles of the Catalan Statute of Autonomy,[5] a decision which was highly controversial in Catalonia, the Court declared:[6]

> The people of Catalonia is not … a legal subject that competes with the holder of national sovereignty … The expression *people of Catalonia* … [is] totally different from … the expression *Spanish people*, the only bearer of the national sovereignty which gives origin to the Constitution and to all the norms whose validity derives from the Constitution.[7]
>
> [Even more], the only nation that here matters is the nation in the legal-constitutional sense. And in that particular sense, the Constitution knows of no other nation than Spain.[8]

This means that, despite the fact that in a sociological or cultural sense the term nation is commonly used to refer to Catalonia or the Basque Country,

> In light of the categorical meaning of Article 2 of the Constitution … the reference to the national reality of Catalonia has no legal interpretive scope … even though, out of the legal-constitutional context, there is room in a democratic order for the self-representation of a group as a national reality, understood in an ideological, historical and cultural sense. It expresses a perfectly legitimate idea.[9]

self-government of the different nationalities and regions of which Spain is composed, the unity of the state and the solidarity among its peoples.'

As can be seen, the preliminary version of Art 2 mentioned 'the unity of the *state*,' rather that the 'indissoluble unity of the *Spanish Nation*.' The recognition of the unity of the state is compatible with the existence of a plurality of nations within it, all of which are entitled to decide the type of relationship they want to build together. Secession would not be allowed, but self-determination is not limited to this outcome.

But how and why was Art 2 changed? One of the seven members of the panel that wrote the Constitution, J Solé-Tura, *Nacionalidades y nacionalismos en España. Autonomías, federalismo y autodeterminación* (Madrid, Alianza, 1985) 99–100, tells an extremely revealing anecdote about the factual genesis of Art 2. One day he was presiding over the session, a courier delivered a message containing the current wording of Art 2, and the stipulation that the future of the Constitution would depend on the inclusion of that new draft with no corrections. Solé-Tura speculates on a military authorship of the manuscript note.

[5] Organic Law 6/2006, 19 July 2006, on the Reform of the Statute of Autonomy of Catalonia. English version available at www.parlament.cat/document/cataleg/150259.pdf.

[6] Constitutional Court Judgment (CCJ) 31/2010, 28 June 2010. Available at boe.es/diario_boe/txt.php?id=BOE-A-2010-11409&lang=es.

[7] Legal Basis 9.

[8] Legal Basis 12.

According to V Ferreres, 'The Spanish Constitutional Court Confronts Catalonia's "Right to Decide" (Comment on the Judgment 42/2014)' (2014) 10 *European Constitutional Law Review* 571, 575, 'the Court was probably too strict when it insisted on the legal impossibility of defining Catalonia as a nation', and certainly it 'did not choose the most felicitous phrase when it asserted that "the Constitution only knows of the existence of the Spanish nation."'

[9] CCJ 31/2010, Legal Basis 12.

Of particular relevance is the judgment which declared partially unconstitutional the Declaration of sovereignty and of the right to decide of the people of Catalonia, which was issued by the Catalan Parliament on 23 January 2013.[10] The judgment contains two interesting statements.[11]

First, the Court invalidated the principle of sovereignty enshrined in the Declaration, because according to the Constitution 'national sovereignty belongs to the Spanish people.'[12] The Court drew two conclusions from the idea that the Spanish nation is sovereign: Catalonia cannot secede unilaterally, or hold a referendum on independence unilaterally.[13] Despite the fact of citing in its favour the Opinion rendered by the Supreme Court of Canada on the secession of Quebec,[14] the Spanish Constitutional Court went further, since the Canadian Court did not question the legality of the two referenda held in Quebec.[15]

Second, the Constitutional Court stated that a right to decide, different from a right to self-determination and not entailing sovereignty, is compatible with the Constitution. The exercise of such right would be two-fold:[16] in a first phase, the proposal of reforming the territorial order would be formulated, whereas in a second moment, the reform would be implemented. For doing it, constitutional amendment would be required. Therefore, in its judgment 42/2014, the Constitutional Court recognised that the capacity to call an independence referendum falls within the state's remit,[17] and also that before starting the process of constitutional amendment a referendum or other kind of non-binding consultation in

[10] Resolution 5/X of the Parliament of Catalonia, adopting the Declaration of sovereignty and of the right to decide of the people of Catalonia, 23 January 2013. English version available at www.parlament.cat/document/intrade/7176.

[11] CCJ 42/2014, 25 March 2014.

[12] Art 1.2.

[13] CCJ 42/2014, Legal Basis 3. The independence referendum held in Catalonia on 1 October 2017 was accordingly declared illegal by the Spanish Government which sought to prevent it taking place.

[14] Reference re Secession of Quebec, [1998] 2 SCR 217. Available at scc-csc.lexum.com/scc-csc/scc-csc/en/item/1643/index.do.

[15] Quebec is a province of Canada with strong national feelings. Although the Canadian Constitution does not acknowledge the right of self-determination, the federal government allowed two referenda to be held (it did not intervene, which in that situation was equivalent to permit): in 1980 and 1995. In both cases the results were against independence, but by a narrow margin. In 1998 the Federal Government submitted a request to the Supreme Court for an advisory opinion on the legality of the secession of Quebec. The Court stated that 'there is no right, under the Constitution or at international law, to unilateral secession, that is secession without negotiation' (Reference re Secession of Quebec, para 155). However, 'the continued existence and operation of the Canadian constitutional order cannot remain indifferent to the clear expression of a clear majority of Quebecers that they no longer wish to remain in Canada. .... The rights of other provinces and the federal government cannot deny the right of the government of Quebec to pursue secession, should a clear majority of the people of Quebec choose that goal, so long as in doing so, Quebec respects the rights of others. Negotiations would be necessary to address the federal government, of Quebec and the other provinces, and other participants, as well as the rights of all Canadians' (para 92).

[16] M Barceló, 'Reconocimiento y construcción del derecho a decidir en el sistema constitucional español' in M Barceló et al, *El derecho a decidir. Teoría y práctica de un nuevo derecho* (Barcelona, Atelier, 2015) 104.

[17] CCJ 42/2014, Legal Basis 3.

which only the citizens of a particular Autonomous Community would vote can be held.[18]

Nonetheless, its subsequent case law modified this idea,[19] coming back to the criterion stated in 2008:[20] the only referendum which can be held to change the territorial order is the referendum established in Article 168 for constitutional amendment, in which all the Spanish people is entitled to vote. Not even the Spanish government is authorised to call an independence referendum, according to the Court. In this sense, the Constitutional Court is deactivating the institution of consultative referendum established by the Constitution[21] and the power to call referenda.[22]

In short, it can be said that the Constitution favours Spanish nationalism over any other, leaving a narrow margin for the self-determination of nationalities. Besides, the Constitutional Court interprets the territorial Constitution in a very restricted sense: peripheral[23] nations are not entitled either to self-determination or to call a referendum to decide on their integration within Spain. The referendum needs to be authorised by the Congress of Deputies. However, when the Catalan Parliament asked for the delegation of that power, the majority of deputies refused to transfer the power to call a referendum.[24] Therefore, along with a monist Constitution construed by a radically (Spanish) nationalist Constitutional Court, Spain is also characterised by a parliamentary majority and a government even more centralist and dogmatic than the Court.

[18] See J Ridao, 'La juridificación del derecho a decidir en España. La STC 42/2014 y el derecho a aspirar a un proceso de cambio político del orden constitutional' (2014) 91 *UNED. Revista de Derecho Político* 91, 96; JM Castellà, 'Derecho a decidir, secesión y formas de democracia. Un diálogo constitucional entre Italia y España' in L Cappuccio and M Corretja (eds), *El derecho a decidir. Un diálogo ítalo-catalán* (Barcelona, IEA, 2014) 48; and M Corretja, 'El derecho a decidir en clave económica' in ibid 191.

[19] CCJ 31/2015, 25 February 2015 (Legal Basis 6b), and particularly, CCJ 138/2015, 11 June 2015 (Legal Basis 3a).

[20] CCJ 103/2008, 11 September 2008, which declared unconstitutional the Act 9/2008, 27 June, of the Basque Parliament convening and regulating a popular consultation for the purpose of ascertaining public opinion in the Autonomous Community of the Basque Country on commencing negotiations for achieving peace and political normalisation.

[21] Art 92 of the Constitution establishes: '1. Political decisions of special importance may be submitted to all citizens in a consultative referendum. 2. The referendum shall be called by the King on the President of the Government's proposal after previous authorisation by the Congress. 3. An organic act shall lay down the terms and procedures for the different kinds of referendum provided for in this Constitution.'

[22] Art 149.1,32 of the Constitution reads: 'The State shall have exclusive competence over … [the] authorisation of popular consultations through the holding of referendums.'

[23] The term 'peripheral' refers to the geographical location of these nations: the Basque Country and Catalonia lay, respectively, to the north and north east of Spain, whereas Madrid, the capital, is situated in the centre of Spain.

[24] The Catalan Parliament asked for this delegation on the basis of Art 150.2 of the Constitution: 'The State may transfer of delegate to the Self-governing Communities, through an organic act, some of its powers which by their very nature can be transferred or delegated.'

The Congress of Deputies refused to transfer the power to call a referendum to the Catalan Parliament by a vast majority on 8 April 2014. See Journal of Debates of the Congress of Deputies, no 192.

III. Differences between the Spanish Model of Devolution and a Federation

As asserted before, Spain is not a federal state. The Constitution does not mention federalism even once, and the main principles and institutions of federalism are absent.

Although there are many definitions of federalism, it could be argued that the federal idea is condensed in three basic principles: freedom to enter into the federal compact (*foedus*), a permanent tension between unity and plurality within the federation,[25] and the existence of two levels of government—the federation and the federated states.[26] Should this characterisation be applied to Spain, the conclusion to be drawn would be that none of these principles are present in this country at the moment.

First of all, the territorial organisation in Spain has never been freely decided by either the citizens or their political representatives. This has happened despite of the fact that it is a very contentious issue. The elaboration of the Constitution would have been a good opportunity to make a pact among territories, but in 1978 pragmatic considerations weighed more: democracy was at stake and the army posed a constant threat to its consolidation. However, after 40 years and with a democratic system firmly established, it is not possible to take a free decision on national matters yet. The flat refusal of the central state to call a referendum in Catalonia illustrates it.

Second, unity was de facto imposed over plurality, and the Constitution later sanctioned that *fait accompli*. Neither the parliamentarian approval of the Constitution nor the subsequent constitutional referendum could be interpreted as the outcome of a free decision on national matters. But even now, every decision of the Constitutional Court, the Congress of Deputies, and the government clearly favours centralism to the detriment of peripheral nationalism.

Third, although in Spain there are two different levels of government—the state and the Autonomous Communities[27]—the relationships between them favour the centre. For instance, the Constitutional Court, which is responsible for resolving disputes between the state and the Autonomous Communities, is not a neutral referee, but a highly politicised organ that gives priority to the interests of the

[25] As M Caminal, 'Nacionalismo, federalismo y democracia territorial' (1997) 73 *Claves de Razón Práctica* 10, 13, points out, the federal agreement was originally aimed at building state unity while respecting national plurality. In his opinion, federalism is asymmetric by its very nature, since federal arrangements look for uniting, rather than levelling, different political communities.

[26] This is basically the characterisation of federations given by O Beaud, *Théorie de la Fédération* (Paris, PUF, 2007).

[27] Sala's definition of federalism only includes this element. According to such minimalist concept of federation, she does not hesitate in considering Spain as a fully-fledged federal state. Sala, above n 1, 110–11.

central government.[28] Even more, in the election of the judges of the Constitutional Court territorial considerations play no role at all.[29] This is particularly relevant since 'the Court has been most instrumental in defining the state of autonomies as one with federal arrangements.'[30]

Another example is the Senate. According to the Constitution, 'the Senate is the House of territorial representation';[31] nonetheless, it does not function like a territorial chamber: senators do not form a parliamentary group according to their territorial origin, but by their political affiliation, and they defend the interests of their party rather than those of their Autonomous Community. Furthermore, the Senate has no specific functions related to the territories;[32] on the contrary, it decides on the same issues as the Congress of Deputies, acting as a chamber for the second reading of bills.

A third example is the narrow autonomy that the Autonomous Communities enjoy.[33] They only have executive and legislative limited powers, but are deprived

[28] See J Bengoetxea, 'Seven Thesis on Spanish Justice to Understand the Prosecution of Judge Garzón' (2011) 9 *Oñati Socio-Legal Series*; J Pérez-Royo, 'Avería grave' *El País* (Madrid 13 November 2012) politica.elpais.com/politica/2012/11/13/actualidad/1352832544_039639.html; A Buchanan, 'Prólogo a la edición española' in *Secesión: causas y consecuencias del divorcio político* (Barcelona, Ariel, 2013); and Cagiao, 'El federalismo ante la consulta catalana', above n 1.

[29] According to the Constitution, four of the 12 members of the Constitutional Court shall be nominated by the Congress of Deputies, another four by the Senate, two by the Government and the remaining two by the General Council of the Judicial Power (Art 159.1). The first three are political organs and the last one is as much politicised as the Constitutional Court itself. In Caminal's view, the Constitutional Court will only be neutral and independent if the state plurality is reflected in its composition. M Caminal, 'Diversidad, representación y proceso federal' (2004) 8 *Anuario de la Facultad de Derecho de la Universidad Autónoma de Madrid* 121, 134.

[30] R Agranoff and JA Ramos-Gallarín, 'Toward Federal Democracy in Spain: An Examination of Intergovernmental Relations' (1997) 27 *Publius* 1, 8.

Progressive judges of the Constitutional Court (María-Luisa Balaguer, Cándido Conde-Pumpido, Fernando Valdés and Juan-Antonio Xiol), who currently represent a minority, have been lately expressing in their dissenting opinions how the case law of the Constitutional Court is eroding Autonomic Law and emptying Autonomous Communities of many of their competences in favour of the central state. See, among others, Dissenting Opinion of Judge Juan-Antonio Xiol to the CCJ 74/2016, 14 April.

[31] Art 69.1.

[32] The only Senate exclusive power is contained in Art 155.1, which states what is normally called 'federal coercion:' 'If a Self-governing Community does not fulfil the obligations imposed upon it by the Constitution or other laws or acts in a way that is seriously prejudicial to the general interest of Spain, the Government, after having lodged a complaint with the president of the Self-governing Community and failed to receive satisfaction therefore may, following approval granted by the overall majority of the Senate, take all measures necessary to compel the Community to meet said obligations, or to protect the abovementioned general interest.' Before 2017 this power had never been invoked, although a number of politicians—all of them out of office—suggested the use of this provision to stifle Catalan initiatives for independence. Among others, Rosa Díez (Union Progress and Democracy), Juan-Alberto Belloch (Spanish Socialist Workers' Party) and Aleix Vidal-Quadras (VOX). However, after Puigdemont's speech before the Catalan Parliament and the symbolic signature of a declaration of independence (10 October 2017) whose effects would be suspended for a number of weeks, the Spanish government activated Art 155.

[33] As Agranoff and Ramos-Gallarín, above n 30, 7–8, have pointed out, 'Spain possesses a very strong prime minister and cabinet government and the executive role is central in intergovernmental relations. Executive powers include the right to provide national oversight and control in areas of devolved or concurrent competencies, introduction of organic laws that affect subnational government operations and financing, to establish general instructions regarding budget structure, accounts, taxing and borrowing of local government.'

of judicial powers and, with the exception of the Basque Country and Navarre, of fiscal autonomy. Furthermore, Autonomous Communities do not take part in the process of constitutional reform,[34] and their autonomy could be removed by a decision of the Parliament, which conflicts with the principle of constitutional autonomy vested in federated states.

A fourth example relates to the judiciary, a power which has not been decentralised in Spain, and consequently Autonomous Communities cannot exercise it. Moreover, the self-conception of the judiciary as a power is unitary and has been modelled on an equally unitary state.[35]

IV. Federalism in the Context of Secessionist Claims: Independence Plebiscites in Scotland and Catalonia

As previously stated, Spain is not a federation; however, it would be possible to transform Spain into a federal state by means of a reform of the Constitution. It is important to say that the rationale for federalism in Spain would be the need to accommodate 'strong cultural distinctiveness',[36] so any federal model should try to achieve this goal.

In the Catalan political context, in which support for independence has exponentially increased from 2010 onwards, a number of political parties proposed federal amendments to the Constitution: the Spanish Socialist Workers' Party (PSOE), Citizens Party (Cs), the Socialists' Party of Catalonia (PSC), and Initiative for Catalonia Greens (ICV). The situation poses the following question: can federalism be an attractive alternative to secession in Spain? To answer this question it is important to bear in mind not only the view that Spanish politicians hold, those who argue for a federal evolution of the State of the Autonomies and those who do not, but also the opinion that supporters of independence have.

[34] C Colino, 'Constitutional Change without Constitutional Reform: Spanish Federalism and the Revision of Catalonia's Statute of Autonomy' (2009) 39 *Publius: The Journal of Federalism* 262, 285, interprets the role played by Autonomous Communities in constitutional reform a bit differently. In his opinion, 'although Autonomous Communities are not given a direct role in constitutional reform, because they did not exist when the constitution was approved, constitutionally their power is not totally negligible. Regional parliaments have the right to propose a constitutional reform bill to the national parliament and will also participate through the Senate'. Two objections can be raised against Colino's view. Firstly, the non-existence of Autonomous Communities at the time of the elaboration of the Constitution does not justify why they were excluded from the process of constitutional reform, since the State of the Automomies is established by the Constitution and many constitutional provisions refer to Autonomous Communities and their powers. Secondly, the Senate does not act as a chamber of territorial representation. Therefore, it is not accurate to understand that regions participate in the process of constitutional amendment through the Senate.

[35] Bengoetxea, above n 28, 11.

[36] S Tierney, 'Federalism in a Unitary State: A Paradox too Far?' (2009) 19 *Regional and Federal Studies* 237.

A summary revision of the federal proposals for constitutional reform that some political parties have suggested reveals their different nature.

For PSOE and Cs the State of the Autonomies is an acceptable starting point, so they suggest cosmetic changes to improve and rationalise the overall functioning of the system: the transformation of the Senate in a real House of territorial representation, the clarification of the distribution of powers between the central state and the Autonomous Communities, the fiscal system, and greater cooperation among the different levels of government.

However, the proposals of PSC and ICV reflect the national plurality of Spain, putting all the nations within it on an equal footing. This is a major difference with regard to the federal models supported by PSOE and Cs. The cleavage between PSC and ICV relies on the recognition of a right to self-determination for peripheral nations. On the one hand, PSC accepts Article 2 of the Constitution and does not propose its modification. On the contrary, ICV conceives of federalism as one of the possible outcomes of the exercise of the right of self-determination. The bearers of this right are all the nations within the state: the Spanish nation, but also Catalonia, the Basque Country and Galicia. Citizens will have to decide among a range of options which must include federalism and secession.

Considering that Spain is a plurinational state, any federal proposal should adopt an equally plural character; otherwise, it would be useless in attempting to solve national problems. In this sense, the proposal of ICV recognises freedom for the parties to sign the federal compact. Therefore, the federal model of ICV is the most likely to be accepted by peripheral nations as an alternative to secession. The reason is that the right to decide,[37] a modern version of the right to self-determination, is the central claim made by Catalan nationalists. It was only when the Spanish government, the Congress of Deputies and the Constitutional Court denied Catalans the possibility to decide that independence support steeply increased. Consequently, the recognition of the right to decide may just strike a balance among all the parties involved, and represent a promising beginning for the solution of the perennial national question in Spain.

The right to decide requires the holding of a referendum in order to know citizens' will. In 2014 two popular consultations took place in Scotland and in Catalonia. However, the gap between these two political events is so wide that while the first one could have led to independence for Scotland, the second was not even a referendum, but a 'citizen participation process.'[38] Let us analyse the main differences between the Scottish and the Catalan cases.

In the 2011 election to the Scottish Parliament, the Scottish National Party (SNP) won an absolute majority. Then Alex Salmond stated that it was his decision

[37] On the right to decide, see JM Vilajosana, 'Principi democràtic i justificació constitucional del dret de decidir' (2014) 19 *Revista d'Estudis Autonòmics i Federals*; M Barceló *et al*, *El derecho a decidir. Teoría y práctica de un nuevo derecho* (Barcelona, Atelier, 2015).

[38] For a detailed study of this consultation, see L Payero, 'The "citizen participation process" in Catalonia: past, present and future' (2015) 36 *Liverpool Law Review*.

to hold a referendum. On October 2012 an agreement was reached between both the Scottish and the British government,[39] by which a single-question referendum on Scottish independence was negotiated to be held before the end of 2014. It is interesting to note that the constitutional framework did not allow that referendum, so a legal amendment was necessary. Schedule 5 to the Scotland Act 1998 establishes the reserved matters of the Constitution, 'the Union of the Kingdoms of Scotland and England' being one of them.[40] Nevertheless, by virtue of a modification of Schedule 5 under section 30 (2) of the Scotland Act 1998, the referendum was authorised.[41] Therefore, despite of the fact that Scotland was not entitled to hold an independence referendum, the government of the UK agreed to transfer the power to do it to the Scottish Parliament.

In Catalonia the origin of the current nationalist tension dates back to 2010, when the 2006 Statute of Autonomy[42] was declared partially unconstitutional by the Constitutional Court.[43] In November 2010 Convergence and Union (CiU) won the regional election in Catalonia and one year later the People's Party (PP) did the same in Spain, but by an absolute majority. After the mass demonstration held on the 2012 National Day of Catalonia (*Diada*), CiU called an early election. During the electoral campaign, Artur Mas promised that should CiU win, an independence referendum would be held. The results forced CiU to sign a governability accord with the Republican Left of Catalonia (ERC), which included the commitment of both parties to call a referendum in 2014. The constitutional framework

[39] Agreement between the United Kingdom Government and the Scottish Government on a referendum on independence for Scotland (signed in Edinburgh, 15 October 2012). Available at: www.gov.scot/resource/0040/00404789.pdf.

[40] Scotland Act 1998 (1998 c. 46). Available at: www.legislation.gov.uk/ukpga/1998/46.

[41] The Scotland Act 1998 (Modification of Schedule 5) Order 2013 reads: '(1) Paragraph 1 does not reserve a referendum on the independence of Scotland from the rest of the United Kingdom if the following requirements are met. (2) The date of the poll at the referendum must not be the date of the poll at any other referendum held under provision made by the Parliament. (3) The date of the poll at the referendum must not be later than 31st December 2014. (4) There must be only one ballot paper at the referendum and the ballot must give the voter a choice between only two responses.' Available at: www.legislation.gov.uk/uksi/2013/242/article/3/made.

[42] Organic Act 6/2006, 19 July. English version available at: web.gencat.cat/en/generalitat/estatut/estatut2006/.

The thorniest issues were the recognition of Catalonia as a nation, although it appeared only in the Preamble, and the financial system. For a detailed analysis, see F Requejo, 'Revealing the Dark Side of Traditional Democracies in Plurinational Societies: The Case of Catalonia and the Spanish "Estado de las autonomías"' (2010) 16 *Nations and Nationalism*.

[43] CCJ 31/2010. The ruling was particularly contentious in Catalonia, where it was interpreted as an attack against regional autonomy: the Statute bill had been passed by an absolute majority in the Catalan Parliament (30 September 2005), then a modified version of it had been approved by the Spanish Parliament (30 March 2006 in the Congress of Deputies and 10 May 2006 in the Senate), and finally Catalans ratified the text in a referendum (18 June 2006). Four years after coming into force, the Constitutional Court ruled out several articles of the Statute and stated the correct exegesis of many others. As J Pérez-Royo, 'La STC 31/2010 y la contribución de la jurisprudencia constitucional a la configuración de un Estado compuesto en España: elementos de continuidad y ruptura, e incidencia en las perspectivas de evolución del Estado autonómico' (2011) 43 *Revista catalana de dret public* 121, 142–43, observes, the territorial compact contained in the 1978 Constitution was broken by the 2010 judgment.

in Spain did not entitle an Autonomous Community to call a referendum, just like the UK. That is why the Catalan Parliament requested from the Congress of Deputies that such power be transferred to it (16 January 2014). As the proposal was rejected, the Catalan Parliament started to adopt a set of legislative initiatives aimed to hold the referendum. The most relevant were the Act on non-referendum popular consultations and the Decree for the call of a popular consultation on the political future of Catalonia.[44] Both norms were brought by the central government before the Constitutional Court and the challenge suspended the operation of both legal texts. However, since Article 40.2 of the Act had not been appealed, Artur Mas decided to call a 'citizen participation process' on the basis of this provision.[45] Both the date and the two questions of the initially planned referendum were maintained,[46] but the 'citizen participation process' lacked the legal guarantees of a referendum. Therefore, it bore more resemblance to an opinion poll than to a referendum.

Since the state opposed the celebration of a negotiated referendum, nationalist parties in Catalonia construed the 2015 regional election as an independence plebiscite. The alliance Together for Yes (*Junts pel Sí*, JxSí)[47] and the Popular Unity Candidacy-Constituent Call (*Candidatura d'Unitat Popular-Crida Constituent*, CUP-CC) gained the majority of seats (72 out of 135), but not of votes (47.8 per cent). A parliamentary majority granted pro-sovereign parties a fair amount of leeway to pave the way for 'disconnection.' In October 2016, the Catalan Parliament approved a motion to hold an independence referendum the following year, either reaching an agreement with the central authorities or—in the absence of pact—unilaterally. No compact was signed, and consequently two relevant bills were passed in September 2017: the Act on the referendum of self-determination[48] and the Act on the juridical transition and foundation of the Republic.[49] As expected, the central government appealed both regulations before the

[44] Act of the Parliament of Catalonia 10/2014, 26 September, on non-referendum popular consultations and other forms of citizen participation. Available at: www.boe.es/diario_boe/txt.php?id=BOE-A-2015-2743. Decree 129/2014, 27 September, for the call of a popular consultation on the political future of Catalonia. Available at: noticias.juridicas.com/base_datos/CCAA/536892-d-129-2014-de-27-sep-ca-cataluna-de-convocatoria-de-la-consulta-popular-no.html.

[45] Art 40.2 of the Catalan Act 10/2014 reads: 'Citizen participation processes aim to guarantee debate and deliberation between the citizenry and public institutions, so that citizens' opinion on a specific political action is collected regarding the stages of proposal, decision, implementation or evaluation.'

[46] The consultation took place on 9 November 2014 (9-N). Two questions were posed: 'Do you want Catalonia to become a state? If so, do you want that state to be independent?'

[47] JxSí was an electoral coalition created in 2015. It was composed of Democratic Convergence of Catalonia (CDC)—in 2016 this party was substituted for the Catalan Democratic Party (PdeCAT)—ERC, Democrats of Catalonia (DC), and the Left Movement (MES). After winning the 2015 regional election, JxSí became a parliamentary group in the Catalan legislature.

[48] Act of the Parliament of Catalonia 19/2017, 6 September, on the referendum of self-determination. Available at: http://portaldogc.gencat.cat/utilsEADOP/PDF/7449A/1633375.pdf.

[49] Act of the Parliament of Catalonia 20/2017, 8 September, on the juridical transition and foundation of the Republic. Available at: http://portaldogc.gencat.cat/utilsEADOP/PDF/7451A/1633636.pdf.

Constitutional Court, thus suspending their operation.[50] On 1 October 2017 (1-O) more than two million Catalans voted for secession, according to the organisers.[51] Article 4.4 of the Act on the referendum stated that should a majority support independence, the Parliament would declare it in a formal session two days after the official results were known. On 10 October, President Puigdemont addressed the Catalan legislature to ask for a suspension of the effects of such declaration with the aim of initiating a period of dialogue with the Spanish government. Just after his speech, MPs of JxSí and CUP-CC signed a symbolic declaration of independence outside the plenary room, which triggered the legal response of the government: the resort to federal coercion. It remains to be seen what specific measures are adopted under Article 155, but there is no doubt that the main difference between 9-N and 1-O lies in the strategy used by the central executive to confront Catalan nationalism: whereas in 2014 the consultation was neutralised by legal and judicial means, in 2017 police violence[52] and violations of civil rights[53] have also been employed against secessionism.

As can be observed, under quite similar legal constraints, the UK and Spain reacted very differently. Whereas the British government came to a compromise with the Scottish political representatives and agreed to give extra powers under the Scotland Act 1998, the Spanish government flatly refused to negotiate a new territorial arrangement for Catalonia. Precisely one of the main arguments used to justify this course of action was based upon law: the Constitution forbids Catalan self-determination.[54] Constitutional reform is so complex that it becomes

[50] The Constitutional Court declared the Act 19/2017 unconstitutional on 17 October 2017 (CCJ 114/2017). Judgment available at: http://hj.tribunalconstitucional.es/docs/BOE/BOE-A-2017-12206.pdf. On 8 November 2017 the Act 20/2017 was equally repealed by CCJ 124/2017 (available at: http://hj.tribunalconstitucional.es/docs/BOE/BOE-A-2017-13228.pdf).

[51] Official data available at: http://premsa.gencat.cat/pres_fsvp/docs/2017/10/06/14/43/64cb2841-373e-46da-af51-e5c4a847cc97.pdf.

[52] Three out of four Spanish anti-riot police officers were deployed in Catalonia with the aim of preventing citizens from voting on 1-O. Law enforcement officials acted on the ruling of the High Court of Justice of Catalonia (*Tribunal Superior de Justicia de Catalunya*), which bid to thwart the holding of a referendum. Nonetheless, any voting event that had taken place on 1-O could not have been a referendum. According to the Spanish law, the state's authorisation is required, since the calling of a referendum is among the reserved matters. From a material point of view, the consultation did not fulfill criteria that referenda must meet (see, for instance, the 'Code of good practice on referendums' adopted by the Venice Commission: http://www.venice.coe.int/webforms/documents/default.aspx?pdffile=cdl-ad(2007)008-e).

[53] The weeks previous to 1-O a number of events (namely, talks and speeches scheduled in public premises) were banned on the basis of their connection with a referendum which had been suspended by the Constitutional Court. In addition, law enforcement officials used their power of search and seizure against individuals, citizen movements, political parties and private companies (regardless of the fact that the Constitutional Court ruling which suspended the Act on the referendum only bound public authorities, particularly those who are mentioned in it—see Providencia of the Constitutional Court, 7 September 2017: https://www.boe.es/boe/dias/2017/09/08/pdfs/BOE-A-2017-10287.pdf) in order to confiscate graphic material aimed to be employed for the referendum.

[54] Political conflicts cannot be addressed by using legal tools. The resort to Criminal law to combat secessionism in Catalonia is generating serious problems, such as the politicisation of justice, the breach of the principles of minimal intervention and *ultima ratio* that characterise Criminal law, the end of the separation of powers as a model of governance, let alone the excesses numerous zealous public servants are committing (law enforcement officers, public prosecutors, judges) when applying law.

materially non-viable.[55] Nonetheless, the transfer of the power to call a non-binding referendum complies with the Constitution, but even so, the Congress of Deputies opposed it. A non-binding referendum would represent an excellent opportunity to know how many Catalans support independence; if a majority favours secession, either constitutional reform—regardless its difficulty—or additional possibilities should be explored in order to accommodate territorial claims in a democratic sense. As Nicolaïdis pointed out, 'where there is a (political) will, there is a (legal) way.'[56] Moreover, if there is a real intention of finding a solution, it will always be in accordance with law.[57]

The Spanish authorities are facing the challenge posed by Catalan demands of self-determination in a non-democratic way. In the twenty-first century, liberal democratic states' approach to national problems should give priority to democracy and respect for minorities over any other considerations, such as state territorial integrity or a long history living together. The experience of plurinational states that confronted independence claims by means of a referendum should serve as guidance to be followed in Spain. Otherwise, Catalonia will predictably end up unilaterally seceding, sooner rather than later.

V. Italy's Territorial Organisation

Federalism has been a heavily debated issue in Italy, but it has never been contemplated in designing the institutional settlement of the legal order. When the Italian Kingdom was created in 1861 thanks to a process of fusion of different kingdoms to the Kingdom of Sardinia and Piemonte, 'Italy was hardly more than a geographical expression'. This expression was used by Metternich to emphasise the extreme fragmentation of small states and territories subject to foreign domination. At that time, the myth of the 'Nation' was used as a glue keeping the different territories together and *federalism* as a concept was rejected.

> After centuries of foreign conquest and division into small entities, the *Risorgimento* was the time when Italian began dreaming of a strong, unitary and undivided state, in the tradition of other European sovereign systems. Anything that would imply an internal division into smaller units (like a federation or a confederation) was seen by many as a return to a past where foreign domination and local fights were the rule.[58]

Moreover, in the late nineteenth century, when the Italian Kingdom was created, the federalist option adopted in the US proved to be a failure: in that very same

[55] P de Vega, *La reforma constitucional y la problemática del poder constituyente* (Madrid, Tecnos, 1985).

[56] K Nicolaïdis, 'Scotland and the EU: Comment' *Verfassungsblog* (9 September 2014) verfassungsblog.de/scotland-eu-comment-kalypso-nicolaidis-2/.

[57] Cagiao, 'El federalismo ante la consulta catalana', above n 1, 123.

[58] E Arban, *Italian Regionalism and the Federal Challenge,* PhD thesis submitted at the Faculty of Law (University of Ottawa, Canada, 2015) 198.

period, the secession war clearly dividing the country and federalism as an institutional arrangement was deemed to bear a strong disaggregating function, inconsistent with the unitary conception of the Nation-State.

It is interesting to note that if—when the Italian Kingdom was created in 1861—the federalist option was excluded fearing its 'decentralizing' and disaggregating forces,[59] when the Italian Republic was born—in 1948—the federalist option was excluded fearing its 'centralizing' force, namely for the opposite reason. Indeed, the Constituent Assembly drafting the Italian Constitution soon after the second world war, looked at the experience of the so called 'coming together' federalism, such as the one developed in the US. The integrationist pull triggered by this model, entailing for example the principle of supremacy of federal laws upon State laws, could not be embraced by a country which experienced the overarching centralisation of the Fascist regime. The regional rather than the federal solution was considered more suitable to secure the unity of the Republic without compromising the promotion of territorial autonomies and their differentiation.[60]

Consistently with the Founding Fathers' aim to remedy the excessive centralisation existing in the totalitarian era, the Italian Republican regional model was drafted bearing in mind both Spanish regionalism and German federalism.[61] According to some scholars, the Spanish Republican Constitution of 1931 was a source of inspiration for the Italian Constituents and the expression 'regional state' was invented by Gaspare Ambrosini looking at a model—such as the Spanish one—where the autonomous regions hold legislative powers.[62] The following paragraphs, after illustrating the main features of the Italian Regional State, will analyse the pace and modalities of the devolution of powers from the central State to the Regions.

Italy can be qualified as a unitary State organised in territorial autonomies. Despite the presence of at least two levels of government (namely the central State and the Regions) sharing legislative and administrative powers,[63] and despite the strong decentralising process which occurred from the 1970s onwards, Italy is not qualified as a 'federal" State, but as a 'Regional' State. Actually, the Constituent Assembly drafting the 1948 Republican Constitution, opted for the 'unitary' rather than for the 'federal' solution. At the same time, the Assembly felt the need to include the 'autonomistic principle' among the fundamental principles of the

[59] It is worth recalling that the Italian Parliament in 1865 approved a law on the municipal and provincial unification of the Kingdom of Italy. This model was clearly inspired from the French scheme of administrative unification.

[60] J Loughlin, 'Federalism, regionalism and local government: comparative perspectives on transforming the Nation-State' (2008) 7 *European Political Science* 472–82.

[61] A D'Atena, 'Between Spain and Germany: the Historical Models of Italian Regionalism' in S Mangiameli (ed), *Italian Regionalism: Between Unitary Traditions and Federal Processes* (Cham, Springer, 2014).

[62] R Bin and G Falcon (a cura di), *Diritto regionale* (Bologna, Il Mulino, 2012) 25–48. The Authors note that the Austro-Hungarian model and the Soviet Union model were also studied.

[63] The Constitution also envisages the Provinces, the Metropolitan Cities and Municipalities as per Art 114 of the Constitution.

Italian Constitution, drafting an article that enshrines at the same time the *unity* of the Italian Republic and the *plurality* of its territorial autonomies.

Indeed, according to Article 5 of the Italian Constitution:

> The Republic, *one and indivisible*, *recognises* and *promotes local autonomies*, and implements the fullest measure of administrative decentralisation in those services which depend on the State. The Republic accords the principles and methods of its legislation to the requirements of autonomy and decentralisation.[64]

The strong recognition of territorial pluralism notwithstanding, Article 5 has often been used by the Italian Constitutional Court as a glue keeping the system together, fostering the Unitarian spirit of the Republic, consistently with the choice made by the Constituent Assembly.

As the working documents of the Constituent Assembly prove, soon after the second world war there was a lively debate on the opportunity to add a new territorial institution to the two territorial forms of government existing since the unity of the Italian Kingdom in 1861 (namely the provinces and the Municipalities).[65] The idea of introducing the Regions—which did not pre-exist the Constitution of the Italian Republic as the States composing Federation—stemmed not only from the pre-republican federal/regional debate, but from the concrete experience of some territories in the post-fascist areas. These territories, indeed, in some cases experienced a sort of local self-government. In other cases (such as Sicily) they started to develop secessionist-independentist feelings or to call for autonomy due to the willingness to protect linguistic minorities (such as Trentino Alto Adige). This is why five out of all the 20 Regions composing Italy were endowed with stronger autonomy.

Up to now, indeed, Sardinia, Sicily, Trentino Alto Adige, Friuli Venezia Giulia and Valle D'Aosta (which, geographically, are also at the periphery of Italy), are 'Regions with a *special* statute' and their legal and political powers are different from all the other 'Regions with *ordinary* statute'. A strong asymmetrical regionalism characterised Italy, if we consider that not only the powers and competences of the Regions differed significantly but also the time and pace of their path towards territorial autonomy. With the exception of Friuli Venezia Giulia (1963) the Regions with special statutes were immediately activated with the entry into force of the Constitution, while the implementation of the ordinary regions took several years, notwithstanding the fact that a final provision of the Constitution

[64] Emphasis added. On the importance of the autonomistic principle see C Esposito, 'Autonomie locali e decentramento amministrativo nell'art. 5 della Costituzione' in C Esposito, *La Costituzione. Saggi* (Padova, Cedam, 1954); G Berti, 'Art. 5' in G Branca (a cura di), *Commentario alla Costituzione* (Bologna-Roma, 1975). More recently, see R Bifulco, 'Art. 5' in R Bifulco, A Celotto, M Olivetti (a cura di), *Commentario alla Costituzione* (Torino, Utet, 2006) and S Staiano, *Costituzione italiana. Articolo 5* (Firenze, 2017).

[65] On the debate during the Constituent Assembly see A D'Atena, *Costituzione e Regioni. Studi* (Milano, Giuffrè, 1991); N Antonetti and U De Siervo (a cura di), *Ambrosini e Sturzo. La nascita delle regioni* (Bologna, Il Mulino, 1998).

called for the election of the regional legislative assemblies within one year from the entry into force of the Constitution.[66] As a matter of fact, it was only in the 1970s, namely more than 20 years after the entry into force of the Constitution, that the 'ordinary' Regions were created.

A. The 1948 Constitution and the Vertical Division of Competences

Despite the fact that Article 5 of the Constitution protected both the unity of the Republic and the plurality of territorial autonomies, the allocation of powers provided by the Italian Constitution paved the way for a strong asymmetry between the State and the Regions, which lead some commentators to talk about a hierarchical relationship between the State, on the one hand, and territorial autonomies, on the other.

The article of the Constitution dedicated to the vertical division of power, namely Article 117, enumerated the list of subject areas in which the Regions could share the legislative competence with the State. This choice impliedly limited Regional legislatures for two basic reasons. First, the listing of regional competences made clear that the State was the exclusive legislator in all the others areas not mentioned by the Article. Second, even within the listed areas, the Regions were not at all sovereign legislators. The model of 'shared competences' envisaged by the Constitution entailed the following 'division of labour': the central State was the one entitled to set out the general principles governing the subject area, while leaving to the Regions the possibility to define the details.[67]

Moreover, two other constitutional provisions constrained the activity of the Regions. On the one hand, the same article 117 stated that Regional laws could be made only as long as they 'did not conflict with the national interest or with the interest of other regions'. This limit of 'national interest' brought some scholars to consider the constitutional text as a 'white page',[68] assuming that the State could basically re-define the constitutional allocation of competences by legislating any time that a national interest seemed to be at stake.[69] By its token, the Constitutional Court case law on competence conflicts did not challenge this sort of encroachment upon Regions' legislative power. Indeed, in one of its first rulings,

[66] F Bassanini, *L'attuazione delle regioni* (Firenze, Nuova Italia, 1970); E Rotelli (a cura di), *Dal regionalismo alla regione* (Bologna, Il Mulino, 1973); AA.VV, *Le regioni tra Costituzione e realtà politica* (Torino, ed della Fondazione Agnelli, 1977).

[67] This was one of the categories of competences envisaged also by the German Constitution, allowing the Länder to legislate within a framework law provided by the Federation. This category was abolished in 2006.

[68] L Paladin, 'Problemi legislativi e interpretativi nella definizione delle materie di competenza regionale' (1971) III *Il Foro amministrativo* 3.

[69] This was nevertheless not endorsed by the text of the Constitution, which said that any other 'subject-areas' could be added by constitutional law.

the Court anchored 'national interest' limitations upon the Regions on the necessity to ensure the 'unity' of State activity in light of Article 5 of the Constitution which states that, although promoting territorial autonomies, the Republic is 'one and indivisible'.[70]

Last but not least, the activity of the Regions was strongly circumscribed by the possibility of pre-enactment scrutiny of regional laws, envisaged by Article 127 of the Italian Constitution. Accordingly, any bill passed by the regional council needed to be communicated to a governmental Commissioner—who would examine it within 30 days of notification—and required his consent to enter into force. This shows that, although Italy shares with fully-fledged federal States the guarantee that the division of power between central State and territorial autonomies is enshrined within the Constitution—and that there could not be a unilateral act of the national Parliament giving or revoking the competences of a devolved legislature as can happen in other unitary States such as the UK—the 1948 Constitution itself created an imbalance between the State and the Regions. As we have seen, many provisions allowed the State to intrude into the legislative autonomy of regional councils.

B. The Decentralising Drift of the 2001 Constitutional Reform: Devolving More Powers to the Regions

The vertical division of powers envisaged by the Constitution has been significantly reshaped through the years. Starting from the 1990s, the legal order experienced a process of administrative decentralisation from the State to lower levels of government (Regions, Provinces and municipalities)[71] in the name of the principle of subsidiarity, aimed at bringing public administration closer to the citizens. The process of decentralisation culminated with the constitutional reform of 2001, which significantly bolstered also the legislative role of the Regions. This reform partially responded to some of the 'federalist' claims of new political parties (such as Lega Nord) calling for more territorial autonomy and more fiscal powers to the Regions.[72]

At a general level, the intent of the reform was that of accommodating the claims of territorial autonomies while keeping the unity of the Republic through a form of 'cooperative regionalism' able to produce genuine cooperation between levels of government and to overcome the hierarchical relationship which often imposed the supremacy of one interest (namely the national one) upon others (namely regional ones). Against this backdrop, many important principles helping to guide

[70] Italian Constitutional Court, Judgment No 39 of 1971.

[71] The so called 'Bassanini reforms' (see in particular Law No 59 and 127 of 15 March 1997).

[72] During 1995 the party 'Lega Nord' becomes determinant in the construction of the political majority. This is why, in order to preserve the stability of the government, other political parties tried to accommodate the federalist vocation and requests of Lega Nord.

the balancing of interests between levels of government—such as *subsidiarity* and *loyal cooperation*—were brought to the fore and acquired constitutional relevance by being included in the constitutional text.[73]

Besides this general attempt, at least two specific innovations potentially increasing regional autonomy deserve to be mentioned. First of all, the constitutional way of allocating power significantly changed to resemble the one typical of federal states. Differently from the 1948 Constitution, which listed the subject areas in which the Regions had shared competences while leaving the general law-making power to the central State, the new version of the Constitution listed the 'exclusive' competences of the State, listed the 'shared' competences between State and the Regions, and left the residual law-making power to the Regions.[74] Both the listing of the exclusive powers of the state and the consequential allocation of residual powers to territorial autonomies, are typical of the federal states.

Second of all, most importantly, almost all the State constraints upon regional legislatures were abolished. The political pre-enactment scrutiny by the Governmental Commissioner (Officer) was dismissed since it intruded too far upon the discretion of regional legislatures, which necessitated the Government to turn regional bills into regional laws. Only after their entry into force could the Government challenge regional laws allegedly exceeding their competence before the Constitutional Court. Also the textual limit related to 'national interest'—according to which Regions could legislate in the field of shared competences only insofar as they did not affect it—was erased from the Constitutional text.

Despite the allocation of competences being drafted to favour the regions, and despite the abolishment of almost all State constraints on regional legislatures, the reality turned out to be disappointing for the autonomy of the regions. Some of the problems arose from the lack of concrete implementation of the reform. The national legislator, indeed, did not implement many of the reforms contained in the draft constitutional bill, which required its intervention. First of all, there was not concrete application of Article 119,[75] which would have required financial autonomy of the Regions (which were so entitled with many new competences without the financial resources to carry out policy outputs). Most importantly, the requirement to integrate the national Parliamentary Committee for Regional Affairs with representatives of territorial autonomies, was not activated.[76] In the

[73] As per Art 118 of the Italian Constitution, 'Administrative functions are attributed to the Municipalities, unless they are attributed to the provinces, metropolitan cities and regions or to the State, pursuant to the principles of subsidiarity, differentiation and proportionality, to ensure their uniform implementation'.

[74] A Barbera, 'La polverizzazione delle materie regionali e la (ormai necessaria) clausola di supremazia' (2011) 2/3 *Le Regioni* 558, said to be one of the supporters of the reform.

[75] As per the first provisions of Art 119, 'Municipalities, provinces, metropolitan cities and regions shall have revenue and expenditure autonomy. Municipalities, provinces, metropolitan cities and regions shall have independent financial resources. They set and levy taxes and collect revenues of their own, in compliance with the Constitution and according to the principles of coordination of State finances and the tax system'.

[76] It was envisaged by Art 11 of the Constitutional law n 3/2001.

absence of a Second Chamber with territorial representation, this Article was supposed to be crucial to allow territorial autonomies to participate in the legislative process at the central level. It is remarkable that the strong impetus of the 2001 reform toward a genuine system of 'cooperative regionalism' was not followed by the concrete creation of appropriate instruments and settings for promoting cooperation.

The result was that—without clear boundaries between competences and without any political forum, such as a 'federal' Second Chamber, to settle the issue—the Italian Constitutional Court was soon after the reform overloaded by constitutional conflicts between the State and the Regions. It will suffice here to recall that the number of competence conflicts before the Constitutional Court rose from 5.9 per cent of all cases in 2000 to 45.7 per cent in 2013.[77]

C. The Centralising Twist of the 2014 Constitutional Reform

The 2014 constitutional reform was launched by the Government also with the intent to decrease the huge competence conflicts between central State and the Regions before the Constitutional Court. Indeed, a constitutional bill aimed at amending the Italian Constitution was presented by the Government on 8 April 2014,[78] but it failed because of the popular vote against it, through the referendum of 4 December 2016.[79] If it had entered into force, the constitutional reform could have affected two pivotal features of the Italian legal order, namely the 'perfect bicameralism'—by creating a Second Chamber representative of territorial autonomies—and the vertical division of power between the central State and territorial autonomies characterising Italian regionalism.[80]

As to the abolition of the perfect bicameralism, which sees the two Chambers of the Parliament being both directly elected and performing the same functions, the Constitutional Bill deeply changed both the functions and the composition of the Senate of the Republic. While not calling it 'Senate of Autonomies' as the Government initially proposed, the Senate, consistently with one of the functions

[77] The data are available on the website of the Italian Constitutional Court www.cortecostituzionale.it.

[78] Disegno di legge costituzionale N. 1429, 'Disposizioni per il superamento del bicameralismo paritario, la riduzione del numero dei parlamentari, il contenimento dei costi di funzionamento delle istituzioni, la soppressione del CNEL e la revisione del titolo V della parte seconda della Costituzione' (herein after 'constitutional bill').

[79] With a turnout of 65.5 per cent, the Yes to the constitutional reform scored 40.9 per cent, and the No scored 59.1 per cent.

[80] Early comments on the draft constitutional bill presented by the Government in R Bifulco, 'A New Senate? A First Look to the Draft Constitutional Bill' (2014) 1 *Italian Journal of Public Law*; V Cerulli Irelli, 'On the Constitutional Reform in the Process of Being Approved in Italy' (2014) 1 *Italian Journal of Public Law*; G della Cananea, 'The End of (Symmetric) Bicameralism or a Novus Ordo?' (2014) 1 *Italian Journal of Public Law*; GE Vigevani, 'The Reform of Italian Bicameralism: the First Step' (2014) 1 *Italian Journal of Public Law*; L Violini, 'The Reform of Italian Bicameralism: Current Issues' (2014) 1 *Italian Journal of Public Law*.

performed by Second Chambers in other constitutional systems,[81] should have represented territorial autonomies. Each Region was not represented in the Senate in an equal number. The numbers of Senators attributed to each Region were proportional to the varying size of the population of the Regions, although each Region had no less than two Senators. Against this backdrop, the constitutional bill amended the notion of political representation provided by the 1948 Republican Constitution, and specified that while the House of Deputies kept on representing 'the Nation', the Senate of the Republic represented 'territorial institutions'.[82] For this reason, the members of the new Senate were no longer directly elected by citizens. They were elected by regional councillors—namely by the members composing regional Councils (ie the legislative assemblies of the Regions). The members of the Senate were chosen among the regional councillors themselves and among the mayors of the local municipalities belonging to each Region. It is worth emphasising that this major change to the constitutional settlement was also functional to the decreasing of competence conflicts. A Senate representative of territorial autonomies allowed a previous intervention of Regions within the law-making process, and the possibility to solve possible conflicts at the ex ante political level, thus preventing many of the competence conflicts to reach the Constitutional Court. The 2014 reform, in other words, wanted to realise the institutionalisation of appropriate instruments guaranteeing loyal cooperation between levels of government that the 2001 reform failed to implement.

As to the vertical division of power, the new division of competences between the State and the Regions challenged the 'federal' allocation of powers introduced by the 2001 constitutional reform. At that time, enumerating the subject areas in which the State holds exclusive and shared competences, leaving to the Regions the exclusive power to legislate on the remaining subject areas, had the express intent to bolster the powers of territorial autonomies, leaving them with significant residual legislative powers.

The revision of the V title of Part II of the Constitution envisaged by the 2014 constitutional bill significantly reshuffled these provisions. First of all, the 2014 constitutional reform abolished the possibility for the State and the Regions to share legislative powers in the same subject areas: this overlapping, indeed, overloaded the role of the Constitutional Court as the 'arbiter' of increasing competence conflicts. The new competence catalogue was 'dual', creating a dividing line between the exclusive competences of the State, on the one hand, and the exclusive competence of the Regions, on the other.

While the attempt to streamline the allocation of powers should be welcomed, at least two problematic aspects arose from the new vertical division of competences. First, the reform seemed to be characterised by a 'centripetal' taste running counter

[81] S Mannoni, 'The "Second Chamber": a Historical and Comparative Sketch' (2014) 1 *Italian Journal of Public Law*.

[82] Art 1 of the Constitutional Bill, modifying Art 55 of the Italian Constitution.

to the spirit of the 2001 reform and its decentralising force. The constitutional amendment brought back significant powers to the Government at the expense of territorial autonomies. Indeed, the subject areas previously belonging to the (abolished) category of shared competences were added to the list of subject areas in which the State holds exclusive powers. It must be acknowledged that in some cases this was a mere codification of the constitutional praxis of the Italian Constitutional Court which, in resolving the competences conflicts between the State and the Regions, sometimes favoured the State whenever there were functional interferences between the two levels of government.[83] Nevertheless, in addition to the traditional subjects reserved to the state such as foreign policy, defence and security policy, organisation of the State etc, the list of the exclusive powers of the State revised by the constitutional bill also included the general rules on administrative procedures and on public employment, general provision for health protection, food safety and workplace safety, the educational system, and, most importantly, the coordination of public finance.[84]

The second problematic aspect of the new vertical division of competences was that, at first glance, the 'double enumeration model'[85] listing, on the one hand, the powers of the State and, on the other, the powers of the Region, was not so clear-cut. In other words, the abolition of the category of shared competences did not eliminate the overlapping functions between the two levels of government. The reform, indeed, envisaged other elements of flexibility to the system which could easily trigger possible constitutional conflict before the Constitutional Court. Just to give an example, on the side of the State, the reform allowed the Government to initiate legislation in areas not belonging to the exclusive power of the State, should this be necessary to protect the national interest and the legal and economic unity of the State. By way of contrast, on the side of the Regions, the reform seemed not to consider the list of the exclusive powers of the Regions as exhaustive. Indeed, the constitutional bill also included in this list 'all subject areas not explicitly reserved to the exclusive competence of the State'. It is submitted that both the 'residual' nature of regional powers and the 'national interest' clause could create several functional overlaps between the competences of the State and the competences of the Regions, thus not decreasing the amount of constitutional conflicts before the Court as it was intended by the amended vertical division of powers.[86]

[83] For a recent general overview of the constitutional jurisprudence of Italian Constitutional Court see V Barsotti, P Carozza, M Cartabia and A Simoncini, *Italian Constitutional Justice in Global Context* (Oxford, Oxford University Press, 2015).

[84] Report of the Government attached to the constitutional bill, 18–19, available at https://www.senato.it/service/PDF/PDFServer/DF/302471.pdf.

[85] On the manner in which legislative powers can be allocated in compound legal orders (single and double enumeration model) see P Craig and M Walters, 'The courts, devolution, and judicial review' (1999) *Public Law* 293.

[86] Similar criticism have been expressed in B Guastaferro, 'Constitutional Reform in Italy: the Senate as a Second Chamber Representative of Territorial Institutions' (2016) *Tijdschrift voor Constitutioneel Recht (TvCR)* 3.

VI. Differences between the Italian Model of Devolution and a Federation

It has been argued that the regional State can be

> distinguished, on the one hand, from the Napoleonic model of State, to the extent that Regions are invested with legislative, and not only administrative functions, and, on the other hand, from the federal model, usually presupposing a fusion into a Federation of formerly sovereign States.[87]

As to the latter aspect, Italian Regions do not hold the same degree of autonomy and cultural and historical identity as the formerly sovereign States of a fully-fledged federation. According to some authors, the Regions have never been a 'significant expression of territorial identity',[88] in that the territorial boundaries currently representing the regions were an artificial creation dating from 1864 with a statistical aim, namely that of allowing the first census in the unified Italy. In this respect, the history of Italian regionalism is characterised by a sort of 'ambivalence'. In some cases, especially regarding the 'Regions with *special* status', Regions have expressed their 'identitarian' claim, resulting in a propensity for differentiation of objectives and rules in their policy-making choices.[89] In many other cases, Regions have been conceived as an essential instrument of the political decentralisation of the central State, namely as a sort of 'governmental' branch. They could not be compared to the pre-existing States of a Federation 'coming together' to share their sovereignty and join the Federal union through a bottom-up approach.

Another element which differentiates the Italian Regional State from the Federal State, is that, although the legislative power seems to be divided between the State and the Regions since from the 1948 Republican Constitution, ordinary Regions were created only 20 years after the entry into force of the Constitution and clashed with a strong centralistic bureaucracy and constitutional culture inherited by the totalitarian regime. Indeed, the degree of legislative and administrative autonomy of the Regions significantly increased over the years, starting with the decentralisation processes of the 1970s and 1990s and culminating with the 2001 constitutional reform. This reform, abolishing the pre-enactment scrutiny of regional laws by the Government and empowering the competence of the Regions through a Constitution attaching only enumerated powers to the central State, seemed to deliver a 'federal' institutional design, similar to the definition given by Wheare:

> In a federal constitution the powers of government are divided between a government for the whole country and governments for parts of the country in such a way that each government is legally independent in its own sphere. The government for the whole

[87] C Pinelli, 'The 1948 Italian Constitution and the 2006 Referendum: Food for Thought' (2006) 2(3) *European Constitutional Law Review* 333.

[88] M Cammelli, 'Regioni e regionalismo. La doppia impasse' (2012) *Le Regioni* 4.

[89] GC De Martin, 'Le autonomie regionali tra ambivalenze, potenzialità, involuzioni e privilegi' (2013) *Amministrazione in Cammino*.

> country has its own area of powers and it exercises them without any control from the governments of the constituent parts of the country, and these latter in their turn exercise their powers without being controlled by the central government. In particular the legislature of the whole country has limited powers, and the legislatures of the states or provinces have limited powers. Neither is subordinate to the other; both are coordinate.[90]

In other words, while the wave of 'first regionalism' during the 1970s implemented the Constitution by creating the Regions and *devolving* them some of the central competences exercised by the State, the 2000 wave of 'second regionalism' re-wrote the Constitution in a way which seemed to *divide* powers between the State and the Regions, as if they were political entities of a federal order, and called for their cooperation. Nevertheless, the vertical division of power envisaged by the reform—significantly strengthening the Regions—was to a certain extent narrowly interpreted by the Constitutional Court, that in the competence conflicts between the State and the Regions usually favoured the first at the expense of the latter. Moreover, in the following years, a constitutional reform which was labelled as 'federal' by its supporters failed in that it was rejected by a popular referendum in 2006. The right party promoting the constitutional reform increased the areas in which Regions could have exclusive powers and introduced fiscal federalism[91] in order to accommodate the request of the Lega Nord (a political party belonging to the right coalition) and, to a certain extent, to temper their secessionist desires, namely the desire to split the Northern (richest) part of Italy from the Southern one.

Besides the failure of the federalist reform of 2006, the 2014 constitutional reform represents a move back to centralism, and it does not have any federal impetus. To a certain extent, the vertical division of power is reshaped in a way that gives more power to the central State. Indeed, territorial governments did not live up the expectation of producing policy outcomes more sensitive to citizens' needs as the 2001 constitutional reform hoped. Often, Regions became centres of mismanagement and corruption, this paving the way to a significant reflection on the 'crisis of regionalism',[92] coupled with a strong criticism of the Regions as a territorial form of government, nurtured by both public opinion and scholarly literature.

VII. Devolving Powers in the Shade of Unitary Sovereignty: Insights for the UK

The analysis of the way in which powers have been devolved in Italy, proves to be interesting for the UK. First of all, both Italy and the UK can be defined as unitary States. Second, both countries have experienced significant processes of

[90] KC Wheare, *Modern Constitutions* 2nd edn (Oxford, Oxford University Press, 1966) 19.

[91] The 1948 Constitution gave full autonomy with regards to expenditures and a much more limited autonomy with regards to revenues.

[92] R Bin, 'La crisi delle regioni. Che fare?' (2012) 4 *Le Regioni* 735–50; V Onida, 'Le cause profonde della crisi del regionalismo' (2012) 4 *Le Regioni* 791–98.

decentralisation from the centre to the periphery, starting to devolve legislative and executive competences to Regions and local autonomies, in the case of Italy, and to the devolved legislatures of Scotland, Wales and Northern Ireland in the case of the UK.[93] Third, differently from Spain, the territorial Constitution of both Italy and the UK is asymmetric, in the sense that some Regions/devolved institutions hold more autonomy than the others, because the process of devolution was 'demand-led' and, consequently, tried to accommodate the specific needs and requests of territorial autonomies. Despite these similarities, the instruments envisaged to transfer powers to devolved legislatures and territorial autonomies slightly varied. In the UK, devolution occurred through ordinary statutes of the Parliament, such as the Scotland Act 1998 etc, which, notwithstanding their constitutional significance, are considered to be statutes that Westminster Parliament could in any event repeal (thus putting an end to the existence of the devolved Parliaments) or simply amend to confer or withdraw competences to devolved legislatures.[94] By way of contrast, even if several times ordinary statutes have been used to decentralise administrative functions, the articulation of the Italian Republic into territorial autonomies is a fundamental principle enshrined within Article 5 of the Constitution, which might not be subject to constitutional amendment.

In sum, despite some dissimilarities, both Italy and the UK are unitary States which experienced a strong decentralisation process. Nevertheless, none of them found in federalism a possible solution to organise their territorial Constitution. On the one hand, from the original drafting of the Republican Constitution in 1948 to the last constitutional reform of 2014, Italy can still be defined as a 'decentralized state with some federal features yet nested within a bureaucratic organization and political culture that remains highly centralized'.[95] We saw in the previous paragraphs that federalism, as an idea, never held a strong appeal. Along similar lines, the federal solution has been explicitly rebuffed at several stages of UK legal history. Indeed, the 1973 Royal Commission on the Constitution dismissed the federal option as inappropriate for Great Britain. Many of the characterising features of federalism—such as a written Constitution, a Constitutional Court entitled to police the division of powers, and, most importantly the idea of shared sovereignty—were considered to be alien to the British experience. Also more recently, despite the suggestions coming from scholars, wondering if and to what extent federalism could be a solution to the constitutional tensions created by devolution,[96] many official documents

> concur with the conclusion of the Kilbrandon Commission in 1973 that there is no federal structure currently proposed that could accommodate England as a discrete entity. Nor is

[93] If we consider devolution to Scotland, both in Italy and in the UK, the process of decentralisation started during the seventies and reached its pick at the end of the nineteens.

[94] But see nevertheless the 'permanent nature' of the existence of the Scottish Parliament in Scotland Act 2016. See chapters by Schutze, Tierney and Tomkins in this book.

[95] F Palermo and A Wilson, *The Dynamics of Decentralization in Italy: Towards a Federal Solution?* (2013) European Diversity and Autonomu Papers, EDAP 4/2012, 5.

[96] S Tierney, 'Is a Federal Britain Now Inevitable?' (27 November 2014) (available at http://ukconstitutionallaw.org).

> there public or political support at present for the creation of regional assemblies within England which may otherwise provide a viable basis for a federal system. Federalism does not, therefore, provide a solution to the tensions in the UK's territorial constitution.[97]

The first lesson that can be drawn from the comparison is that, notwithstanding the (even far-reaching) level of decentralisation and transfer of powers to territorial autonomies, the dogma of unitary sovereignty shared by both the unitary States, seems to prevent any federal outcome for these institutional arrangements. If in the UK federalism has been deemed inconsistent with the orthodoxies of Dicey's conception of the unity of parliamentary sovereignty,[98] in Italy the Constitutional Court has been very jealous in protecting the unitarian concept of sovereignty, making clear that the unitary character of the Republic should not be questioned. In one judgment where the Regione Sardinia drafted a regional Statute mentioning the 'sovereignty of the people of Sardinia' the Court insisted on the unitary concept of sovereignty, which, as per article 1, belongs to '*the* Italian people'. In this reading, Regions can be accorded a degree of *autonomy*, but not of sovereignty.[99] More recently, the attempts of Regione Veneto to propose a referendum for the independence of the Region from the Italian Republic, was declared unconstitutional by the Court (2015).[100] The very same question that was framed for the possible referendum—namely 'Do you want that Veneto becomes an *independent sovereign Republic*?'—was judged by the Court an 'institutional upheaval inconsistent with Article 5 of the Constitution', which promotes local autonomies but enshrines the principle of the 'unity and indivisibility' of the Republic.[101]

Against this backdrop, it is possible to conclude that Italian legal order, despite according a high level of 'constitutional entrenchment' to territorial autonomies, developed some sort of 'safeguard of Unitarianism' any time that the decentralisation process went too far. After the 2001 constitutional reform which significantly increased the legislative competences of the Regions, the Constitutional Court counter-balanced these possible disaggregating forces by favouring the State at the expense of the Regions in the context of competence conflicts. Along similar lines, and more recently, the Constitutional Court defended the unity and indivisibility of the Republic which was under threat by the independence claims of one Region.

[97] House of Lords, Select Committee on the Constitution, *The Union and Devolution* (published on 25 May 2016) 114, point 45 of the Summary.

[98] J Kendle, 'The Federal solution is not possible for us' ch 8 of the book *Federal Britain. A History* (London and New York, Routledge, 1997).

[99] Italian Constitutional Court, Judgment No 365/2007. For a case note see A Anzon Demming 'Sovranità, processi federalistici, autonomia regionale. In margine alla sentenza n. 365 del 2007 della Corte Costituzionale', in *Giurisprudenza Costituzionale* (2007).

[100] Italian Constitutional Court, Judgment No 118/2015. For a case note see G Ferraiuolo, 'La Corte costituzionale in tema di referendum consultivi regionali e processo politico: una esile linea argomentativa per un esito (in parte) prevedibile', in *federalismi.it* (28 ottobre 2015).

[101] On 22 October 2017 citizens living in Regione Veneto and in Regione Lombardia will be consulted again through a regional referendum. Nevertheless, they will not vote upon the (unconstitutional) hypothesis of independence but upon the (constitutional) possibility to be granted further autonomy (particularly in the fields belonging to the shared competence of State and Regions), as provided by Art 116, par 3 of the Italian Constitution.

The lessons to be drawn from the Italian experience is that if devolution is pushed forward without counter-balancing the decentralisation with appropriate concerns for the Unity of the legal order, the disaggregation of the United Kingdom is at risk. If federalism is not the favourite option, new political or judicial solutions should be found to address the tensions between the unity of the kingdom and the plurality of the nations composing it.

VIII. Final Remarks

This chapter has analysed the territorial organisation of two regional states in Europe, Spain and Italy, and their differences with federal states. As explained before, the unity of both states is constitutionally enshrined and firmly guaranteed, and under no circumstances may autonomy conferred on regions endanger such a unitarian conception. The Constitutional Court plays an important role in protecting national unity.

The study of Spain and Italy reveals useful lessons for the UK in two different aspects. On the one hand, the UK can use these cases as a model to be followed when it comes to the constitutional entrenchment of territorial autonomy and the formalisation of devolved powers. On the other hand, the UK should take careful consideration of the mistakes made by Italy and Spain in their respective processes of devolution, particularly regarding their reluctance to embrace federalism. For the UK it would be interesting to explore the federal path and its possibilities to reorganise the state in a new fashion. The replacement of the doctrine of parliamentary sovereignty for the Scottish doctrine of popular sovereignty would help to carry out this operation.

Part II

In Particular: The External Dimension

6

The UK's Reluctant Relationship with the EU: Integration, Equivocation, or Disintegration?

JO ERIC KHUSHAL MURKENS

I. Introduction

Britain's relationship with Europe has ebbed and flowed over the centuries. From 1066 until the mid-fifteenth century, after the Hundred Years' War, the Kingdom of England was deeply entangled with the European continent. In the Age of Discovery, England diverted its attentions overseas and became a maritime power. Its trade routes with the colonies criss-crossed the oceans and stretched around the globe. Its European objectives were limited to preventing any one nation from upsetting the balance of power. Long-standing European alliances were considered a threat to Britain's independence, as encapsulated by its foreign policy of 'splendid isolation'.[1] Its relationship with the Continent became 'semi-detached'.[2] Britain only started to break its pattern of looking down on the Continent from the lofty heights of imperial rule after the empire had gone.

After World War II, Britain had to choose between the 'special relationship' with the USA and the prospect of 'ever closer union' with European countries. The intuitive reaction was to try to have both by supporting the USA and NATO as well as the European Community. The ideal result would have combined maximum economic benefits with minimal loss of sovereignty. Charles de Gaulle torpedoed this strategy, and UK membership was successfully negotiated only after his death. Joining the European Economic Community late, after its rules had been written

[1] 'It is the duty of the Government of this country, placed as it is with regard to geographical position, to keep itself upon terms of goodwill with all surrounding nations, but not to entangle itself with any single or monopolising alliance with any one of them; above all to endeavour not to interfere needlessly and vexatiously with the internal affairs of any foreign country.' The Earl of Derby, *Parliamentary Debates*, House of Lords, 9 July 1866 (London, Cornelius Buck, 1866) 736.

[2] N Davies, *Europe: A History* (London, Pimlico, 1997) 13.

and its finances agreed, was 'Britain's biggest mistake'.[3] It was a mistake not simply because it cast Britain forever to the edge of Europe,[4] but also because the subsequent legalistic attempts to transform Britain into a European country could be interpreted by sceptics as a form of deception. In Hugo Young's words: 'The full-hearted consent of the people was never obtained, for the simple reason that the true nature of the contract was never put to them. This was subterfuge most foul'.[5]

This contribution challenges the idea that Britain was somehow duped by the project of European integration. The key domestic legal and political actors understood both the project and the implications of joining it very well. Deception, however, did take place—by the very same actors who misled the British public by prioritising economic benefits over constitutional implications. Splendid ignorance echoed Britain's earlier policy of splendid isolation.

From a British perspective, European integration could only proceed and succeed under two conditions. First, the domestic political system, the Westminster model of government, had to remain unchanged. Second, the UK had to stay convinced of the economic benefits of accessing the single market. Since the Treaty of Maastricht, if not before, Euroscepticism has defined itself not in opposition to the common market that the UK voluntarily joined in 1973, but in opposition to the unsolicited forms of further political integration. The dynamism and scope of European integration since 1992 destabilises and delegitimises British membership, all the more if membership is simply refracted through the supposed stability and constrictions of parliamentary sovereignty. This lop-sidedness creates the perfect conditions for Eurosceptics to reclaim 'control' and to claim that the UK had only ever joined a common market, not a 'federal superstate'.

The Eurosceptics conveniently, but woefully, forget to mention four central points. First, the project of European integration was never purely economic and always political. British politicians knew that from the start, but played it down in public for strategic reasons. Second, it is true that parliamentary sovereignty is customarily proclaimed as static, absolute and timeless. However, the normative justifications for sovereignty have changed since 1689 and need to be assessed on a recurring basis. Third, the legal relationship between the UK and the EU defies the solipsistic understanding of Eurosceptics. No other Member State has secured more opt-outs than the UK. No other Member State is more detached from the core objectives of integration. Finally, and most importantly, the UK's Constitution has itself transformed since 1998. The assertion of Westminster sovereignty rings increasingly hollow in the regions. Before the UK starts to unpick the carefully-drafted devolution legislation in preparation for outright withdrawal, thereby damaging Anglo-Irish relations, risking a border poll in Northern Ireland,

[3] S. Wall, *A Stranger in Europe: Britain and the EU from Thatcher to Blair* (Oxford, Oxford University Press, 2008) 215.

[4] A Geddes, *Britain and the European Union* (London, Palgrave Macmillan, 2013) 8.

[5] H Young, *This Blessed Plot: Britain and Europe from Churchill to Blair* (London, Macmillan, 1998) 2.

and a second referendum on Scottish independence, should the priority of those in power not be to identify and secure the national interest? Should the national interest, at a minimum, not stand for upholding carefully tailored constitutional arrangements and preventing the disintegration of the United Kingdom?

II. Economics

British participation in the European project has always been driven by the overriding concern of the national interest. But what is the national interest? From the start there were two competing considerations: economics and sovereignty. Looking at the debates, the economic argument was clearly the primary motivation for joining and remaining part of the Common and then Single Market. But prioritising economics was as much about national interest as about strategy: the political establishment in the 1960s deliberately framed the debate in economic terms so as to avoid any discussion about constitutional impact. Both Conservative and Labour governments insisted that European membership was essential for the British national interest, whilst giving numerous political assurances that 'nothing in [the European Communities Act 1972] abridges the ultimate sovereignty of Parliament'.[6] In other words, the establishment created and sustained a diversionary tactic that deflected attention from the changes and adjustments that membership would bring for British politics, government and the Constitution. These will be discussed in the later sections. Having sidelined any constitutional obstacles to accession, the UK government could focus solely on the economic benefits of membership, which would, incidentally, also enhance the UK's standing in the world. (There is an irony in that Brexiters today are fond of claiming that Britain could enhance its role in the world by leaving the EU.)

Yet even on purely economic grounds the case for membership was not straightforward. Britain had existing trade agreements with Commonwealth countries. It imported wool and dried fruits from Australia, deep-frozen lamb and butter from New Zealand, steel from Canada, spices from India, tobacco from the Americas, and sugar from the Caribbean. However, the Commonwealth was no longer a viable alternative for two reasons: European economies were starting to outperform the Commonwealth, and the UK's per capita GDP relative to the original six members' had declined steadily from 1945 to 1972. With declining interest from the former Empire, the UK needed easy access to Western European markets. Having eschewed participation in the European project in the 1950s, UK policy changed in 1961 when Macmillan announced Britain's intention to join the EEC.

[6] Sir G Rippon 831 HC Debates 278 (15 Feb 1972). See also the 1967 White Paper: *Legal and Constitutional Implications of United Kingdom Membership of the European Communities* (Cmnd 3301); and in 1971 *UK and European Communities* (Cmnd 4715) where the Government insisted that there was 'no question of any erosion of essential national sovereignty' (at para 29).

The economic case for membership explains why New Zealand had such sway over the UK in the 1960s. Its size, location and agrarian economy made New Zealand uniquely vulnerable to the EEC's common agricultural policy. Without a special deal, its produce would have faced punitive import tariffs imposed by the EEC. Britain acknowledged that New Zealand's vital interests had to be protected before the UK could accede to the EEC. Astonishingly from a 'national interest' perspective, New Zealand effectively had a veto over British membership with the EEC. In the end, the Luxembourg Agreement of 1971 produced a favourable deal for New Zealand. Although limited in time, it allowed the New Zealand economy to diversify. In 1970 Britain took more than 90 per cent of New Zealand's butter exports and 75 per cent of cheese exports, which over the course of the decade were substantively reduced.[7]

These examples demonstrate that the Treasury, not the Foreign Office, was driving membership. They further illustrate the primacy of economics and the urgency of gaining access to the common market. By way of contrast, economics was not the main factor for the original six. They began the process of integration within the European Community on a political imperative to make war between France and Germany 'not merely unthinkable, but materially impossible.'[8] It was PM Harold Macmillan who designated economics as the prime sphere of action of the Treaty of Rome. The common market was exactly that: a common market, not a political entity.

> I ask hon. Members to note the word 'economic'. The Treaty of Rome does not deal with defence. It does not deal with foreign policy. It deals with trade and some of the social aspects of human life which are most connected with trade and production.[9]

It is precisely because the European project was a political one from the start that the UK government resorted to economic argument to sugar the pill. It allowed politicians to claim that membership was vital for the national interest. Focusing on economic benefits also conveniently deflected from the question whether participation in European integration might necessitate changes to the domestic legal and political system.

The absence of constitutional awareness in the 1960s is not complete, but nonetheless striking. The summer of 1961 saw two debates on EEC membership (in July and August). On neither occasion were constitutional considerations prominent. PM Macmillan made no reference to the Constitution, preferring to compare the EEC to NATO and to the Organisation for Economic Co-operation and Development (OEEC). Nor did he assume that joining the EEC would commit UK to a federal Europe. The constitutional implications are dressed down to

[7] 'Britain's Entry Into the European Community', Report by Sir Con O'Neill (London, Frank Cass, 2000).

[8] The Schuman Declaration, 9 May 1950.

[9] H Macmillan, HC Deb 02 August 1961 vol 645 c1481.

draw attention to the social and economic benefits and to Britain's standing in the world.

> We have to consider the state of the world as it is today and will be tomorrow and not in outdated terms of a vanished past. There remain only two national units which can claim to be world powers in their own right, namely the United States and Soviet Russia. To these may soon be added what Napoleon once called the 'sleeping giant' of China, whose combination of a rapidly multiplying population and great natural resources must increasingly be reckoned as a potent force in world affairs ... It is true of course that political unity is the central aim of those European countries and we would naturally accept that ultimate goal. But the effects on our position of joining Europe have been much exaggerated by the critics. Accession to the Treaty of Rome would not involve a one-sided surrender of sovereignty on our part but a pooling of sovereignty by all concerned, mainly in economic and social fields. In renouncing some of our sovereignty we would receive in return a share of the sovereignty renounced by other members. The form which political unity of the Community should take is now under active discussion in Europe, where opinions on it are strongly divided. There is a school which ardently believes in the unitary concept of a European federation, a new European state. I myself believe that the bulk of public opinion is firmly against the extinction of separate national identities and would choose a Europe which preserved and harmonised all that is best in our different national traditions. We would, I think, favour a more gradual approach worked out by experience, instead of a leap in the dark, and this is a view shared by many leaders of opinion in Europe.[10]

Interestingly, Macmillan had sought to secure an 'association' with the EEC. Had European integration been primarily an economic undertaking, he might have achieved it. In the end, Macmillan claimed to have considered and rejected the proposal. Being a free-trading associate would 'raise all the same problems for British agriculture and Commonwealth trade without giving us any position in which we could share in the decisions of the Community in all its aspects'.[11] In truth, it was not Macmillan who rejected the proposal, but de Gaulle who in 1958 vetoed a British effort to get a free trade area throughout Europe. In 1961 Edward Heath articulated the suspicion on the Continent 'that we want all the advantages of the developments in Europe without undertaking any of the obligations of the other members of the Community'.[12]

In short, those who supported Common Market membership were not motivated by the thought of pooling sovereignty, but instead were guided by boosting the economy and protecting British influence in the world. This economic focus fuels the concern that European integration only ever amounted to an elite project that by-passed the people and did not need to be explained to them. One of the reasons for Euroscepticism relates to basic communication. Successive

[10] H Macmillan, *Britain, the Commonwealth and Europe* (London, Conservative and Unionist Central Office, 1962).

[11] HC Deb 02 August 1961 vol 645 c1492.

[12] HC Deb 03 August 1961 vol 645 c1683.

UK governments have not been forthcoming in explaining the implications of decisions they help reached in the EU. As Stephen Wall notes:

> … their lack of candour is outdone by that of many of the opponents of British EU membership who do the British people an even greater disservice by distorting the nature of issues under debate in Brussels and by presenting a vision of an alternative world in which Britain could successfully operate without the rest of Europe or, even more insidiously, simply pick and choose at will which bits of European policy Britain chose to adhere to.[13]

The flip-side of the elitist argument is that European integration has not been achieved by targeting the people, but by concentrating on national rules and practices that are obstacles to integration. In that sense, European integration always was an elite project, but one from which everyone stood to benefit. Three examples of integration will suffice. First, the EU breaks down barriers to trade, most prominently internal tariffs, trade quotas, and with the single European currency. However, it continues to abolish many technical barriers relating to consumer protection and health and safety. Second, the EU integrates Member States through a process of national deregulation and EU reregulation, for instance the deregulation of airlines in 1992. The democracy deficit in this context is remote. Domestically, most regulatory measures take the form of delegated legislation, which is not enacted by Parliament but by a Minister. Finally, the European Union integrates citizens by outlawing laws and practices that discriminate on grounds of nationality, age, sex, sexual orientation. EU laws are, therefore, much more compatible with constitutional democracies than much national legislation. To conclude, discussing EU membership solely in terms that relate to volume of trade ignores the wider social and political dimension. However, welcoming or even acknowledging that dimension also misses the point: after all, those laws still come from Brussels! The question of sovereignty remains unanswered and needs to be addressed.

III. Sovereignty

The current crop of Eurosceptics argues that the European project is no longer an economic one. It has gone far beyond the organisation of a common or single market, which is what Britain had signed up to when it joined in 1973 and when the British electorate last had a vote in a nationwide referendum in 1975. As a result, the British electorate was duped. The EU enjoyed many of the trappings of a political and federal union on its way to becoming a 'superstate', whilst lacking institutions that were recognisably democratic, legitimate, transparent and accountable. Based on this logic, the UK needed to withdraw from the EU in order to rejuvenate democracy, revitalise voters and rebuild 'sovereignty' (shorthand for

[13] Wall, above n 3, 212.

political control) in the Westminster Parliament. In this section, I will interrogate the premise of this argument. Was the EEC in the 1970s merely an economic community? Did UK politicians lack sufficient information during the accession phase? Was the British electorate kept in the dark during the referendum of 1975? In the next section, I will deconstruct the conclusion that sovereignty could be restored to Westminster.

British politicians knew right from the start that the European project transcended economic integration. As leader of the opposition Hugh Gaitskill in 1962 decried membership as 'the end of Britain as an independent European state'.[14] For Gaitskill, joining the European project meant 'the end of a thousand years of history'. It did not mean sharing sovereignty, but a loss of it. In essence, Gaitskill's analysis of the EEC did not differ from that of Walter Hallstein, the first president of the European Commission—although their final assessments could not have been further apart: 'By its very nature, the Community must be an ever-growing, ever-developing organism … Essentially, [it] may be described as a federation in the making … History is on our side'.[15]

The UK's reservations about supranationalism, which it shared with de Gaulle, were offset by a vision of transatlanticism, which it shared with Washington. The US unequivocally wanted the UK to join the European Community wholesale and to embrace supranationalism, the CAP, and make no concessions for the Commonwealth. For the US, non-membership of the UK was, and remains, 'politically awkward'.[16] The questions of supranationalism and the supremacy of European Community laws raised technical questions that UK politicians might have been forgiven for not grasping fully. Danny Nicol argues that Members of Parliament knew very little of the constitutional implications when they conducted the debate as to EEC membership.[17] Nicol argues that the political nature of the UK Constitution makes it harder for politicians to ascertain the legal implications of their actions and, regarding the European Union, to appreciate fully the legal aspects of membership. However, this view is contradicted by a closer examination of the position of the government before and during the negotiations of the European Communities Act 1972.[18]

Lord Dilhorne, Lord Chancellor under Macmillan, explained to the House of Commons in 1962 that the Community organs 'have in the spheres in which they

[14] 'Britain and the Common Market', Texts of speeches made at the 1962 Labour Party Conference by the Rt Hon Hugh Gaitskell MP and the Rt Hon George Brown MP together with the policy statement accepted by Conference (London, Labour Party, 1962) 3–23.

[15] W Hallstein, 'The European Economic Community' (1963) 78(2) *Political Science Quarterly* 167–68.

[16] D Dinan, *Europe Recast: A History of European Union* (Houndsmills, Palgrave Macmillan, 2014) 100.

[17] D Nicol, *EC Membership and the Judicialization of British Politics* (Oxford, Oxford University Press, 2001).

[18] See eg J Forman, 'The European Communities Act 1972' (1973) 10 *Common Market Law Review* 39.

operate ... certain supra-national powers which override those of the national constitutional bodies, and which are also incapable of challenge in the national courts of the member States'.[19] He continued:

> I fully accept that [Community] regulations would have to be given effect to in our law as they stand. Should they conflict with existing Statute or Case Law they would override it; and, as regards regulations which may come to be made after our accession, we should have to provide in advance that they should have effect as part of our municipal law.[20]

What is noteworthy about Lord Dilhorne's statement is that he not only recognises the existence of supranational powers within the EEC, but fully accepts the supremacy of Community law *well in advance* of the actual articulation of that doctrine by the ECJ in *Costa v ENEL*.[21] In short, the legal and political establishment had a full decade to think about the constitutional implications of membership, and chose not to. Lord Dilhorne might have set out the problems for the UK Constitution that stemmed from having to recognise i) a new source of law ii) with the power to override domestic law. But Lord Dilhorne clearly did not think this was necessary. After all, membership 'does not involve our having to adopt anything in the nature of a written Constitution. That is quite unnecessary ...'[22]

A handful of backbenchers noted that joining the EEC would involve a substantial loss of sovereignty, ie control over domestic affairs. Sir Derek Walker-Smith noted in 1961 that the case for membership was not just economic, but that it raised 'issues which concern our constitutional practices, our national institutions and our future as a sovereign State'.[23] He drew attention to Article 3 Treaty of Rome, which placed Member States under a duty to alter domestic law 'to the extent necessary for the functioning of the Common Market'. He made the point that arguments about Community membership ought to consider 'the wider implications of the long-term effect in relation to our sovereignty and our constitutional machinery'.[24]

> Friends must ask themselves and answer questions such as these. If we adhere to the Economic Community now and the Six proceed, as they are entitled to proceed, to the next stage of political union, what then is our position? If we do not want to go along with them on the political side, could we stay in on the economic side, or could we get out at that stage even if we wanted to? Or is the real position this, that if the decision is taken now we forfeit the power of political decision? And what is the intention of the Government in this regard? Do they want to take a step forward into political union or not? So far we have not had an answer to that question. If we tried to come out of the Community in those circumstances, would not the Six be justified in saying to us, 'But you knew all along of our enthusiasm for the next political step. If you did not share it,

[19] HL Deb 02 August 1962 vol 243 c418.
[20] HL Deb 02 August 1962 vol 243 c420.
[21] Case 6/64 *Costa v ENEL* [1964] ECR 585.
[22] HL Deb 02 August 1962 vol 243 c421.
[23] HC Deb 2 August 1961 Hansard, vol 645, col 1507; and again: HC Deb 16 November 1966 Hansard vol 736 c476.
[24] HC Deb 2 August 1961 Hansard, vol 645, col 1511.

> why did you join us in the first place?' Then the last state of our relations with Europe would be worse than the first.[25]

This statement from August 1961 gives the lie to those politicians and journalists who are fond of claiming that the UK only joined, and the British electorate by plebiscite in 1975 only sanctioned membership in, a common market. The UK was fully apprised of the political ambitions of the original six, and not just in the early 1970s but from the outset. If there is a persistent sense that the UK joined the common market on purely economic grounds, then the reasons can be traced directly to a domestic political strategy that treated European integration in such terms and ignored all the evidence to the contrary.

It is true that the Treaty contains no express commitment on constitutional matters, such as the supremacy of European law or a federal Europe that have bedevilled British Eurosceptics for decades. However, anyone who gave a moment's thought to the matter, like Walker Smith, realised that being a member of the Community would one day mean that

> … the decision about federation would not be one of our own choosing so much as of the will of others, because our arrangements would be so inextricably involved with those of the Community that it would be difficult to the point of impossibility in practice—though not impossible in theory—to dissociate ourselves from a supranational federation if our partners decide that they want it.[26]

Taking a closer look at Article 189 of the Treaty, Walker Smith drew the Common's attention to the fact that European Regulations would be directly applicable in the UK. That provision would reduce the Commons to a 'conduit pipe' which, together with courts, would be 'powerless to intervene'. Walker Smith pondered that the British people may even be prepared to pay this 'heavy price' of membership, but he insisted that

> they should not be asked to pay it in ignorance. It is a mistake to assume that the British people are interested only in the economic, bread and butter aspects of this matter. It is a mistake to assume that they are not interested in these great political and constitutional matters. I know, of course, that terms like 'sovereignty' are not part of the everyday idiom of the British people; but they represent things which are long-established and deeply cherished. They are like the air we breathe—little noticed in its presence but valued beyond price in the event of deprivation.[27]

The debates reveal concerns over Community membership that are expressed in terms relating to British history, national identity, and British autonomy and independence. But the vast majority of members did not address Community membership from the perspective of the British legal and political system. As JC Jennings MP noted during the 1966 debates, the constitutional question of

[25] Sir Derek Walker-Smith, HC Deb 2 August 1961 Hansard, vol 645, col 1513.
[26] HC Deb 16 November 1966 Hansard vol 736 c475.
[27] HC Deb 16 November 1966 Hansard vol 736 c478.

national sovereignty in a political union 'has been swept nicely, beautifully and quietly under the carpet. It is almost a sin to talk about it.'[28]

Geoffrey Howe, the main drafter of the European Communities Bill, also chose to play down the implications of membership for the doctrine of parliamentary sovereignty. That issue had been dealt with by the European Communities Act (ECA) 1972 and was effectively a non-issue.

> ... I believe sovereignty is not some pre-defined absolute, but a flexible, adaptable, organic notion that evolves and adjusts with circumstances. It is to explain how sovereignty constitutes a resource to be used, rather than a constraint that inhibits or limits our capacity for action.[29]

Howe shared Macmillan's view that the transfer of sovereignty to the EEC was not a one-way deal that would cause its erosion. Instead, sovereignty was transferred instrumentally in the national interest.

The Commons debates of 1971–72 show that, although ministers did not mislead Parliament, they were also not forthcoming with details on the supremacy doctrine of Community law that had by then been firmly established in the jurisprudence of the European Court of Justice. 'Scarcely any interest was shown in 1971 in the details of exactly how EEC membership might affect the working of the British political system'.[30] This is reflected in the European Communities Act 1972, which does not contain a section, as it might have done, on the priority of application of Community law over national law. Anthony King attributes this to the reluctance of ministers 'to air in public the constitutional issues that would inevitably arise if and when Britain's application for membership succeeded'.[31] Stephen Wall acknowledges that ministers carefully shielded MPs from the supremacy doctrine 'for fear of the adverse reaction'.[32]

The reason why the supremacy of Community law was not debated was, therefore, entirely political, and certainly not because the implications for domestic law were not properly understood. There was a real sense that the sovereignty question had the potential to derail Britain's membership application. Hugo Young recounts an anecdote that fully exonerates the legal service from the charge of being asleep at the wheel:

> Community supremacy would have had explosive possibilities. The Government lawyers knew perfectly well what the legal consequences were. 'Does he think we were all complete idiots?' one of them riposted, when a professor suggested many years later that the degree of subordination of British law to European law had comes as a surprise. Of course they knew. But the draftsmen has been instructed to tread carefully, knowing ... that full and open admission of what was being done to parliamentary sovereignty would be 'so astounding' as to put the whole Bill in danger.[33]

[28] HC Deb 16 November 1966 Hansard vol 736 c496.
[29] G Howe, 'Sovereignty and Interdependence: Britain's Place in the World' (1990) 66(4) *International Affairs* 675–95, 676.
[30] A King, *The British Constitution* (Oxford, Oxford University Press, 2007) 95.
[31] ibid, 92; Young, above n 5, 247.
[32] Wall, above n 13, 206.
[33] Young, above n 5, 247.

The failure to discuss European membership in constitutional terms amounts to a serious policy error. Outside the political realm, most academics also did not assess correctly the constitutional impact of membership. PB Keenan assumed erroneously that Britain, upon joining the Communities, would have to incorporate the Treaty of Rome into English law.[34] On the one hand, there were those provisions, 'which are immediately and legally binding' and could be easily incorporated. On the other hand, there were statements of future intent or those which established the organs of the Community, which could not 'sensibly be enacted as part of English law and yet it would be dangerous to ignore them because it is in the light and context of these parts of the Treaty that the legal obligations which are incorporated should be interpreted'.[35] Keenan touches upon the toughest constitutional question of the past 50 years. How should the courts treat future British legislation that is found to be inconsistent with the relevant Treaty or Community law? Fully aware of the problem, Lord Gardiner, the Lord Chancellor, dismissed it as 'academic' and 'unprofitable'.

> There is in theory no constitutional means available to us to make it certain that no future Parliament would enact legislation in conflict with Community law. It would, however, be unprofitable to speculate upon the academic possibility of a future Parliament enacting legislation expressly designed to have that effect. Some risk of inadvertent contradiction between United Kingdom legislation and Community law could not be ruled out; but, of course, we must remember that if we joined the Community we should be taking part in the preparation and enactment of all future Community law and our participation would reduce the likelihood of incompatibility.[36]

Stanley de Smith considered the case for limiting Parliament's sovereignty in order to give priority of application to Community law and preclude a future Parliament from legislating inconsistently with Community law. In line with the dominant tradition of the 'political constitution', he concludes that the formalisation of 'so far-reaching an innovation' is not called for. Nonetheless, Parliament and the courts will be 'expected' to conform to the Treaty obligations and give priority to Community law.[37]

In contrast, JDB Mitchell's output in the mid to late 1960s stands out for viewing membership as an opportunity for constitutional renewal. He draws on section 4 of the Statute of Westminster 1931, and the subsequent Independence Acts, which disabled Parliament from legislating on behalf of the members of the Commonwealth. If Parliament could accept a territorial limitation on its power, then there was no reason in logic why Parliament could not also accept

[34] Interestingly, in the first case in which the Court of Appeal had to consider the Treaty of Rome, the Treaty was understood to have been incorporated into domestic law 'precisely as if the terms of the Treaty were contained in an enactment of the Parliament of the United Kingdom': *Application des Gaz v Falks Veritas* [1974] Ch 381, 399 E, per Stamp LJ.

[35] PB Keenan, 'Some Legal Consequences of Britain's Entry into the European Common Market' [1962] *Public Law* 327, 331–35.

[36] HL Deb, Hansard, 8 May 1967, vol 282, cols 1202–03.

[37] S de Smith, 'The Constitution and the Common Market: A Tentative Appraisal' (1971) 34(6) *Modern Law Review* 597–614, 609.

a limitation on legislative content 'where coupled with a transfer of matching legislative capacity'.[38]

Mitchell took issue with the economic tenor of British negotiations in the 1960s and highlighted the opportunities for public law. In relation to courts, Mitchell argued that they ought to be fully integrated into the working of the new legal order. Two reasons stood out. First, the domestic courts had become too deferential to parliamentary and governmental activity.[39] The Community system, by contrast, depended upon active courts for its development. Second, domestic courts needed to attune themselves to a new system of public law, with distinctive techniques and concepts that were without counterpart in the UK. He wished that the White Paper on the Legal and Constitutional Implications of United Kingdom Membership of the European Communities, published by the Labour government in 1967, had 'delivered more of a shock, or conveyed more excitement to lawyers'. It limply sought guarantees from the Community that 'the special needs of our legal system would be taken into account'.[40] Instead, Mitchell argued that the UK must adhere to the philosophy underlying the Treaty of Rome. 'When you jump into a swimming bath you learn to swim, and you don't expect water to behave like dry land'.[41]

IV. Opt-outs

If Britain had joined the European Community under false pretences the Eurosceptics mission to take back control would sound more credible. To be sure, Britain had to sign up to the *acquis communautaire* and to the supervisory jurisdiction of the European Court of Justice like every other Member State. However, the UK also sought to reconcile Mitchell's tension, between the dry land of sovereignty and the open waters of integration, by negotiating and obtaining opt-outs and special clauses. This clashes with the standard European account that posits the uniform application of EU law as a necessary condition for the continued existence of the EU. As a result no other Member State is today more detached from the core project of integration as the UK. What are the prospects of further deepening this fudge so as to produce the semblance of sovereignty (Brexit) whilst mirroring European regulatory standards? In a country as politically divided as the UK, and on a matter as technically complicated as unpicking four decades of European law, continuing constitutional equivocation might be preferable to clarity either way.

[38] JDB Mitchell, 'What Do You Want To Be Inscrutable For, Marcia?' (1967) 5 *Common Market Law Review* 112, 119–20.

[39] See generally JDB Mitchell, 'The Causes and Effects of the Absence of a System of Public Law in the United Kingdom' [1965] *Public Law* 95.

[40] Para 27.

[41] Mitchell, above n 38, 122.

The viability of constitutional equivocation needs to be discussed in the context of opt-outs, which tend to receive a mixed reaction. On the one hand, allowing Member States to argue for and obtain a permanent 'ring-fence', for example based on specific national constitutional provisions or sensitive domestic policies, creates a Europe á la carte from which Member States are free to pick and choose their favourite policies. Opt-outs, therefore, symbolise the 'negation of the idea of European cooperation'[42] and pose a direct threat to 'the entire cohesiveness of the Community system'.[43]

On the other hand, opt-outs are pragmatically preferable to the national veto. If a Member State is unable to sign up to a specific policy, it could *in extremis* withhold assent and halt the entire integration process. By providing for special exemptions, the EU allows Member States to preserve some sense of their sovereignty, in return for which the Member State permits the EU to advance the integration process.[44]

The UK secured opt-outs in four areas that are central to its conception of sovereignty. The first one is monetary union with respect to which the UK and Denmark secured permanent opt-outs under Protocol 25 of the Maastricht Treaty. By extension, the UK has also not participated in other forms of closer Eurozone integration, such as the Euro Plus Pact, the Fiscal compact or the banking union.

The second opt-out relates to the Schengen Agreement, which abolishes border controls and allows travel across the EU without the need for visas or passports. Neither the UK nor Ireland are members. From a domestic perspective, this opt-out is justifiable. As islands, the Schengen Agreement affects the UK and Ireland differently. Border controls are also more important as British citizens do not carry ID cards. Finally, the UK and Ireland operate common law systems, which grant comparatively more power to courts and judicial precedents than is the case in civil law systems.

Relatedly, the third opt-out pertains to justice and home affairs policy. Under Protocol 36 of the Lisbon Treaty, the UK is entitled to opt-in/out of individual legislative measures passed under Title V. In 2013 the UK opted out of all 130 Justice and Home Affairs (JHA) measures that came into force prior to the Lisbon Treaty. A year later, the UK opted back in to 35 measures that matched its national interests, including Europol, the sharing of information with countries in the Schengen area, and the European Arrest Warrant.

Finally, with the Lisbon Treaty the UK has also obtained not an opt-out, but a 'clarifying protocol', which states the Charter 'does not extend' the ability of the European Court of Justice to find UK law inconsistent with the Charter. This exemption was obtained because the UK was concerned about the Court of Justice's ability to change domestic labour law using the Charter.

[42] G Verhofstadt, *The United States of Europe* (London, Federal Trust, 2006) 214.

[43] Deirdre Curtin, 'The Constitutional Structure of the Union: A Europe of Bits and Pieces' (1993) 30 (1) *Common Market Law Review* 17–69, 49, 57.

[44] R Adler Nissen, *Opting Out of the European Union: Diplomacy, Sovereignty and European Integration* (Cambridge, Cambridge University Press, 2015).

Taken together, these opt-outs are neither technical nor insignificant. Moreover, if one considers for a moment the recent themes and crises of the EU, from the sovereign debt crisis, Russia, Ukraine and mass migration to the Commission proposal to introduce a financial transaction tax, the UK has used its status as permanent outsider either to oppose or to pass over significant parts of EU policy responses.

A cynic would deride the opt-out system as a fudge: not in, but not out either. It symbolises the UK's arm-length relationship with the EU. It is precisely this fabricated distance that the UK could put to good use during the Brexit negotiations. Denmark has since 1959 precluded non-nationals from purchasing second homes unless they reside in Denmark. When Denmark acceded to the EEC in 1973, the domestic summer homes regulations ran contrary to the ethos of Community law. It discriminated on grounds of nationality, and infringed the freedom to provide services and the free movement of capital.[45] But Denmark eventually secured a permanent opt-out in the Maastricht Treaty 1992.[46] In similar fashion, it seems inevitable that the EU will have to make concessions on free movement of EU nationals to the UK. Even pro-Europeans, like the Liberal Democrat Vince Cable, have expressed 'serious doubts that EU free movement is tenable or even desirable'.[47] Given the number of existing opt-outs the 'ethos' argument has also lost much of its potency. Bruno de Witte argues that, under the 'framework for its future relationship' referred to in Article 50 TEU, the UK could become a 'partial Member State' by remaining part of the EU but extending its opt-outs and special protocols.[48] As the Prime Minister of Luxembourg Xavier Bettel commented on the UK government's Brexit strategy: 'Before, they were in and they had many opt-outs; now they want to be out with many opt-ins'.[49] One person's fudge is another person's pragmatic response. It is certainly more sensible than outright withdrawal. The EU has a rich tradition of political compromises and the UK has a long tradition of constitutional equivocation. Combined, these are potent forces to guard against further UK participation in European integration, and to prevent complete national disintegration.

V. Constitution

In the first three decades of the EEC, hardly anyone viewed the issue of membership primarily as a constitutional issue. From a domestic perspective, EU membership

[45] Curtin, above n 43, 46–47.

[46] Protocol No 1 in the Maastricht Treaty, now Protocol 32 in the Lisbon Treaty.

[47] V Cable, 'Why it's time to end EU free movement' *New Statesman*, 4 January 2017.

[48] B de Witte, 'Near-membership, partial membership and the EU constitution' (2016) 41(4) *European Law Review* 471–72.

[49] Harry Cooper, 'Luxembourg PM: EU countries should shut borders to teach lesson' *Politico*, 11 October 2016.

or withdrawal is a non-issue anyway: Westminster decides. However, if it is correct that the Westminster model of government has changed, possibly beyond recognition, then three points follow: first, it is no longer possible to restore sovereignty in the way Eurosceptics want; second, the constitutional implications of EU withdrawal will be far more complex than Eurosceptics expect; third, in addition to pursuing opt-outs as part of the UK's external relations with the EU, the UK will also need to consider domestic constitutional reform as a matter of urgency. A radically re-modelled Constitution would create buffers that could resist the urge to view EU law in opposition to Westminster statute. EU law would simply become another source of law alongside local, regional and national laws in a more diverse legal system.

After four decades of European integration and after 20 years of devolution, the Westminster model of government is still the lodestar for legal and political scholars. I use the word 'model' loosely: some refer to it as a model,[50] whereas for others it forms a critical reference point.[51] The Westminster model differs in crucial respects from the central tenets of modern Western liberal constitutionalism. Constitutional laws are not entrenched against change by means of an ordinary statute. The judiciary enjoys comparatively weak powers of judicial review. These aspects are not viewed as deficits, but as a means of keeping the Constitution flexible rather than rigid.[52] Political power is concentrated in a single-party executive. In addition, Parliament's authority as the 'sovereign' law-maker is served by an electoral system ('first past the post') that artificially boosts the strength of the two main parties. The government, therefore, dominates Parliament. Far from being removed from the ordinary politics, as liberal constitutional theory demands, the Westminster model has been shaped directly by organic political processes.

'The Westminster model has not, and will not, evaporate'.[53] However, today it only offers a partial understanding in a post-industrialised context. Since 1945 Britain has changed from a unitary state to a differentiated polity. The political system has witnessed shifts from a strong executive (and the tradition of 'leaders know best') to a segmented executive, which is characterised by bargaining games within and between networks.[54] Moreover, the traditional Westminster model cannot accommodate the introduction of market mechanisms in the public sector

[50] I Jennings, *The British Constitution* (Cambridge, Cambridge University, 1966); A Lijphart, *Patterns of Democracy: Government Forms and Performance in Thirty-six Countries* 2nd edn (New Haven, CT, Yale University Press, 2012) Ch 2.

[51] See for instance the contributions to the special issue 'Devolution: Ten Years On' in (2010) 63(1) *Parliamentary Affairs*; D Richards and M Smith, 'The Tensions of Political Control and Administrative Autonomy: From NPM to a Reconstituted Westminster Model' in T Christensen and P Lægreid (eds), *Autonomy and Regulation: Coping with Agencies in the Modern State* (Cheltenham, Edward Elgar, 2006); D Marsh, 'Understanding British Government: Analysing Competing Models' (2008) 10(2) *The British Journal of Politics and International Relations* 251–68.

[52] G Marshall and GC Moodie, *Some Problems of the Constitution* 5th rev edn (London, Hutchinson, 1971) 17–18.

[53] RAW Rhodes, *Understanding Governance: Policy Networks, Governance, Reflexivity and Accountability* (Maidenhead, Open University Press, 1997) 200.

[54] ibid, 3.

(New Public Management); it does not reflect the growth in judicial power since the 1960s; and it cannot explain the parcelling out of sovereign powers to subnational and supranational polities. In short, the Westminster model no longer describes how government works, nor can it prescribe how it ought to work in a 'differentiated polity'.[55] The Westminster model and its rhetorical outposts ('sovereignty', 'take back control') have lost their explanatory power and sound increasingly implausible in the rest of the UK.

That said, the model still enjoys a degree of relevance and reverence: it provides central government with the stability, capacity and justification to govern and for its ministers to be held to account in Parliament. The Westminster model provides ministers and civil servants with a legitimating foundation for their final decision-making powers.[56] The model still provides a (false?) sense of unity in the place of state fragmentism.[57] According to Richards and Smith, 'the enduring importance and relevance of the model rests in the way in which ministers rhetorically appeal to it, often implicitly, sometimes unwittingly, as the cornerstone framing their understanding of the political world'.[58]

The major constitutional changes over the past half-century have decentralised political authority in the United Kingdom. Political and legal powers have been devolved, and new institutions have been created. The UK Supreme Court enjoys jurisdictional competence regarding the delineation, definition and dispute resolution over devolved and reserved matters. In that area the court operates in the manner of a constitutional or supreme court.[59]

Put differently, the major political changes and constitutional reforms of the past 20 years have transformed the British political system. The sharing of power, the decentralisation of authority, and the coordination of policy between different parties and governments are more typical of a federal system than of the unitary Westminster model.[60] The Westminster model has in piecemeal fashion devised and executed many of the constitutional changes it was supposed to guard against. In the absence of a better name to formalise the paradigm shift, Vernon Bogdanor refers to the new settlement as the New British Constitution[61] and RAW Rhodes to the 'differentiated polity', ie shift from strong centre and unified polity to a complex maze of institutional arrangements in a differentiated polity.

[55] ibid, 4–7.

[56] D Marsh, D Richards and M Smith, 'Unequal Plurality: Towards an Asymmetric Power Model of the British Polity' (2003) 38 (3) *Government and Opposition* 306–32; T Nairn, 'UKania under Blair' (2000) 1 *New Left Review* 69–103.

[57] JS Migdal, *State in Society Studying How States and Societies Transform and Constitute One Another* (Cambridge, Cambridge University Press, 2001).

[58] D Richards and M Smith, 'Back to the Future: New Labour, sovereignty and the plurality of the party's ideological tradition' (2010) 5(3) *British Politics* 239–64, 242.

[59] R Masterman and JEK Murkens, 'Skirting Supremacy and Subordination: the constitutional authority of the United Kingdom Supreme Court' [2013] *Public Law* 800–20.

[60] S Tierney, 'Federalism in a Unitary State: A Paradox too Far?' (2009) *Regional and Federal Studies* 237–54, and his contribution to the present volume.

[61] V Bogdanor, *The British Constitution* (Oxford, Hart, 2009).

The changes to the UK Constitution over two decades of devolution have arguably gone much deeper than those due to European membership over four decades. Despite top-level rhetoric asserting the contrary, uniform parliamentary sovereignty, the unitary state and executive centralism have become illusionary and have given way to power-sharing and divided government. What have emerged are three devolved polities which, for different reasons and in varying degrees, were established to depart from the Westminster model. The most radical departures are found in Northern Ireland where the Good Friday Agreement provided for institutions based on power-sharing, though this term was expunged to avoid association with past failed efforts at reform. An electoral system and rules governing the creation of an Executive were instituted that ran contrary to the power-hoarding Westminster model. Similarly the Welsh Assembly was elected by a more proportional system than that used for Westminster and initially was based more on a local government model. Much rhetoric surrounded the idea of 'new politics' but this was given little institutional form. In Scotland, an electoral system was adopted that was designed to make it highly unlikely that any one party would have a majority in Parliament necessitating coalition or minority government.[62] More importantly, the Scotland Act 2016 opens with the following provision: 'The Scottish Parliament and the Scottish Government are now permanent features of the United Kingdom's constitutional arrangements.'[63] This section purports to entrench devolution against the legislative reaches of the Westminster Parliament, which is nothing short of revolutionary in constitutional terms.

The Westminster model has effectively ceased to exist with respect to the government of regions. Devolution has positively laid to rest any remaining Victorian notion that the British parliament is the supreme law maker. This is the point where all the Eurosceptic claims unravel. It is simply no longer possible to restore sovereignty and to take back control. Moreover, and irony upon irony, the political and constitutional consequences of Brexit are nothing short of disastrous for the future of the United Kingdom as a state. The 62 per cent of voters in Scotland, and the 55.8 per cent in Northern Ireland, who voted for the UK to remain within the EU, have turned their nations into potential veto players. If either withholds consent, it is difficult to see how the UK as a whole could proceed with EU withdrawal in any constitutionally sustainable way. And yet, the implications of this transformative change have not yet been fully incorporated. 'Reinventing the Westminster model of representative democracy for a differentiated polity in the twenty-first century is a task scarcely begun, in either theory or practice'.[64]

The decaying Westminster model underpinned the UK Supreme Court's decision in *Miller* in January 2017.[65] The attempt to bypass Parliament over Article 50 TEU was comprehensively thwarted as unconstitutional. However, the

[62] The Scottish Parliament election of 2011 nonetheless delivered a majority SNP government.

[63] See also the new Wales Act 2017, and its analysis by S Tierney in this volume.

[64] Rhodes, above n 53, 198.

[65] *R (Miller) v Secretary of State for Exiting the European Union* [2017] UKSC 5.

government secured a strong victory on the second 'devolution' question, which was whether any UK legislation that sought, for instance, to repeal the ECA 1972 would be subject to the Sewel Convention, according to which the UK government will not normally invite Westminster to legislate on devolved matters or on the extent of devolved powers without first obtaining the consent of the relevant devolved legislature.

This question opened up a gulf between constitutional law and constitutional politics. The UK government claimed, correctly, that EU law falls within the jurisdiction of the Westminster Parliament. Westminster may repeal the ECA 1972 or amend the devolution legislation at any time. The devolution legislation in Scotland, Wales and Northern Ireland merely *assumed* that the UK would be a member of the EU, but did *not require* the UK to remain a member. It follows that there can be no 'parallel legislative competence' by which the devolved legislatures could withdraw from the EU.[66]

However, the devolved administrations pointed out, equally correctly, that to give effect to EU withdrawal Westminster would have to relieve the devolved legislatures of their statutory obligation to respect EU law. This would require changing the devolution legislation, which in the context of Northern Ireland would involve a delicate three-way power sharing structure between the Republic of Ireland, the devolved administrations and legislatures, and the UK. Amending the NIA 1998 unilaterally would be especially reckless, if not actually impossible as a matter of international relations and constitutional politics.

If constitutional law on this question is straightforward and simple, the constitutional politics is anything but. The Sewel Convention is a fundamental organisational principle that exists in two forms: first, as an uncodified constitutional convention for Northern Ireland; second, in statutory form for Scotland and Wales.[67] The UKSC is undoubtedly correct that the consent of the devolved legislatures is not legally required for the purposes of triggering Article 50 TEU—or for the purposes of amending the devolution legislation. However, so long as the Sewel Convention is in place, it is a constitutional requirement that the devolved assemblies pass a legislative consent motion under the Sewel convention before those parts of the devolution legislation incorporating EU law can be amended. Politically, there is a danger that the UKSC's retreat to constitutional formalism will be interpreted as constitutional intransigence in the regions. Withdrawing from the EU will certainly alter the general and special arrangements of the Northern Irish peace process.

The single most important constitutional requirement for the UK lies in prioritising the Northern Irish and Scottish questions. Devolution happens to be intrinsically tied up with the UK's membership of the EU. It is unfortunate that the British tradition steadfastly refuses to discuss politics through a constitutional

[66] ibid [129].

[67] s 28(8) Scotland Act 1998, as amended by s 2(2) Scotland Act 2016; s 2 Wales Act 2017.

matrix. Finding an answer to the devolution question is not just indispensable to working out the legal process of the UK's withdrawal. More than that, it is constitutionally important, politically urgent and, with an eye on preventing national disintegration, vital.

The Westminster model is too unilinear and unrefined to capture the sophistication and subtlety of devolution. The changes of the past two decades call for a new framework to understand the changing nature of the New British Constitution. Its central aspects are, first, the triadic relationship between devolved regional government, central government, and supra-national governance;[68] and second, the modernisation of the public sector on the basis of new public management.[69] The phenomena of multi-level government and administrative devolution have diluted the unitary and all-pervasive qualities of the Westminster model. From a constitutional perspective, the UK looks like a 'centreless society'[70] 'an ever looser union',[71] and like 'an increasingly disunited kingdom'.[72]

How can the UK be saved? A recent thought-provoking and workable proposal was put forward by the Constitution Reform Group (CRG).[73] It calls for a reversal of the UK's current constitutional arrangements and proposes to re-imagine the Constitution as a federal one. The premise should be that England, Scotland, Wales and Northern Ireland represent autonomous units with fully devolved governments that determine the majority of their own affairs. It would be up to each unit to decide what competences to share centrally with a leaner and more efficient United Kingdom.

In political science terms, the UK would transform from a general-purpose to a special-purpose jurisdiction. Special-purpose bodies would be created to discharge particular functions or tackle particular problems. The CRG remarks that a reworked House of Commons could become the English Parliament, and a reworked House of Lords could become the UK Parliament.[74] To be sure, such a federal-style arrangement may give rise to jurisdictional disputes. These already exist under the current devolution arrangement. Such disputes are a feature of all power-sharing regimes for which institutions and procedures can be devised to settle them.[75]

The main hurdle is the absence of a universally-agreed way to split central, regional and local functions. Under the CRG proposals, the functions of central

[68] I Bache and M Flinders, 'Multi-Level Governance and the Study of British Politics and Government' (2004) 19(1) *Public Policy and Administration* 38; L Hooghe and G Marks, 'Types of Multi-Level Governance' (2002) 3 *Cahiers européens de Sciences Po* 1–31.

[69] C Crouch, *Post Democracy* (Cambridge, Polity, 2004).

[70] N Luhmann, *The Differentiation of Society* (New York, Columbia University Press, 1982) xv.

[71] J Mitchell, 'The Westminster Model and the State of Unions' (2010) 63(1) *Parliamentary Affairs* 85–88, 87.

[72] A Geddis, *Britain and the European Union* (London, Palgrave Macmillan, 2013) 15.

[73] Constitution Reform Group, *Towards A New Act of Union*, Discussion Paper DP01, September 2015.

[74] ibid, 55.

[75] See generally Hooghe and Marks, above n 68.

government are critical to the new constitutional arrangements. Rather than working out which powers to devolve to regional and local institution, 'and then trying to invest them with sufficient powers and duties to justify their existence', the CRG reforms assume that 'default competence' lies with the centre.[76] Producing lists is always difficult and unsatisfactory. But they also help focus the mind as to what the overall purpose of the Union ought to be. Commenting on the proposals, Professor Arthur Aughey summed up the constitutional challenge in one sentence:

> The historical objective of central government, or Westminster, has been to secure common rights of citizenship within the shared space of the UK, where expressions of national difference need not conflict with the achievement of multi-national purpose.[77]

Without prejudice to differential administration in the constituent countries, the CRG suggests the following areas as ones that would most likely fall to the centre: i) the Crown; ii) the constitutional settlement itself; iii) foreign affairs; iv) defence; v) national security; vi) overarching fiscal, economic and monetary policy; vii) currency; viii) immigration; ix) citizenship; x) extradition; xi) emergency powers.[78] The CRG also notes that a final list of central powers needs to reflect the allocation in practical terms. However, it also needs to consider other functions, such as broadcasting or the universal state pension. After all, 'that the United Kingdom is not just a legal constitutional construct, but a cultural and political one'.[79]

A federal UK would be able to absorb EU law much more smoothly than the current centrist model. The electorate in Scotland and Northern Ireland are used to the idea that some competences are exercised locally, regionally, nationally and supranationally. English voters, by contrast, have not experienced any devolution of powers since 1998. Asymmetrical devolution was, in Bogdanor's words, 'the price England pays to keep Scotland within the union'.[80] However, this has also contributed to the English sense that power-sharing is tantamount to a loss of 'sovereignty' and 'control'. Federalism would institutionalise power-sharing across the board. On the plus side, EU law would no longer stand out as a constitutional abnormality. On the downside, English politicians and journalists would have to find a new scapegoat for unpopular legislation.

VI. Conclusion

The competitive advantage of the Leave campaign, with slogans along the lines of 'We want our country back' and 'Let's take back control', enhanced the mendacities,

[76] Which is not the case in the federal arrangements of the European Union, United States, or Germany: CRG, above n 73, 11.
[77] ibid, 10, fn 16.
[78] ibid, 13–14.
[79] ibid, 14.
[80] V Bodganor, 'Why English votes for English laws is a kneejerk absurdity' *The Guardian*, 24 September 2014.

myths and misinformation that pro-European commentators complained about over the course of the two-month long referendum campaign. However, as I have sought to show in this chapter, the project of European integration has been willfully and skillfully distorted by British politicians and journalists from the very beginning, and especially since the date of accession in 1973. Based on Britain's torturous relationship with the EU, it is fair to ask whether a referendum on membership could ever have been won since the signing of the Maastricht Treaty. Put differently, should we not be positively surprised by the 48 per cent who elected to remain in the EU?

The other point that I wanted to highlight is that the referendum ultimately did not amount to a verdict on the European Union. Instead, it revealed the fragility of the United Kingdom. The United Kingdom did not unite against the EU, but split down the middle: Scotland and Northern Ireland voted to remain, England and Wales voted to leave. In the aftermath of the referendum, the two main political parties did not put forward helpful proposals regarding Britain's future relationship with the EU, let alone proposals about the future of Britain. Rather, they descended into open meltdown over the Europe question. The reason Britain had set itself up to fail over a serious policy choice was because only few people understood that the British Constitution cannot be separated from EU membership. 'There is now only one thing: the British constitution, which today incorporates … the EU's principal rules and institutions'[81]—most visibly in the context of devolution and the Belfast Peace Agreement.

Away from the political rhetoric regarding economics and sovereignty, the real trials facing all European states in years to come will be transnational and existential. Stephen Wall lists poverty, disease, migration, terrorism, energy, climate change and economic competitiveness as the main issues:

> [A]ll of them requires Britain to work with her European partners and many of them will require, not the lengthy, lowest common denominator, approach of intergovernmental negotiation but the effective decision-making and subsequent enforcement, which can only be achieved by the so-called Community method.[82]

Contrary to assertions by PM Theresa May to the contrary,[83] the British electorate did choose to turn its back on European cooperation. The politics of the referendum result means that the UK's relationship with the EU must change. However, over four decades, and despite deep reservations, distrust and scepticism, British politics has absorbed European integration organisationally and conceptually: the 'politics of time' means that decisions have become locked-in and difficult to change.[84] The government now faces two stern challenges. First, in order to preserve the UK it must bring about complex and considerate constitutional reform.

[81] King, above n 30, 110.
[82] Wall, above n 13, 219.
[83] 'We may be leaving the European Union, but we are not leaving Europe': PM's Florence speech: a new era of cooperation and partnership between the UK and the EU, 22 September 2017.
[84] Geddes, above n 4, 8.

Second, preserving the UK will necessitate equivocating the relationship with the EU. The biggest lapse of the Leavers lies not in their failure to understand the intricacies of European integration; it lies in their failure to understand the basics of the Constitution they sought to save and which their actions may inadvertently destroy. To re-write Hugo Young: this is subterfuge most foul! The full-hearted consent of the people was never obtained, for the simple reason that the true nature *of EU withdrawal* was never put to them.

7

Britain and the European Union: Federalism and Differentiation

SIONAIDH DOUGLAS-SCOTT

I. Introduction

On 23 June 2016 a majority, albeit a slender one, of the UK electorate voting at the national EU in-out referendum, voted to leave the European Union (EU). This may well become a defining moment in the constitutional politics of the United Kingdom (UK)[1] as well as a landmark or stumbling post in the history of European integration. Undoubtedly, untangling and re-establishing a relationship with the EU (and perhaps the wider world) will have legal, economic, social and cultural effects within the UK, as well as in the remaining Member States. But Brexit also seems to be provoking a constitutional crisis and a challenge to a Constitution that is already 'unsettled.'[2] The essence of the British Constitution has long been characterised as resting on the sovereignty of Parliament—unwritten, flexible, uncodified in nature, with political conventions and ministerial accountability often taking the place of hard law or a constitutional court. A phenomenon whose very uncodified and sometimes tacit nature somehow gave rise to a holistic constitutional identity.

Nonetheless, this organic Constitution has in recent decades undergone a creeping and gradual reform process. This has been provoked by certain developments which have affected sovereignty and lines of authority. These include: EU membership, which has challenged Parliamentary supremacy; the 'weak entrenchment' of the Human Rights Act, bringing increased judicial power to shape a human rights culture; and devolution in Scotland, Wales and Northern Ireland challenging any notion of a 'unitary' UK. All of this has rendered the Constitution (and Britain) less unitary and more heterogeneous, more willing to recognise centres

[1] I also use the term 'Britain' loosely as a collective term for the four disparate parts of Scotland, England, Wales and Northern Ireland, while recognising that the 'UK', while being the official state in international law, is a more recent designation, only becoming official in 1801.

[2] N Walker, 'Our Constitutional Unsettlement' (2014) *Public Law* 529–48.

of power elsewhere, without however bringing any coherence or consolidation of constitutional form.

This constitutional transformation has gone hand in hand with the development of multi-dimensionality and pluralism within law more generally, within and beyond the UK, undermining law's connection with the state. For a brief period (from roughly the midseventeenth century to mid-twentieth century) the 'Westphalian' order of sovereign states governed the order of things in western Europe. Before that, a shared Christianity under the ultimate Catholic tutelage of the Pope, feudalism, and such arcane entities as the Holy Roman Empire, ensured that sovereignty was a complex and fragmented entity. However, to some extent, a new order of sovereign states took over from this. The Peace of Westphalia, which ended the Thirty Years War,[3] one of the most brutal wars in history, marked the end of the Holy Roman Empire as an effective institution and initiated huge power shifts in Europe, inaugurating the modern state system which is founded on the notion of national sovereignty and borders, as well as the beginnings of some religious toleration.[4] The Peace of Westphalia has been described as marking 'the end of an epoch and the opening of another', as well as 'the genesis of the inter-state order.'[5] It was not, however, an era of continuous peace and good will, and unmitigated national sovereignty was not always a force for the good.

However, since earlier last century, and certainly by the end of the Second World War, the post-Westphalian order has been breaking down. In a speech at Humboldt University Berlin in 2000, then German foreign minister, Joschka Fischer, suggested that:

> The core of the concept of Europe after 1945 was and still is a rejection of … hegemonic ambitions of individual states that had emerged following the Peace of Westphalia in 1648, a rejection which took the form of … the transfer of nation-state sovereign rights to supranational European institutions.[6]

It appeared that borders were not what they used to be. Since 1945, there have been shifts to supra-national institutions, and international law has become more important. But there have been demands for self-government from sub-state nations as well—for a 'downwards devolution'. These also concern the nature and bounds of the political community and locus of ultimate authority. However, there has not always been a claim for full statehood, but sometimes a push for greater self-government within the existing state.

[3] CV Wedgwood, *The Thirty Years War* (Abingdon, Routledge, 1990, original edition 1936).

[4] V Gerhardt, 'On the historical significance of the Peace of Westphalia: 12 theses' in *1648—War and Peace in Europe I* (Council of Europe Exposition: Münster, Osnabrück 1998/99); W Spellman, *European Political Thought* (London, Macmillan, 1998).

[5] L Gross, 'The Peace of Westphalia, 1648–1948' (1948) 42 *American Journal of International Law* 28; A Eyffinger, 'Europe in the Balance: an appraisal of the Westphalian system' (1998) 45 *Netherlands International Law Review* 164.

[6] 'From Confederacy to Federation—Thoughts on the finality of European integration' Speech by Joschka Fischer at the Humboldt University in Berlin, 12 May 2000.

The philosophical underpinning for these movements is the idea of 'post sovereignty'.[7] This does not argue that sovereignty has disappeared, rather that it is transformed and is no longer the dominant mode of political organisation. Post-sovereign approaches argue that states must share their powers with supra-state, sub-state and trans-state systems. Neil MacCormick's work has been very influential in this area. His view was that

> sovereignty and sovereign states, and the inexorable linkage of law with sovereignty and the state, have been but the passing phenomena of a few centuries, that their passing is by no means regrettable, and that current developments in Europe exhibit the possibility of going beyond all that.[8]

The argument is that, in contrast to the earlier Westphalian world, the contemporary legal space is one of overlapping jurisdictions, segmented authority and multiple loyalties, characterised by an increasing number of transnational, supranational and subnational legal orders, and a tendency to heterarchical rather than hierarchical relationships. Many theorists now believe legal pluralism, which describes a state of affairs in which two or more legal orders occupy the same legal space, to be the most convincing theory of law.[9]

So it might seem that the idea of the unitary state is in retreat. Yet Brexit challenges this vision of post-sovereignty. Perhaps the most common constitutional idea to feature in the Brexit debates was the notion of sovereignty, of 'taking back control',[10] an apparent yearning for a parliamentary sovereignty that cannot be reconciled with continuing EU membership, a desire for a clearly national constitutional architecture. However, such an anachronistic notion of sovereignty is too simplistic. It fails to capture the way in which a pooling of sovereignty in one area, such as is enabled by EU membership, may actually empower a state. Indeed, rather than 'taking back control', perhaps Brexit imperils national sovereignty. This is because, as well as threatening Britain's economic security (which itself impacts on Britain's sovereignty) it risks shattering the UK's balance and stability by threatening the peace settlement in Northern Ireland and possibly inciting a further independence referendum in Scotland. In these circumstances, Brexit heralds a period of potentially profound uncertainty and change, during which many of the foundations of the UK constitutional settlement will be tested.

Just what was it that Britons who voted Leave in the EU Referendum were rejecting? What was it about Britain's constitutional relationship with the EU, and indeed the EU's own constitutional status, that was seen as undesirable? There is

[7] N MacCormick, 'On Sovereignty and Post-Sovereignty' in N MacCormick, *Questioning Sovereignty: Law, State, and Nation in the European Commonwealth* (Oxford, Oxford University Press, 1999).

[8] N MacCormick, 'Beyond the Sovereign State' (1993) 56 *MLR* 1.

[9] See eg J Griffiths, 'What is legal pluralism?' (1986) 24 *Journal of Legal Pluralism*, 2–55 at 2.

[10] For example, the very domain name of the Vote Leave website was http://www.voteleavetakecontrol.org/why_vote_leave.html.

no one clear identifiable rationale for the Leave vote,[11] and a closer look at the heterogeneous and variegated EU settlement may undermine the claim that in leaving the EU, Britain is successfully 'taking back control'. In an era where sovereignty claims are fuzzy and diluted, this simply may not be possible. In contrast, this chapter considers the many and varied legal relationships and forms that exist both between the EU and its Member States, but also internally, within those states, and between their sub-state parts and the EU. In this way, it considers whether existing structures, forms of federalism, federacy and other legal orderings, and a greater legal imagination, may provide solutions to the problems of Brexit.

II. The EU and Federalism

The EU can be a difficult polity to fathom. Perhaps, for eurosceptics, this is part of its problem. If it appears too close in its structures to a sovereign state, then it is prone to censure as an unwanted 'superstate', undermining national sovereignty. On the other hand, if its configuration is perceived as too unwieldy, its processes too diffuse, then it is dismissed as ineffective and unworkable. Can it really be both? Part of the problem is that, in spite of the 'post sovereignty' evolution detailed in the introduction, too many (in Britain especially) continue to interpret governance as something irredeemably connected to national sovereignty and a strong central state. So they do not appreciate what has been described as Europe's 'Sonderweg'.[12] To understand the EU properly, we need to consider its governance arrangements, to interrogate its relationship to federalism, and also the complex and multiple relations that states may have within and beyond themselves. This reveals that the EU's relations with the UK are far more complex, but also more nuanced, and delicately balanced, than eurosceptics ever allowed.

As Halberstam has commented, 'Federalism' can be a charged and confusing word,[13] and indeed there seems to be no agreed criteria for what makes a legal order federal. Whereas for some, it is a means of decentralisation, for others it may mean a strong central government. Federalism in its modern sense was born in the USA, in the late eighteenth century, a means of dividing power to ensure greater liberty, and preserve both central and state governance. James Madison asserted

[11] For example, polls carried out by Lord Ashcroft revealed a variety of reasons why those voting leave did so, 'How the United Kingdom voted on Thursday ... and why', available at http://lordashcroftpolls.com/2016/06/how-the-united-kingdom-voted-and-why/.

[12] JHH Weiler, 'Federalism Without Constitutionalism: Europe's *Sonderweg*' in Kalypso Nicolaidis and Robert Howse (eds), *The Federal Vision: Legitimacy and Levels of Governance in the United States and the European Union* (Oxford, Oxford University Press, 2001) 54–70.

[13] D Halberstam, 'Federalism: Theory, Policy, Law' in M Rosenfeld and A Sajó (eds), *The Oxford Handbook of Comparative Constitutional Law* (Oxford, Oxford University Press, 2012) at 578.

his classic caution in the *Federalist Papers* that 'we will not be governed by angels, or even enlightened statesmen'. Madison's conclusion was clear: 'Ambition must be made to counteract ambition. The interest of the man must be connected with the constitutional rights of the place.'[14] This meant dividing power and 'splitting the atom of sovereignty'.[15]

The suggestion that early US federalism ('the Union as a *confederacy* of sovereign states')[16] might even have appeared more 'confederal' than 'federal' prompts the question of what the difference between these two terms might be. It is a salient distinction, connoting on the one hand, a looser alliance (confederation) with lesser implications for national sovereignty, and on the other hand, something more closely knit (federation). It is also a distinction acknowledged by German literature,[17] which employs the terms *Staatenbund* (confederation) and *Bundesstaat* (federation), but also highlighted by EU scholars, politicians and lawyers, who have questioned whether the EU is a federal state, federation, confederation or *sui generis* entity.[18]

Wheare's notable work, *Federal Government*, proposed an understanding of federalism as 'the method of dividing powers so that the general and regional governments are each, within a sphere, coordinate and independent.'[19] However the problem with this account is that it ignores the *cooperative* elements of federalism. In federal states, various levels of governance are not necessarily autonomous from each another but compete and intermingle.[20] This is relevant in the EU, where Member State courts and authorities apply and interpret much EU law in practice. In contrast, Daniel Elazar's definition of federalism as a combination of 'self-rule plus shared rule' extends the scope of federalism beyond US structures to other systems that might include Union, Federation, Confederation, Federacy,

[14] J Madison, *The Federalist No 51*.

[15] *See United States Term Limits, Inc v Thornton*, 514 US 779, 838 (1995) (Kennedy, J, concurring) (stating 'The Framers split the atom of sovereignty'). For an analysis of the US American conception of 'divided sovereignty' and its relation to the European Union, see: R Schütze, 'Federalism as Constitutional Pluralism: 'Letter from America' in M Avbelj and J Komárek (eds), *Constitutional Pluralism and Beyond* (Oxford, Hart, 2012).

[16] J Madison, *The Federalist No 39*. Emphasis added.

[17] See further Robert Schütze, *From Dual to Cooperative Federalism* (Oxford, Oxford University Press, 2009); see also Karl M Meessen, 'Hedging European Integration: The Maastricht Judgment of the Federal Constitutional Court of Germany' (1994) 17 *Fordham International Law Journal* 511, 525–26. The term 'Staatenverbund' has sometimes been credited to Paul Kirchhof, the judge rapporteur in the German Constitutional Court Maastricht case (see *Brunner v European Union Treaty* CMLR [1994] 57), who stated his preference for that term for the EU as opposed to 'supranational organisation', which in his view, implied an erosion of the statehood of its members.

[18] See eg R Bellamy, 'Sovereignty, post-sovereignty, and pre-sovereignty: Three models of the state, democracy, and rights in the EU' in N Walker (ed), *Sovereignty in Transition* (Oxford, Hart Publishing, 2003); A Føllesdal, 'Democracy and federalism in the European Union' in A Føllesdal and P Koslowski (eds), *Democracy in the European Union* (Berlin, Springer, 2004).

[19] KC Wheare, *Federal Government* (Oxford, Oxford University Press, 1946), 11.

[20] Schütze, above n 17.

Associated Statehood, Condominium and League within this interpretation[21]—rendering it perhaps too vague.

Undeniably, Federalism can function in an upward as well as a downward direction. In the eighteenth century, Kant's 'On Perpetual Peace'[22] considered the notion of world federation, although saw obstacles to its realisation. More recently, David Held and others have asserted the possibility of global, hierarchically organised, multilevel rule.[23] Koen Lenaerts, judge at the European Court of Justice, suggests that federalism might be 'characterised by the existence of a central authority that manages the fields of competence entrusted to it',[24] which is certainly capable of catching the EU.

Nonetheless, within EU studies, the European Union has often been regarded as *sui generis*, as something more than an international organisation but still not a state. There has certainly been no consensus of opinion among scholars as to its legal status.[25] This needs some further explanation.

A. Is the EU a Federal Polity?

Lord Beloff, writing in the 1990s, in somewhat eurosceptic vein, suggested that 'the EEC was the basis for a federal system.'[26] In this context, Beloff referred to HG Wells' idea of 'an open conspiracy' suggesting, 'if ever there was one, this was it.'[27]

To be sure, integrationists in the twentieth century hoped that federalism might provide both a uniting factor in Europe, and an attractive form of government. The early European federalists, such as Spinelli, were clearly aware of the benefits of a federalist structure for Europe. The requirement of different spheres of public authority, what Madison described as a 'compound republic',[28] can build a political system sensitive to a wide diversity of cultural, social, geographical differences, as well as promoting democracy by the separation of powers, but also by a system of 'checks and balances'.[29]

[21] D Elazar, *Exploring Federalism* (Tuscaloosa, University of Alabama Press, 1987); see also Riker's definition, whereby two levels of government regulate the same land and people, but whereby each level has at least one area of action in which it is autonomous, and some guarantee of autonomy in its own sphere, which has also proved influential (W Riker, *Federalism: Origin, Operation, Significance* (Boston, Little Brown and Co, 1964)).

[22] I Kant, 'Perpetual Peace: A Philosophical Sketch' in H Reiss (ed), *Kant's Political Writings* (Cambridge, Cambridge University Press, 1970).

[23] eg D Held, *Cosmopolitanism: Ideals and Realities* (Cambridge, Polity, 2010).

[24] K Lenaerts, 'Constitutionalism and The Many Faces of Federalism' (1990) 38 *American Journal of Comparative Law* 205.

[25] see eg D Curtin and I Dekker, 'The EU as a "layered" international organisation' in P Craig and G de Burca, *The Evolution of EU Law* (Oxford, Oxford University Press, 1999).

[26] Lord Beloff, *Britain and European Union: Dialogue of the Deaf* (London, Macmillan, 1996) at 35.

[27] ibid.

[28] J Madison, *The Federalist, No 51*.

[29] The EU does not operate a system of checks and balances, but does have a somewhat underdeveloped concept of 'institutional balance'.

However, the very word 'federal'—in an early draft of the Maastricht treaty—was enough to cause apoplexy in certain quarters, so it has usually been avoided in the EU context. For many British, it connoted the creation of a European super-state. Yet if the spectre of the word 'federalism' provoked fear at the Maastricht Inter Governmental Conference (IGC), it probably should not have done so. Not only may we cite as examples of federal government some of those among the most stable in the world: US (since 1787), Switzerland (since 1848), Canada (since 1867) and Australia (since 1901) but federalism has proved sufficiently agreeable to be revived as a political solution in the 1990s (in Belgium, which became a fully-fledged federal system in 1993, and in South Africa in 1996).

Yet, aside from mere avoidance of an issue unpalatable to some, there are two reasons why the EU's relation to federalism is a difficult question to answer. The first is that, as we have seen, the concept of federalism is itself complex and contested. The second reason, closely related to the first, is that of the complex multidimensional nature of the EU: trying to pigeonhole it within a single concept may simply not do it justice. So it is helpful to carry out a short audit of the EU, considering which 'typical' features of federalism might apply to it, and what conclusions to draw from that.

The first such feature is the division of competences between federal and state components. In the undoubtedly federal US, a major feature is the division of powers, set out in Article 1, section 8 US Federal Constitution, which lists the subjects that lie under federal authority. In the EU, the division of powers between the EU and its Member States has been set out since the Treaty of Lisbon. The Treaty on the Functioning of the EU (TFEU) clarifies the division of competences between the EU and Member States. These competences are divided into three main categories: exclusive competences under Article 3 TFEU (whereby Member States have no right to legislate on their own); shared competences under Article 4 TFEU (whereby the EU can legislate only if it conforms with the principle of subsidiarity, but if the Union does legislate, EU law has primacy over national law); and supporting, coordinating and supplementing competences under Article 6 TFEU (whereby the EU has no legislative power in these fields and can only intervene to support, coordinate or complement the action of Member States).

Lest there be fear that such a division of competences clearly illustrates a federal, power grabbing exercise, we should remember that the UK Government's 'Balance of Competences review', comprised of 32 volumes, 3000 pages of evidence, and more than 1500 independent sources, concluded there was no evidence that the EU had excessive competence nor that its competences need be repatriated.[30] It noted that most of the EU's competences are shared with Member States and not exclusive to the EU. Indeed, the EU has few exclusive competences, and those

[30] See eg FCO, *Review of the Balance of Competences between the United Kingdom and the European Union*, Cm 8415, July 2012: https://www.gov.uk/government/uploads/system/uploads/attachment_data/file/35431/eu-balance-of-competences-review.pdf.

that exist fall mainly in international trade, the eurozone, and where exclusivity is driven by practical reality, given neither the Customs Union nor Economic and Monetary Union (EMU) could function if there were multiple national policies. This Review was launched to prepare the ground for the UK Government to define its policy on the EU, and described as 'an audit of what the EU does and how it affects the UK',[31] although, regrettably, it was overshadowed by the renegotiation and EU referendum processes in 2016, and then generally ignored.

The concept of subsidiarity is also relevant to competences. Subsidiarity, with some of its origins in Catholic theory, was an unfamiliar term to Anglo-Americans, at least prior to its explicit introduction by the Maastricht treaty. In the EU context, subsidiarity is a means of determining the appropriate level of action, and is closely related to the concepts of necessity, effectiveness, proportionality, or even good government. It has been promoted as a means of reconciling the conflicting needs of unity and diversity within the EU. As it is set out in Article 5 TEU, subsidiarity permits EU institutions to act in areas of concurrent competence 'only if and insofar as the objectives of the proposed action cannot be sufficiently achieved by the member states'.

There are further components of EU law which are indicative of some federal drift: recognition of the doctrines of supremacy, direct effect and preemption, for example, which all provide scope for strengthening the EU against its Member States.[32] Indeed, the EU has been criticised for being too conscious of the need for its legal supremacy and autonomy, at the expense of other interests, even of human rights.[33] The decision-making processes of the EU, which lend a role both to the Member States acting in the Council, but also to peoples of Europe as represented in the Parliament, is also capable of looking federal. There are also treaty provisions which protect the identity of the member states, for example Article 4(2) TEU, which requires the EU to respect the national identities of its Member States, an indication of a federal concern with protecting the diversity of the parts.

However, some aspects of the EU seem less than federal, given the amount of intergovernmental decision-making that they involve. Foreign and security policy, usually the preserve of the central government in federal systems, is such an example. Nonetheless, the EU's Common Foreign and Security Policy is to be a *common* foreign and security policy, constructed according to the principles set out in Articles 23–46 TEU. Decision-making is unanimous, and thus in the hands of the Member States, but the Commission and Parliament do play some role, however, so it is not just intergovernmental. The EU's common currency,

[31] See *Review of the Balance of Competences* 'Introduction' available at: https://www.gov.uk/guidance/review-of-the-balance-of-competences.

[32] Compare the Supremacy Clause of the United States Constitution (Art VI, Clause 2) which establishes that the Constitution, federal laws made pursuant to it, and treaties made under its authority, constitute the supreme law of the land.

[33] Case 6/ 64 *Flaminio Costa v ENEL* [1964] ECR 585; *Opinion 2/13 on EU Accession to the ECHR* [2014] ECR nyr.

the euro, also poses some questions. On the one hand, a common or single currency has traditionally been a feature of the federal state. The EU now has such a currency, although of course not all of its members participate in it. On the other hand, the USA had a federal government and federal Constitution before it had a central bank and uniform dollar currency, so a uniform currency is perhaps not a must.

However, it is not just institutional arrangements which are indicative of federalism. Dicey, for example, argued that a successful federal system required a singular state of sentiment among the inhabitants of the countries which it was to unite: 'They must desire union and not desire diversity.'[34] This is somewhat tendentious given that the clearly federal US system permits both. Nonetheless, the social forces underlying federal systems are clearly very important. According to WS Livingston, 'The essential nature of federalism is to be sought for, not in the shadings of legal and constitutional terminology; but in the forces—economic, social, political and cultural—that have made the outward forms of federation necessary.'[35] Common values for the EU are asserted in Article 2 TEU, which states that:

> The Union is founded on the values of respect for human dignity, freedom, democracy, equality, the rule of law and respect for human rights, including the rights of persons belonging to minorities. These values are common to the Member States in a society in which pluralism, non-discrimination, tolerance, justice, solidarity and equality between women and men prevail.

Notwithstanding, it has been argued that Europe lacks a *demos* and there may be little affective support for the EU.[36] Yet a lack of affective support may also exist in individual states—there may be little support for Westminster in Scotland, little support for Ottawa in parts of Canada, but still linking social, economic and cultural forces and work. This may be the case in the EU too.

B. The *Sui Generis* Character of EU Law

So the EU is at least not straightforwardly federal. Nor is federalism an agreed goal for the EU. Many Europeans are suspicious of a premature federalism, of unifying structures which might endanger the pluralism of Europe, stultifying diversity and stunting difference. There is certainly evidence of this in the UK, a fear or warning of a European 'superstate' being a familiar card in the eurosceptics' toolbox. On the other hand, there are clear counterbalances to unifying and harmonising

[34] AV Dicey, *The Law of the Constitution* (vol 1, Oxford Edition of Dicey, JWF Allison (ed), Oxford, Oxford University Press, 2013) at 144.

[35] WS Livingston, *Federalism and Constitutional Change* (Oxford, Clarendon Press, 1956) 1–2.

[36] eg D Grimm, 'Does Europe Need a Constitution?' (1995) *European Law Journal* 282–302.

tendencies in European law.[37] The TEU introduced opt-outs, protocols and differentiated integration.[38] Subsequent EU treaties continued this, and increased flexibility looks set to stay.

EU law illustrates its own ambivalence to categorisation of its status as federal. Indeed, in spite of treaty provisions setting out a division of competences, competence is not neatly divided between the EU and its Member States, but instead is overlapping, symbiotic, incremental and unpredictable in nature. This cannot easily be accommodated within the terminology of federalism, nor indeed that of functionalism, neo-functionalism, supranationalism, intergovernmentalism or consociationalism—theories which usually apply in the context of a bilateral relationship between two fixed units: Member States, and international organisations or sub-national components. Such a two-dimensional analysis no longer seems sustainable in the EU. Instead, Europe has become a 'multi-dimensional configuration of authority'.[39]

This is scarcely a new or radical perception,[40] but has become more of a preoccupation. New approaches to this complex European legal space are being developed, whether in the context of MacCormick's 'overlapping legal orders', the assertion of a constitutional pluralism,[41] or the belief that the European Union is an essentially contested project,[42] in an attempt to come to grips with this complexity.

In the end, it surely matters not whether we call the EU a federal system or not. It exhibits enough federal features to satisfy those who are determined to find it federal, and lacks some which would entitle purists to reject the title. It is perhaps simply misplaced to call the EU federal. While the concept of federalism is too rich and contested to be condensed into a simple explanation, it also does not feel quite right as an explanation of the EU, which is too *sui generis*, too complex, too multidimensional, to fit into any such categorisation. It has, as Weiler suggested, its own *Sonderweg*.

What this brief investigation into federalism and the EU does, however, suggest is that relations between the EU and Member States defy straightforward hierarchical relationships of EU centre to state periphery. This problematises Brexit as a zero-sum exercise of taking back control.

[37] See eg F Tuytschaever, *Differentiation in European Law* (Oxford, Hart, 1999); N Walker, 'Sovereignty and differentiated integration of the European Union' in Z Bankowski and A Scott (eds), *The European Union and its Legal Order* (Oxford, Blackwell, 2000).

[38] Although these actually predated the TEU. Art 94(5) EEC, introduced by the SEA gave member states the chance to opt out of harmonisation on certain grounds.

[39] Per Walker, above n 37, 32.

[40] The first President of the Euratom Commission, Armand, would often refer to a 'Europe a la Carte', cited in F Duchêne, *Jean Monnet: The First Statesman of Interdependence* (New York, Norton, 1996) at 397.

[41] eg N MacCormick, *Questioning Sovereignty. Law, State and Nation in the European Commonwealth* (Oxford, Oxford University Press, 1999); N Walker, 'The Idea of Constitutional Pluralism' (2002) 65 *MLR* 317; M. Kumm, 'The Jurisprudence of Constitutional Conflict: Constitutional Supremacy in Europe before and after the Constitutional Treaty' (2005) 11 *ELJ* 262.

[42] Z Bankowski and A Scott, 'The European Union as an essentially contested project' in Z Bankowski and A Scott (eds), *The European Union and its Legal Order* (Oxford, Blackwell, 2000).

III. The UK: Federalism, Devolution and EU Membership

UK Devolution has a symbiotic relationship with both the EU and Brexit. Devolved nations have benefited from Britain's EU membership, and a large part of the problems caused by Brexit relate to Britain's internal Constitution.

A. The Status of the 'UK'—A Rejection of Federalism?

Britain is not a federal state. Although, in the period immediately preceding the First World War there was a brief enthusiasm for 'home rule all round',[43] in fact federalism has never operated within the UK, even if the idea of a grand federation, as applied to Britain's Empire-Commonwealth, did attract supporters until the 1930s.

The Union of Scotland and England was the founding act of the UK in 1707. Surprisingly, there has been little debate about what the 'Union' or 'Britain' is, or should be, even in the context of the first Scottish independence referendum. Must there be a shared constitutional identity for a Union to exist or flourish, in which case both the EU and the UK appear to suffer a problematic lack? The Treaty of Lisbon requires the EU to 'respect' the constitutional identity of states, but what is the UK's constitutional identity?

A salient question is whether it is correct to view the UK as a 'union state' rather than unitary in nature. The term 'union state' was forged by Rokkan and Urwin to connote a polity distinct both from the unitary and the federal state.[44] Although the concept of union is widely used in political and constitutional studies to refer to the consolidation of existing units into one, it is not the same as a unitary state, a term which implies a constitutional order with a single, unrivalled, legal competence, from which may be derived a fundamental 'rule of recognition' which places a central agency, the Queen in Parliament, in a position of unequivocal authority.

Britain therefore might be described as a 'union' state, as there is a strong argument that it lacks an unequivocal, unitary sovereignty (although many traditionalists would contest this point). There exist very different constitutional settlements in the different parts of the UK. Devolution is not symmetric.[45] Since 1998,

[43] See eg JE Kendle, 'The Round Table Movement And "Home Rule All Round"' (1968) XI *The Historical Journal* 332–53; also JE Kendle, *Federal Britain: A History* (New York, Routledge, 1997).

[44] S Rokkan and D Urwin, *Economy, Territory, Identity: Politics of West European Territories*, (London, Sage Publications, 1983); see also N Walker, 'Beyond the Unitary Conception of the United Kingdom Constitution' (2000) *Public Law* 384.

[45] AJ Ward, 'Devolution: Labour's Strange Constitutional Design' in J Jowell and D Oliver (eds), *The Changing Constitution* (Oxford, Oxford University Press, 2000) 111–36.

Scotland has developed some progressive constitutional forms,[46] as well as more pro-European inclinations that challenge the unitary constitutional approaches of London. The Scottish Parliament is for all intents and purposes permanent,[47] (yet many still adhere to the doctrine of the Parliamentary sovereignty of the Westminster Parliament). Although the Act of Union with Ireland in 1801 set up direct rule from Westminster, during the nineteenth century there was a campaign for Irish Home Rule (in which Dicey participated, arguing against it). Home Rule never came, rendered pointless by subsequent events, such as the Easter Rising of 1916, and the creation of the Irish Free State. However, Acts of Union may be too rigid and perfunctory for Ireland, where a variegated but pragmatic settlement of consociation and compromise has proved more successful in Northern Ireland in recent decades.[48] The EU has played its role in the peace process, providing structures for its continuation and Brexit now presents considerable challenges for Northern Ireland and the Republic. Such variegated Devolution illustrates competing constitutional narratives.

Therefore, as well as being a Union state, the UK is a *devolved* state, and the rise of 'post sovereignty' arguments referenced in the introduction raise issues about the relationship of Britain's component parts to the centre, to each other, and to the EU.

However, if we place the devolved nations of the UK in the context of sub-state communities elsewhere, it is apparent that self-government is not a cut and dried matter—ie either of complete independence or unitary state. In fact, there exist possibilities across the spectrum, eg: 'Independence lite'; 'Devo max'; or a quest for greater autonomy without necessarily becoming fully independent. There are comparisons to be made with Catalonia, or Quebec, but also precedents from elsewhere. Federalism is not the only solution. For example, Federacies,[49] such as the Åland Islands or Greenland, are instructive. Federacies share many features with traditional 'federal' systems, in that the sub-state unit and a larger state are linked in a federal relationship in which the sub-state unit has constitutionally guaranteed autonomy.

These examples might offer solutions to Britain's future relations with the EU,[50] but instead, there has been a tendency to perceive the UK's Constitution as singular. Federalism is so often ruled out. British experience in former transfers of power—whether in the case of Irish independence, or past constitutional relationships with former colonies, is rarely considered. Yet there are lessons to be learned. For example, between 1764 and 1776, the British Empire confronted a political

[46] Such as proportional representation for elections to the Holyrood Parliament. The Scottish Parliament is also bounded —its legislation must comply with human rights and EU law.

[47] s 1 Scotland Act 2016 states: 'The Scottish Parliament and the Scottish Government are a permanent part of the United Kingdom's constitutional arrangements.'

[48] See eg C McCrudden, 'Northern Ireland' in J Jowell and D Oliver (eds), *The Changing Constitution* 5th edn (Oxford, Oxford University Press, 2004).

[49] For further on federacies, see s III of this chapter.

[50] See further under s III for an exploration of this.

crisis over parliamentary sovereignty—the authority of the British Parliament over America. The Declaratory Act of 1766 asserted the right of the UK Parliament to legislate for the colonies 'in all cases whatsoever'.[51] However, by 1774, most American spokesmen argued that Parliament exercised no authority by right and asserted the failure of the British Constitution to provide for the governance of colonies. On this basis, Americans determined they were in a truly revolutionary situation. Warnings, such as Burke's, who argued it was better to allow American legislatures some independence than force compliance from afar were ignored.[52] These earlier debates on sovereignty are worth revisiting in the light of Brexit and renewed independence demands from Scotland. The lesson is that inflexibility over sovereignty is liable to have unfortunate consequences.

Some further comparisons (albeit tentative) between the British Empire-Commonwealth and the EU can be made. In the nineteenth and early twentieth centuries, Westminster was often known as the 'Imperial Parliament', passing legislation that affected any or all constituent parts of the British Empire. This 'Imperial legislation' predominated if faced with incompatible colonial laws, a situation in some ways comparable to the supremacy of EU law established in *Costa v ENEL* in 1966. However, unlike the EU Parliament, Westminster only contained representatives from UK constituencies, not all the other members. A further analogy can be found in the Privy Council, with its supreme legal jurisdiction over almost the entire British Empire, thus maintaining some uniformity over laws, in the same way the ECJ has attempted for the EU. Yet there was also resistance to placing Britain under the same final jurisdiction as the rest of the Empire, revealing doubts as to the competence of colonial judges and hostility to determination of British cases by 'foreign' judges,[53] a situation that persists to this day with Theresa May's 'red line' barring the post Brexit ECJ from jurisdiction over the UK.

Imperial federalists also argued the Empire must 'federate or disintegrate'.[54] The European Union faces similar dilemmas today in coping with competing centripetal and centrifugal forces.[55] Yet Imperial federation never succeeded and a lesson to be drawn is that British resistance to greater integration in a community of nations is nothing new, even where Britain was at the apex of that Empire.

The Commonwealth was popularly perceived as based on unwritten conventions with a minimum of written law,[56] which contrasts with the common image

[51] See D Ammerman, 'The British Constitution and the American Revolution: A Failure of Precedent' (1976) 17 *William and Mary Law Review* 473.

[52] E Burke, 'Speech on Conciliation with America', 1775, in Ian Harris (ed), *Pre-Revolutionary Writings* (Cambridge, Cambridge University Press, 1993).

[53] See eg T Mohr, 'The United Kingdom and Imperial federation, 1900 to 1939: a precedent for British legal relations with the European Union?' (2016) *Comparative Legal History* 131.

[54] See eg N Aroney, *The Constitution of a Federal Commonwealth: The Making and Meaning of the Australian Constitution* (Cambridge, Cambridge University Press, 2009); Maurice Ollivier, 'The Colonial and Imperial Conferences: From 1887 to 1937' 3 vols (Ottawa, Queen's Printer Cloutier, 1954).

[55] Mohr, above n 53.

[56] see eg H Duncan Hall, *Commonwealth: A History of the British Commonwealth of Nations* (London/New York, Von Nostrand Reinhold, 1971) 927.

of the EU as a vast network of rules and regulations.[57] The EU might be open-ended, without a clearly defined *telos,* but one way of distinguishing it from the UK is as a community of law, with treaties that serve as its written Constitution and an ECJ with power to declare national law ineffective if incompatible with EU law. It could and has been described as a *Rechtsgemeinschaft*.[58] The EU and European Convention on Human Rights (ECHR) also provide external guarantees and entrenchment of human rights, many of which will be critically at risk on Brexit when human rights law will be subject to UK parliamentary sovereignty, political override and repeals.

Churchill had the idea of three majestic overlapping circles (the US, the Commonwealth and Europe), stating 'we are the only country that has a great part in every one of them.'[59] Had Britain been less distracted by maintaining its global power in the 1950s, perhaps it might have played a larger role in reconstruction of Europe, and helped to shape an EU closer to British interests and inclinations. Rather, the EU developed as a source of disunion for Britain, and of disagreement between different parts of the UK. The product has been Brexit and the constitutional challenges it now poses.

B. The UK, the EU and Sovereignty

The EU prompts animosity from sectors of the UK population. It is just too 'foreign' for some. In particular, there is animosity that a newly developed foreign law can override such an ancient, organic system as the British Constitution, and debilitate Parliamentary sovereignty. Further, the EU's complex, confusing structures, going beyond mere 'red tape', may have the feel of an Escher construction, thus prompting further animosity. Yet, if the EU's constitutional structures may appear labyrinthine, the Brexit process is rendered highly problematic by the lack of any coherent conception of the British Constitution. Different parties settle on interpretations of constitutional law that support their case, but often there is no determinative answer.[60]

This point may be illustrated with the example of sovereignty. There is some irony in recognising that, just as scholars have proclaimed a post-sovereignty era, sovereignty claims seem to be escalating. There has been much talk of sovereignty in the Referendum context, with certain parties employing a mantra of 'Take back control', but there has been less clarity as to what sovereignty actually means.

[57] Mohr, above n 53, 159.

[58] This term was popularised by Walter Hallstein in the 1960s (W Hallstein, *Der unvollendete Bundesstaat* (Econ, Dusseldorf/Wien, 1969) 33–38): 'Sie ist Schopfung des Rechts, sie ist Rechtsquelle und sie ist Rechtsordnung'.

[59] WS Churchill, *Europe Unites: Speeches 1947 and 1948* (London, Cassell, 1950).

[60] For further on this see S Douglas-Scott, 'Brexit, Article 50 and the Contested British Constitution' (2016) 79 *MLR* 1019.

This confusion has obscured what is at stake in Britain's EU membership, in its insistence that sovereignty can be simplified into one message of 'Take Back Control'. However, at its most basic, there are at least three notions of sovereignty relevant in the context of Brexit, and they are often confused. The first is *parliamentary sovereignty*, which is said to have particular resonance in the UK because, due to the vagaries of the uncodified UK Constitution, the Westminster Parliament has been recognised as a body with unlimited legislative power. Yet the parliamentary sovereignty of a representative democracy may seem to be at odds with *popular sovereignty* as exercised in a referendum. Popular sovereignty also has other implications, such as in Scotland, where an indigenous Scottish tradition claims that sovereignty resides in the Scottish people, in spite of the alternative claims of Diceyan parliamentary sovereignty.[61] Third, there is *external sovereignty*: whereby a country may be sovereign and recognised as independent by the international community. But states recognise that international agreements such as NATO, or EU treaties, curb sovereignty in practice. However, these constraints are willingly accepted by states because of the benefits that pooling or ceding some sovereignty can bring—indeed it can even enhance sovereignty in another sense of a state's power or ability to deal with certain issues.[62]

The surprising thing is that there was so little clarity on the issue of sovereignty in the UK prior to Brexit (and the lack of clarity continues). The *Miller* case[63] may well be the last occasion on which the UK Supreme Court interprets the *nature* of EU law, an issue given perhaps less consideration in UK courts than it merited, even in the pivotal 1991 House of Lords *Factortame* judgment.[64] The relationship of EU law to national law has been a murky area of the British Constitution, and it is ironic that the most far reaching and definitive statement on the status of EU law within UK law was given by the Supreme Court in *Miller* when Britain is on the point of leaving the EU. For the majority of the Court, EU law is a 'source of UK law', a holding crucial to its analysis. The ECA is a 'conduit pipe' for EU law, which is 'an *independent* and overriding source of domestic law.' EU law was 'grafted onto', and so became a facet of, UK law.[65] This judgment recognises the special nature of EU law, and its distinction from international law more generally, because of its capacity for direct effect, and to act as an independent source of national law.[66] The judgment recognises that EU law is not a foreign body, but has

[61] See eg JDB Mitchell, 'Sovereignty of Parliament—Yet Again' (1963) 79 *Law Quarterly Review* 196.

[62] See further on this S Douglas-Scott, 'Brexit, the Referendum and the UK Parliament: Some Questions about Sovereignty', UK Constitutional Law Blog (28 Jun 2016) (available at https://ukconstitutionallaw.org/).

[63] *R (Miller) v Secretary of State for Exiting the European Union* [2017] UKSC 5.

[64] *Regina v Secretary of State for Transport, ex parte Factortame (No 2)* HL [1991] 1 AC 603.

[65] *Miller*, above n 63 at para 90.

[66] Contrast this view to that of the dissenting judges, for example Lord Reed, who held that 'EU law *not* itself an independent source of domestic law, but depends for its effect in domestic law on the ECA' (*Miller*, above n 63 at 228). Because Lord Reed perceived EU law as distinct from domestic law, triggering Article 50 could be a prerogative act, as it did not involve the removal of domestic rights in a traditional sense, nor the removal of a source of UK law.

become part of UK's national law, thus rejecting any straightforward dualist categorisation of EU law as international law. This is important because, if EU law is not just like any provision of international law,[67] it is different, special, *sui generis*, part of UK domestic law, and inevitably very complicated to dispose of, or convert into national legislation.[68]

C. The Problem of Brexit for Devolution

In the referendum on the UK's EU membership, the UK as a whole voted to leave. However, 62 per cent of Scotland's voting electorate, and 56 per cent of those voting in Northern Ireland, voted to remain. Yet the devolved nations have no formal role in the Article 50 withdrawal proceedings, and thus no means of ensuring that their constitutional interests are protected.

Further, although not always acknowledged, EU membership has provided an external support system for UK devolution, facilitating common approaches within the UK and conciliation between the UK and Ireland, and a venue for bilateral discussions. Somewhat ironically, Europe has provided a framework for alleviating sovereignty issues in practice, allowing a looser form of UK union. Indeed, EU membership has insulated devolved nations from a unitary UK wide approach, by, for example, distributing EU funds on a basis more beneficial to some parts of the UK than others (as with agriculture) an approach unlikely to continue post-Brexit, where a unified UK approach is likely to predominate, however unfavourable this may be to devolved interests.

Brexit, whatever its final form, risks undermining an already brittle devolution settlement and forcing it to change. The UK Government's 'Great Repeal Bill' White Paper[69] states: 'As powers are repatriated from the EU, it will be important to ensure that stability and certainty is not compromised, and that the effective functioning of the UK single market is maintained'[70] and that it will 'replicate the current frameworks provided by EU rules through UK legislation'.[71] This has been described as a 'holding pattern'[72] which would continue until it is decided whether a UK-wide framework is appropriate. It is unclear what the UK Government

[67] For an argument that EU law could be compared to double taxation treaties, see J Finnis, 'Terminating Treaty-based UK Rights', UK Constitutional Law Blog (26 Oct 2016) (available at https://ukconstitutionallaw.org/).

[68] A feat which will be attempted by the UK Great Repeal Bill and other legislation to domesticate EU law.

[69] Dept for Exiting the European Union, *Legislating for the United Kingdom's withdrawal from the European Union*, (30 March 2017) at 8, 28.

[70] ibid, at 27.

[71] ibid at 27, Para 4.4.

[72] Per Alun Cairns, Welsh Secretary, see 'Brexit holding pattern for EU Laws in Great Repeal Bill' *BBC News*, 30 March 2017.

means by 'frameworks'. In any event, any adjustments to the devolution settlement would require the consent of the Scottish Parliament and use of a LCM (Sewel) and are discussed below.

The problem is that UK devolution took place within the structures of the larger EU Internal Market, so it was not necessary to provide a detailed framework for a UK Internal Market. Prior to the UK's accession to the (then) EEC, the 1973 Kilbrandon Report on the Constitution was able to state that

> the UK is a unitary state in economic terms ... It has, for example, a single currency and a banking system responsible to a single central bank. Its people enjoy a right of freedom of movement of trade, labour and capital and of settlement and establishment anywhere within the UK.[73]

However, almost immediately, the UK joined the (then) EEC and the EU presently controls much of the UK's economic union, relocating the machinery that might be needed for a UK Internal Market to EU level, also facilitating a less intrusive devolution settlement than might otherwise have been required.

Federal and other non-unitary states have had to make provision to ensure policy harmonisation or prevent barriers to trade. For example, the US has its commerce clause, which states that the United States Congress shall have power 'To regulate Commerce with foreign Nations, and among the several States, and with the Indian Tribes.'[74] Article 73 (1) (5) German Constitution states that

> The Federation shall have exclusive legislative power with respect to: ... the unity of the customs and trading area, treaties regarding commerce and navigation, the free movement of goods, and the exchange of goods and payments with foreign countries, including customs and border protection.

However, post Brexit, it is difficult to determine what the UK Government has in mind—whether it plans to set up some new intra-governmental machinery or to legislate to put in place UK wide free movement principles which courts could enforce. However, whatever the mechanism, the UK Government will need to act with attention to the devolutionary settlement and Sewel convention.

James Bryce, an Oxford professor and a rival of Dicey in the nineteenth century, wrote of the *centripetal* and *centrifugal* forces that operate on Constitutions.[75] Devolution may be a centrifugal force—pulling (if unsuccessfully) towards

[73] *Royal Commission on the Constitution 1969–1973*, Vol 1 Report, HMSO, London 1973 (Cmnd 5460) para 57.

[74] United States Constitution (Art I, s 8, Clause 3).

[75] J Bryce, 'The Action of Centripetal and Centrifugal Forces on Political Constitutions' in J Bryce, *Studies in History and Jurisprudence, vol 1* (Oxford, Clarendon Press, 1901). For a specific analysis of Bryce in the EU context, see D Edward, 'The Community's Constitution—Rigid or Flexible? The Contemporary Relevance of the Constitutional Thinking of James Bryce' in D Curtin and T Heukels (eds), *Institutional Dynamics of European Integration: Essays in Honour of Henry G Schermers*, vol II (Dordrecht, Martinus Nijhoff, 1994) 58.

complete independence as in Scotland's first independence referendum, and raising the possibility of another such referendum. Centrifugal currents carry a risk of dissolution, whereby small sections of the population can determine futures—Scots could vote for independence (and in 2014, this could have been accomplished by 50.01 per cent of those voting in an already small nation); Brexit is interpreted as requiring the UK to leave the EU on the back of an 'advisory' referendum in which only 37 per cent of eligible UK voters voted to leave the EU;[76] and the Northern Ireland peace settlement could collapse, leading to a vote for unification of Northern Ireland with the Republic of Ireland.

As far as the constitutional structures of the UK are concerned, Brexit may have centripetal or centrifugal effects. There are impulses towards recentralisation and a reassertion of Westminster sovereignty, as powers are repatriated from the EU. English, Scottish, Irish and Welsh unionists prefer the UK union to that of the EU, discarding Leave or Remain affiliations. In such a situation, Scottish and Irish nationalists are marginalised, without support in Westminster to stop the process.

Yet, on the other hand, there exist centrifugal forces. There is the possibility of UK disintegration with Scottish independence and Irish reunification. To be sure, neither of these potential scenarios is uncomplicated. A united Ireland would be within the EU;[77] an independent Scotland would have a good chance of joining.[78] This prospect maintains both Scotland and Ireland within the EU, but at the expense of new borders with the remaining United Kingdom, which will may or may not be hard depending on the rest of the UK (rUK)'s future relationship with the EU Single Market. Further, independence and reunification are divisive and factious within Scotland and Northern Ireland.

D. A Federal UK?

Might a federal plan, or written Constitution, for a post-Brexit Britain provide a solution to some of the conundrums outlined above? Is there any evidence that Brexit will provide a 'constitutional moment' in which a common solution will be found to these constitutional conundrums? It is unlikely that the framework of the 1688 constitutional settlement, which gave rise to parliamentary supremacy, can resolve the revolution unleashed by Brexit, not least because devolved nations have already undergone a form of constitutional transformation, more accepting of qualified and circumscribed sovereignty than the rest of the UK. Yet advocates of Scottish independence, or a united Ireland, may have little enthusiasm

[76] eg Unlock Democracy, 'Brexit: One Year on,' available at http://www.unlockdemocracy.org/blog/brexit-one-year-on.

[77] 'Europe could allow a united Ireland to join EU after Brexit' *The Guardian*, 28 April 2017.

[78] See eg S Douglas-Scott, 'How Easily Could an Independent Scotland Join the EU?' Oxford *Legal Studies Research Paper No* 46/2014.

for an arrangement that would anchor them into the UK, even if it provided authoritative and legally enforceable constitutional procedures for protecting different national communities within the state. And those satisfied with the prospect of Brexit are unlikely to desire a written Constitution or federal option, given that a desire for strong parliamentary sovereignty is likely to have motivated their euroscepticism in the first place. Such approaches, and distinct political identities, may militate against a comprehensive approach which would address the capacity of the British Constitution to deal with issues of disputed authority and challenges of Brexit.

Although the UK Liberal Democrat party has long favoured a federal UK, other parties have not done so to date. However, post-Brexit, things might have changed. In 2016, the Constitution Reform Group, led by former Conservative cabinet minister Lord Salisbury, argued for radical constitutional change in the UK.[79] They argued that Devolution should be 'turned upside down' to create a federal Britain, contending that the existing union should be replaced with fully devolved government in each part of the UK, each with complete sovereignty over its own affairs. Such a construction would require transformation of the UK's current constitutional arrangement, in which sovereignty formally rests in the centre and has been devolved on a partial and incremental basis. The group proposed that shared UK functions would include the monarchy as head of state, foreign affairs, defence, national security, immigration, international treaties, human rights, the supreme court, a single currency, a central bank function, financial services regulation, income and corporation tax powers, and the civil service. Other functions of the existing UK would be controlled by the nations and regions, similar in effect to the 'devo-max' proposal often promoted in Scotland.[80] The Group's proposals were drafted into an Act of Union bill promoted as a basis for discussion.[81]

The Constitution Reform Group is one of several proposals that emerged since Brexit for a more federal UK. A further example is that of Welsh First Minister Carwyn Jones, who suggested that Brexit provided an opportunity to 'reinvent and strengthen' the United Kingdom.[82] Jones suggested that a proposed UK Council of Ministers would take over from the current Joint Ministerial Council, which he dismissed as a 'talking shop'. He also called for a convention looking at the wider questions about the future of the UK once it leaves the EU.

[79] 'Brexit vote paves way for federal union to save UK, says all-party group', *The Guardian* 10 July 2016.

[80] 'Devo-max' would give Holyrood the power over most reserved matters, except defence and foreign affairs. It was discussed but not offered on the ballot in the 2014 Scottish Independence Referendum.

[81] Available at: http://www.constitutionreformgroup.co.uk/wp-content/uploads/2015/09/CRG-Act-of-Union-Bill.pdf; see also See Bingham Centre for the Rule of Law, *Draft Charter of the Union with Explanatory Notes*, 2016.

[82] 'Brexit an opportunity to reinvent the UK—Carwyn Jones' *BBC News*, 17 June 2017.

IV. Differentiated Relationships

A. Scotland's Place in Europe: Single Market Membership for Scotland?

In December 2016, the Scottish Government published a White Paper, *Scotland's Place in Europe.*[83] This Paper attempts to provide a solution to the problem caused by the EU Referendum vote, whereby although the UK voting public voted by 51.9 per cent to leave the EU, 62 per cent of Scots voted to remain.[84] This White Paper contemplates continued Single Market membership for Scotland, even in the absence of Single Market membership for 'rUK'.[85] However, the UK Government appeared to have rejected this approach, leaving very little space for Scotland to protect its interests in the context of the withdrawal process, where it is the UK that will do the negotiating, thus apparently embracing a unitary and top down approach.[86] But, at time of writing, given the unstable minority Government situation, the prospect of a new and different UK Government, more willing to accommodate a differentiated solution, may not be ruled out. Further, the UK Government has acknowledged that a special solution must be found for Northern Ireland, in order to prevent the return of a 'hard' border, between Northern Ireland and the Irish Republic, so it would seem that some sort of differentiated solution must be contemplated there, at least.

B. EU Law

First, let us start with EU membership. The EU treaties suggest that only States can be members of the EU (Article 49 TEU: 'Any European *State* ... may apply to become a member of the Union.'[87]) Neither Scotland, nor Northern Ireland, are independent States, but part of the UK, and while this situation continues, their relationship with the EU is linked to that of the UK. In traditional international law, the 'state' is a formal recognisable category, with legal personality, in a way that

[83] *Scotland's Place in Europe*, available at: http://www.gov.scot/Resource/0051/00512073.pdf. The Welsh and Northern Irish Governments also provided proposals, but this chapter focusses on the Scottish Paper for reasons of space.

[84] The EU Referendum Act itself failed to include a 'quadruple lock' guarantee, whereby a leave vote would be required in each nation of the UK in order for the UK to leave the EU.

[85] Although *Scotland's Place in Europe* starts by recommending continued Single Market access for the whole UK.

[86] See eg *The United Kingdom's exit from and new partnership with the European Union* White Paper, Cm 9417, 2 February 2017.

[87] Emphasis added.

the region usually is not.[88] The EU itself was founded as an entity of international law, set up by an intergovernmental Treaty, within which sovereign states dominated (although it is accepted that the EU has now evolved beyond a classic international law model.)[89] The EU has not tended to acknowledge many opportunities for involvement of sub-national regions in its government and administration, even where those regions exercise extensive, or even exclusive, power over a policy area. If the UK withdraws from the EU, it might seem that devolved nations have no legal route to remaining in the EU.

C. EU Provisions Allowing Sub-state Participation

However, there do exist provisions in the EU treaties that permit sub-state entities to participate in certain EU institutions. The main problem, however, is that all of these provisions are dependent on a state already being a member of the EU, and allowing greater regional empowerment within that membership, so they are hard to apply in the context of a UK that is negotiating to leave. However, these provisions are evidence of a growing view that the EU should be less concerned with imposing uniform laws across its Member States, and more concerned with flexibility, differentiation and accommodation of regional variation.

The 1992 Maastricht Treaty first introduced measures to accord a clearly regional dimension of integration within the EU, partly under pressure from regional actors, especially the German Länder. It was then that the principle of subsidiarity[90] was first formally introduced into EU law (although at that stage without its later clarification that policy requirements can also be satisfied at regional and local level), and provision was also made for regional, and not only central, government ministers to represent a Member State in the Council.[91] A new institution, the Committee of the Regions, was created,[92] which some hoped would stimulate a 'Europe of the Regions' as a next step in European integration, that would enable direct engagement between EU institutions and the regions.

[88] eg Montevideo Convention on Rights and Duties of States 1933, Art 1. As with the EU, under UN Charter Art 4, only 'States' can be admitted to UN membership. However, the PCIJ analysis in the *Western Sahara* case is a good example of the clash between the classical concept of statehood and other cultural concepts of control over territory (ICJ Reports (1975) 10); see also R Portman, *Legal Personality in International Law* (Cambridge, Cambridge University Press, 2013); M Koskeniemmi, 'The Future of Statehood' (1991) 32 *Harvard Journal of International Law* 397; H Michelmann, P Soldatos (eds), *Federalism and International Relations, the Role of Subnational Units* (Oxford, Oxford University Press, 1990); C Schreuer, 'The Waning of the Sovereign State: Towards a New Paradigm for International-Law?' (1993) 4 *EJIL* 447–71.

[89] See further on this, Case 26/62 *van Gend en Loos* ECR [1963] 1.

[90] Former EC Treaty, Art 5—see now Art 5(3) TEU.

[91] Although the Treaty did not specifically refer to regional ministers, it made provision for the participation of a 'representative of each Member State at ministerial level, authorised to commit the government of that Member State'—Former EC Treaty, Art 203—see now Art 16(2) TEU.

[92] Former EC Treaty, Art 263—see now Arts 305–07 TFEU.

However, 25 years later, the Committee of the Regions is still not acknowledged as an EU formal institution under Article 13 TEU.

It has been claimed[93] that approximately 80 per cent of devolved policies fall within EU competences—eg fisheries, agriculture, environmental policy and economic development. Regional considerations may require a distinctive policy approach from devolved administrations and potentially differential implementation of EU law obligations to that of the other parts of the Member State. So there already exists within the UK an increasing body of differently implemented laws, reflecting different and distinct devolved policies, such as under the Water Framework Directive.[94] The issue of differentiated implementation of EU law within a Member State was also raised in the *Horvath* case,[95] decided by the ECJ in 2009, where the European Court held that that Member States are free to allocate powers internally as they see fit, so long as the law is implemented correctly.

Other examples are provided by further treaty provisions and protocols. For example, Article 4(2) TEU provides that 'the Union shall respect the Member States' national identities inherent in their fundamental structures, political and constitutional, *inclusive of regional and local self-government*.' However, notably, Article 4(2) continues, 'It shall respect their essential State functions, *including ensuring the territorial integrity of the State*, maintaining law and order and safeguarding national security' (emphases added). On the other hand, Protocol No 2 to the Lisbon Treaty on Subsidiarity and Proportionality, while identifying central parliaments of the Member States as key players, leaves scope for further co-ordination with sub-state parliaments.

However, all in all, existing provisions of EU law are premised on a sub-state entity being part of a larger Member State which is itself already part of the EU, so they seem less relevant for the question of how the varying interest of the different sub-states of the UK could be accommodated in the Brexit context.

D. EEA Membership

However, *Scotland's Place in Europe* argued not for EU membership, but for continued Single Market membership, possibly through the European Economic Area (EEA).[96] Would this be achievable? The EEA is not part of the EU, although does

[93] See eg J Hunt, 'Devolution and differentiation: regional variation in EU law' (2010) 30 *Legal Studies* 421–41; C Carter, 'The Formulation of UK-EU Policy Post-Devolution: A Transformative Model of Governance?' Manchester Papers in Politics MPP 9/2002, 1, available at http://www.socialsciences.manchester.ac.uk/disciplines/politics/publications/workingpapers/documents/manchester_working_papers/MPP092002.pdf.

[94] Directive 2000/60/EC of the European Parliament and of the Council of 23 October 2000 establishing a framework for Community action in the field of water policy, [2000] OJ L327/1.

[95] Case C-428/07 *R (Horvath) v Secretary of State for Environment, Food and Rural Affairs* [2009] ECR I-6355.

[96] For further on the EEA see eg T-I Harbo, 'The European Economic Area Agreement: A Case of Legal Pluralism' (2009) 78 *Nordic Journal of International Law* 201.

apply many EU Single Market laws. For example, the same legal principles may apply in the context of EU law and EEA law but with different enforcement and adjudication mechanisms. A special EEA court (the EFTA[97] court) rather than the ECJ adjudicates. New terminology has evolved—eg EEA institutions engage in 'decision shaping' rather than the 'decision making' of the EU bodies.[98]

Nonetheless, admitting a sub-state such as Scotland, or Northern Ireland, to the EEA raises some problems.

First, there would have to be a change to EFTA and EEA rules to allow in a sub-state (whether as full or associate member or member 'through' the UK). For example, Scotland, although a nation in its own right, lacks the legal personality and external legal competence to enter into treaties on its own behalf—unlike some other sub-state entities, for example, the Belgian regions.[99]

Second, Scotland's application for EEA membership would depend on 'UK sponsoring', as the UK Government would have to negotiate this as part of a UK withdrawal treaty. *Scotland's Place in Europe* gives the example of the Faroe Islands, which explored the EEA option under Danish sponsorship. However, this has not yet been achieved. In any case, it is not clear that the political will exists for this purpose in the UK government. The Scottish Paper, however, also argues from analogy that, whatever solutions might be found for the Irish border (promised by UK government) should also be applied to relations between Scotland and 'rUK'.

Third, there would need to be a wider-ranging devolution of powers to Scotland to enable it to comply with Single Market rules ranging from employment and social policy to product and professional standards, health and safety, consumer protection and migration. For example, powers over immigration might need to be devolved. Such a transfer of power could not be achieved by the Repeal Bill but would require separate UK primary legislation, devolving powers to Scotland, and providing it with legal personality and the ability to conclude international agreements in its own right, as well as subsequent Scottish legislation on EU Single Market matters. So far, there is little evidence that the UK Government is contemplating this. For example, although the notion of 'regional visas' could also be explored for other parts of the UK,[100] devolution of immigration is something Theresa May seems to have ruled out.[101]

More generally, there are issues with a differentiated settlement for Scotland that require, in the words of the Scottish Government, some legal 'engineering'. *Scotland's Place in Europe* suggests that Scotland would remain in a Customs

[97] EFTA being the acronym for the 'European Free Trade Association'.

[98] For these terms, see C Harding, 'The Identity of European Law: Mapping out the European Legal Space' (2000) 6 *European Law Journal* 128, at fn 99, at 138.

[99] See eg D Criekemans (ed) *Regional Substate Diplomacy Today* (Dordrecht, Martinus Nijhoff, 2010).

[100] Price Waterhouse Cooper: *Regional Visas—A Unique Immigration Solution* (October 2016) prepared for the City of London Corporation.

[101] 'Theresa May rules out Scots deal on immigration despite warnings', *The Herald*, 5 February 2017.

Union with 'rUK' so that the internal border between Scotland and rUK would not be a customs border, thus avoiding the potential problems facing the island of Ireland. However, it would still be necessary to distinguish Scottish exports to the EU from 'rUK' exports which would need to pay EU tariffs. The situation would be more complicated still with non-tariff barriers, as the situation of 'rUK' goods which are non-compliant with EU standards reveals. These could be sold in Scotland under what the Paper terms 'parallel marketability'[102] but not to other EEA countries. But there would be a need for some system to ensure these goods were not then exported to the EU, thus circumventing EU rules.

E. Differentiated EU Membership

Beyond contemplating EEA membership, there are also further examples of ways in which diverse parts of a state may have different relationships with the EU. Some of these examples come from Britain itself. One such example is the Isle of Man and Channel Islands. These are not part of the UK or EU, but possessions of the British Crown. Nonetheless, Protocol 3 Accession Treaty of the UK to the (then) EEC permits trade for their goods without non-EU tariffs. However they are excluded from the provisions governing free movement of people.[103] Another example is that of Gibraltar, which is a British overseas territory with its own Constitution and self-government, except for defence and foreign affairs for which the British Government is responsible. Although part of the EU, Gibraltar is outside the Customs Union and VAT area, exempted from the CAP, and does not form part of Schengen. Gibraltar has no option of cancelling its EU membership separately from the UK, but has stated that it wishes to remain in the EU, notwithstanding the Brexit vote. Yet while the Northern Irish border was mentioned in the letter triggering the UK's withdrawal under Article 50 TEU, Gibraltar was not. On 1 April 2017, a draft document on the EU's Brexit strategy said no agreement on the EU's future relationship with the UK would apply to Gibraltar without the consent of Spain, giving it a potential veto.[104] This situation remains to be resolved.

A last example (although one could give many others) of the differentiated membership of the EU is provided by the no longer extant West Berlin. In 1955, the Federal Republic of Germany (FRG) had no governmental authority over Berlin[105] and the Allied Control Authority, City Council and Senate were the only governing bodies in Berlin.[106] At the time of the Treaty of Rome in 1957, which set up the EEC, Berlin was not treated as a European territory for whose external

[102] *Scotland's Place in Europe*, above n 83, at para 152.

[103] Their relationship with the EU generally is set out under Art 355(5)(c) TFEU, and Protocol 3 of the Act of Accession, annexed to the Treaty of Accession 1972.

[104] 'Brexit: Gibraltar angered by Spain's EU "veto"', *BBC News*, 1 April 2017.

[105] See eg P Jessup, 'The Rights of the United States in Berlin' (1949) 43 *AJIL* 92.

[106] See *Hartje v Yugoslav Military Mission* (1954) 21 ILR 116, 119.

relations the FRG was responsible under the treaties.[107] Instead, the treaties were extended to Berlin by special declaration annexed to the Treaty of Rome. This distinct status of Berlin, separate from the FRG, was confirmed by a Quadripartite Agreement and Associated Arrangements of 3 September 1971.[108] This agreement declared that West Berlin was 'not to be a constituent part of the Federal Republic of Germany and not to be governed by it'. Shortly before German reunification, the British Government stated to the House of Commons Foreign Affairs Committee that: 'Germany as a whole continues to exist as a State in international law, and the special Berlin area remains subject to a special quadripartite status.'[109]

The point of this excursus into the status of a now defunct territory is that a significant territory, such as West Berlin, closely linked to the FRG, and yet subject to government by different states' authorities altogether, could enjoy membership of the EEC up to 1990, in spite of (then) Article 237 EEC treaty, which declared 'Any European *State* may apply to become a member of the Community' (emphasis added).

F. 'Reverse Greenland'

For a while, immediately after the 2016 EU Referendum, the 'reverse Greenland' option was floated as a possibility for Scotland. In 1985, Greenland, which is part of Denmark, withdrew from the (then) EEC, although Denmark remained.[110] As the EEC treaties at that time contained no provision for the withdrawal either of a Member State or a part thereof, the necessary arrangements had to be negotiated.[111] The basis for Greenland's withdrawal was former Article 236 EEC (now Article 48 TEU). Following withdrawal, Greenland became associated with the EU as an Overseas Country and Territory through the Greenland Treaty.

Therefore, it was suggested that the EU treaties might be similarly amended, enabling Scotland to remain a member of the EU, even if England/'rUK' were to leave. However, there are obstacles to this. The main issue to be negotiated at the time of Greenland's departure concerned fishing rights, whereas there are multiple issues of contention in the case of Brexit. Furthermore, the part of Denmark that remains within the EU contains its central government, in Copenhagen. However, if 'rUK' were to withdraw and Scotland remain in the EU, the UK's central government would be located in England.

[107] (former) EEC Treaty, Art 227(4), 298 UNTS 11.

[108] Quadripartite Agreement, Berlin, 3 September 1971, 10 ILM 895, 880 UNTS 123.

[109] FCO Memorandum to House of Commons Foreign Affairs Committee on the Status of the Two German States, March 1990, reprinted (1991) 61 *BY* 494.

[110] This took a considerable time—three years. See further on the Greenland case, eg F Weiss, 'Greenland's Withdrawal from the European Communities' (1985) *ELRev* 173; also M Nash, 'Could Britain Leave the European Union? The Greenland Option' 46 *NLJ* 6752.

[111] See on this eg *Status of Greenland: Commission Opinion*, COM (83) 66 final, 2 February 1983, 12.

However, the Greenland case at least provides a precedent. It is possible for only part of a state to secede from the EU. Article 29 of the Vienna Convention on the Law of Treaties provides: 'Unless a different intention appears from the treaty or is otherwise established, a treaty is binding upon each party in respect of its entire territory'.[112] This implies it would be possible for a new amendment treaty to redefine which parts of UK territory fall within the scope of EU law. Indeed, when the Federal Republic of Germany enlarged in 1990, (then) EEC Member States accepted that the treaties could apply to its expanded territory without even being specifically amended, thus avoiding the lengthy and risky amendment procedure.

G. Federacies and Associate States

One reason that explains why the Greenland example might seem fanciful in the Brexit context relates to Greenland's legal status, which is different from that of Scotland or Northern Ireland. Greenland has greater autonomy than the UK's devolved nations, and is in fact a federacy, a status similar to but legally distinct from federalism. If we look more closely at the position of sub-state nations and federacies there are some useful examples.[113] Federacies (and associate states)[114] have much in common with situations of asymmetrical devolution such as that in Scotland or Northern Ireland, in that they concern a relationship between a smaller territorial unit and a larger state, in which the smaller unit shares the benefits of association with the larger polity but retains internal autonomy and self-government.

Federacies are usually small populations, and are often islands. There are less than 20 of them in existence. Stepan, Linz and Yadav define a *federacy* in the following way:

> [A] federacy is a political-administrative unit in an independent unitary state with exclusive power in certain areas, including some legislative power, constitutionally or quasi-constitutionally embedded, that cannot be changed unilaterally and whose inhabitants have full citizenship rights in the otherwise unitary state.[115]

[112] See further eg O Dörr, K Schmalenbach (eds), *The Vienna Convention on the Law of Treaties: A Commentary* (Berlin, Springer, 2012).

[113] Dr Eve Hepburn and I addressed this issue in our written evidence to the Scottish Parliament inquiry into the 'Scotland Clauses' in 2015 (Scottish Parliament Devolution (Further Powers) Committee Implementing the Smith Agreement: The UK Government's Draft Legislative Clauses). Our evidence, *The 'Permanence' Issue: A Question of Symbolism or Power?* is available here at: http://www.scottish.parliament.uk/S4_ScotlandBillCommittee/General%20Documents/Dr_E_Hepburn.pdf.

[114] According to Ronald Watts, examples of federacies are the Aaland Islands (Finland), Azores Islands (Portugal), Faroe Islands (Denmark), Greenland (Denmark), Guernsey (United Kingdom), Isle of Man (United Kingdom), Jammu and Kashmir (India), Jersey (United Kingdom), Madeira Islands (Portugal), Northern Marianas (United States), and Puerto Rico (United States). Examples of associated states are Bhutan (India), Cook Islands (New Zealand), Liechtenstein (Switzerland), Monaco (France), Netherlands Antilles (Netherlands), Nieue Island (New Zealand), and San Marino (Italy) (R Watts, 'Foreword: States, Provinces, Lander, and Cantons: International variety among Subnational Constitutions' (1999–2000) 31 *Rutgers Law Journal* 941).

[115] A Stepan, J Linz, Y Yadav, *Crafting State-Nations: India and Other Multinational Democracies* (Baltimore, Johns Hopkins University Press, 2011).

In such arrangements, there is considerable *self-rule*, but much less *shared-rule* than in federal states such as Germany, for example.

So, for example, Denmark and Finland have both legislated Autonomy (also called Self Government or Home Rule) Acts that constitutionally protect the self-governing powers of some of their sub-state units, including Greenland, the Faroe Islands and the Åland Islands.[116] These sub-state units can veto any competence transfer away from them and thus escape the constitutional uncertainty of their powers being revoked, unlike in the case of devolved states which endure a hierarchical relationship with the centre, which is Scotland's current status in the UK due to the ongoing doctrine of the sovereignty of the Westminster Parliament (even following the most recent Scotland Act 2016, which includes a 'permanence' clause for the Scottish Parliament).

Associate states are similar to federacies, in that the smaller unit benefits from a high level of internal self-determination and its autonomy is constitutionally guaranteed. In the associate statehood model, the sub-state unit has substantial autonomy over a range of competences (indeed, often more extensive than those of a federacy), whilst the larger power often assumes control for foreign policy and defence. However, in contrast to federacies, the relationship 'can be dissolved be either of the units acting alone on prearranged terms.'[117] As a result, as Watts states, their stability is less secure. Among their number are European examples—for example, Monaco is associated with France, and Liechtenstein with Switzerland. Other examples are provided by the relationships between the United States and the Marshall Islands, and New Zealand and the Cook Islands.

So, if UK devolution were to develop further, and for example Scotland evolve into federacy status, then it is perhaps conceivable that with that greater degree of autonomy, it could form its own relationship with the EU or EEA, including even the sort of differentiated relationship we see between the EU and Denmark and Greenland. However, what distinguishes 'federacies' from other traditional federal models—such as Germany, Canada, Belgium or the USA—is that in federacies the autonomous institutions of a sub-state territory in an otherwise unitary state may be made permanent, *but without the necessity of dividing the rest of the state into separate sub state political units*, and therefore 'federalising' the rest of the country. In the present circumstances, it is not so likely that the UK will undertake a more profound and radical process of federal reform across the entire territory, and thus the federacy model is more appropriate to understand for example Scotland's evolving status in the UK.

[116] For Greenland, see the Greenlandic Self Government Act (Act no 473 of the Danish Parliament 12 June 2009). For the Faroes see the Faroese Home Rule Act (Act 137 of the Danish Parliament of 23 March 1948). The Faroe Islands have around 45,000 inhabitants and are located in the Atlantic Ocean, west of Norway and north of Scotland. The Faroe Islands are not a part of the European Union.

The current Self-Government (Autonomy) Act of the Åland Islands was enacted by the Parliament of Finland in 1991 (No 1144/1991).

[117] RL Watts, *Comparing Federal Systems in the 1990s* (Belfast, Queen's University Press, 1999) 8–9.

Federacies and associated states may provide some useful examples concerning a sub-state entity's relationship with a unitary state and with an international organisation. However, they enjoy only limited shared rule, and have limited powers in foreign policy matters. This is a problem, while EU subject matter, although concerning many devolved areas, is treated as a foreign policy matter and thus for determination by the unitary state overall.

V. Conclusion

There are many legal, constitutional and transnational forms and battles in our present age. The reality is not coherent but messy. The British Constitution is an 'old building' and it is hard to renovate. The EU may be a 'post sovereign' entity, but its structures are often inchoate and unclear. International and national institutions overlap and vie for supremacy.

Brexit has produced a legal and constitutional headache for the UK and EU. This chapter has explored some of the possibilities suggested by devolution, federalism, federacy and other structures as solutions to these conundrums. It attempts to build on the spirit of 'post sovereignty' while acknowledging that there are no easy answers. Brexit presents a challenge, not just to constitutional law and international relations, but also to the legal imagination. How to bring about these legal and constitutional futures? Is constitutional law too limited in its imagination to conceive governance structures separate from the state? Is EU law overly focused on its own autonomy and supremacy? There is a need for trust, fair dealing and mutual respect between institutions of jurisdictions, and for less preoccupation with autonomy and unity.

It has been suggested that the British built up an Empire and then decolonised in a 'fit of absence of mind'.[118] The same may be true of Brexit, where Britain joined the EEC without any real enthusiasm, and now risks leaving the EU in a state of insouciance as to the consequences. A closer look at the solutions outlined above, however, suggests that there are other possibilities.

[118] JR Seeley, *The Expansion of England* (London, 1883) 8.

8

Federal Dynamics of the UK/Strasbourg Relationship

ROGER MASTERMAN*

I. Introduction

In his 1989 essay '"Federal" aspects of the European Convention on Human Rights' (ECHR), Colin Warbrick examined the 'extent to which or the manner in which federal concerns make a difference to the interpretation of bills of rights.'[1] Specifically, Warbrick asked:

> How is State autonomy to be maintained against a centralising tendency of the federal judiciary ... which extends the reach of protected rights into areas previously regulated by States? How is the contest between demands of national uniformity and the ability of the States to respond to local needs to be resolved?[2]

Taking as his starting point the nationalising tendencies of the United States Supreme Court in the sphere of individual rights in the post-New Deal era, Warbrick queried the extent to which the European Court of Human Rights could be said to be pursuing a similarly centralising approach, 'Europeanising' standards of individual rights at the expense of variation and policy autonomy across the Member States. Observing the expansion by the United States Supreme Court of the protections afforded by the Bill of Rights during that period,[3] Warbrick suggested that a state-level counter-reaction had become evident, with the 'perception now being that the national intervention has extended into matters "properly" falling within the power of the States.'[4] At the time of writing, Warbrick was able to conclude that, while the reach of the European Convention into domestic affairs

* My thanks are due to Janneke Gerards, Alan Greene, Colin Warbrick and Se-shauna Wheatle for their comments on an earlier draft.

[1] C Warbrick, '"Federal" Aspects of the European Convention on Human Rights' (1989) 10 *Michigan Journal of International Law* 698.

[2] ibid, 699.

[3] For an overview see: WH Rehnquist, *The Supreme Court* (New York, Vintage Books, 2002), ch 10.

[4] Warbrick, above n 1, 703.

was extensive, the interventions of the Strasbourg Court had not (yet) provoked comparable counter-dynamics; the reach of the Convention had not 'threatened the "States as States"'.[5]

But given contemporary debates in the UK—and elsewhere—surrounding the relative influence of domestic authorities and the European Court of Human Rights within the Convention scheme,[6] Warbrick's unease was prescient. As the jurisprudence of the Strasbourg court added depth and greater specificity to the Convention's requirements, Warbrick was concerned that the Court would transgress the divide, 'however difficult it may be to define exactly, between international and constitutional interpretation' and in doing so 'transform the Convention into a constitutional bill of rights rather than an international convention.'[7] The consequences of this, Warbrick wrote, would be significant:

> The delicate and subtle relationship between the Convention system and the national legal system for the assurance of individual rights is a developing one. ... There are indications ... that a majority on the Court might want to abandon the constraints of this international relationship and aspire to a supra-national or constitutional role. The greater good of protecting individual rights would swamp the limitations imposed by considering contrary State interest, whether general or particular. The costs of this process, if pursued too enthusiastically, are not only likely to be a weakening of the legitimacy of the Convention system but, in the short term, an undermining of the national systems for protecting individual rights.[8]

For Warbrick, the tension between the centralising and decentralising characteristics of the Convention system provided insight into its 'federal' qualities, and its ability to effectively accommodate national interests and initiatives into an overarching multi-jurisdictional scheme for the protection of individual rights. In the context of the relationships between the European Court of Human Rights and national authorities within the UK, the growing perception of a power imbalance—of an *inability* on the part of the Court and Convention to accommodate such difference—animates deliberations over a UK Bill of Rights.[9]

[5] ibid, 723.

[6] On which see: P Popelier, S Lambrecht and K Lemmens (eds), *Criticism of the European Court of Human Rights—Shifting the Convention System: Counter-Dynamics at the National and EU Levels* (Antwerp, Intersentia, 2016).

[7] Warbrick, above n 1, 714. For a survey of the 'constitutionalisation' of international human rights instruments more generally see: S Gardbaum, 'Human Rights as International Constitutional Rights' (2008) 19 *EJIL* 749.

[8] Warbrick, above n 1, 723. Concern that the legitimacy of the European Court—and of the Convention system—would be threatened as a result of the Strasbourg Court's adjudicative approach was also a theme of Warbrick's later work (see: C Warbrick, 'The European Convention on Human Rights and the Human Rights Act: the view from the outside' in H Fenwick, G Phillipson and R Masterman (eds), *Judicial Reasoning under the UK Human Rights Act* (Cambridge, Cambridge University Press, 2007).

[9] See for instance: *Protecting Human Rights in the UK: The Conservatives' Proposals for Changing Britain's Human Rights Laws* (October 2014) (available at: https://www.conservatives.com/~/media/files/downloadable%20Files/human_rights.pdf); M Pinto-Duschinsky, *Bringing Rights Back Home:*

The consequences of the perceived trend towards centralisation have been to unsettle the balance between state and centralised authority that is inherent in the Convention system to the extent that—in the context of current UK political discourse at least—it is questionable whether the narrative of the Convention's architecture as 'subsidiary to the national systems'[10] retains widespread credibility. These debates have prompted calls for revision of both the internal and external dimensions of the UK/Strasbourg relationship. As to the external, it has become commonplace for the European Court of Human Rights to be accused of over-reach, of utilising the 'living instrument' doctrine to develop the Convention's protections illegitimately and, as a consequence, of increasingly interfering with national sovereignty.[11] The European Court's jurisprudence is amplified internally through the provisions and application of the Human Rights Act 1998 (HRA), which collectively affords—critics argue—an overly prominent role to the (European) 'Convention rights'[12] and Strasbourg jurisprudence[13] to the detriment of genuinely municipal solutions to the questions posed by rights adjudication.[14]

A desire to reassert national sovereignty in the face of perceived Strasbourg encroachment lies behind Conservative Party proposals to repeal the HRA and enact as its replacement a UK Bill of Rights.[15] This debate—which it is impossible to distinguish in its entirety from eurosceptic concerns regarding the influence of the European Union—is premised primarily on the sense that the Strasbourg Court is increasingly intervening in matters of policy that should rightly sit within the remit of national decision-makers.[16] Through the application of the Convention

Making Human Rights Compatible with Parliamentary Democracy in the UK (London, Policy Exchange, 2011). Concerns relating to the extent of the Strasbourg Court's influence over 'domestic' affairs pre-date the enactment of the HRA (see: E Bates, 'British Sovereignty and the European Court of Human Rights' (2012) 128 *LQR* 382).

[10] *Handyside v United Kingdom* (1979–1980) 1 EHRR 737, [48].

[11] As the former UK judge on the European Court of Human Rights, Sir Nicholas Bratza, has summarised: 'It is said that the "living instrument" doctrine has increasingly been used as a fig-leaf to cover the Court's enthusiasm for judicial activism, at the expense of the Convention's scope which its drafters had intended, and that the Court has overreached itself in its methods of interpretation of the Convention and transgressed into the realm of policy-making.' (N Bratza, 'Living Instrument or Dead Letter—the Future of the European Convention on Human Rights' [2014] European Human Rights Law Review 116, 118).

[12] s 1, Human Rights Act 1998.

[13] s 2(1), Human Rights Act 1998.

[14] *Protecting Human Rights in the UK: The Conservatives' Proposals for Changing Britain's Human Rights Laws*, above n 9, 5. Cf R Masterman, 'Taking the Strasbourg Jurisprudence into Account: Developing a "Municipal Law of Human Rights" under the Human Rights Act' (2005) 54 *International and Comparative Law Quarterly* 907.

[15] The Conservative Party is committed to 'consider our human rights legal framework when the process of leaving the EU concludes' (The Conservative Party, *Forward, Together: Our Proposals for a Stronger Britain and a Prosperous Future* (May 2017), 37). See also: House of Commons Justice Committee, Oral Evidence, The Work of the Secretary of State HC620, 7 September 2016, Q78–Q91; HC Debates, Vol.618, Col.355, 8 December 2016 (Jeremy Wright QC MP).

[16] The debate over prisoner voting following *Hirst v United Kingdom (No 2)* 42 EHRR 41 provides the paradigm example (for analysis see: CRG Murray, 'A Perfect Storm: Parliament and Prisoner Disenfranchisement' (2013) 66 *Parliamentary Affairs* 511).

rights to situations unforeseen at the time of their drafting and the progressive interpretation of the Convention as a 'living instrument', the policy autonomy of the States parties has—it is argued—been jeopardised by the perceived inability of the European Court to 'resist the temptation to aggrandise its jurisdiction and to impose uniform rules on Member States.'[17] The promise of a UK Bill of Rights responds to this tension through calls for rights adjudication to be repatriated and for supremacy over questions of rights to be restored to UK national institutions.[18] Discord between the UK Government and the European Court of Human Rights is therefore reflective of what Dicey identified as one of the potential costs of federalism, namely, 'the denial of national independence to every state' within the overarching federal structure.[19] Though one of the animating concerns of a federal structure is that the central authority should not be competent to arrogate powers to itself at the expense of the federation's component parts,[20] this is precisely the accusation levelled at the Strasbourg court.[21]

This chapter examines the federal pressures of the ECHR regime as manifested in the debate over the adoption of a UK Bill of Rights, arguing that, in spite of movement on the part of the Strasbourg court towards embracing a constitutionalised function, co-operation remains fundamental to the effectiveness of the ECHR regime. The core centralising difficulties of the growing reach of the ECHR and domestic amplification of the Convention jurisprudence via the HRA will be contrasted with evidence of the upward influence of national decision-making and moves—at the European level—to reiterate the subsidiarity integral to the Convention regime. In the light of the continued scope within the Convention system for subsidiarity to be realised in practice, it will be argued that the adoption of a UK Bill of Rights—and its promise of a clear demarcation of autonomous national decision-making—would mark a movement towards expression of exclusive competences and thereby contain potential to destabilise the co-operative constitutionalism which underpins the Convention system.

II. The 'Federal' Character of the ECHR

While the Convention system cannot be regarded as being fully federalised, it nonetheless displays significant federal—or pseudo-federal—characteristics.

[17] Lord Hoffmann, 'The Universality of Human Rights' (2009) 125 *LQR* 416, 424.

[18] *Protecting Human Rights in the UK: The Conservatives' Proposals for Changing Britain's Human Rights Laws*, above n 9, 5; J Forsyth, 'Chris Grayling: "I want to see our Supreme Court supreme again"', *The Spectator*, 28 September 2013.

[19] AV Dicey, *An Introduction to the Study of the Law of the Constitution* 8th edn reprint (Indianapolis, Liberty Fund, 1982) xcvii.

[20] E Barendt, *An Introduction to Constitutional Law* (Oxford, Clarendon Press, 1998) 64.

[21] For a robust defence of the Court in the face of these criticisms see: R Spano, 'Universality or Diversity of Human Rights? Strasbourg in an Age of Subsidiarity' (2014) 14(3) *Human Rights Law Review* 487.

Roots of the federal notion can be found in international law and relations; Locke's conception of the federative power was concerned with governmental powers beyond the state, and with the relations between otherwise autonomous state units on the international plane.[22] Though federal structures have subsequently evolved to regulate the internal dynamics of national and regional governance, parallels can clearly be drawn between the characteristics of internal federal structures and those inter-state arrangements which seek to distribute powers between centralised governance structures and otherwise autonomous state units.[23] If the legal relationship between state/national units and overarching multi-state/national institution(s) can be accepted as providing the bare minimum of a federal structure, it is certainly arguable that that in structuring cross-jurisdictional rights protections around an international (federal/centralised) court exercising a supervisory jurisdiction over national (states) authorities, linkages between the Convention system and explicitly federal systems can be drawn and that quasi-federal parallels can be identified.

The federal account of the Strasbourg Court and Convention is however subject to a number of qualifications. The fact that the Convention system rests upon an international structure that is not by design, avowedly federal, raises particular issues for those seeking to compare it to a single-state federal configuration. It should be acknowledged for instance (as Warbrick did) that, in contradistinction to a system of divided powers within a sole state, the 'functional demand for uniformity in a system of international States is less than that within a national federal system.'[24] As much is reflected in the competence of the Court, whose decisions—rather than formally acting as cross-jurisdictional precedents—demand a response only from the *respondent* State and may be tempered by any margin of appreciation exercisable at the domestic level. In spite of the hierarchical positioning of the European Court of Human Rights 'above' the structures of national legal systems, Warbrick wrote that in the Convention context:

> [I]t has to be conceded that the division of power is vastly asymmetrical in favour of the States and is not uniform across the range of governmental powers. There is nothing equivalent to the Supremacy Clause in the European Convention. What degree of direct/domestic effect is given to the Convention or to the decisions of its institutions is a matter of national constitutional law ... [and] the Court has made it clear that it is for the State to choose the means it adopts to secure compliance.[25]

[22] J Locke, *Two Treatises of Government* (1690) Ch XII. For a survey of the interrelationship between federalism, international and national laws see: R Schütze, *From Dual to Cooperative Federalism: The Changing Structure of European Law* (Oxford, Oxford University Press, 2009) 16–22.

[23] Of which the European Union provides a salient example. On which see: Schütze, ibid.

[24] Warbrick, above n 1, 705. Indeed, as Warbrick later observed: '[i]t was not the object of the Convention to establish a uniform set of rights for all the party states, still less to set an optimum standard' (Warbrick, above n 8, 29).

[25] Warbrick, above n 1, 699–700. See also: S Greer, *The European Convention on Human Rights: Achievements, Problems and Prospects* (Cambridge, Cambridge University Press, 2006) 56.

This limitation is integral to the status of the Convention as an agreement between States; a 'co-operative'[26] endeavour that is politically and legally reliant on the continuing acquiescence of its State membership. The success of the Convention system remains contingent on a (rudimentary) division of power that entrusts primary responsibility for the realisation of the Convention's standards to the Member States:[27] the supervisory jurisdiction of the Court comes into play only once domestically-available avenues towards redress have been exhausted.[28]

But engagement of the Strasbourg organs does not automatically come at the expense of State autonomy. Judgments of the European Court of Human Rights are in form 'essentially declaratory',[29] stating whether a given decision, action or omission of the national authorities in question is either compatible with, or in breach of, the Convention standards (or falls within the State's margin of appreciation). While in a federal Constitution a supreme court 'must be able to strike down *state* legislation'[30] that is inconsistent with the Constitution, the Strasbourg court's enforcement mechanisms are comparably weak, with the execution of judgments subject to the executive supervision of the Committee of Ministers.[31] The Strasbourg court does not enjoy the ability to invalidate national legislation deemed to be inconsistent with the requirements of the Convention and, as such, 'does not exercise *direct* authority within national legal orders.'[32] Further, that the Strasbourg authorities recognise that a certain amount of adaptation may be necessary to give effect to judgments at the national level is evident from the allowance that a State is free to implement such decisions 'in accordance with the rules of its national legal system'.[33] This 'highly decentralised'[34] approach to remedial action provides a further structural limitation on the nature of the Court's central authority and emphasises that responsibility for upholding the Convention's standards was therefore to be a joint enterprise, reliant on the positive engagement of both national authorities and the Strasbourg institutions.[35] Such an approach

[26] Warbrick, above n 1, 700.

[27] N Krisch, 'The Open Architecture of European Human Rights Law' (2008) 71 *MLR* 183, 206–08.

[28] Art 35(1) ECHR. And see: *Vučković v Serbia* (2014) 59 EHRR 19, [69]–[77].

[29] *Marckx v Belgium* (1979) 2 EHRR 330, [58].

[30] Barendt, above n 20, 55.

[31] The UK, for instance, resisted addressing the breach of Art 3 of Protocol No 1 of the Convention highlighted in *Hirst v United Kingdom (No 2)* ((2006) 42 EHRR 41) for over a decade.

[32] A Stone Sweet, 'The European Convention on Human Rights and National Constitutional Reordering' (2011–12) 33 *Cardozo Law Review* 1859, 1860 (emphasis added).

[33] DJ Harris, M O'Boyle, EP Bates and CM Buckley, *Harris, O'Boyle and Warbrick, Law of the European Convention on Human Rights* 3rd edn (Oxford, Oxford University Press, 2014) 30 (where the example givern is *Vermeire v Belgium* (1993) 15 EHRR 488).

[34] J Christoffersen, 'Individual and Constitutional Justice: Can the Power Balance of Adjudication be Reversed?' in J Christoffersen and MR Madsen (eds), *The European Court of Human Rights Between Law and Politics* (Oxford, Oxford University Press, 2011) 195.

[35] S Greer and L Wildhaber, 'Revisiting the Debate about "Constitutionalising" the European Court of Human Rights' (2012) 12 *Human Rights Law Review* 655, 674.

is entirely consistent with the view—recently reiterated in Protocol 15[36]—that it is the national authorities of the Member States that provide the foundations on which the Convention and the jurisdiction of the Court rests.

In the absence of a clear articulation that decisions of the Strasbourg court are both binding and of general applicability (and consistently with its partial division of powers), the vision of federalism that emphasises *separation* of governmental competences and the detached sovereignties of component units and central authority does not accurately capture the spirit of the Convention system. Wheare's famous account of the federal principle—'the method of dividing powers so that the general and the regional governments are each, within a sphere, coordinate and independent'[37]—emphasises autonomy, arguably at the expense of co-operation.[38] Yet it is the latter characteristic which better reflects the animating concerns of the Convention system; the notion of the 'shared responsibility'[39] of the Member States and the European Court for the maintenance of the Convention's protections enjoys a firm grounding in the text of the Convention,[40] the jurisprudence of the Court,[41] and has provided a recurring theme in ongoing political deliberations regarding its modernisation, case-management and jurisprudential technique.[42] The self-perception of the Court in this regard is that of a body whose role and function is supplementary—secondary—to that of the Member States:

> [The] task of ensuring respect for the rights enshrined in the Convention lies first and foremost with the authorities in the contracting states rather than with the Court. The Court can and should intervene only where the domestic authorities fail in that task.[43]

[36] Art 1 of Protocol 15 ECHR reads: 'Affirming that the High Contracting Parties, in accordance with the principle of subsidiarity, have the primary responsibility to secure the rights and freedoms defined in the Convention and the Protocols thereto, and that in so doing, they enjoy a margin of appreciation, subject to the supervisory jurisdiction of the European Court of Human Rights established by this Convention.'

[37] KC Wheare, *Federal Government* (London, Oxford University Press, 1953) 11.

[38] D Halberstam, 'Federalism: Theory, Policy, Law' in M Rosenfeld and A Sajó, *The Oxford Handbook of Comparative Constitutional Law* (Oxford, Oxford University Press, 2012) 579.

[39] On which see: J Gerards, 'The European Court of Human Rights and the National Courts: Giving shape to the notion of "shared responsibility"' in J Gerards and J Fleuren (eds), *Implementation of the European Convention on Human Rights and the judgments of the ECtHR in national case law: A Comparative Analysis* (Cambridge, Intersentia, 2014).

[40] Art 1 ECHR ('The High Contracting Parties shall secure to everyone within their jurisdiction the rights and freedoms defined in … this Convention'); Art 35 ECHR (the European Court of Human Rights will only enjoy jurisdiction in relation to cases in which, inter alia, 'all domestic remedies have been exhausted').

[41] See eg: *SAS v France* (2015) 60 EHRR 11, [129].

[42] See for instance: Council of Europe Steering Committee for Human Rights, *CDDH report on the longer-term future of the system of the European Court of Human Rights* (11 December 2015) (available at: http://www.coe.int/t/dghl/standardsetting/cddh/reformechr/CDDH(2015)R84_Addendum%20I_EN-Final.pdf/).

[43] Jurisconsult of the European Court of Human Rights, *Interlaken Follow-up: Principle of Subsidiarity* (8 July 2010), available at: http://www.echr.coe.int/Documents/2010_Interlaken_Follow-up_ENG.pdf.

In consequence—as the States and Court should be seen as 'mutually complementary'[44] components of the ECHR system—parallels may be more readily drawn between the Convention and systems of co-operative federalism, rather than the mutually exclusive spheres of dual federalism.

Though the fact that the Convention mechanisms lack the capacity to *enforce* uniformity provides one ground on which recognised federal systems might be distinguished, the fact that subsidiarity is built into the fabric of the Convention system underlines a structural similarity to formalised federal systems:

> Federal systems across the world are generally designed according to the principle of subsidiarity, which in one form or another holds that the central government should play only a supporting role in governance, acting only if the constituent units of government are incapable of acting on their own.[45]

Accordingly, while the primary responsibility for upholding the requirements of the Convention lies with the Member States, the system demands recourse to centralised authority where those requirements may not have been satisfied. The empowerment of the central authority is a necessary consequence of subsidiarity for the reason that the principle implicitly justifies 'central involvement in affairs that *cannot be adequately handled* at the local level.'[46]

III. The 'Centralising' Influence of the European Court of Human Rights

Assessing the jurisprudence of the Strasbourg Court, Warbrick highlighted the following as 'federal' techniques of reasoning, indicative of the centralising tendencies of the Convention system:

1. The suggestion that there should be no national authority to limit or reduce rights as defined by the Strasbourg court (ie in those cases where the right in question might be said to enjoy a clearly-defined and irreducible minimum);
2. In determining the content of the right in question, the Strasbourg court finds a 'strong majority practice' across its jurisdiction;
3. A concern that the 'localization' of rights will result in unjustifiable differences in treatment as between the states.[47]

Warbrick was careful to observe that—aside from the first argument—the European Court had developed no theory that made the application of any of

[44] ES Corwin, 'The Passing of Dual Federalism' [1950] 36 *Virginia Law Review* 1, 19.

[45] D Halberstam, 'Federal Powers and the Principle of Subsidiarity' in VD Amar and M Tushnet, *Global Perspectives on Constitutional Law* (Oxford, Oxford University Press, 2009) 34.

[46] ibid, 35 (emphasis added).

[47] Warbrick, above n 1, 707.

the 'federal' contentions mandatory.[48] But each of these characteristics remains of relevance, and speaks to the (centralised) interpretative function of the Court in articulating the meaning of the Convention rights.[49]

It is a core element of the Court's role to articulate the minimum standards required by the Convention. The visible function of the Court is therefore to adjudicate the complaints of individuals alleging interference with their rights at the hands of the state or its agents, but in doing so it must also seek to expound the level of protection that should be afforded to those rights across the Convention system. The individual complaint mechanism is the means by which the concurrent purpose of the Convention—the administration of 'constitutional justice' through the articulation of minimum standards of compliance in response to serious defects at the national level—is realised.[50] There is considerable tension between these two core elements of the Court's function,[51] but it is in discharging this (constitutional) interpretative function that the Court can be most clearly seen to wield a clear centralising influence; '[*o*]*nly* a central institution … can uniformly establish the meaning of fundamental rights and define a minimum level of fundamental rights protection that must be guaranteed' across each of the Member States.[52] That the Convention, and the European Court of Human Rights, undertake constitutional functions is not therefore open to question; the Court is both descriptively and normatively 'a constitutional, or "quasi-constitutional" court, in the sense of being the final authoritative judicial tribunal for a specific constitutional system designed to ensure that the exercise of public power throughout Europe is constitution-compliant.'[53]

And yet, since publication of Warbrick's essay the Court has, in the process expounding the Convention, also adopted characteristics of an overtly constitutional court.[54] Though the Court is not the creature of a national constitution, the Convention has come to be viewed as a 'European Bill of Rights'[55] or—as the Court has recognised—an analogous 'instrument of European public order ("*ordre public*").'[56] And while decisions of the European Court may lack the supremacy or finality typically enjoyed by those of domestic constitutional courts, they

48 ibid, 708–09.

49 Art 32(1) ECHR.

50 Greer, above n 25, 59.

51 On which see: K Dzehtsiarou and A Greene, 'Restructuring the European Court of Human Rights: Preserving the right of individual petition and promoting constitutionalism' [2013] *PL* 710; F de Londras, 'Dual functionality and the persistent frailty of the European Court of Human Rights' [2013] *European Human Rights Law Review* 38.

52 Gerards, above n 39, 16 (emphasis added).

53 Greer, above n 25, 190.

54 See for instance: ibid, 165–89; D Nicol, 'Lessons from Luxembourg: Federalisation and the Court of Human Rights' (2001) 26 *European Law Review (Human Rights Survey)* 3. Cf Krisch, above n 27, 183.

55 On which see: E Bates, *The Evolution of the European Convention on Human Rights: From its Inception to the Creation of a Permanent Court of Human Rights* (Oxford, Oxford University Press, 2010).

56 *Loizidou v Turkey* (1995) 20 EHRR 99, [75].

otherwise enjoy significant gravitational pull.[57] As (domestically) acknowledged by Lord Bingham in the influential decision of the House of Lords in *Ullah*, 'the Convention is an international instrument, the correct interpretation of which can be authoritatively expounded *only* by the Strasbourg court.'[58] When this 'pull' is taken in combination with the dynamic approach to interpretation employed by the European Court, then the potential reach of the Strasbourg jurisprudence into 'domestic' affairs is considerable. The transition between the relatively 'fixed' and 'consensual' obligations of a treaty regime towards making requirements of Member States 'that are neither' indicates—for Gardbaum—the confirmation of the ECHR system as a 'federalized or constitutionalized regional human rights system' exercising significant normative influence within its component legal systems.[59]

The consequent tendency toward viewing the Convention system as being highly centralised, to the detriment of national self-government or sovereignty, is clearly apparent in discourse surrounding the role of the Convention jurisprudence in domestic law and in the projected replacement of the HRA with a UK Bill of Rights. It would be wrong however to assume that this centralisation narrative is solely a product of the Convention system itself. In addition to those centralising characteristics of the Convention system highlighted above, UK experience emphasises further difficulties at the international level *and* in the interpretation of the existing mechanism for vindicating the Convention rights in domestic law, the HRA. Current debate is in particular animated by two core concerns: the adoption by the European Court of an expansionist approach to the Convention and the increased prominence—or amplification—of the Convention jurisprudence in domestic law following the adoption of the HRA.

A. An 'Expansionist' Approach to the Convention

It is now well-established in the jurisprudence of the European Court of Human Rights that 'the Convention is a living instrument which … must be interpreted in the light of present day conditions.'[60] Thus, the Strasbourg Court is not formally bound to follow its own judgments[61]—allowing the Court to 'have regard to the changing conditions in contracting states and respond … to any emerging consensus as to the standards to be achieved.'[62] The precise content of or, perhaps

[57] Gardbaum characterises the Convention case-law as having '*de facto* rather than *de jure* direct effect' within the Member States as a result (S Gardbaum, 'Human Rights as International Constitutional Rights' (2008) 19 *EJIL* 749, 760).

[58] *R (on the application of Ullah) v Special Adjudicator* [2004] UKHL 26; [2004] 2 AC 323, [20] (emphasis added).

[59] Gardbaum, above n 57, 759–60.

[60] *Tyrer v United Kingdom* (1979–1980) 2 EHRR 1, [31].

[61] See eg *Cossey v United Kingdom* (1991) 13 EHRR 622, [35].

[62] *Stafford v United Kingdom* (2002) 35 EHRR 32, [68].

more accurately, the minimum level of protection afforded by a Convention right, may therefore develop over time.[63] While the adoption of the living instrument doctrine pre-dated Warbrick's assessment of the federal aspects of the Convention,[64] he voiced a concern regarding the stretching of this interpretative method. Looking to the decision of the minority of the European Court in *Feldbrugge v Netherlands*, Warbrick highlighted the suggestion that 'evolutive interpretation ... does not allow entirely new concepts of spheres of application to be introduced into the Convention: that is a legislative function that belongs to the Member States of the Council of Europe.'[65] Warbrick observed that such an approach:

> [S]eems to me to stay clearly within the international (and even federalist) tradition. It recognizes the peculiar characteristics of the treaty under consideration without letting them overwhelm the legal basis of the Convention, the agreement of sovereign States.[66]

The development of the European Court's jurisprudence—as the Convention's meaning has been articulated in response to contemporary challenges to rights—has resulted in its application to new spheres of governmental activity (and indeed inactivity).[67] The judgment of Judge Costa in *Hatton v United Kingdom*[68]—concerning whether permitted night flights out of Heathrow airport constituted an interference with local residents' rights under Article 8 ECHR—attempts to explain and contextualise the need for the Court's adoption of the living instrument approach:

> [A]s the Court has often underlined: 'The Convention is a living instrument, to be interpreted in the light of present-day conditions' ... This 'evolutive' interpretation by the Commission and the Court of various Convention requirements has generally been 'progressive', in the sense that they have gradually extended and raised the level of protection afforded to the rights and freedoms guaranteed by the Convention to develop the 'European public order'. In the field of environmental human rights, which was practically unknown in 1950, the Commission and the Court have increasingly taken the view that Article 8 [the right to privacy] embraces the right to a healthy environment, and therefore to protection against pollution and nuisances caused by harmful chemicals, offensive smells, agents which precipitate respiratory ailments, noise and so on.[69]

These statements have been singled out for criticism by one critic of the HRA and of the European Court as betraying the 'blatantly expansionist' tendencies of

63 That the Convention is a 'living instrument' has been acknowledged by domestic courts in litigation under the HRA: see eg *Brown v Stott* [2003] 1 AC 681, 727 (Lord Clyde).

64 *Tyrer v United Kingdom* (1978) 2 EHRR 1. See also: *Marckx v Belgium* (1979–80) 2 EHRR 330; *Dudgeon v United Kingdom* (1982) 4 EHRR 149. Warbrick's piece also pre-dates the abolition of the Commission and establishment of the European Court as a permanent institution following the implementation of Protocol No.11.

65 *Feldbrugge v Netherlands* (1986) 8 EHRR 425, [24].

66 Warbrick, above n 1, 713.

67 For instance: *Goodwin v United Kingdom* (2002) 35 EHRR 18; *EB v France* (2008) 47 EHRR 21.

68 *Hatton v United Kingdom* (2003) 37 EHRR 28.

69 ibid, [O-I5].

the latter.[70] It should be noted in response that the judgment of Judge Costa came in dissent and that the violation found by the European Court in *Hatton* was—as a result of the case arising prior to the implementation of the HRA—that domestic law failed to provide an effective remedy in respect of the complaint made. No violation of the applicants' substantive Article 8 rights was found, and no damages were awarded.

The expansionist—or centralising—narrative in relation to the extent of the Convention's protections has, however, increasingly gained traction. The decision of the European Court in *Hirst (No 2)*[71] has been seized upon by critics as providing evidence of the extension of the meaning of the Convention to include rights originally 'excluded' from the Convention and therefore of the imperialising tendencies of the Court.[72] In the resulting February 2011 House of Commons debate on prisoner voting, the former Secretary of State for Justice and Lord Chancellor Jack Straw argued that, 'through the decision in the *Hirst* case and some similar decisions, the Strasbourg court is setting itself up as a supreme court for Europe with an ever-widening remit.'[73] Senior judicial figures have made similar observations. Extra-judicially, Lord Sumption has described the European Court of Human Rights as having become 'the institutional flag-bearer for judge-made fundamental law extending well beyond the text which it is charged with applying.'[74] The effect of the application by the Court of the living instrument approach has, Sumption continued, been 'to take many contentious issues which would previously have been regarded as questions for political debate, administrative discretion or social convention, and transformed them into questions of law to be resolved by an international judicial tribunal.'[75] The consequence of then applying—at the domestic level—that jurisprudence, is to preclude the courts 'from respecting the proper role of Parliament as a representative body and of Ministers as officers answerable to Parliament and the electorate.'[76]

So while the living instrument doctrine is argued by many to provide one of the essential underpinnings to the Convention's relative longevity—permitting the Court to 'breathe life into the words of the instrument so as to make it relevant to contemporary European society'[77]—others perceive the steady encroachment

[70] M Pinto-Duschinsky, *Bringing Rights Back Home: Making Human Rights Compatible with Parliamentary Democracy in the UK* (London, Policy Exchange, 2011) 31.

[71] *Hirst v United Kingdom (No 2)* (2006) 42 EHRR 41.

[72] On which see: CRG Murray, 'A Perfect Storm: Parliament and Prisoner Disenfranchisement' (2013) 66 *Parliamentary Affairs* 511.

[73] HC Debs, Vol 523, Col 502, 10 February 2011. See also: Nicol, above n 54, 3; F de Londras, 'Dual functionality and the persistent frailty of the European Court of Human Rights' [2013] *European Human Rights Law Review* 38, 46.

[74] Lord Sumption, 'The Limits of Law', The 27th Sultan Azlan Shah Lecture, Kuala Lumpur, 20 November 2013.

[75] ibid.

[76] Lord Sumption, 'Judicial and Political Decision-Making: The Uncertain Boundary' 2011 FA Mann Lecture. See also: Lord Hoffmann, 'The Universality of Human Rights' (2009) 125 *LQR* 416.

[77] N Bratza, 'Living Instrument or Dead Letter—The Future of the European Convention on Human Rights' [2014] *European Human Rights Law Review* 116, 118.

of the Court upon areas of law and policy for which constitutional responsibility could previously be said to lie within the domestic domain.[78] Though the Court has repeatedly stressed that it is not open to it to rewrite the terms of the Convention,[79] those terms have been extended to include meaning that its framers—it is said—cannot possibly have envisaged,[80] or rather less charitably (and in the words of the UK Government's former Minister for Human Rights), have been ignored as the Court has taken it upon itself to 'invent' new rights.[81] In the light of this, proposals for a UK Bill of Rights reflect a distinctly originalist vision of the Convention rights.[82]

But the interpretative function of the Court is not administered in splendid isolation of the concerns arising within and across the Member States. The capacity of the Court as a constitutional actor in this regard is limited by those cases that come before it. And though the living instrument doctrine permits the incremental development of the Convention jurisprudence, it does so only—if operating consistently with the subsidiary role of the Court and in order to retain a linkage to the notion of State consent—where a consensus can legitimise a direction of travel.[83] The interpretative role of the Court is, even in the incremental development of the Convention case law, doubly parasitic upon trends and developments within the Member States.

B. The Domestic Amplification of the Convention Jurisprudence

Any assessment of the federal character of the UK/Strasbourg relationship is complicated by the fact that one of the core centralising arguments in the case for a UK Bill of Rights is the consequence of a legislative exercise in decentralisation taken by the Westminster Parliament. It has become trite to recall that the purpose of enacting the HRA was to 'bring rights home', but the problem to which the Act was the proposed solution was that the Convention rights were seen as being both practically and jurisprudentially alien. The Act therefore sought to deliver on the promises to make rights accessible to litigants in domestic courts—saving the

[78] See eg: *Marckx v Belgium* (1979–1980) 2 EHRR 330, dissenting opinion of Sir Gerald Fitzmaurice.

[79] See eg: *Quark Fishing v United Kingdom* (2007) 44 EHRR SE4.

[80] *Protecting Human Rights in the UK: The Conservatives' Proposals for Changing Britain's Human Rights Laws*, above n 9, 3.

[81] This suggestion is made on multiple occasions in D Raab, *The Assault on Liberty: What went wrong with rights* (London, Fourth Estate, 2009) esp 123–68.

[82] *Protecting Human Rights in the UK: The Conservatives' Proposals for Changing Britain's Human Rights Laws*, above n 9, 5.

[83] Just as consensus might underpin a jurisprudential development on the part of the Court (eg *Goodwin v United Kingdom* (2002) 35 EHRR 18), an absence of consensus may inhibit the Court (eg *A, B and C v Ireland* (2011) 53 EHRR 13). See generally: K Dzehtsiarou, 'Does Consensus Matter? Legitimacy of European Consensus in the case law of the European Court of Human Rights' [2011] *PL* 534.

delays and costs associated with making an application to the Strasbourg court—and to bring the Convention rights 'much more fully into the jurisprudence of the courts throughout the United Kingdom' so that they might be 'more subtly and powerfully woven into our law.'[84] The 1998 Act therefore was, and remains, an essentially pro-subsidiarity measure. This state-led exercise in decentralisation has, however, ironically given rise to a heightened perception of central control held by the Strasbourg court.[85]

In adjudication under the HRA, the centralising interpretative aspect of the Convention system has been amplified by domestic courts in their application of the Convention rights. In discharging obligations under section 2(1) of the Act—the duty to 'take into account' decisions of the European Court of Human Rights in its resolution of disputes arising in connection with the protected rights—domestic adjudication has highlighted the potential paradox that the 'Convention rights' are simultaneously creatures of both statute (the HRA[86]) and of the Convention itself. Those readings of the Act which emphasise its domestic credentials decentralise interpretative authority over the protected rights, understanding them as standards that are subtly distinct from those adjudicated by the European Court and whose 'meaning and application is a matter for domestic courts, not the court in Strasbourg.'[87] The (initially) prevailing 'internationalist'[88] approach to the interpretation of the Act casts domestic courts as local proxies for the Strasbourg court,[89] replicating the requirements of the Strasbourg jurisprudence in the domestic context.[90] As a consequence, domestic courts applying the HRA have deferred to (and implicitly acceded to) a rather more centralised understanding of the role of the European Court, and have treated its decisions—if deemed to be relevant and applicable to the dispute in question—as effectively setting precedential standards, regardless of the UK's involvement in the proceedings before the Strasbourg court.[91] Treatment of any and all relevant decisions of the European

[84] *Rights Brought Home: The Human Rights Bill*, Cm.3782 (October 1997), [1.14].

[85] Beyond the UK, Greer and Wildhaber have noted that incorporation of the ECHR rights into national laws is a factor contributing to the broader 'constitutionalisation' of the Convention regime (Greer and Wildhaber, above n 35).

[86] Human Rights Act, s 1(1).

[87] *Re McKerr* [2004] UKHL 12, [65] (Lord Hoffmann).

[88] B Dickson, *Human Rights and the United Kingdom Supreme Court* (Oxford, Oxford University Press, 2013) 56.

[89] *R v Secretary of State for Foreign and Commonwealth Affairs, ex parte Quark Fishing Ltd* [2005] UKHL 57; [2006] 1 AC 529, [34] (Lord Nicholls): 'The [Human Rights] Act was intended to provide a remedy where a remedy would have been available in Strasbourg. Conversely, the Act was not intended to provide a domestic remedy where a remedy would not have been available in Strasbourg.'

[90] On which see: J Lewis, 'The European Ceiling on Rights' [2007] *PL* 720; R Masterman, 'Aspiration or Foundation? The Status of the Strasbourg Jurisprudence and the "Convention Rights" in Domestic Law' in H Fenwick, G Phillipson and R Masterman (eds), *Judicial Reasoning under the UK Human Rights Act* (Cambridge, Cambridge University Press, 2007).

[91] R Masterman, 'Section 2(1) of the Human Rights Act 1998: Binding Domestic Courts to Strasbourg?' [2004] *PL* 725. See also: Lord Irvine of Lairg, 'A British Interpretation of Convention Rights' [2012] *PL* 237, 240.

Court of Human Rights as being presumptively to be followed distorts—in its translation into domestic law—the requirements of the Convention in two core ways. First, by regarding decisions taken by the Court against States other than the UK as being of greater coercive force than the Convention organs themselves would. Second, by treating what could be seen as a decentralised system of constitutional review in a rather more centralised manner.

In treating the judgments of the European Court of Human Rights as setting standards to be applied under the HRA, the individual justice dispensing elements of the Court's role have been emphasised at the expense of its ability to deliver constitutional justice.[92] Individual decisions of the European Court are treated as being domestically applicable, rather than contributing—collectively—to a broader understanding of the Convention's minimum standards. Regardless of the specific language adopted in the HRA itself, the result of this is a tendency to view the decisions of the European Court of Human Rights as determinative (rather than persuasive), and to see the Court itself as an *appellate* (rather than supervisory) body, in turn encouraging the sense that the Strasbourg court *overrules* decisions taken at the national level (rather than declaring such decisions to be in contravention of the Convention's requirements). The symbolism of this perceived appellate (as opposed to supervisory) role is as potent in discussions regarding the role and function of the European Court of Human Rights as it is to the distinction between review and appeal as drawn in the domestic law of judicial review of administrative action and is reinforced by the hierarchical symbolism of the Court's extra-jurisdictional position. In the UK context at least, the sense that the European Court of Human Rights operates effectively as a court of fourth instance will be difficult to displace.[93] It is a view of the Court which is underlined by years of pre-HRA practice—during which time substantive judicial consideration of the Convention could *only* be achieved (following the exhaustion of domestic 'remedies') through an application to the European Court[94]—has been implicitly (and explicitly)[95] endorsed in judicial practice since implementation of the Act,[96] and has been conveniently assimilated in the anti-Strasbourg narrative as 'evidence' of an over-mighty institution.[97]

[92] It must be acknowledged that the Court itself, in the determination of decisions such as *Von Hannover* ((2006) 43 EHRR 7) has, perhaps inadvertently, contributed to this perception.

[93] See: R Masterman, 'Deconstructing the Mirror Principle' in R Masterman and I Leigh (eds), *The United Kingdom's Statutory Bill of Rights: Constitutional and Comparative Perspectives* (183 *Proceedings of the British Academy*) (Oxford, Oxford University Press, 2013) 136–37.

[94] *R v Secretary of State for the Home Department, ex parte Brind* [1991] 1 AC 696.

[95] *Secretary of State for the Home Department v AF (No 3)* [2009] UKHL 28; [2010] 2 AC 269, [98] (Lord Rodger): 'Strasbourg has spoken, the case is closed.'

[96] Including, on occasion, by the Strasbourg Court itself (for instance *Axel Springer AG v Germany* (2012) 55 EHRR 6, cf dissenting opinion of Judge Lopez Gueva joined by Judges Jungwiert, Jaeger, Villiger and Poalelungi).

[97] *Protecting Human Rights in the UK: The Conservatives' Proposals for Changing Britain's Human Rights Laws*, above n 9, 3: 'There is mounting concern at Strasbourg's attempts to *overrule* decisions of our democratically elected Parliament and *overturn* the UK courts' careful applications of Convention rights' (emphasis added).

IV. Decentralisation through Subsidiarity

Given that symbiosis between the Member States and European Court is a necessary consequence of the Convention architecture, it is to be expected that the centralising force of the Strasbourg court will be tempered by factors tending towards the devolution of responsibility to the component parts of the Convention's 'federal' structure. In favour of a more decentralised application of the Convention's protections, Warbrick highlighted the following considerations:

1. That the sovereignty of States as 'significant autonomous units' requires that certain matters fall to be resolved at the national level, especially where there is uncertainty regarding the reach or extent of the protected right;
2. That any system of divided powers implies a degree of diversity;
3. That there is an intrinsic interest in 'preserving the leeway for States to experiment on social and political questions'; and
4. That—especially in cases dealing with qualified rights—national authorities may be the 'best judges, both more sensitive and more effective, of such issues.'[98]

Given that the Convention system regards national authorities as the primary level of rights protection, it is no surprise that the margin of appreciation—the central mechanism employed in the name of promoting the autonomy of the Member States—encompasses each of the above and continues to figure prominently in the Court's jurisprudence and in attempts to reform the Convention system more broadly. In the light of domestic criticisms of the Court however, it is arguable that the idea of the margin of appreciation as a recognition of 'the latitude which signatory States are permitted in their observance of the Convention'[99] lacks currency. Warbrick's decentralising characteristics emphasise the positive role to be played by the State in upholding the Convention. A narrative which speaks of the imperialising, expansionist, tendencies of the Court contains little space for consideration of those aspects of the Convention system designed to empower the Member States.

Conscious of current controversy, former Judge Mahoney has reiterated that the

> object of the Convention system, unlike that of the legal order of the European Union, is not to bring about uniformity of national law or rigorously uniform implementation of the internationally accepted engagements (that is, the guaranteed rights and freedoms) in each one of the participating states.[100]

It follows that the Court grants not only a margin of appreciation but also does not—as noted above—prescribe specific responses, allowing States the scope to

[98] Warbrick, above n 1, 708.

[99] TH Jones, 'The Devaluation of Human Rights under the European Convention' [1995] *PL* 430, 430–31.

[100] P Mahoney, 'The relationship between the Strasbourg court and the national courts' (2014) 130 *LQR* 568, 582.

determine the most appropriate mechanism by which the Convention's minimum standards might be secured within the jurisdiction in question. The European Court itself has, in a similar vein, taken the opportunity to reject the suggestion that it is in the process of attempting to homogenise the legal and political systems of the Member States: 'There [are] a wealth of differences, inter alia, in the historical development, cultural diversity and political thought within Europe which it is for each contracting State to mould into its own democratic vision.'[101]

While the very notion of the margin of appreciation suggests that an allocation of powers as between the States and the European Court might be possible (for instance in questions engaging questions of public morals, national security or where national authorities have attempted a proportionate balancing of rights) the division would, in practice, appear to be highly porous. Though a wider margin of appreciation may, for instance, be permitted to the States in decisions taken in support of upholding 'the rights of others',[102] this does not mean that States have a monopoly on all limitations taken on such grounds. That the dividing line between the Court's duty to uphold the Convention rights, and the State's duty to uphold individual and group interests as best it sees fit, is therefore reliant on a contextual analysis of proportionality means that no clear division of responsibility can be asserted in the abstract with any precision. Though this is consistent with the shared responsibility of national authorities and the Strasbourg court, it is also problematic—especially for those States concerned with the cession of sovereignty over questions of national law and policy—for the perceived autonomy of the Member States. As a consequence, the repeated emphasis by the Court that the Convention system permits domestic variance and considerable flexibility in the realisation of the protected rights has done little to mollify critical factions in the UK.[103]

Given the apparent devaluation of the margin of appreciation, other mechanisms of acknowledging decentralisation within the Convention system are worthy of consideration. They are noteworthy because, instead of taking the form of a concession afforded by the Strasbourg court, they provide evidence of the direct influence of national decision making on the reasoning of, and outcomes determined by, the Court.

A. Demonstrating Jurisprudential Subsidiarity

Contrary to the broad tenor of much conservative critique of the Strasbourg Court, recent UK experience provides a number of illustrations of the upward

[101] *Shindler v United Kingdom* (2014) 58 EHRR 5, [102].

[102] See for instance: *Handyside v United Kingdom* (1979–1980) 1 EHRR 737; *Otto-Preminger Institute v Austria* (1995) 19 EHRR 34.

[103] That similar sentiments were expressed in *Hirst v United Kingdom (No 2)* ((2006) 42 EHRR 41, [61]) appears to indicate that the mollifying effect of such statements is, or can be, rather limited.

influence of national decision-making on that of the European Court. In contrast to those domestic views of the Strasbourg court that emphasised its determinative role in the articulation of effectively binding standards, recent decisions have seen a greater prominence given over to the distinctive role played by the Court as an *international* actor:

> It must be remembered that the Strasbourg court is an international court, deciding whether a Member State, as a state, has complied with its duty in international law to secure to everyone within its jurisdiction the rights and freedoms guaranteed by the Convention.[104]

In recognition of this fact (which also speaks to the role of the Court as a body which reviews domestic compliance rather than by which domestic decisions might be overturned on appeal), it has also—and perhaps belatedly—been recognised by the UK Supreme Court that the Convention rights 'have to be fulfilled at national level through a substantial body of much more specific domestic law [than that emanating from the European Court].'[105] As a result, the willingness of domestic courts to engage in 'creative dialogue'[106] with the European Court of Human Rights has become gradually more pronounced.[107] Such interactions have been evident both in the iterative refinement of the implications of the Convention rights in domestic law, and—illustrating the point most clearly—on those occasions on which the European Court has effectively adopted the reasoning of the domestic court as to the requirements of the Convention in the relevant national context.

As to the first of these categories, domestic courts have increasingly sought to identify the flexibility in their HRA-imposed obligation to 'take into account' the Convention jurisprudence, and have held that in the light of various circumstances, otherwise applicable Convention case law need not be followed. The UK Supreme Court decision in *Moohan* provides, in the judgment of Lord Hodge (with whom four of the seven Supreme Court Justices were in full agreement), evidence of this more nuanced approach:

> The courts of the United Kingdom are not bound by the judgments of the Strasbourg court in interpreting the ECHR. In section 2 of HRA 1998 the courts are obliged only to 'take into account' that jurisprudence. There is room for disagreement and dialogue between the domestic courts and the Strasbourg court on the application of provisions of the ECHR to circumstances in the UK. None the less, it is consistent with the intention of Parliament in enacting HRA 1998 that our courts should follow 'a clear and constant line of decisions' of the Strasbourg court, 'whose effect is not inconsistent with some

[104] *Re P* [2008] UKHL 38; [2009] 1 AC 173, [32].

[105] *Osborn v Parole Board* [2013] UKSC 61; [2014] AC 1115, [55].

[106] Lord Steyn, '2000–2005: Laying the foundations of human rights law in the United Kingdom' [2005] *European Human Rights Law Review* 349, 361.

[107] On which see: M Amos, 'From Monologue to Dialogue: The Relationship between UK Courts and the European Court of Human Rights' in R. Masterman and I Leigh (eds), *The United Kingdom's Statutory Bill of Rights: Constitutional and Comparative Perspectives* (183 *Proceedings of the British Academy*) (Oxford, Oxford University Press, 2013).

> fundamental substantive or procedural aspect of our law, and whose reasoning does not appear to overlook or misunderstand some argument or point of principle' ...[108]

Moohan, considered alongside the earlier decision in *Pinnock* (upon which Lord Hodge relied) provides a rejection of the precedential approach to the Strasbourg jurisprudence, instead envisaging a relationship between national authorities and the European Court in which greater space for critical jurisprudential collaboration is permitted.[109]

That the European Court can also be seen to positively engage with, and take a lead from, national authorities, further emphasises the co-operation that many argue to be lacking from the Convention system. The decision of the Supreme Court in *R v Horncastle* provides perhaps the most compelling authority to date for both the suggestion that domestic courts will not simply apply even relevant and clear Strasbourg case law as a matter of course, *and* that critical engagement with the Strasbourg jurisprudence in domestic adjudication can lead to a reconsideration and refinement of European Court's own stance.[110] Following that decision, the willingness of the Strasbourg court to reconsider its earlier position on the compatibility of hearsay evidence with Article 6(1),[111] demonstrates the principle of subsidiarity in practice and illustrates that national authorities can—and do—play a decisive role in shaping the content of the Strasbourg case law.[112]

The increasing turn of the European Court towards procedural review[113] also provides an example of the preparedness of the Strasbourg Court to accommodate—and potentially defer to—domestic decision-making. Thus, for example, in *Animal Defenders International*—a case concerned with the limitation of political expression, and therefore typically an area in which any margin of appreciation would be relatively narrowly drawn[114]—the Court thoroughly considered the process by which the UK's challenged ban on political advertising[115] had been enacted (and subsequently found not to be incompatible with the requirements of Article 10 in domestic adjudication).[116] The Strasbourg court noted that:

> The prohibition was ... the culmination of an exceptional examination by Parliamentary bodies of the cultural, political and legal aspects of the prohibition as part of the

[108] *Moohan v Lord Advocate* [2014] UKSC 67; [2015] AC 901, [13] (the latter quote being from *Manchester City Council v Pinnock* [2010] UKSC 45; [2011] 2 AC 104, [48]).

[109] For instance: *Poshteh v Royal Borough of Kensington and Chelsea* [2017] UKSC 36, [32]–[37].

[110] *R v Horncastle* [2009] UKSC 14; [2010] 2 AC 373.

[111] *Al-Khawaja v United Kingdom* (2009) 49 EHRR 1.

[112] ibid, *Al-Khawaja v United Kingdom* (2012) 54 EHRR 23. A similar accommodation of national-level judicial reasoning is also in evidence in *Hutchinson v United Kingdom*, App No 57592/08, 17 January 2017 (responding to *R v McLoughlin* [2014] EWCA Crim 188; [2014] 1 WLR 3964).

[113] On which see: J Gerards and E Brems (eds), *Procedural Review in European Fundamental Rights Cases* (Cambridge, Cambridge University Press, 2017).

[114] See eg: *Lingens v Austria* (1986) 8 EHRR 407.

[115] Communications Act 2003, s 321(2).

[116] *R (on the application of Animal Defenders International) v Secretary of State for Culture, Media and Sport* [2008] UKHL 15; [2008] 1 AC 1312.

> broader regulatory system governing broadcasted public interest expression in the United Kingdom, and all bodies found the prohibition to have been a necessary interference with art.10 rights. …
>
> The proportionality of the prohibition was, nonetheless, debated in some detail before the High Court and the House of Lords … both levels endorsed the objective of the prohibition as well as the rationale of the legislative choices which defined its particular scope and each concluded that it was a necessary and proportionate interference with the applicant's rights under art.10 of the Convention.
>
> The Court, for its part, attaches considerable weight to these exacting and pertinent reviews, by both parliamentary and judicial bodies, of the complex regulatory regime governing political broadcasting in the United Kingdom, and to their view that the general measure was necessary to prevent the distortion of crucial public interest debates and, thereby, the undermining of the democratic process.[117]

The European Court of Human Rights found that national authorities were 'best placed' to determine what should be regarded as a 'country specific and complex assessment' of the balance to be struck.[118]

Affording weight to the considered judgment of a national legislature (and/or courts) could be said to illustrate in practice that '[s]ubsidiarity is at the very heart of the Convention' and is demonstrative that the European Court is 'intended to be subsidiary to the national systems'.[119] Instead of affording a concession to national authorities, the European Court demonstrates that the decision-making process of the domestic legislature will be material, and that decisions adopted following 'extensive debate by the democratically elected representatives',[120] or which can be shown to be 'the culmination of … detailed examination of the social, ethical and legal implications of developments'[121] may be more likely to fall within any margin of appreciation afforded by the Strasbourg Court. It is clear also however, that deference to the decisions of national authorities—especially in those circumstances in which there exists only limited scope for policy autonomy—may be perceived as being detrimental to the necessary standard-setting (and maintaining) function of the Court.[122]

B. Embedding Structural Subsidiarity

The UK Government's chairing of the Committee of Ministers of the Council of Europe provided, in early 2012, a clear opportunity to see concerns relating

[117] *Animal Defenders International v United Kingdom* (2013) 57 EHRR 21, [114]–[116].

[118] *Animal Defenders International v United Kingdom* (2013) 57 EHRR 21, [111].

[119] *Austin v United Kin*, [61]. And see: M. Saul, 'The European Court of Human Rights' Margin of Appreciation and the Processes of National Parliaments' (2015) HRLR 1.

[120] *Friend v United Kingdom* (2010) 50 EHRR 51, [50].

[121] *Evans v United Kingdom* (2008) 46 EHRR 34, [60].

[122] On which see the dissenting judgment of Judge Pinto de Albuquerque in *Hutchinson v United Kingdom*, App No 57592/08, 17 January 2017, esp [35]–[50].

to the perceived diminution of national authorities' influence over those areas of law falling within the purview of the European Court raised at a High Level Conference on the Future of the European Court of Human Rights. The discussions and outcomes of the Brighton conference, held in April 2012, were explicitly animated by concerns relating to the perceived dilution of the importance of national authorities within the Convention system. Entering into the Brighton conference, the UK Government sought to promote revisions to the Convention system in order to emphasise the primary role of national authorities in the protection of the Convention rights, to reinforce the concept of subsidiarity, to work towards increasingly efficient case law management on the part of the European Court and to ensure consistency in the quality of European Court decisions through improvement to the processes by which national judges were appointed.[123] UK Government efforts to confine the jurisdiction of the Strasbourg court to cases in which national courts could be demonstrated to have 'seriously erred' in their interpretation of the Convention, or to only those which raise 'a serious question' relating to the interpretation of the Convention rights, were ultimately unsuccessful.[124] Nonetheless, the Brighton process did lead to a notable reiteration of the vital place of national decision-making within the Convention system.

The Brighton Declaration saw the shared responsibility of the States parties to the Convention and the Courts for 'realising the effective implementation of the Convention, underpinned by the fundamental principle of subsidiarity' reasserted. The text of the declaration sought to undercut suggestions that the European Court had usurped the position of national-level protections as the core of the Convention system by reaffirming that 'the States Parties enjoy a margin of appreciation in how they apply and implement the Convention' and 'that national authorities are in principle better placed than an international court to evaluate local needs and conditions.'[125] Protocol 15's subsequent revision to the Preamble to the Convention[126] might be interpreted as little more than a formalisation of concepts of interpretation that have been commonplace in the jurisprudence of the European Court of Human Rights since at least the *Handyside* decision in 1976.[127] But given that the additional protocol is the product of agreement

[123] For an accessible summary see House of Commons Library, *The UK and Reform of the European Court of Human Rights*, SN/IA/6277 (27 April 2012). See also: D Cameron, Speech to the Parliamentary Assembly of the Council of Europe (25 January 2012).

[124] M Elliott, 'After Brighton: Between a Rock and a Hard Place' [2012] *PL* 619, 622–23.

[125] *The Brighton Declaration* (available at http://www.echr.coe.int/Documents/2012_Brighton_FinalDeclaration_ENG.pdf), [11].

[126] Art 1 of Protocol 15 reads: 'Affirming that the High Contracting Parties, in accordance with the principle of subsidiarity, have the primary responsibility to secure the rights and freedoms defined in the Convention and the Protocols thereto, and that in so doing, they enjoy a margin of appreciation, subject to the supervisory jurisdiction of the European Court of Human Rights established by this Convention.'

[127] *Handyside v United Kingdom* (1979–1980) 1 EHRR 737, [48]–[50].

amongst the Member States it should also be interpreted as an indicator of broad consensus as to the political trajectory of the ECHR regime.[128]

The Joint Parliamentary Committee on Human Rights has welcomed the amendment to the Preamble to the Convention prompted by the Brighton process saying that it 'signifies a new era in the life of the Convention, an age of subsidiarity, in which the emphasis is on States' primary responsibility to secure the rights and freedoms set out in the Convention.'[129] While the European Court of Human Rights' continuing commitment to the subsidiarity principle had begun to be perceived as being increasingly in tension with the expanding scope of its jurisprudence, recent cases have hinted that the European Court's respect for the democratic decision making processes of the Member States runs deeper than critics of the Court would concede. In the *RMT* decision, the European Court reiterated that:

> In the sphere of social and economic policy ... the court will generally respect the legislature's policy choice unless it is 'manifestly without legal foundation.' Moreover, the Court has recognised the 'special weight' to be accorded to the domestic policy-maker in matters of general policy on which opinions within a democratic society may reasonably differ.[130]

Though the UK Government was successful at Brighton in securing support for a number of its initiatives, this did not in practice diminish dissatisfaction with the European Court within the Conservative membership of the (then) Coalition Government. The Conservative 2015 General Election manifesto duly committed to introduce a UK Bill of Rights and 'break the formal link between British courts and the European Court of Human Rights.'[131]

V. Conclusion: Towards the Re-nationalisation of Human Rights?

In sum, as Nicol has argued, the European Court of Human Rights has traditionally occupied a space on the 'spectrum of federalism' between that held by a 'classical international tribunal' and that of a 'quasi-federal sui generis entity' such as the Court of Justice of the European Union; the interventions of the Court are

[128] Similar sentiments are evident in the 2015 Brussels Declaration, which, inter alia, reiterated the role of the Court in 'upholding the States Parties' margin of appreciation' (http://www.echr.coe.int/Documents/Brussels_Declaration_ENG.pdf).

[129] Joint Committee on Human Rights, *Protocol 15 to the European Convention on Human Rights*, HL 71/HC 837 (2 December 2014), [3.17].

[130] *National Union of Rail, Maritime and Transport Workers v United Kingdom* (2015) 60 EHRR 10, [99]. See also: *James v United Kingdom* (1986) 8 EHRR 123, [43].

[131] The Conservative Party Manifesto 2015, 60.

'perceived as going to the core of national sovereignty' but lack the 'hierarchical pre-eminence' of those of the Luxembourg Court.[132] The gradual expansion of the reach of the Convention, and the 'general acceptance of [the Strasbourg Court's] authority as the ultimate arbiter of human rights disputes in Europe',[133] has however resulted in the weakening of the narrative of co-operation and an increased sense of centralisation (and constitutionalisation) within the Convention system.[134] In such circumstances, while the ongoing 'consent' of the signatory States cannot provide a comprehensive underpinning to the interventions of the Court,[135] it nonetheless remains a vital ingredient in relation to the remedial capacity of the Convention and to the broader political stability of the ECHR enterprise. As a result, it is unsurprising to find pro-subsidiarity initiatives—emphasising the investment of national authorities in the Convention regime—in evidence in the jurisprudence of the Court *and* in ongoing political initiatives to stabilise the Convention system.

In spite of the evidence of the continuing Strasbourg-level efforts to accommodate, and respond to, the decentralising pull of the Convention's States membership, there remains a powerful sense—within UK constitutional and political discourse—that the centralising influence of the European Court of Human Rights remains too great. For their part, domestic courts have begun to address the perceived imbalance between national and European protections for rights—partially at least a product of their own interpretation of the provisions of the HRA—through examination of those circumstances in which departure from the Convention jurisprudence might be possible. This subtle movement in the domestic courts' understanding of the Act has been accompanied by more direct attempts to accentuate the continuing utility of the common law as a means by which rights can be protected[136] and, in so doing, re-emphasise the capacity of *national* laws to complement the Convention's protections.[137] This common law 'resurgence' provides partial evidence of a trend towards recalibration of the United Kingdom's position within the Convention system,[138] but it is also arguably a self-correction on the part of the domestic judiciary of what came to be seen as an overly-limiting interpretation of the provisions of the HRA itself.

[132] D Nicol, above n 54, HR3. And see: R Masterman, 'A Tale of Competing Supremacies' UK Constitutional Law Blog, 30 September 2013.

[133] Krisch, above n 27, 184.

[134] See: Greer and Wildhaber, above n 35, 655; W Sadurski, 'Partnering with Strasbourg: Constitutionalisation of the European Court of Human Rights, the Accession of Central and East European States to the Council of Europe and the Idea of Pilot Judgments' (2009) 9 *Human Rights Law Review* 397, 445–50.

[135] A Von Bogdandy and I Venzke, 'In whose name? An investigation of international courts' public authority and its democratic justification' (2012) *European Journal of International Law* 7, 8.

[136] *R (Osborn) v Parole Board* [2013] UKSC 61; [2014] AC 1115, [57].

[137] *A v British Broadcasting Corporation* [2014] UKSC 25; [2015] AC 558, [57].

[138] R Masterman and S Wheatle, 'A Common Law Resurgence in Rights Protection?' [2015] *European Human Rights Law Review* 57. See also: P Scott, 'On "Domestic" Law and the Law of Human Rights' (2014) 25 *King's Law Journal* 147; S Stephenson, 'The Supreme Court's Renewed Interest in Autochthonous Constitutionalism' [2015] *PL* 394.

In spite of such developments, advocates of a UK Bill of Rights seek a more radical realignment of State power vis-à-vis that of the Strasbourg Court.[139] Indications are that such a UK Bill of Rights would seek to diminish the influence of the Strasbourg case law on domestic proceedings, giving the UK Supreme Court the 'final say' over domestic human rights questions.[140] More radically, Strasbourg findings of a UK breach of the Convention would be rendered 'advisory' and subject to Parliamentary approval prior to any remedial action.[141] The push for a UK Bill of Rights implicitly rejects much of the co-operative narrative of the Convention regime, adopting a 'politically-unidirectional, sovereigntist'[142] stance towards the notion of shared responsibility. The adoption of a UK Bill of Rights would—its supporters hope—be a firm assertion of decentralisation and an attempt to recapture national powers ceded to (or accumulated by) the European Court of Human Rights. It is a project premised on the need to reclaim 'sovereignty' and cement a relationship in which the (potentially exclusive) competences of States and European Court are more carefully demarcated and policed. As such, it is a defensive step towards a dualised model of federal relationship that seeks to underscore the autonomy of the Member State at the expense of the Convention's still-vital sense of pan-European co-operation.

[139] The UK Supreme Court has acknowledged that the common law will yield to the Convention, where the latter would provide for a more generous protection of rights: '... although the Convention and our domestic law give expression to common values, the balance between those values, when they conflict, may not always be struck in the same place under the Convention as it might once have been under our domestic law. In that event, effect must be given to the Convention rights in accordance with the Human Rights Act' (*A v British Broadcasting Corporation* [2014] UKSC 25; [2015] AC 558, [57]).

[140] *Protecting Human Rights in the UK: The Conservatives' Proposals for Changing Britain's Human Rights Laws*, above n 9, 6.

[141] ibid.

[142] *Hutchinson v United Kingdom*, App No 57592/08, 17 January 2017, dissenting judgment of Judge Pinto de Albuquerque, [40].

9

The UK's Status in the WTO Post-Brexit

LORAND BARTELS*

I. Introduction

It has become conventional wisdom that once the UK leaves the EU it will have to renegotiate core aspects of its World Trade Organization (WTO) rights and obligations, and in particular its concessions under Article II of the General Agreement on Tariffs and Trade (GATT) 1994 and Article XX of the General Agreement on Trade in Services (GATS). Quite how difficult this is likely to be is in dispute. Probably the most pessimistic voice, at one point at least,[1] was that of WTO Director-General Azevêdo, who said during the Brexit referendum campaign that '[the UK] will be a member with no country-specific commitments'.[2] Others have adopted the more limited view that the UK will have to negotiate its share of the EU's quantified commitments not to subsidise agricultural production above a certain level and to permit fixed quantity of imports of agricultural products from WTO Members under preferential tariff rate quotas.[3] Beyond this, it is also generally assumed, including, it seems, by the UK Government,[4] that the

* I am very grateful to Tomer Broude, Lothar Ehring, Alberta Fabbricotti, Tom Grant, Holger Hestermeyer, Gary Horlick, David Kleimann, Andrew Lang, Petros Mavroidis, Federico Ortino, David Roberts, and Peter Ungphakorn for comments and discussion. All opinions and errors remain mine.

[1] Azevêdo subsequently changed his position, as documented by David Allen Green, 'Brexit and the issue of the WTO schedules', Financial Times, 28 February 2017 (https://www.ft.com/content/42b59126-794c-3a0b-b19a-6d4b0a11c990).

[2] Larry Elliot, 'WTO chief says post-Brexit trade talks must start from scratch', *The Guardian*, 7 June 2016 (www.theguardian.com/business/2016/jun/07/wto-chief-brexit-trade-talks-start-scratch-eu-referendum). Azevêdo's view was echoed by others, eg Piet Eeckhout, 'Brexit and trade: the view over the hill', 16 June 2016 (https://londonbrussels.wordpress.com/2016/06/16/brexit-and-trade-the-view-over-the-hill/).

[3] Richard Eglin and Piet Eeckhout, Oral Evidence, Brexit: future trade between the UK and the EU, Select Committee on the European Union—External Affairs and Internal Market Sub-Committees, 8 September 2016 (http://data.parliament.uk/writtenevidence/committeeevidence.svc/evidencedocument/eu-external-affairs-subcommittee/brexit-future-trade-between-the-uk-and-the-eu/oral/37864.pdf).

[4] Cl 1 of the Trade Bill (UK), published 7 November 2017.

UK will have to accede as a new party to the plurilateral Government Procurement Agreement (GPA),[5] which establishes obligations with regard to UK public entities, and to which the EU—but not the UK—is a party. In general, the governing assumption appears to be that the UK's legal position within the WTO depends on the positions of other WTO Members, who can hold it to ransom, in particular by withholding consent to the certification of any new UK schedules of concessions.

It is contended here that, in different ways, these views are mistaken. As far as the multilateral WTO agreements are concerned, it is argued (section II) that what changes are not the UK's underlying rights and obligations, but solely the EU's exercise of these rights on behalf of the UK (a question of autonomy) and the EU's assumption of responsibility for the performance of these obligations by the UK (a question of attribution). It follows that the UK's rights and obligations are, as a matter of legal theory, complete, even if, at least in the case of the quantified commitments noted above, they are presently undetermined (section III). Identifying these rights and obligations is not necessarily difficult. All WTO rules that apply to WTO Members on an *erga omnes partes* basis also apply to the UK without any further complications (section III.A). The key questions, addressed here, concern the identification of the UK's rights to access the country-specific EU tariff rate quotas bound by other WTO Members under the GATT 1994 (section III.B), the identification of the UK's scheduled commitments in relation to current EU tariff rate quota commitments (section III.C) and agricultural subsidies (section III.D) under the GATT 1994, the identification of the UK's scheduled commitments under the GATS (section III.E), the procedural mechanism that should be used to establish the UK's commitments in new schedules of commitments (section IV), and the UK's legal position in relation to the Revised Government Procurement Agreement (section V).

The chapter concludes that, based upon WTO law, practice under the GATT 1947, and customary international law, the position is relatively clear even on these more complicated issues. First, the UK is entitled to its share of any tariff rate quotas offered by other WTO Members in accordance with Article XIII:2 of the GATT 1994. Second, and more complicated, its tariff rate quota commitments should be determined in line with the principle underlying Article XIII:2, but, in addition, the expected benefits of other WTO Members under those tariff rate quotas are protected via the possibility of a non-violation complaint. Both of these factors mean that the UK should offer tariff rate quotas based on the more generous of initially expected benefits and recent patterns of trade, including from the EU-27. Third, the UK's agricultural subsidy commitments should be based upon recent payments out of the EU's Common Agricultural Policy. Fourth, GATS commitments should be easily transposed to an independent schedule, with the deletion of the stipulation that the existing schedule only applies within EU territory.

[5] ibid; Michael Bowsher, 'Procurement law after Brexit?', 16 March 2016 (http://publicsectorblog.practicallaw.com/procurement-law-after-brexit/).

Fifth, all of these commitments should be established in a new UK schedule submitted as an 'other change', usually but inaccurately called a 'rectification', as opposed to a 'modification' of the current EU schedule. Sixth, the UK succeeds to the Government Procurement Agreement, and is entitled to be registered as a party to this agreement. None of this means that negotiations will not or should not take place. However, they should take place within the framework of the UK's existing rights and obligations.

II. The UK's Status as an Original WTO Member

On 1 January 1995 the UK became an original WTO Member pursuant to Article XI:1 of the WTO Agreement. This provision states:

> The contracting parties to GATT 1947 as of the date of entry into force of this Agreement, and the European Communities, which accept this Agreement and the Multilateral Trade Agreements and for which Schedules of Concessions and Commitments are annexed to GATT 1994 and for which Schedules of Specific Commitments are annexed to GATS shall become original Members of the WTO.

This applies to the UK in a straightforward way. The UK was a contracting party to the GATT 1947 and it 'accepted' the WTO Agreement and the multilateral trade agreements, in accordance with Article XIV:1 of the WTO Agreement, by ratification on 30 December 1994.[6] Further, the EU annexed a schedule of concessions to the GATT 1994 'for'[7] the UK,[8] in accordance with its practice since the UK joined the EU[9] in 1974.[10] For the GATS the situation is a little different, in that the EU and its Member States, including the UK, jointly submitted a schedule of specific commitments.[11] Accordingly, all of the conditions set out in Article XI:1 have been

[6] Note 1 to the Marrakesh Agreement Establishing the World Trade Organization (1995) 1867 UNTS 155, in force 1 January 1995; also WTO, *Status of WTO Legal Instruments* (Geneva, WTO, 2015) at 41.

[7] Para 1 of the Marrakesh Protocol to the General Agreement on Tariffs and Trade 1994 (the 'Marrakesh Protocol') states that '[t]he schedule annexed to this Protocol relating to a Member shall become a Schedule to GATT 1994 relating to that Member'.

[8] The EEC-12 schedule attached to the Marrakesh Protocol, ibid, was Schedule LXXX. The current certified EU-25 Schedule CLXXIII dates from 1 December 2016 (WT/Let/1220, 14 December 2016).

[9] For convenience, this article uses the term 'European Union' (EU), effective both generally and in the WTO (WT/Let/679) from 1 December 2009, also for its predecessors, the European Communities ('EC') (1993–2009), the European Coal and Steel Community ('ECSC') (1952–2002), and the European Economic Community ('EEC') (1958–1992).

[10] The UK's schedule for its metropolitan territory had been Schedule XIX, Section A, Parts I and II. The EEC withdrew the schedules of the EEC-6 and the UK (and Denmark and Ireland) as of 1 August 1974, and a new EEC-9 Schedule LXXII was circulated on 6 August 1974. See GATT, Art XXIV:6 Renegotiations—Entry into Force of Schedules LXXII and LXXII*bis*, L/4067, 6 August 1974.

[11] European Communities and their Member States—Schedule of Specific Commitments, GATS/SC/31, 15 April 1994. Article XX:1 of the GATS states that '[e]ach Member shall set out in a schedule the specific commitments it undertakes under Part III of this Agreement'. This language is personal to

met for the UK, and the UK will remain a WTO Member unless it withdraws from the WTO Agreement in accordance with Article XV of the WTO Agreement.[12]

Article XI:1 of the WTO Agreement is an unusual provision, although not unique,[13] insofar as it allows for the possibility that original WTO Members will lack autonomy in at least some of the areas covered by the WTO agreements. Specifically, this provision was designed for the EU and its Member States, each of which lacked full autonomy in areas covered by the WTO agreements.[14] This contrasts with Article XII of the WTO Agreement, according to which newly acceding WTO Members must have full autonomy in matters covered by the WTO agreements. But Article XI:1 has no effect on the rights and obligations of the EU and its Member States, which remain those of ordinary WTO Members.[15] There is no suggestion anywhere in the WTO Agreement, or in any relevant instruments, that the WTO rights and obligations of the EU Member States, or of the EU, are in any way limited to their areas of autonomy.[16] Indeed, there are indications to the contrary. The Marrakesh Final Act states that 'the WTO Agreement shall be open for acceptance as a whole, by signature or otherwise, by all participants pursuant to Article XIV thereof',[17] and Article XVI:5 of the WTO Agreement specifies that

each WTO Member, and seemingly does not permit one Member to submit a schedule 'for' another Member, contrary to Art XI:1 of the WTO Agreement. On the other hand, Art XVI:3 of the WTO Agreement states that '[i]n the event of a conflict between a provision of this Agreement and a provision of any of the Multilateral Trade Agreements, the provision of this Agreement shall prevail to the extent of the conflict.'

[12] It is also possible for a WTO Member to be expelled if it refuses to accept certain amendments to the WTO agreements under Art X:3 and Art X:5 of the WTO Agreement.

[13] Art 3 of the UN Charter states that '[t]he original Members of the United Nations shall be the states which … sign the present Charter and ratify it in accordance with Article 110.' Among the 49 original UN Members were Belarus, Ukraine, India and the Philippines, which, seemingly in contradiction to Art 3, were not independent states at that time.

[14] It was known that the EU Member States had no autonomy in the area of trade in goods, but it was uncertain whether they also lacked autonomy in the areas of services and intellectual property. On 15 April 1994 the WTO Agreement was signed separately by the EU and the EU Member States. On 15 November 1994 the European Court of Justice decided that, apart from cross-border services, the EU and its Member States possessed a shared competence for GATS and a joint competence for TRIPS: *Opinion 1/94*, paras 98 and 105. On 30 December 1994 the EU and its Member States each accepted the WTO Agreement in accordance with Art XIV:1 of the WTO Agreement: WTO, *Status of WTO Legal Instruments*, above n 6, at 16–42. Subsequent treaty changes have meant that, at present, except for transport services, all areas covered by the WTO are now within exclusive EU competence. See *Opinion 1/08 (GATS)* EU:C:2009:739 (GATS) and Case C-414/11, *Daiichi Sankyo* EU:C:2013:520 (TRIPS).

[15] I would like to thank Tomer Broude for insisting upon this point. See also Joni Heliskoski, 'EU Declarations of Competence and International Responsibility' in Malcolm Evans and Panos Koutrakos (eds), *The International Responsibility of the European Union* (Oxford, Hart, 2013) 192–96.

[16] As to whether the EU or its Member States could claim that their consent to be bound to the WTO Agreement was invalid on the grounds that it was in manifest violation of a constitutional norm of fundamental importance see Eva Steinberger, 'The WTO Treaty as a Mixed Agreement: Problems with the EC's and the EC Member States' Membership of the WTO' (2006) 14 *European Journal of International Law* 837, at 856–57.

[17] Para 4 of the Final Act Embodying the Results of the Uruguay Round of Multilateral Trade Negotiations.

'[n]o reservations may be made in respect of any provision of this Agreement.' Moreover, the WTO Agreement refers to the votes of the EU Member States, without limiting these to specific areas.[18]

The conclusion that the EU Member States have full WTO rights and responsibilities has also been endorsed in WTO jurisprudence.[19] In *EC/Certain MS—Large Civil Aircraft*, the Panel rejected an EU request to remove five EU Member States as respondent, which would have left the EU as the sole remaining respondent. It said that '[e]ach of these five is, in its own right, a Member of the WTO, with all the rights and obligations pertaining to such membership, including the obligation to respond to claims made against it by another WTO Member'. The Panel added that '[w]hatever responsibility the European Communities bears for the actions of its member States does not diminish their rights and obligations as WTO Members, but is rather an internal matter concerning the relations between the European Communities and its member States.'[20] The point is clear, and, it is submitted, correct. (It is also to be distinguished from the separate question whether conduct of the EU Member States can be attributed to the EU, and whether, if this is the case, such attribution is shared or exclusive.[21] Autonomy vis-à-vis rights and responsibility vis-à-vis obligations relate to law; attribution relates to acts.)[22]

It is worth noting that the arrangement set out in Article XI:1 is somewhat unusual, not only in international law generally, but also in the treaty practice of the

[18] fn 2 of Art IX:1 of the WTO Agreement.

[19] See Gracia Marín Durán, 'Untangling the International Responsibility of the European Union and Its Member States in the World Trade Organization Post-Lisbon: A Competence/Remedy Model' (2017) 28 *European Journal of International Law* 697.

[20] WTO Panel Report, *EC and Certain Member States—Large Civil Aircraft (Airbus)*, WT/DS316/R, adopted 1 June 2011, paras 7.174–7.175. See also WTO Panel Report, *EC—Selected Customs Matters*, adopted 11 December 2006, WT/DS315/R, para 7.548, stating that 'it would appear that the [EU] as well as its constituent member States concurrently bear the obligations contained in the WTO Agreements, including those contained in Article X:3(b) of the GATT 1994'. Further, Marín Durán, above n 19, at 708–21.

[21] For an argument in favour of exclusive attribution, based on the division of competences between the EU and the EU Member States, see Frank Hoffmeister, 'Litigating against the European Union and Its Member States—Who Responds under the ILC's Draft Articles on International Responsibility of International Organizations?' (2010) 21 *European Journal of International Law* 723, at 728 and 734 and Pieter-Jan Kuijper and Esa Paasivirta, 'EU International Responsibility and its Attribution: From the Inside Looking Out' in Evans and Koutrakos, above n 15, at 60–63. For an argument against, see Giorgio Gaja, ILC Special Rapporteur on responsibility of international organizations, Third Report, UN Doc A/CN.4/553, 13 May 2005, para 12 and, expressing a sceptical view, James Flett, 'The World Trade Organization and the European Union and its Member States in the WTO' in André Nollkaemper and Ilias Plakokefalos (eds), *The Practice of Shared Responsibility in International Law* (Cambridge, Cambridge University Press, 2016) at 896–97. See also WTO Panel Report, *Russia—Tariff Treatment*, WT/DS485/R, adopted 26 September 2016, para 7.46, in which the Panel said that 'the act of applying the duty rates (ie the levying of duties at the time of importation) is directly attributable to Russia' even though Russia was arguably acting as an organ of the Eurasian Economic Union (EAEU) in so doing.

[22] This is sometimes confused by reference to a party assuming 'responsibility' for the measures of another party.

EU and its Member States. Typically, when the EU and its Member States conclude so-called 'mixed agreements', they seek to limit their respective responsibilities to their areas of autonomy (or, in EU language, 'competence'). There are several ways by which this is sought to be achieved. One, common in multilateral treaties, is by making a 'declaration of competences' in relation to the various subject matters covered by the treaty.[23] Another is to define the 'parties' as 'the EU, or the Member States, or the EU and the Member States, in accordance with their respective powers'.[24] A third, more recent, innovation is to permit the EU to determine the proper respondent in any arbitral proceedings.[25] There is much that can be said about these techniques, but what is presently important is that, in the absence of a statement, effective in international law, that limits the respective responsibilities of the EU and its Member States under a given treaty, they will each be fully responsible for performing that treaty.[26] At most, one might argue that their liability would be joint in terms of quantum, an issue which is of little relevance to WTO law.[27]

III. Identifying the UK's Separate Rights and Obligations

A. Introduction

If the UK already possesses all of the rights and obligations of an original WTO Member, it will continue to possess all of these rights and obligations once it leaves

[23] See, eg, Heliskoski, above n 15.

[24] There has been virtually no academic commentary on these provisions. Hoffmeister considers that they determine responsibility according to whether a treaty provision specifies that it relates to an EU or Member State competence, and that in cases of shared responsibility or silence both the EU and its Member States (or State) might be responsible. See Frank Hoffmeister, 'The Contribution of EU Practice to International Law' in Marise Cremona (ed), *Developments in EU External Relations Law* (Oxford, Oxford University Press, 2008) 65.

[25] Art 8.21(3) of the Comprehensive Economic and Trade Agreement (CETA) between Canada and the EU and its Member States [2017] OJ L11/23.

[26] Piet Eeckhout, 'The EU and its Member States in the WTO—Issues of Responsibility' in Lorand Bartels and Federico Ortino (eds), *Regional Trade Agreements and the WTO Legal System* (Oxford, Oxford University Press, 2006) 457.

[27] At present, financial compensation is not available in WTO law, although it can form part of an agreed settlement. The question of quantum might also however be relevant for determining 'appropriate countermeasures' under the SCM Agreement in terms of the amount of a prohibited subsidy rather than by the injury caused. This approach was adopted in Arbitrator, *Brazil—Aircraft (Article 22.6—Canada)*, WT/DS46/ARB, 12 December 2000, para 3.60. But it has not been followed, inter alia because of the difficulties that would arise in the case of multiple complainants. See eg Arbitrator, *US—FSC (Article 22.6—US)*, WT/DS108/ARB, 30 August 2002, para 6.27. On joint and joint and several liability between the EU and its Member States in the WTO, see Flett, above n 21.

the EU. What will change is the EU's role in exercising these rights and assuming responsibility for performing these obligations, a role which will henceforth be exercised by the UK. What remains is to identify the UK's rights and obligations. Accordingly, the UK has declared its intention of submitting new schedules which replicate, as far as possible, the UK's existing obligations.[28]

This is relatively unproblematic in relation to WTO rights and obligations that apply on an *erga omnes partes* basis with respect to all WTO Members, or to WTO Members within an established category, such as developing countries, or when the UK is specifically named.[29] No more, therefore, needs to be said about the UK's rights and obligations under the WTO Agreement, the GATT 1994 (except for Article II), the GATS (except for Articles XX), the Agreement on Trade-Related Aspects of Intellectual Property Rights (TRIPS), or the Dispute Settlement Understanding (DSU). However, questions arise in relation to rights and obligations concerning the UK's commitments under Article II of the GATT 1994 and Article XX of the GATS, in particular when these commitments give the EU, by name, rights or obligations that are quantified, for example, in the form of quotas and money (such as the right to subsidise agricultural production up to a certain amount). It is these difficulties that explain why the UK proposes to replicate its existing commitments only 'as far as possible'.

B. The UK's Share of Import Tariff Rate Quotas of Other WTO Members

A first difficulty concerns the identification of the UK's share of tariff rate quotas offered by other WTO Members to the EU on a country-specific basis, such as the US tariff rate quota for cheese. Article XIII:2 of the GATT 1994, which applies to tariff rate quotas,[30] permits an importing WTO Member to allocate quotas, in the first instance, according to its chapeau, on a non-discriminatory basis.[31]

However, Article XIII:2(d) also offers an importing WTO Member the option of reaching an 'agreement with respect to the allocation of shares in the quota with all other contracting parties having a substantial interest in supplying the product concerned' or to allocate a quota to such parties based on their share

[28] Letter to all Permanent Representatives to the WTO from the UK and EU Permanent Representatives to the WTO, 11 October 2017.

[29] This includes special safeguard measures in the form of increased customs duties as permitted under Art 5 of the WTO Safeguards Agreement. See WTO Committee on Agriculture, Notification—European Union, G/AG/N/EU/39, 4 October 2017.

[30] Art XIII:5 of the GATT 1994.

[31] Art XIII:2(a) of the GATT 1994. Art XIII:2 aims to 'mimic' the comparative advantages of all WTO Members producing like products which might participate under a quota: WTO Appellate Body Report, *EC—Bananas III (Article 21.5—Ecuador II)*, WT/WT/DS27/AB/RW/ECU, adopted 22 December 2008, para 338.

of total imports[32] during a previous representative period,[33] 'due account being taken of any special factors which may have affected or may be affecting the trade in the product.'[34] In *EC—Bananas III (Article 21.5—Ecuador II)*, the Appellate Body stated that 'Article XIII:2(d) is a permissive "safe harbour"; compliance with the requirements of Article XIII:2(d) is presumed to lead to a distribution of trade as foreseen in the chapeau of Article XIII:2, as far as substantial suppliers are concerned.'[35]

Accordingly, as between these two options, there is a clear incentive for WTO Members with a substantial interest in supplying a given product to reach an agreement on the allocation of a quota. This is because, in the absence of such an agreement, pursuant to the chapeau of Article XIII:2, an importing WTO Member must allocate quota shares to WTO Members with a substantial supplying interest and to WTO Members without such an interest.[36] With such an agreement, however, an importer does not need to take any account of imports from WTO Members without a substantial supplying interest.

This does not mean that the UK has a clear right to access another WTO Member's tariff rate quota even when it has a substantial interest in those exports. In *EU—Poultry Meat*, the Panel determined that agreements under Article XIII:2(d) are not subject to revision simply because another WTO Member acquires a substantial supplying interest. It noted that Article XIII:4 imposed a procedural obligation on an importing country to consult on adjustments to the agreed quota, upon request, with any other WTO Member having a substantial supplying interest. However, the Panel was reluctant to read into this provision any substantive obligation to adjust this quota in any way. It accepted that 'a Member does not have unfettered discretion to refuse to reallocate the TRQ shares upon the request of a Member holding a substantial supplying interest following a change in import shares'.[37] However, the Panel avoided providing any further detail. All it said was that:

> the prevalence and centrality of historical market shares in TRQ share allocations also suggest that, insofar as there is indeed an obligation to reallocate the shares allocated

[32] WTO Appellate Body Report, *EC—Poultry*, WT/DS69/AB/R, adopted 23 July 1998, para 106.

[33] The representative period will typically be a three year period, which can be the three years preceding the commencement of negotiations, rather than the three years preceding the implementation of the TRQ: WTO Panel Report, *EU—Poultry Meat (China)*, WT/DS492/R, adopted 19 April 2017, para 7.353, although other periods may also be used: WTO Arbitrator, *EC—Bananas III*, WT/DS27/ARB/US, 9 April 1999, paras 5.29–5.33.

[34] According to the Note Ad Art XI:2 of the GATT 1994 (which applies also to Art XIII:2(d) and Art XIII:4 of the GATT 1994), 'special factors' include changes to the relative productive efficiencies of exporters and domestic producers. They do not include reductions in imports due to legitimate trade measures but can include increases following the withdrawal of such measures, even after the end of the representative period. See WTO Panel Report, *EU—Poultry Meat (China)*, WT/DS492/R, above n 33, paras 7.343 and 7.363.

[35] WTO Appellate Body Report, *EC—Bananas III (Art 21.5—Ecuador II)*, above n 31, para 338 and n 408.

[36] WTO Panel Report, *EU—Poultry Meat (China)*, above n 33, paras 7.402–406.

[37] ibid, para 7.478.

among supplying countries upon the request of a Member holding a substantial supplying interest under Article XIII:4, there is no obligation to do within any specified time frame, or with any particularly frequency.[38]

This means that, providing the UK has a substantial supplying interest in respect of a quota maintained by another WTO Member, it has an undoubted procedural right to consultations with a view to gaining a share of that quota, and it seems to have a substantive right to such a share, but when it might be entitled to enjoy that right remains unclear.

C. The UK's Share of EU-25 Import Tariff Rate Quotas

A more complicated question concerns the identification of the UK's commitment to provide certain country-specific tariff rate quotas as listed in the EU's existing schedule.[39] There are two practical solutions. One would be for the UK to bind a commitment to cover all products currently the subject of an EU tariff rate quota at the duty rate of that quota; the other would be for the UK (and, optionally, the EU) to reach an agreement with all suppliers, or all suppliers with a substantial interest, which would then be protected under the first sentence of Article XIII:2(d) of the GATT 1994. The UK and the EU have announced their intention to proceed on this basis,[40] although this proposal has already encountered opposition from WTO members concerned by a loss in both the quantity and the 'quality' of the existing tariff rate quota if it is split.[41]

Against this background, it is important to note that the UK has existing legal obligations in respect of its share of the tariff rate quotas that are currently set out in the EU-25 schedule. As this schedule is part of the GATT 1994,[42] the identification of the UK's share of these obligations, as expressed in this schedule, is a question of treaty interpretation. There are several key questions. One is the basis on which the UK's share can be determined. In the first instance, this must be seen in terms of the UK's territory (or at least that part of the UK's territory to which the

[38] ibid, para 7.480.

[39] See above n 8 for the EU's schedules. Tariff rate quotas are notified in WTO Committee on Agriculture, Notification—European Union (tariff rate quotas: imports), G/AG/N/EU/30, 2 September 2016 and WTO Committee on Agriculture, Notification—European Union (tariff rate quotas: administration), G/AG/N/EU/31, 2 September 2016. Quotas were filled above 70 per cent for the following products, not all of which are produced in the UK: beef, lamb, chicken, turkey, garlic, millet, sugar, cheddar, potatoes, carrots and turnips, sweet peppers, dried onions, grapes, apples, pears, almonds, maize, rice, manioc starch, pasta, chocolate, cereals, preserved fruit, fruit juices, wine, corn gluten, dog, cat and certain animal feed: WTO doc G/AG/N/EU/30, ibid.

[40] Letter, 11 October 2017, above n 28.

[41] Letter from the Permanent Representatives to the WTO of Argentina, Brazil, Canada, New Zealand, and the Chargés d'Affaires of the United States and Uruguayan Missions to the WTO, 26 October 2017. Australia has reportedly also rejected the UK-EU proposal.

[42] Art II:7 of the GATT 1994.

shared schedule applies). This follows from the rule of customary international law reflected in Article 29 of the Vienna Convention on the Law of Treaties, as well as from the rule, reflected in Article 34 of the same Convention, that treaties cannot affect third parties without their consent.[43]

As for the means by which the UK's share of the common commitment might be identified, it is certainly true that there is no express WTO rule on this point. It would however seem reasonable to adopt a method inspired by the principle by which quotas are apportioned, which, as discussed, is on the basis of trade flows over a representative three year period, taking into account any special factors. On this basis, it would seem reasonable to identify the UK's share of the EU-25 quota in terms of trade flows in the three years previous to the certification of that schedule in December 2016, again, taking account of any special factors. What is not relevant, however, at least to the UK's obligations, are any commitments affecting territory for which the UK is not responsible under WTO law. This, at least for the UK, should dispose of the objection that splitting the shared quota reduces the 'quality' of its commitment.

A second question is whether the EU-27 could access the UK's share of the EU-25 tariff rate quota (and vice versa). The difficulty is that, provided that there is no other basis on which the EU-27 exports those products to the UK, such as a free trade agreement or a waiver,[44] then, as an ordinary WTO Member, the EU-27 would have a right to request access to any UK tariff rate quota for any product for which it has a substantial supplying interest (and vice versa). That, of course, would reduce the value of any tariff rate quota for existing Members with a substantial supplying interest. As discussed, *EU—Poultry Meat* favoured the stability of any country-specific quota over the rights of newcomers, at least for a certain (unspecified) period. To that extent, WTO Members with country-specific quota rights have a certain degree of protection. But that protection is not indefinite, and in any event it does not extend to WTO Members supplying the UK under a general quota. It is arguable that, at least after a certain period for country-specific quotas and perhaps immediately for others, both the UK and the EU-27 will have the right to access each other's quotas. Interestingly, the UK and EU letter offering to divide their shared quotas does not address this point.[45]

[43] Arts 29 and 34 of the Vienna Convention on the Law of Treaties, (opened for signature 23 May 1969; entered into force on 27 January 1980) (1980) 1155 UNTS 331. See Case C-104/16 P, *Council v Polisario*, ECLI:EU:C:2016:973, paras 94–100 and Matthew Kennedy, 'Overseas Territories in the WTO' (2016) 65 *International and Comparative Law Quarterly* 741, at 746–47.

[44] GATT 1947 Panel Report, *EEC—Newsprint*, L/5680, adopted 20 November 1984, para 55; WTO Arbitrator, *EC—Bananas III*, above n 33, para 5.8.

[45] Letter, above n 41.

D. The UK's Share of the EU-25 Agricultural Subsidy Commitments

A next question concerns the UK's share of the EU's commitment not to subsidise agricultural production beyond a given annual quantum, or, to describe this from the other direction, the UK's share of the EU's liberty to subsidise up to that quantum. In reality, this question is unlikely to be very controversial,[46] as the EU's actual domestic subsidies are only seven per cent of its scheduled amount[47] and the EU has already abolished export subsidies,[48] in line with the 2015 WTO Nairobi Ministerial Decision on Export Competition.[49] Nonetheless, the theoretical question remains.

Once again, WTO law supplies no direct rules or principles for determining the UK's share of a shared liberty to subsidise agricultural production. One might wonder whether the origins of the UK's and EU's respective subsidy commitments would be a suitable basis for this calculation. As with tariff rate quotas, this might be relevant with respect to a non-violation complaint. Given the reduction in commitments over time, however, it is unlikely that any WTO Member would make such a claim. A more realistic option would be based on the UK's existing shares of the EU's subsidisation policy, either in terms of its (higher) contributions or its (lower) receipts.[50] As between these two options, given that the purpose of the commitments is to reduce distortions in the domestic marketplace, it is suggested that the stronger basis for determining the UK's right to subsidise would be the UK's receipts from the EU's Common Agricultural Policy, rather than its contributions to that policy, which are based on the UK's share of EU gross national income.[51]

[46] Alan Matthews, 'WTO dimensions of a UK "Brexit" and agricultural trade', http://capreform.eu/wto-dimensions-of-a-uk-brexit-and-agricultural-trade/, 5 January 2016. Statistical issues resulting from transit of products to the UK via other EU ports (the 'Rotterdam issue') may add a certain practical difficulty; see Yorkshire Agricultural Society, *The Implications of 'Brexit' for UK Agriculture*, 2016 (http://yas.co.uk/uploads/files/YAS_FSN_Brexit_-_Full_Report.pdf), at 29.

[47] In the marketing year 2013/14, domestic support was €5.9bn of a possible €72.3bn: WTO Committee on Agriculture, Notification—European Union, WT/G/AG/N/EU/34, 8 February 2017.

[48] In the marketing year 2015/16, export subsidies were zero except for on sugar, WTO Committee on Agriculture, Notification—European Union, G/AG/N/EU/38, 25 April 2017.

[49] WTO Ministerial Conference, Decision on Export Competition, 19 December 2015, WT/MIN(15)/45, para 6. For discussion of the legal value of this decision see Lorand Bartels, 'The Relationship between the WTO Agreement on Agriculture and the SCM Agreement: An Analysis of Hierarchy Rules in the WTO Legal System' (2016) 50 *Journal of World Trade* 7, at 17–19.

[50] Lars Brink, 'UK Brexit and WTO farm support limits', 13 July 2016 (http://capreform.eu/uk-brexit-and-wto-farm-support-limits/).

[51] If one were prepared to draw an analogy between a right to subsidise agricultural production and movable property related to territory, this would also accord with the rule in the Vienna Convention on Succession of States in Respect of State Property providing that 'movable State property of the predecessor State connected with the activity of the predecessor State in respect of the territory to which the succession of States relates shall pass to the successor State'. Art 14(2)(b) and Art 15(1)(d) of the 1983 Vienna Convention on Succession of States in Respect of State Property, Archives and Debts (done 8 April 1983, not yet in force).

E. The UK's GATS Schedules

A next question concerns the UK's commitments under Article XX of the GATS.[52] The UK, the EU and the other EU Member States share a generic set of commitments, subject to limitations on an EU Member State basis. These can easily be transposed to a new exclusive UK GATS schedule.

There is a slightly niche issue concerning the territorial limitation to the schedule annexed by the EU and the UK to the GATS, according to which '[t]he specific commitments in this schedule apply only to the territories in which the Treaties establishing the European Communities are applied and under the conditions laid down in these Treaties'.[53] Read strictly, this clause would have the effect that, after leaving the EU, the UK would have no commitments in respect of its own territory, even though it would continue to have rights vis a vis other WTO Members in respect of their territories. This is far from desirable, even if it is not legally impossible for such an unbalanced situation to exist. It appears to be assumed that the WTO agreements apply to territories of WTO Members that are not subject to a schedule (such as the Faroe Islands, a dependency of Denmark).[54]

There is however a different approach. It is a principle of customary international law that a treaty only binds a state in respect of its territory 'unless a different intention appears from the treaty or is otherwise established'.[55] It might be argued that the territorial application clause represents just such a different intention.[56] However, it is readily apparent that this clause was predicated upon the EU Member States continuing as such. It is therefore suggested that, once the UK leaves the EU, that clause be read either as applying to UK territory described in that clause, or else ignored entirely, with the result that the UK's commitments would extend to all UK territory unless expressly limited.

This is not as radical a suggestion as might be thought. According to the 'moving frontiers' principle, a rule of customary international law,[57] when territory passes from one state to another, the treaties of the former state cease to apply to that territory and the treaties of the latter state commence applying to that territory.

[52] European Communities and their Member States—Schedule of Specific Commitments, GATS/SC/31, above n 11.

[53] ibid.

[54] Kennedy, above n 43 at 745.

[55] Art 29 of the Vienna Convention on the Law of Treaties, above n 43.

[56] Schedules of concessions are an integral part of the GATT 1994, according to Art II:7 of this agreement.

[57] The 'moving frontiers' rule is codified in Art 15 of the 1978 Vienna Convention on the Succession of States in Respect of Treaties (1978) 1946 UNTS 3, in force 6 November 1996. In 1990 Germany notified the GATT 1947 contracting parties that it was now applying the GATT 1947 to the territory of the former German Democratic Republic and East Berlin, which it had absorbed. See GATT Doc L/6759, 31 October 1990. There were no objections.

Importantly, this rule includes limitations on treaties, such as reservations,[58] and there is no reason why this rule would not likewise apply to territorial limitations. The result, which accords with common sense, would be that the territorial application clause in the current EU schedule would simply cease to be relevant to the UK once its leaves the EU, and this could be reflected by means of a rectification to that schedule.

In any case, one might doubt whether, in practice, this territorial application is likely to cause much controversy. As a rule, WTO Members are unlikely to complain that another Member's schedule covers too much, rather than too little. For example, when the UK notified the WTO that its commitments now covered the Isle of Man, it made no exception for services[59] notwithstanding the fact that the EU treaties do not apply to the Isle of Man in respect of services,[60] and this passed without any objections by any other WTO Members.

IV. Procedures for Rectifying and Modifying Schedules of Concessions

These considerations inform the procedure applicable to the UK in annexing new schedules to the GATT 1994 and the GATS.

With one relevant exception, discussed shortly, the current procedure for making changes to a GATT 1994 schedule is set out in the 1980 Decision on Procedures for Modification and Rectification of Schedules of Tariff Concessions,[61] which is binding as part of the GATT 1994.[62] This Decision distinguishes between modifications, on the one hand, and 'other changes,' on the other. Paragraph 1 describes modifications, relevantly, as follows: 'Changes in the authentic texts of Schedules annexed to the General Agreement which reflect modifications resulting from action under Article II, Article XVIII, Article XXIV, Article XXVII or Article XXVIII shall be certified by means of Certifications'.

It is notable that each of the provisions listed in this paragraph is concerned with negotiations reflecting an intention by a WTO Member to increase duties or other barriers to trade. Article II:5 grants an affected WTO Member a right to consult another WTO Member if the first Member considers that a product is

[58] First report on succession of States in respect of treaties, by Sir Francis Vallat, Special Rapporteur, International Law Commission, Commentary to Article 14 [later 15], UN Doc A/CN.4/278 (1974) II(1) Yearbook of the International Law Commission 1, at 210, para 11.

[59] Confirmed by email communication with the UK Foreign and Commonwealth Office.

[60] Art 355(5)(c) of the Treaty on the Functioning of the European Union, discussed in Fiona Murray, *The European Union and Member State Territories* (The Hague, TMC Asser, 2012) 152.

[61] GATT Contracting Parties, Procedures for Modification and Rectification of Schedules of Tariff Concessions, Decision of 26 March 1980, L/4962.

[62] Introductory language to the GATT 1994, para 1(b)(iv).

not receiving the expected treatment contemplated by a concession; Article XVIII grants developing country WTO Members a right to raise trade barriers for the purposes of infant industry production, subject to compensation; Article XXIV:6 refers to the procedure in Article XVIII for WTO Members wishing to raise duties as a result of forming a regional trade agreement; Article XXVII grants WTO members the right to withdrawing or withholding concessions initially negotiated with a party that never became or ceased to become a WTO Member; and Article XXVIII establishes a right for a WTO member wishing to modify or withdraw a concession, and a mechanism for consulting and negotiating compensation with certain other affected WTO Members.

Other 'changes' are described in paragraph 2 of the 1980 Decision, which states, relevantly, as follows:

> Changes in the authentic texts of Schedules shall be made when amendments or rearrangements which do not alter the scope of a concession are introduced in national customs tariffs in respect of bound items. Such changes and other rectifications of a purely formal character shall be made by means of Certifications.[63]

It is to be emphasised that paragraph 2 describes not only formal rectifications, which are concerned with accuracy, but also 'other amendments and rearrangements which do not alter the scope of a concession'. Given that paragraph 1 is concerned with modifications that negatively affect concessions, it is submitted that this phrase must refer both to changes that are neutral, and to those that lead to improvements to bound concessions. The equivalent 2000 GATS Council Decision makes this even clearer by distinguishing between ordinary modifications, on the one hand, and 'modifications … which consist of new commitments, improvements to existing ones, or rectifications or changes of a purely technical character that do not alter the scope or the substance of the existing commitments'.[64]

This said, one might wonder whether the submission of a new schedule by a newly autonomous WTO Member, such as a post-Brexit UK, can be treated as a 'change' in a schedule not amounting to a modification as described in paragraph 1 of the Decision. In this respect, however, it is relevant to refer to paragraph 5 of the 1980 Decision, which states that:

> The procedure of Certification under this Decision may be applied for the establishment of consolidated Schedules or of new Schedules under paragraph 5(c) of Article XXVI, wherein all changes are modifications or rectifications referred to in paragraphs 1 or 2.

Article XXVI:5(c) of the GATT 1947 permitted newly autonomous customs territories, which in practice was mainly decolonised independent states, to which the GATT 1947 had been made applicable, to succeed to GATT contracting

[63] See above at n 60.

[64] WTO Council for Trade in Services, Decision on Procedures for the Certification of Rectifications or Improvements to Schedules of Specific Commitments, adopted 14 April 2000, S/L/83, 18 April 2000. The Procedures are set out in S/L/84, 18 April 2000.

party status,[65] upon request and with the sponsorship of the responsible (or formerly responsible) GATT contracting party.[66] Upon succession, the newly autonomous territory inherited all of the rights and obligations that were previously applicable to its territory, including scheduled commitments (and qualifications)[67] which the formerly responsible contracting party had made effective in respect of its territory.[68] Sometimes, this meant that succeeding contracting parties preferred not to inherit these rights and obligations, and rather accede to the GATT 1947 as a new contracting party.[69] Importantly, and relevantly to the present situation, the submission of new GATT 1947 schedules in this context was

[65] Alberta Fabbricotti, 'Article XXVI' in Rüdiger Wolfrum, Peter-Tobias Stoll and Holger Hestermeyer (eds), *WTO—Trade in Goods*, Max Planck Commentaries on World Trade Law, Vol 5 (Leiden, Brill, 2011). The right of succession—to be deemed a contracting party—was automatic, on request, provided that the request was sponsored by the responsible (or formerly responsible) contracting party. See GATT Council, Minutes of Meeting 25 April to 1 May 1963, GATT Doc C/M/15, 15 May 1962, at 7. The automaticity of this procedure is reflected in the more accurate use, at least after 1963, of the terminology of 'succession': Tatsuro Kunigi, 'State Succession in the Framework of GATT' (1965) 59 *American Journal of International Law* 268, at 272 and 275. Going beyond the usual rules in some respect, newly autonomous territories were also permitted a grace period prior to deciding whether to apply for succession (during which, to a limited extent, they were treated as de facto GATT contracting parties): GATT Contracting Parties, Application of the Provisions of Article XXVI:5(c), Recommendation adopted by the Contracting Parties on 1 November 1957, GATT Doc L/748, 21 November 1957. This reflection period was later extended indefinitely, until the WTO required that all Members submit schedules. See para 1(a) of the WTO Ministerial Decision on the Acceptance of and Accession to the Agreement Establishing the World Trade Organization, and, extending the period, WTO General Council, *Decision on the Finalization of Negotiations on Schedules on Goods and Services*, 31 January 1995, WT/L/30, 7 February 1995. Craig VanGrasstek, *The History and Future of the World Trade Organization* (Geneva, WTO, 2013) 125, notes that '[s]everal of the countries that were still negotiating by the time the WTO came into being might well have regretted not taking advantage of this option.'

[66] The criterion of sponsorship was solely evidentiary. It was to clarify for other GATT 1947 contracting parties that the territory at issue was, in fact, autonomous in matters covered by the GATT 1947.

[67] As the 1961 Working Party on the application of Art XXXV to Japan said, 'there could be no doubt that a government becoming a contracting party under Article XXVI:5(c) does so on the terms and conditions previously accepted by the metropolitan government on behalf of the territory in question.' See GATT Contracting Parties, Report of the Working Party on Article XXXV Review, GATT Doc L/1545, 6 September 1961, para 19. See also below at 246 for an example of a state leaving a customs union that is a GATT contracting party and assuming its commitments. This is in accordance with the rule stated in Art 20(1) of the 1978 Convention on the Succession of States in Respect of Treaties.

[68] Contrary to earlier practice, the GATT Panel on *Jamaica—Margins of Preference*, GATT Doc L/3485, adopted 2 February 1971, para 13, determined that the date for determining the application of GATT obligations (in casu, preference margins under Art I:4 of the GATT 1947) was the date on which the original obligations were undertaken (in casu, 1947), not the date on which autonomy was acquired (in casu, 1962). The assumption of previously applicable commitments contrasts with Art 20(2) of the 1978 Convention, according to which newly independent states were permitted to formulate new reservations upon their notification of succession to a multilateral treaty.

[69] An example was Cambodia, which preferred not to commit to the high scheduled commitments that had been applied to its territory (as part of the Indo-China customs union) under France's schedule of concessions. See GATT Contracting Parties, Accession of Cambodia: Statement by Cambodia, GATT Doc L/900, 1 November 1958. It was similar for Tunisia, as discussed by Kunigi, above n 64, at 279.

treated as 'other changes', except when the schedule required an increase in duties beyond the bound rate.[70]

One must, of course, be careful in drawing an analogy between the situation presented by the UK's departure from the EU and the situation described by Article XXVI:5(c) of the GATT 1947, which concerned the acquisition by a customs territory of full autonomy in matters covered by the GATT 1947. In particular, the UK is already a WTO Member, whereas the purpose of Article XXVI:5(c) was to establish a right of succession to contracting party status. However, the facts that are described by Article XXVI:5(c) are the same as those presented by the UK's departure from the EU. That is to say, the UK will become, once again, a customs territory with full autonomy in matters covered by the WTO agreements. It is submitted that for this reason, practice under Article XXVI:5(c) of the GATT 1947 in relation to the identification of the commitments of the newly autonomous customs territories should 'guide' the WTO, in accordance with Article XVI:1 of the WTO Agreement, even though, of course, technically this practice only applies to cases falling under Article XXVI:5(c), which is no longer operative. This is therefore a second reason for suggesting that the UK should submit a new schedule to the GATT 1994 as a 'change' not amounting to a modification, which would enable the UK to avoid having to go through the procedures for modification.

The issue is somewhat easier in relation to subsidy commitments, as it would appear that there is no right to modify these commitments, at least in the sense that they can be increased.[71] There is therefore no alternative but to see the UK's submission of a new schedule with respect to agricultural subsidies as an 'other change' within the meaning of paragraph 2 of the 1980 Decision. As for services, the relevant procedure for the necessary rectifications and other 'changes'—these being name, schedule number and removal of the territorial application clause—is set out in paragraph 1 of the equivalent GATS Council Decision.[72]

The significance of submitting new UK GATT 1994 and GATS schedules for certification as 'changes' and rectifications within the meaning of the respective procedures is that other WTO Members have limited grounds on which they may object. Paragraph 3 of the 1980 Decision states as follows:

> The draft containing the changes described in paragraphs 1 and 2 shall be communicated by the Director-General to all the contracting parties and shall become a Certification

[70] For example, Cameroon accepted that it would have been required to renegotiate its schedule under Art XXIV:6 of the GATT 1947 if it had to increase its tariff bindings due to its membership of a customs union. See GATT, Accession by Newly-Independent African States to the GATT, INT(62)142, 3 November 1962, para 18.

[71] Bernard Hoekman and Petros Mavroidis, 'MFN Clubs and Scheduling Additional Commitments in the GATT: Learning from the GATS' (2017) 28 *European Journal of International Law* 387, at 397–98.

[72] GATS Council, Decision, S/L/84, above n 63.

> provided that no objection has been raised by a contracting party within three months on the ground that, in the case of changes described in paragraph 1, the draft does not correctly reflect the modifications or, in the case of changes described in paragraph 2, the proposed rectification is not within the terms of that paragraph.

The 2000 GATS Decision does not expressly restrict the grounds on which objections may be made, but it does specify that '[a] Member making an objection should to the extent possible identify the specific elements of the modifications which gave rise to that objection.'[73] By implication, the same grounds should be relevant here, or else there would be no need to distinguish between modifications and other changes. On the other hand, there is no practice of rejecting an improperly grounded objection, even if the WTO Director-General by implication has this power, in order to administer these procedures.

This means that, regardless of the UK's proposed schedules, and even if they represent, on a proper analysis, other 'changes' and rectifications and not modifications, it is likely that other WTO Members will object in any case.

Given this, it is important to note that the legal effect of certification is less than is conventionally thought. The right of WTO Members to modify or withdraw their commitments is 'absolute',[74] and stems from the relevant provisions of the GATT 1994 and GATS,[75] not from any secondary instruments on certification or renegotiations. There are several consequences to certification, among which is an evidentiary consequence. In the event of an objection to certification, as a matter of practice it will either be the last certified schedule that is applicable or, should this be contested, the schedule that, legally, reflects the commitments made by a WTO Member in accordance with proper procedures.[76]

In the present case, it matters little if WTO Members refuse to certify the UK's new schedule. What counts is that the UK accurately reflects its existing commitments, as they are currently expressed in the shared EU and UK GATT 1994 and GATS schedules. Ultimately, if there is any dispute as to whether a UK measure violates a scheduled commitment, the matter, including the definition of that commitment, will fall to be interpreted in WTO dispute settlement proceedings.

[73] ibid, para 2.

[74] Anwarul Hoda, *Tariff Negotiations and Renegotiations under the GATT and the WTO* (Cambridge, Cambridge University Press, 2001) 15.

[75] See the lengthy discussion in WTO Panel Report, *EU—Poultry Meat (China)*, above n 33, paras 7.496–7.550. Cf John Jackson, *World Trade and the Law of GATT* (Cambridge, MA, The MIT Press, 1997) 75.

[76] See, eg, WTO Panel Report, *Russia—Tariff Treatment*, WT/DS485/R, above n 21, para 7.54; GATT Panel Report, *Jamaica—Margins of Preference*, above n 67, para 13; WTO Council for Trade in Services, above n 63, para 4 (by implication).

V. Government Procurement Agreement

A final question concerns the UK's status under the revised WTO Government Procurement Agreement (GPA), a plurilateral WTO agreement.[77] Article XXII:1 states that:

> This Agreement shall enter into force on 1 January 1996 for those governments[1] whose agreed coverage is contained in the Annexes of Appendix I of this Agreement, and which have, by signature, accepted the Agreement on 15 April 1994, or have, by that date, signed the Agreement subject to ratification and have subsequently ratified the Agreement before 1 January 1996.
>
> [1] For the purpose of this Agreement, the term 'government' is deemed to include the competent authorities of the European Union.

It is the EU alone, and not the UK, that is the relevant party to this agreement. Accordingly, it is at present the EU that is solely responsible for its obligations under the agreement, including in respect of the actions of government authorities that are organs of its Member States.

The UK Government has adopted the view that the UK should seek to accede to the GPA as a newly acceding party.[78] The following explains why this route—which will involve negotiations that might leave the UK worse off than before—is not necessary. More specifically, it is submitted that on leaving the EU, the UK is entitled to succeed to the GPA in its own right, in accordance with rules of customary international law on the succession of states to treaties, and practice under the GATT 1947, which 'guides' the WTO.[79]

There are two preliminary points. First, whether states succeed to treaties is independent of whether they succeed to the membership of international organisations, where practice is mixed.[80] Second, while it is true that the 1978 Convention

[77] Agreement on Government Procurement (1996) 1915 UNTS 103, n 2. Four EU Member States, but not the UK, ratified the GPA 1995: ibid. The revised Agreement on Government Procurement was however only accepted by the EU, not by these Member States: WTO, *Status of WTO Legal Instruments*, above n 6, at 128–29. Switzerland is a party to the original but not the revised GPA. For brevity, this article refers only to the 'GPA' as the Brexit-related issues relating to both are identical.

[78] See above n 4.

[79] Art XVI:1 of the WTO Agreement.

[80] Konrad Bühler, *State Succession and Membership in International Organizations* (The Hague, Kluwer, 2001) 309–12, concludes his book with the proposition that international organisations that are functionally limited, particularly in relation to political issues, recognise the succession of membership, while others, such as the United Nations, do not. Practice under the GATT 1947, a functionally specific quasi-organisation, is open to interpretation. Most cases of direct succession involve the independence of former colonies, which was specifically regulated under Art XXVI:5(c) of the GATT 1947. Beyond this, there examples of unions that succeeded to the contracting party status of a constituent entity, such as the Federation of Rhodesia and Nyasaland; however, there are also examples of contrary practice, such as that concerning the Czech and Slovak Republics, which acceded as new GATT contracting parties upon the dissolution of Czechoslovakia, which had been a GATT contracting party. On the other hand, these new contracting parties were permitted to retain the Czechoslovakia's rights and obligations without any need for negotiations; so de facto this can be considered a case of succession, supporting Bühler's argument, though he does not refer to this example.

on Succession of States in respect of Treaties is, strictly speaking, inapplicable to predecessors which are international organisations and not states, there is practice concerning the succession of states from unions and federations formed by them with other states. This practice is virtually uniform: in almost all cases the state resuming its autonomy succeeded to the rights and obligations in treaties entered into by that federation or union.[81] This includes, in particular, trade agreements. A 1971 study by the UN Secretariat, having reviewed state practice, concluded that 'in general the members of a union remain bound by the trade agreements of the union following its dissolution, at least if there is a clear continuity of the entity involved.'[82] This accords with the basic rule in the 1978 Convention, which is that new states formerly part of a predecessor state succeed to treaties concluded by the predecessor state that apply to them or, where relevant, their territory.[83] (There is a possible exception for newly independent ex-colonies (and perhaps others in a similar situation),[84] for which succession may not be automatic, but which may rather be at their election.[85] This is a controversial rule, but for present purposes this does not matter, as this rule mirrors, and is in part drawn from, the practice under Article XXVI:5(c) of the GATT 1947 which, as mentioned above, is no longer operative.)

There is also GATT 1947 practice to the same effect. This concerned the Federation of Rhodesia and Nyasaland (also called the Central African Federation), which was formed by Southern Rhodesia, Northern Rhodesia and Nyasaland in 1953, and which succeeded to the contracting party status of Southern Rhodesia.[86] The United Kingdom, which at the time retained a measure of sovereignty over all of these parties under general international law, certified that the Federation had the requisite autonomy in matters covered by the GATT 1947.[87] It would seem,

[81] DP O'Connell, *State Succession in Municipal Law and International Law*, vol II: International Relations (Cambridge, Cambridge University Press, 1967) 164–78, discussing the dissolutions of the Union of Colombia (1829–31), the German Confederation (1866), the United Arab Republic (1960), the Mali Federation (1960), the Federation of Rhodesia and Nyasaland (1963), and the separation of Singapore from Malaysia (1965). O'Connell is critical of cases in which a succeeding state did not assume the obligations incurred by the federation or union, such as Mali (ibid, at 172). He distinguishes these cases from those of secession involving dismemberment, such as the dismemberment of the Austro-Hungarian monarchy (1919) and Rwanda-Burundi (1962), but even here a general principle can be discerned, with anomalies explained on their facts, in favour of the continuity of treaties for the newly emerged states (ibid, at 178–82).

[82] UN Secretariat, Succession of States in respect of bilateral treaties: third study prepared by the Secretariat [trade agreements], UN Doc A/CN.4/243/Add.1, 24 March 1971, para 182.

[83] Art 34 of the Vienna Convention on the Succession of States in Respect of Treaties, above n 56.

[84] See, for example, Eritrea: Ethiopia–Eritrea Claims Commission, Prisoners of War—Eritrea's Claim 17, Partial Award (2003) 26 RIAA 23, para 35.

[85] Arts 16 and 17 of the 1978 Vienna Convention on the Succession of States in Respect of Treaties, above n 56 (with some exceptions).

[86] GATT, Central African Federation—Joint Statement issued by the United Kingdom and Southern Rhodesian Delegations for the Information of the Contracting Parties, L/132, 22 September 1953, discussed in GATT Contracting Parties, Summary Record of the Thirteenth Meeting, 6 October 1953, SR.8/13, 12 October 1953. See also GATT, Central African Federation—Joint Notification by the Governments of the United Kingdom and Southern Rhodesia, L/172, 6 November 1953 and GATT Contracting Parties, Federation of Rhodesia and Nyasaland—Declaration of 1 November 1954, L/278, 11 November 1954.

[87] GATT Contracting Parties, Federation of Rhodesia and Nyasaland—Declaration, L/278, ibid.

however, that this was not a case of succession under Article XXVI:5(c) of the GATT 1947 but rather a case of straightforward succession under international law. The relevant decision contains a preamble stating that 'by the said Declarations [of the United Kingdom and Southern Rhodesia], the Government of Southern Rhodesia has notified the CONTRACTING PARTIES that the Federal Government has succeeded to the rights and obligations under the Agreement formerly accepted by Southern Rhodesia'.[88] It is only after this that the contracting parties declared that the Federation was 'deemed to be a contracting party'. The Federation therefore apparently succeeded as a contracting party on two bases: first, as the successor to Southern Rhodesia, which took effect as of the unilateral declaration by Southern Rhodesia, and second, independently, by declaration of the GATT contracting parties, most likely (although this provision was not cited in relevant respects) under Article XXVI:5(c). For present purposes, of course, it is the first element of this practice that is relevant. It should suffice that the UK declares unilaterally that it succeeds to the EU's status as a party to the GPA in respect of itself and its territory.

This precedent also has a second dimension. The Federation dissolved in 1963, at which point Southern Rhodesia notified the GATT contracting parties as follows:

> In resuming its former status as a contracting party to the GATT, the Southern Rhodesian Government accepts, in respect of the territory of Southern Rhodesia
>
> (i) the rights and obligations incurred by the former Federal Government under various protocols, declarations and recommendations, including the disinvocation of Article XXXV in respect of Japan;
> (ii) that Schedule XVI once again becomes Southern Rhodesia's Schedule in the GATT and that the rights and obligations of the former Federal Government in relation to the concessions negotiated with other contracting parties will be applicable to Southern Rhodesia; and
> (iii) the base date provisions of the Decision of 19 November 1960 and the provisions of the further Decision of 19 November 1960 relative to the Customs Treatment for Products of United Kingdom Dependent Territories.[89]

There was no objection from other GATT 1947 contracting parties, which may be taken as acquiescence in this claim. For present purposes, the relevance of

[88] ibid.

[89] GATT, Submission by the Southern Rhodesian Government for the Information of Contracting Parties, GATT Doc L/2167, 4 March 1964. This claim also had a practical incident, insofar as Southern Rhodesia notified the GATT contracting parties shortly after this declaration that it was withdrawing a safeguard measure that had been imposed by the Federation. GATT, Southern Rhodesia—Article XIX—Modification of Restrictions on Certain Textile Piece-Goods, GATT Doc L/2213, 28 April 1964.

Southern Rhodesia's assumption of the rights and obligations incurred by the Federation is that this occurred by way of right. Again, this supports the proposition that the UK is entitled at its election to succeed to the GPA in its own name.

Additionally, it is relevant that other GPA parties have, at least to some extent, acknowledged that the EU is a party to the GPA in part on behalf of its Member States. In a GPA Committee Decision approving the modification by the EU of its Annexes by adding entities of new EU Member States, the GPA Committee '[r]ecogniz[ed] that … these ten countries will, as member States of the European Communities, form part of the European Communities for the purposes of the Agreement and be bound by the Agreement'.[90] Strictly speaking, this cannot mean that these EU Member States are bound directly by the GPA. It probably refers to the fact that the EU Member States are bound under EU law by the GPA. However, what this also means, it may be suggested, is that other WTO Members have expressly recognised that the EU's status as party to the GPA is at least in part on behalf of its Member States in respect of their territory. This should be sufficient to estop those other GPA parties from rejecting a UK claim to succeed to this agreement in its own name.

One final issue should be mentioned. Sue Arrowsmith has observed that succession might run into difficulties because the scope of GPA parties' obligations is in part determined by bilateral agreements.[91] She adds that 'the GPA does not currently apply at all to govern the rights and obligations of the EU Member States inter se, but only includes commitments relating to the rights and obligations of those states vis-à-vis third country Parties to the GPA.'[92] On the first point, it is important to distinguish the UK's right to succeed to the EU's rights and obligations in respect of UK territory, and the identification of those rights and obligations. The fact that the latter task may be difficult does not mean that it cannot (or need not) be undertaken. On the second, one can assume, as an inevitable consequence of succession, that the UK and the EU would be considered as ordinary third country GPA parties vis-à-vis each other. Nor, in practice, should this raise any particular difficulties, as their obligations to each other are (with certain non-material exceptions) applicable to all third country GPA parties on

[90] WTO Committee on Government Procurement, Decision Pursuant to Article XXIV:6(a) of the Agreement on Government Procurement, 23 April 2004, GPA/78, 4 May 2004 (EU-25), WTO Committee on Government Procurement, Decision Pursuant to Article XXIV:6(a) of the Agreement on Government Procurement, 8 December 2006, GPA/90, 11 December 2006 (EU-27) and WTO Committee on Government Procurement, Decision Pursuant to Article XXIV:6(a) of the Agreement on Government Procurement, 27 June 2013, GPA/118, 27 June 2013 (EU-28).

[91] Sue Arrowsmith, *Consequences of Brexit in the Area of Public Procurement* (Brussels: European Parliament, 2017), at 30. Similarly, see Maike Schäfer, 'Die Rechtsstellung des Vereinigten Königreiches der WTO nach dem Brexit: Verfahren, Rechtslage, Herausforderungen', Paper 147, in Christian Tietje, Gerhard Kraft and Christoph Kumpan (eds), *Beiträge zum Transnationalen Wirtschaftsrecht*, at 26–27.

[92] Arrowsmith, ibid.

a most-favoured-nation basis. It is difficult, therefore, without more detailed argument, to see why succession to the GPA poses problems any greater than succession to any other multilateral treaty.

VI. Conclusion

To summarise, on the basis of the analysis offered here, the UK possesses full WTO rights and performs obligations under the WTO multilateral trade agreements, which are currently, for the most part, exercised and performed on its behalf by the EU, and that the UK also succeeds to the rights and obligations under the Government Procurement Agreement, which are currently held in respect of itself and its territory by the EU. In many respects it is not complicated to identify the UK's rights and obligations under these agreements. Its rights (currently exercised by the EU) are easy to identify insofar as they correspond to obligations owed *erga omnes partes* by other WTO Members; its obligations (currently performed by the EU, and at times by the UK) are likewise easily identified insofar as they are owed by the UK (including via the EU's schedules of concessions) on an *erga omnes partes* basis to all other WTO Members. The main detail on this point concerns the territorial limitation in the UK's GATS schedule, according to which the schedule only applies to EU territory, but this can with justification be ignored in the UK's new schedule.

Complications arise where the UK's rights correspond to part of a right or obligation, determined on a quantified basis, that is currently set out in the EU's schedules. This is the case for the EU's right to subsidise agricultural production up to a set limit, and for the EU's rights to export agricultural production to other WTO Members on a preferential basis under certain of their tariff rate quotas. It was suggested that the UK should adopt a subsidy commitment corresponding to recent receipts from the EU's Common Agricultural Policy over the past three years, and that it has an automatic right, under Article XIII:2 of the GATT 1994, to access its share of any such tariff rate quotas.

As to the UK's quantified obligations corresponding to the EU's country-specific tariff rate quotas, it is likely that, in practice, quotas are likely to be established with relevant WTO Members by agreement, in accordance with Article XIII:2 of the GATT 1994. However, such an agreement should be reached against the background of the fact that the UK currently possesses obligations with respect to these tariff rate quotas; it is just difficult to know what these obligations mean in practice. It was also suggested that the UK could offer tariff rate quotas corresponding to recent imports, including from the EU-27, over a representative three year period, to forestall a potential non-violation complaint.

Finally, as to the procedure to be followed, it was contended that the UK should submit new schedules under Article II of the GATT 1994 and Article XX of the

GATS as other 'changes' and rectifications to the current EU schedule, in respect of itself and its territory. Importantly, any objections to such schedules would not entitle other WTO Members to require renegotiation of the UK's entire schedule, as is sometimes thought to be the case (and certainly not under Article XXVIII of the GATT 1994, which is in any case irrelevant to this situation). At most, it will lead to dispute settlement proceedings in respect of a given measure alleged to violate the UK's commitments or that otherwise nullifies or impairs benefits under the GATT 1994 or the GATS.

10

A Willing International Federalist? The UK's Pivotal Role within the United Nations

NIGEL D WHITE

I. Introduction

At the outset of his 2006 analysis of the past, present and future of the United Nations, the historian Paul Kennedy cites the poem by Alfred Lord Tennyson, 'Locksley Hall', published in 1837. A few lines from that poem are quoted here:

> For I dipt into the future, far as human eye could see,
>
> Saw the vision of the world, and all the wonders that would be;
>
> ...
>
> Till the war-drum throbb'd no longer, and the battle flags were furl'd
>
> In the Parliament of Man, the federation of the world.
>
> There the common sense of most shall hold a fretful realm in awe,
>
> And the kindly earth shall slumber, lapt in universal law.

Kennedy concludes that the UN General Assembly comes closest to the idea of a 'Parliament of Man',[1] seating representatives of all 193 Member States, but its powers are weak in comparison to the Security Council, the 'executive' organ of the UN, which in turn seats the executives of the five permanent members (including the UK), along with those of 10 non-permanent members. Nonetheless, the composition, functions and powers of the principal political organs of the United Nations seem to fall a long way short of the 'federation of the world' dreamt of by Tennyson.

[1] P Kennedy, *The Parliament of Man: The Past, Present and Future of the United Nations* (London, HarperCollins, 2006) 208.

It is unusual to discuss the United Nations as the central component in a federalising international order but it must be remembered that 'federalism' is not a precise concept. Livingston wrote in 1952 of a 'spectrum of federal societies'; stating further:

> This is no less true of federalism than it is of any other form of political organisation. Federalism is a function not of constitutions but of societies. Viewed in this way, it will be seen that federalism is not an absolute but a relative term; there is no specific point at which a society ceases to be unified and becomes diversified.[2]

Eschewing any standard definition of 'federalism' at the outset, this chapter explores the use of the term, and other forms of organisation, in the context of the League of Nations and the United Nations, focusing in particular on the UK's role in shaping those organisations and being a key member of them. The question then raised is whether harnessing the coercive powers of enforcement given to the Security Council is evidence of a federalising international order, moreover one with the potential to by-pass the rule of law in the UK? As with federalism, the concept of the 'rule of law' is contested but for the purposes of this chapter is deployed in the broad sense identified by Waldron: that 'respect for the law can take the edge off human political power, making it less objectionable, less dangerous, more benign and more respectful'.[3] Rule of law compliance is a term used in this chapter to indicate that the balance between politics and law, particularly in the context of decision-making, leans more towards compliance with legal principles, norms and rules than policies, power, political expediency or discretion.

The chapter considers how the UK combines arguments of the supremacy of security obligations produced by decisions of the Security Council with executive expediency with the result that decisions at the level of the Security Council are implemented in a way that is not rule of law compliant. The chapter could have centred upon decisions to use force under UN auspices, when arguments that deployments of UK troops or military assets take place under a UN mandate win over Parliament and the Courts.[4] Rather the choice has been to focus attention on non-forcible measures mainly because they go further than authorisations to use force in that they impact internally within the domestic legal order.

The danger highlighted in this chapter is that, rather than the earth being covered by universal laws agreed to by all nations as envisaged by Tennyson,

[2] WS Livingston, 'A Note on the Nature of Federalism' (1952) 67 *Political Science Quarterly* 81 at 88. See also I Bernier, *International Legal Aspects of Federalism* (London, Longman, 1973) 3–6.

[3] J Waldron, 'Is the Rule of Law an Essentially Contested Concept?' (2002) 21 *Law and Philosophy* 137 at 159.

[4] See ND White, *Democracy Goes to War: British Military Deployments and International Law* (Oxford, Oxford University Press, 2009) 82–112.

188 nations are being ruled by five, at least on security matters and, moreover, ruled by an organ whose responsibility is for enforcing and keeping the peace rather than upholding international law. The chapter examines the UK's engagement and interaction with the UN's political and legal order in order to discern evidence of the development of a rudimentary international federal structure. In particular, the move since 1999 towards targeted sanctions as well as more general Security Council legislation against terrorism has enabled the UK to implement laws without any real accountability. Judicial accountability has increased, however, but is either readily by-passed or is not strong enough. In contrast with its approach to the EU, where it was a reluctant international federalist until the recent referendum in June 2016 and will now withdraw from that federalising order in the next two to three years, the UK's position as a permanent member of the Security Council means that it is a willing participant in such developments, although it would not recognise the use of federal terminology in this context. While the UK is anti-federalist in the context of the EU, it is generally pro-internationalist, but not explicitly pro-federalist, in the context of the UN.

In order to understand and assess the development of a rudimentary form of federalising international legal order through the UN the chapter contrasts the UN Charter with its predecessor, where debates about possible federal structures gave way to a cooperative model. The early sections show how the UN Charter was a radical departure from the consensual approach embodied in the Covenant, which contrasts with the orthodox portrayal of the Charter as simply an improvement on the Covenant. The chapter then examines how non-forcible measures are brought within the UK legal order through the United Nations Act 1946, and how the implementation in the UK of targeted sanctions and legislative measures imposed by the Security Council have departed from the original intent of that Act. The chapter then shows how that change of use has been combined with sustained arguments by the UK government that obligations arising under the UN Charter prevail over other treaty obligations, including under human rights treaties, to introduce a draconian system of sanctions against listed individuals within the UK legal order, and how both the legal and political order has failed to provide these individuals with adequate protection from the state. The chapter concludes by arguing that in order for this growing international form of federalism to be rule of law compliant greater critical scrutiny of executive action by both Parliament and the judiciary is needed.

II. The UK and the League of Nations

At the end of the First World War there was a debate amongst statesmen and other leading figures about ways to secure peace in Europe, whether by a universal association of states (the League of Nations model), which would not threaten sovereignty, or by a regional federation, which might. Giovanni Agnelli, founder of the FIAT motor company, and Attilio Cabiati an Italian economist, argued:

> Without hesitation we believe that, if we really want to make war in Europe a phenomenon which cannot be repeated, there is only one way to do so and we must be outspoken enough to consider it: a federation of European states under a central power which governs them. Any other milder version is but a delusion.[5]

While the experiment in European union did not start until after the Second World War, the League of Nations became a reality in 1919. The League of Nations was not conceived as a federation even by its most ardent supporters, but it did facilitate the continuation of existing federations in the form of empires. US President Wilson, credited with being the idealist behind the Covenant, held views that were tainted with a belief in the supremacy of 'white civilization'.[6] In this respect Wilson shared a vision of the 'civilising' mission of white peoples with the victorious colonial powers—Britain and France—as well as the South African statesman, Jan Smuts, who was very influential in shaping both the League of Nations' Covenant of 1919 and the UN Charter of 1945.

Smuts argued in 1917 that a Commonwealth of Nations should emerge from the British Empire, which he described as the 'only successful experiment in international government', making it clear that the 'Commonwealth' would be a continuation of empire, albeit an 'enlightened' one, where non-white peoples would be under the tutelage of democratic civilised nations.[7] Smuts rejected the autocratic military imperialism of Germany in favour of a liberal form of imperialism offered by Britain, and it was that view which was preserved not only by the Covenant in 1919 but, arguably, also by the UN Charter of 1945,[8] at least until the General Assembly adopted the Declaration on Decolonisation of 1960.[9] As will be seen, the UN Charter contained pro-federal provisions in matters of security but, in 1945 at least, it did not attempt to dismantle empires.

One view of the First World War was that it was a fight for empire: Germany was fighting to gain an empire, while the UK and France were fighting to keep theirs. In August 1916 Wilson spoke of 'England having the earth and of Germany wanting it'.[10] The First World War was in part a battle to continue empires, a dispute over their ownership; it was not a dispute to remove that model at least until the US, in particular President Wilson, became involved. Even his vision did not contain a clear declaration of democracy and self-determination for all, but a

[5] G Agnelli and A. Cabiati, *Federazione europea o lega delle nazioni?* (Turin, Fratelli Bocca, 1918), in (1989) 31 *The Federalist* 71.

[6] A Tooze, *The Deluge: The Great War and the Remaking of World Order* (London, Penguin, 2015) 60, 92.

[7] M Mazower, *No Enchanted Palace: The End of Empire and the Ideological Origins of the United Nations* (Princeton, Princeton University Press, 2009) 37–45.

[8] ibid at 63–65.

[9] UN Doc A/RES/1514 (1960).

[10] Tooze above n 6 at 45.

'gradated view of the capacity for self-government that was typical of nineteenth-century liberalism'.[11] However, ideologically his vision remained a more radical form of liberalism than the 'imperial liberalism' offered by the colonial powers.[12]

The surrender of Germany in 1918 was as much due to a collapse of its economy as it was to a military victory by the Allies,[13] so it is not surprising that the first attempt at a world organisation put emphasis on economic sanctions as a means of ensuring compliance with the norms of the Covenant and that, beyond an acceptance that naval blockades would enforce sanctions, collective military action was kept as a much more vague concept in the background.[14] Prime Minister Clemenceau of France argued for an international army, reflecting French concerns about future German aggression, but these were not acceptable to the British and the Americans.[15] The right to go to 'war', although curtailed by the terms of the Covenant at least, ultimately remained a decision for each sovereign state.[16]

Nonetheless, the Covenant was arguably a purer expression of 'peace through law' than its successor: this was in part explained by the vestiges of Wilsonian idealism that remained in the final draft; in part by a shared belief that correct and open legal procedures would have prevented the outbreak of the Great War; in part because it more accurately reflected the limited nature of international law than its successor; and finally, in part, because it was not premised on a totally vanquished enemy. Although the Treaty of Versailles has since been seen as notorious for the reparations imposed on Germany,[17] it, and the Covenant which was part of it, were premised on respect for Germany as a nation state,[18] (although Germany's period of membership of the League only lasted from 1926–33). In contrast, the total defeat of Germany at the end of the Second World War led to its dismemberment, a condition that prevailed until the end of the Cold War. The Covenant had respect for sovereign equality at its heart, at least amongst what Wilson would have called the nation states of 'white civilisation', while the UN Charter was premised on Great Power supremacy and the complete defeat and rebuilding of 'enemy' states in the liberal democratic mould.

In summary, the League of Nations Covenant was a reaction to the First World War in that it was constructed in a way to prevent such a war, but it was constructed on the basis that what was needed was better inter-governmental cooperation between European rivals rather than the creation of any international federal structure, though it did preserve federal-like empires. It did not anticipate

[11] ibid at 121. See President Woodrow Wilson's Fourteen Points, 8 January 1918, Point 5.
[12] Tooze, ibid 179.
[13] ibid at 39.
[14] Art 16 League of Nations Covenant 1919.
[15] Tooze above n 6 at 264.
[16] See, for example, Art 12 League of Nations Covenant 1919.
[17] Tooze above n 6 at 249.
[18] ibid at 272.

the sort of radical belligerence of Nazi Germany, or indeed the rise of an ideologically driven Soviet Union. While the Allies agreed to an armistice with Germany in November 1918, nothing short of complete annihilation of Germany was acceptable in 1945. While the League was envisaged as a form of cooperation between sovereign equals based on the rule of international law as it then stood (with empire at its heart), the UN was envisaged as a continuation of the international executive created to combat Axis aggression formed by the Allies in 1942;[19] in which stress was given to threats to the peace rather than breaches of international law. In contrast to the UN, the League 'could not be formed during the war since that would make it into an instrument of the victors'.[20] In contrast to the UN Charter, the first draft of the Covenant was 'put together in a matter of a fortnight' by the League of Nations Commission in February 1919, after the war had ended.[21] In some ways the UN could be seen as a move away from law, when compared to the League, but on the other hand the League was seen as a failure and the Covenant too weak to provide anything like a system of collective security. That required a move towards supranationalism in the Security Council of the UN, arguably sowing within it the seeds of federalism.

III. The Covenant and the Charter

It is commonly assumed that the second experiment in universal collective security—the United Nations—remedied the defects of the League of Nations. However, in addressing the deficiencies of the League the founding states of the UN attributed powers to the Security Council that were outside (or exceptional to) the existing structures of international law. Even as the network of consensual international laws rapidly expanded post-1945, the Security Council, though largely inactive during the Cold War, was empowered to make legally binding decisions that could cut through or by-pass that network. It is worth considering the constitutive treaties of the League and the UN as a comparative exercise to demonstrate that, despite changes in nomenclature, they are in some ways different versions of the same thing, but with one profound difference—the insertion of a new form of legal power that combined great power politics and supranationalism.

Writing in 1947, Goodrich, one of the leading commentators on the Charter, was keen to point out that there was clear continuation between the League and the UN. Goodrich saw both as 'cooperative enterprises falling within the category of leagues and confederations',[22] with one exception. The exception was

[19] Declaration by the United Nations, 1 January 1942.
[20] Tooze above n 6 at 223.
[21] ibid at 255.
[22] LM Goodrich, 'From League of Nations to United Nations' (1947) 1 *International Organization* 3 at 8.

the presence of collective enforcement action by the UN Security Council, which could be taken against the will of a member state or states.[23] Nonetheless, Goodrich saw the League as a continuation of the Concert of Europe of 1815, and the UN as a continuation of the League: the UN is seen as 'the continued application of old ideas and methods with some changes deemed necessary in the light of past experience'.[24]

Writing in 1946 Brierly, on the other hand, analysed the UN not as a continuation of the League in terms of improving the cooperative model of collective security, but as a radically different experiment in international organisation.[25] The League of Nations, although based on a constitutional document,[26] only set up an association of states, it did not purport to establish the beginnings of a system of world government. The League's effectiveness depended upon the 'conduct of the members individually', and their willingness to comply with their obligations; meaning that they could 'not be made to act together, and a majority of them' could 'not decide or act for the whole body'.[27] References in the Covenant were to the 'members of the League', who undertook to act in certain ways, except for Article 11(1), which stated that the 'League shall take any action that may be deemed wise and effectual to safeguard the peace of nations'—dismissed as a 'mere slip in drafting' by Brierly.[28] Sovereign equality for independent states meant exactly that under the Covenant; whereas under the UN Charter, there was a distinct move away from 'the purely cooperative basis of international organization',[29] and, it is argued here, from the consensual basis of international law, which is one of the reasons why the Charter is so much longer than the Covenant (111 articles compared to 26). The Covenant contained the outlines of a constitution, enabling members to adjust the workings of the Council and Assembly to suit, whilst the Charter contained details on the powers of each UN organ, and gave decision making competence to the Security Council.[30] In this respect Brierly went much deeper in his analysis of the Charter than Goodrich. For Brierly, the move towards greater constitutionalisation and institutionalisation in the Charter was fraught with problems.

The first draft of the UN Charter, the Dumbarton Oaks proposals of 1944, was essentially predicated on Germany and Japan continuing to pose the greatest threat to world peace, as they were still immensely powerful (at least outwardly) in 1944—hence the draft captured the idea of a police force for the world based on the continuation of the alliance of the Second World War into the post-1945 era.

[23] ibid at 10.

[24] ibid at 5.

[25] JL Brierly, 'The Covenant and the Charter' (1946) 23 *British Yearbook of International Law* 83.

[26] AD McNair, 'The Functions and Different Legal Character of Treaties' (1930) 11 *British Yearbook of International Law* 100 at 112.

[27] Brierly above n 25 at 85.

[28] ibid.

[29] ibid.

[30] Art 25 UN Charter 1945.

In contrast to the First World War that had been stumbled into, the Second World War involved planned aggression and, therefore, required executive-style government to prevent it happening again. The consensus at Dumbarton Oaks and San Francisco wrongly assumed that the 'wartime unity of purpose among the Great Powers would be a permanent feature of their international relations'.[31]

Brierly saw the clear political differences within the permanent membership as a fatal flaw: 'the Covenant scheme had weaknesses … and perhaps it might not have worked even if it had been given a fair trial',[32]

> but we must realize that what we have done is to exchange a scheme which might or might not have worked for one which cannot work, and that instead of limiting the sovereignty of states we have actually extended the sovereignty of the Great Powers, the only states whose sovereignty is still a formidable reality in the modern world.[33]

Brierly's criticism is based on the permanent members failing to cooperate, something which largely proved to be correct for the first 45 years of the UN's existence. Whereas he did foresee the potential for world government within the Charter he did not foresee its actualisation.

The fact that the Charter was more clearly based on the power politics of the post-Second World War period, and that it has helped cement those configurations of power and imbue them with the potential not only to enforce peace and security but also to make binding laws, explains its survival but, unfortunately, it did not signify an advancement in international law. While we might point to the ban on the use of force in the Charter being normatively stronger than the qualified ban on aggression in the Covenant,[34] the fact is that this has not prevented great power aggressions on a regular and continuing basis: not only during the Cold War, but in the post-Cold War period, for example: in Iraq 2003, Georgia 2008 and Ukraine 2014. The Covenant may have been ineffectual, and it may have been flawed, but it did signify the start of an era of constitutionalist thinking in international relations and law, one where a world order built on fundamental principles of law might be envisaged.

In contrast, the normative strengths of the Charter, found particularly in its principles in Article 2, were undermined by the centrality of the Security Council to those principles. The ban on the threat or use of force in Article 2(4) had an exception in the right of self-defence for states in response to armed attacks in Article 51, but had a much broader exception in the shape of military action undertaken by the Security Council under Article 42. The principle of non-intervention by the UN in domestic affairs, found in Article 2(7) of the Charter, was inapplicable when the Security Council was taking enforcement action under

[31] Brierly above n 25 at 91.
[32] ibid at 91–92.
[33] ibid at 93.
[34] Compare Art 2(4) of the UN Charter 1945 with Art 10 Covenant of the League of Nations 1919.

Chapter VII. The triggers for Security Council action were not actual or potential breaches of international law, but threats to or breaches of the peace (Article 39); and, lastly, obligations upon states created under the Charter by Security Council decisions (Article 25) were potentially superior to other conflicting obligations by virtue of the primacy clause (Article 103); meaning that obligations created to deal with security matters potentially prevail over conflicting binding treaty commitments. While in domestic legal orders, rights may be overridden in extreme emergencies (eg to prevent the spread of fire or disease),[35] under the UN system the sense of emergency predominates, meaning that legal rights and duties are weakened and always potentially overridden by political decisions on matters of security, albeit ones having legal effects.

Of course Brierly was right in the sense that the veto provides a real political check on the extensive use of supranational powers by the Security Council under Chapter VII, but the potential is there when the deadlock is broken to create a form of supranationalism, particularly when post 9/11 consensus was achieved over responses to security threats such as terrorism, foreign fighters and weapons of mass destruction. These are indeed security concerns, but the Security Council is empowered to tackle them, not simply as an executive body taking action to enforce existing norms, but rather as a central political organ acting as a 'governing board' with both law-making and executive powers,[36] so that by determining that there exists a threat to the peace, breach of the peace, or act of aggression, it can create obligations binding on the wider membership, and enforceable by means of a range of non-forcible and forcible measures.[37]

IV. The UK and the UN

There were certainly ambitious ideas for international organisation debated in the UK Parliament towards the end of the Second World War. War-time Prime Minister Winston Churchill spoke in visionary terms in May 1944 about the intention to 'set up a world order and organisations, equipped with all the necessary attributes of power, in order to prevent the breaking out of future wars, or the long planning of them in advance, by restless and ambitious nations'. This would require 'a World Council, a controlling Council, comprising the greatest States which emerge victorious from this war' as well as a 'World Assembly of all Powers'.[38] The leader in *The Times* of 27 June 1945 summed up the mixture of

[35] H Kelsen, *Collective Security under International Law* (Washington, Naval War College, 1957) 102.
[36] HG Schermers and NM Blokker, *International Institutional Law* 5th edn (Leiden, Nijhoff, 2011) 310–15.
[37] Arts 25, 39, 41 and 42 UN Charter 1945.
[38] Hansard, HC Debates, vol 400, col 784, 24 May 1944.

'hopes and misgivings' surrounding the debates around the adoption of the UN Charter:

> It is far more widely recognized than it was in 1919 that no international instrument, no constitutional specific, will suffice to maintain peace … The Charter by itself is nothing, if it fails to rally the loyalty of the major Powers who alone can give it body and life.[39]

Nonetheless, in August 1945, in presenting the Charter to the House of Commons for approval, Prime Minister Clement Attlee foresaw the Security Council as embodying the centralisation of force as well as methods of dispute settlement:

> The British delegation [at San Francisco] took a foremost part in seeking to make the Security Council something more than a policeman who is called in when there is already a danger of a breach of the peace. We sought, and sought successfully, to make it a place where the policies of States, and especially the greater States, could be discussed and reconsidered for the time, especially when they showed signs of divergencies as to threaten the harmony of international relations. Collective security is not merely a promise to act when an emergency occurs, but it is active co-operation to prevent emergencies occurring …[40]

There is some evidence that British leaders saw the UN, in particular the Security Council, as a form of supranational power or, perhaps more reluctantly, a federation of great powers, in which the UK, along with the other permanent members, exercised powers rather than being subject to them.

The powers granted to the 'federal government' element of the UN are vast. The right or power of a federal government to use force within constituent states in order to maintain security and stability is a deeply problematic one even within established federal states (eg Russian use of force in Chechnya), but even more so when the right is exercised at the international level. Nonetheless, the Security Council was granted the power to forcefully intervene in Member States under Chapter VII of the UN Charter. However, the UK's position as one of the permanent members of the UN Security Council signifies that it cannot be the direct object of UN intervention against its will, thereby limiting the effects on the UK of the supranational powers of the UN provided for in the Charter.

During the Cold War, the effects of obligations created by the Security Council on the UK were limited to duties to carry out measures in the rare instances when they were adopted against other states. The UK used its permanent seat to protect it from intervention in a variety of ways, not always involving the use of the veto.[41] For instance in 1969, the Republic of Ireland requested a meeting of the Security Council to consider the situation in Northern Ireland with a view to deploying a UN peacekeeping force to the province because of the serious

[39] Cited in GL Goodwin, *Britain and the United Nations* (Oxford, Oxford University Press, 1957) 45–46.

[40] Hansard HC Debates, vol 413, col 665, 22 August 1945.

[41] Contained in Art 27(3) UN Charter 1945.

disturbances caused by the alleged denial of civil rights to the minority Catholic community.[42] Although the question was not even put on the agenda of the Security Council, the UK ambassador, Lord Caradon, was sufficiently perturbed that he justified the closing down of any discussion of Northern Ireland on the grounds that it was purely a domestic matter and so there was no threat to international peace.[43] Any proposal would have been vetoed by the UK in any event but the UK was able to use its position to prevent the matter progressing that far. Similarly in the situation in Southern Rhodesia in 1965, the UK initially used its position to prevent discussion of the matter on the basis that this was a domestic matter,[44] until it had clearly lost control over its colony following the unilateral declaration of independence by the white minority regime in 1965. Thereafter, the UK was active in seeking, and gaining, support for the imposition of comprehensive sanctions against Rhodesia,[45] and also the enforcement of the oil embargo element by means of an authorisation to intercept oil supplies reaching Rhodesia through the port of Beira in Mozambique.[46]

The potential loss of the permanent seat by the UK in a future reformed Security Council would mean that UN-authorised intervention against it would become possible. The referendum on Scottish independence of 2014 caused speculation in regard to the permanent seat.[47] UN practice indicates that when a state breaks away from another, the new state has to apply for membership of the UN, while what remains of the old state continues membership particularly if it is the larger unit.[48] This would indicate that the (rump) UK would continue its seat in the UN, but it might not be able to control challenges to its permanent seat on the Security Council, given that the claims of Germany, Japan, Brazil and many others are simmering not far from the surface as the membership of the Security Council is long overdue a significant overhaul.

V. Legislating for Executive Action: The United Nations Act 1946

The UN Charter's provisions on the centralisation of the use of force under UN command are indicative of an intent to create a central power with military forces

[42] UN Doc S/9394 (1969).

[43] UN Doc S/1503 mtg (1969).

[44] ND White, *Keeping the Peace: The United Nations and the Maintenance of International Peace and Security* 2nd edn (Manchester, Manchester University Press, 1997) 39–40.

[45] UN Doc S/RES/232 (1966).

[46] UN Doc S/RES/217 (1965) UN Doc S/RES/221 (1966).

[47] See, for example, House of Commons Foreign Affairs Committee, 'Foreign Policy Considerations for the UK and Scotland in the Event of Scotland Becoming an Independent Country', Sixth Report of Session 2012–13, HC 643, 23 April 2013.

[48] B Conforti, *The Law and Practice of the United Nations* 3rd edn (The Hague, Kluwer, 2005) 44–45.

at its disposal,[49] but the failure to agree the military arrangements necessary to make this a reality meant that UN authorised military action remained decentralised and based on states volunteering for UN action. The Cold War prevented such actions being authorised, with the singular exception of the Korean War that broke out in 1950 when, in the absence of the Soviet Union, the Security Council recommended that military action be taken to repel the attack against South Korea and to restore international peace and security in the area.[50] The UK supported the resolution and contributed significantly to the campaign against North Korea. Those forces, although US-led, were commonly known as 'United Nations forces'.[51] The UK was also instrumental in drafting a General Assembly Resolution that supported the unification of Korea,[52] leading to military action in the north that provoked massive Chinese intervention, which eventually led to a cessation of hostilities along the 38th parallel in 1953.

The UK's sovereignty was not affected by the Charter's provisions on collective military security in that under the system that has emerged the UK cannot be obliged to provide troops. In contrast, Parliament provided for the rapid incorporation into domestic law of obligations to undertake non-forcible measures (sanctions) arising from decisions made under Article 41 of the UN Charter, in the shape of the United Nations Act 1946. Section 1 of that Act provides:

> If, under Article 41 of the Charter of the United Nations signed at San Francisco on 26 June 1945 (being the article which relates to measures not involving the use of armed force) the Security Council of the United Nations calls upon His Majesty's Government in the United Kingdom to apply any measures to give effect to any decision of that Council, His Majesty may by order in Council make such provision as appears to Him necessary or expedient for enabling those measures to be effectively applied, including … provision for the apprehension, trial and punishment of persons offending against that Order …

It was envisaged that member states would be obliged to enforce UN sanctions against a target state, but that would necessitate incorporation of those obligations into the domestic laws of the sanctioning states; by, for example, prohibiting persons or companies within their jurisdiction trading or having other forms of commercial, economic or financial relations with or within the target state. The target of the sanctions would be a state that the Security Council determined had threatened or breached international peace, not individuals or companies, although if individuals or companies traded or otherwise commercially, financially or economically interacted with the target state they should be punished within the domestic legal orders of member states. This was the basis upon which both the

[49] Arts 42–47 UN Charter 1945.

[50] UN Doc S/RES/83 (1950).

[51] See, for example, memorandum by UK Foreign Secretary Bevin, Cabinet Office Paper CAB 129/41, CP(50) 193, 31 August 1950, paras 5–8; in A Farrar-Hockley, *The British Part in the Korean War: Volume I A Distant Obligation* (London, HMSO, 1990) 192–93.

[52] UN Doc A/RES/376 (1950).

House of Lords and the House of Commons welcomed the United Nations Bill when it was introduced in 1946, the government declaring that Article 41 was the only Charter provision that required immediate legislation to enable the UK to fulfil its obligations under the Charter.[53]

In the *Ahmed* case of 2010,[54] the first case decided by the UK Supreme Court, and one involving a new form of UN sanctions—measures targeted directly at individuals—Lord Hope stated that

> there was no indication during the debates at the Second Reading in either House [in 1946] that it was envisaged that the Security Council would find it necessary under article 41 to require states to impose restraints or take coercive measures against their own citizens.[55]

Parliamentary debates in 1946 indicated that the form of incorporation into domestic law—by an Order in Council made by the executive that was not subject to Parliamentary scrutiny—was a procedure that had 'the necessary combination of speed and authority to enable instant effect to be given to the international obligations to which we are pledged'.[56] Those debates made it clear that non-forcible measures were directed against states.[57] As Lord Hope stated in the *Ahmed* case: 'the use of the power as a means of imposing restraints or the taking of coercive measures targeted against individuals in domestic law is an entirely different matter'.[58]

Targeted sanctions against individuals are implemented in the domestic legal order by the very organ of government that voted for them in the Security Council—the executive; thereby making the Order in Council a formality. In this way they appear to be a manifestation of federalism whereby legal obligations arise in the UK legal order as a consequence of the exercise of the Security Council's discretionary governing powers in matters of peace and security and, when seen in this way, those obligations are a result of executive decisions that are not rule of law compliant. Individuals can be listed by the Security Council or, indeed, by the UK following its obligations under general Security Council resolutions, on the basis of limited evidence (or intelligence) without significant due process and, furthermore, those targeted by such measures can remain listed indefinitely. Those targeted individuals are represented as threats to the peace and, as such, are subject to emergency measures that are exceptional to the normal protections provided by international and domestic human rights norms, civil liberties and criminal justice.

[53] Hansard, HL Debates, 12 February 1946, vol 139, cols 373–75; Hansard HC Debates, 1946, vol 421, col 1516.

[54] *Her Majesty's Treasury v Mohammed Jabar Ahmed and Others* [2010] UKSC 2.

[55] ibid at para 16.

[56] Hansard, HC Debates, 1946, vol 421, col 1517 (Morrison).

[57] *Ahmed* above n 54 at para 44.

[58] ibid.

Following the *Ahmed* case in 2010, the system of executive orders based on the United Nations Act 1946 was replaced by the Terrorist Asset Freezing etc Act 2010. However, even when obligations arising under Article 41 were adopted into UK law by means of this Act of Parliament, there is little willingness in Parliament to scrutinise obligations arising from Security Council decisions in terms of their compatibility with other international obligations accepted by the UK or, indeed, the existing laws of the UK providing for the protection of rights and freedoms.[59] Furthermore, giving the terrorist assets freezing regime a new legislative platform in 2010 did not alter the basic method by which the executive (ie the Treasury) is empowered to either temporarily list individuals on the basis of a 'reasonable suspicion' that they are or have been involved in terrorism or, more permanently, on the basis of a 'reasonable belief'. Even supporters of the Act could discern no clear difference between 'reasonable belief' and 'reasonable suspicion', except that they were both below the 'balance of probabilities' standard of evidence required in civil cases.[60] Only one MP questioned the legal basis upon which the executive and not the courts could impose assets freezing orders.[61] There is little political will in Parliament to challenge executive decisions made on security matters. Indeed, the fact that such obligations result from decisions of the Security Council is almost seen as putting them beyond domestic political scrutiny.[62] Judicial scrutiny has also been hampered by a reluctance to challenge the executive on security matters and, although cases like *Ahmed* suggest greater judicial activism, reluctance remains in cases where the executive is implementing its security obligations arising from the UN Charter.

VI. Targeted Sanctions Regimes

The effects on the civilian population of the UN's comprehensive sanctions regime against Iraq (1990–2003), which severely undermined the rights to life and health of large sections of the civilian population especially children,[63] led to the development of less indiscriminate targeted or smart sanctions against regime elites and non-state actors. As a permanent member, the UK is a strong supporter of this development, often associated with the '1267' regime first imposed in 1999 by the Security Council against the Taliban government in Afghanistan (for its support

[59] Hansard HC Debates, 15 November 2010, col 683 (Vaz).
[60] ibid at col 701 (Opperman).
[61] ibid at col 697 (Llwyd).
[62] ibid at col 676 (Hoban); 681 (Hanson); 687 (Hancock).
[63] J Gordon, *Invisible War: The United States and the Iraq Sanctions* (Cambridge MA, Harvard University Press, 2010) 86–102.

for Al-Qaida),[64] and then directly against Al-Qaida itself. Security Council Resolution 1333 of 2000 required all states (not just Member States) inter alia to

> freeze without delay funds and other financial assets of Usama bin Laden and individuals and entities associated with him as designated by the Committee, including those in the Al-Qaida organization, and including funds derived or generated from property owned or controlled directly or indirectly by Usama bin Laden and individuals and entities associated with him.[65]

The Resolution invoked the language of the primacy clause of the Charter (Article 103) by calling upon all states to

> to act strictly in accordance with the provisions of this resolution, notwithstanding the existence of any rights or obligations conferred or imposed by any international agreement or any contract entered into or any licence or permit granted prior to the date of coming into force of the measures imposed.[66]

However, the absolute primacy suggested by this provision has to be balanced by statements in other Security Council resolutions, which declared that states 'must ensure that any measure taken to combat terrorism comply with their obligations under international law, and should adopt measures in accordance with international law, in particular human rights, refugee and humanitarian law'.[67]

Furthermore, the Security Council has made concessions in the face of judgments of courts around the world, including those discussed below, giving targeted individuals seeking delisting avenues for bringing their claims. However, these concessions are administrative processes rather than judicial protections. It is interesting to note that review of allegedly wrongful listings by the Ombudsperson established by Security Council Resolution 1904 (2009) only applies to those on the Al-Qaida Sanctions List as administered by the Security Council's 1267 Committee and not to any lists beyond that, including the Taliban list. This seemingly curious anomaly is only explicable by the overarching pragmatism of the Security Council on matters of accountability for wrongly listing individuals; in that complaints to international, regional and judicial bodies have largely derived from the 1267 list and the office of the Ombudsperson is a response to that. The lack of remedies elsewhere in the UN system, for wrongly listed individuals, puts the creation of the Ombudsperson in perspective, but it also fits the prevailing view in the Security Council that such measures are administrative ones taken in response to international threats to security caused by the activities of international terrorist organisations and, therefore, any remedial measures should only be of a controlled administrative nature. However, long-term listing of individuals

[64] UN Doc S/RES/1267 (1999).
[65] UN Doc S/RES/1333 (2000) op para 8(c).
[66] UN Doc S/RES/1333 (2000) para 17.
[67] Declaration on Combatting Terrorism in UN Doc S/RES/1456 (2003) op para 6.

constitutes a form of punishment that raises issues of access to legal remedies for violations of due process norms located in the international human rights obligations of states.

Although targeted sanctions imposed against Al-Qaida dominate debates, there were prior instances in the 1990s of targeted sanctions imposed against regime elites in Haiti and non-state armed groups (UNITA in Angola and the Bosnian Serbs).[68] The twenty-first century has seen numerous sanctions regimes against regime elites (in Libya, Guinea-Bissau, Iran, North Korea, Liberia, Sierra Leone, Somalia, Eritrea, South Sudan and Yemen), and non-state actors (in DR Congo, the CAR, Cote D'Ivoire, Lebanon, and Sudan, Libya, and against Islamic State).[69] These non-state actors and the threats they represent are not confined to the boundaries of one state and, therefore, the obligations created could potentially impact on the legal order within the UK. In supporting sanctions against Islamic State (by adding members from that group to the existing Al-Qaida list),[70] the UK representative on the Security Council welcomed the unanimous and rapid adoption of the measures,[71] showing that consensus can readily be achieved on non-forcible measures directed against terrorism.

Security Council resolutions directed at foreign terrorist fighters (individuals travelling from their national state to another state for the purpose of carrying out terrorist activities) demonstrate the broadening legislative scope of its non-forcible measures. Adopted in September 2014, Resolution 2178 was in part directed at the individuals themselves in that it contained a demand 'that all foreign terrorist fighters disarm and cease all terrorist acts and participation in armed conflict'. It was also directed at 'all states', obliging them to ensure 'effective border controls', and encouraging them to 'employ evidence-based traveller risk assessment and screening procedures including collection and analysis of travel data, without resorting to profiling based on stereotypes founded on grounds of discrimination prohibited by international law'. With reference to listing processes already in place and states' general counter-terrorist obligations under Resolution 1373 (2001), Resolution 2178 (2014), inter alia, decided that 'all States shall ensure that their domestic laws and regulations establish serious criminal offences sufficient to provide the ability to prosecute and to penalize' foreign terrorist fighters in a manner duly reflecting the seriousness of the offence. These measures were implemented in the UK within a broader counter-terrorist framework in the Counter-Terrorism and Security Act 2015 that, inter alia, restricted the travel of individuals involved in terrorism-related activity and also provided for their temporary exclusion in order to protect the British public from a risk of terrorism,

[68] Reviewed in detail in ND White, 'Sanctions Against Non-State Actors' in N Ronzitti (ed), *Coercive Diplomacy, Sanctions and International Law* (Leiden, Brill, 2016) 127.

[69] ibid.

[70] UN Doc S/RES/2170 (2014) paras 18–21.

[71] UN Doc S/7242 mtg (2014).

as well as provision for necessary amendments to the TPIM (terrorism prevention and investigation measures) regime.[72]

VII. General International Legislation in Resolution 1373 (2001)

Once a consensus is formed in the permanent membership of the Security Council around a concept as nebulous as terrorism, the power of the Security Council comes close to a form of supranational or central federal government, imposing obligations on all states to take measures against a range of non-state actors, wherever they are located in the world. The focus of the Security Council on peace and security means that it cannot be a world government in any full sense but, given the priority in the UN system for peace and security, and the broad normative meaning given to both 'peace' and 'security' evidenced by an expansive understanding of what constitutes threats to the peace within the Security Council, it has a greater range and impact than an executive organ simply responding to emergencies. Its targeted sanctions regimes against named actors have a longevity that belies emergencies but, moreover, its general legislative-type resolution on terrorism, Resolution 1373 of 2001, has opened up the possibility enabling states to tackle their domestic security problems while purporting to fulfil their obligations arising under the Resolution. This is particularly so given that the Security Council defines all forms of terrorism as threats to international peace and,[73] although the Security Council did offer an understanding of terrorism in a Resolution of 2004, it is not an internationally agreed definition and does not appear to have led to conformity by states in their domestic definitions of terrorism.[74] The Security Council's 'definition' is built on offences already proscribed in the numerous international treaties on various aspect of terrorism, while in contrast, the definition of terrorism in the UK contained in section 1 of the Terrorism Act of 2000 is not so proscribed.

In the case of targeted sanctions imposed against suspected terrorists or terrorist supporters, the temporary freezing of an individual's assets, and restriction of his or her movements, can be construed as administrative measures necessary to prevent threats from terrorism manifesting in indiscriminate acts of violence. As such they are not arguably subject to full due process protections. However, a number of listings appear to be almost permanent without real review, and like indefinite

[72] See discussion on Bill in Hansard HC Debates, 2 December 2015, col 207 et seq; 7 January 2015 col 336 et seq. Hansard HL Debates, 13 January 2015, col 661 et seq; 9 February 2014, col 1024 et seq. See also Terrorism Prevention and Investigation Measures Act 2011.

[73] UN Doc S/RES/1566 (2004) op para 1.

[74] ibid at op para 3.

preventive detention, cease to be responses to imminent existential threats but are rather forms of punishment without due process of law. There is a danger that by creating a legal framework allowing for quasi-permanent listings, the UN is endorsing a system of punishment for wrongs determined by executive organs of states and organisations without any determination or trial before a court. As is the case with targeted killings, the roles of judge, jury and executioner are rolled together. This is even more so as regards the auto-interpretation system of targeted measures triggered by Resolution 1373 of 2001. This piece of UN Security Council law-making has legitimated the development of separate 'lists' of terrorists by member states, fulfilling their obligations under that resolution to: criminalise the financing of terrorism; freeze any funds related to persons involved in acts of terrorism; deny all form of financial support for terrorist groups; and suppress the provision of safe haven, sustenance or support for terrorists.[75] Given that there are no specific terrorist organisations listed in the Resolution, or by a collective process set up by the Resolution, states are given discretion to target those organisations and individuals it considers to be terrorists. The Terrorist Asset-Freezing etc Act 2010 is the current legislative platform for the implementation of Resolution 1373 (2001) in the UK. The 2010 Act provides the UK government (HM Treasury) with powers to freeze the funds and economic resources of those suspected or believed to be involved in terrorist activities, and restricts the making available of funds, financial services and economic resources to, or for the benefit of, such persons. It was adopted as a direct response to the UK Supreme Court's 2010 ruling in the *Ahmed* case.[76]

VIII. Arguing for the Absolute Primacy of UN Obligations

While the UK's permanent seat and right of veto protects it from UN-authorised forcible intervention, the increasing focus of the Security Council, with the UK to the fore, on taking non-forcible measures against non-state actors, has meant that the effects of Charter obligations arising by dint of Security Council decisions have been felt within the UK's legal order. The identification of individuals to be targeted, either at UN level or at national level under the auspices of decisions made by the Security Council, has led to their freedoms being restricted and so to legal challenges that their rights have been violated. The advantage to the UK in securing obligatory Chapter VII resolutions against individuals is that they are not only used to legitimate targeted measures and, thereby, avoid significant Parliamentary scrutiny, but also that the UK government has consistently argued that

[75] UN Doc S/RES/1373 (2001) op para 2.
[76] Above n 54.

the obligations arising thereunder override the UK's other treaty commitments that are in conflict, pointing to Article 103 of the UN Charter by which 'obligations' arising under the Charter 'shall prevail' over conflicting treaty obligations.

The beginning of this line of argument can be traced to the time when the Security Council imposed sanctions against Libya, at the instigation of the US and UK, aimed at forcing Libya to hand over two Libyan agents suspected of the Lockerbie bombing of 1998.[77] In defending itself against a case brought by Libya to the International Court of Justice (ICJ) in 1992, to the effect that Libya had the right to prosecute two suspects under existing international treaty commitments,[78] the UK and US both relied on Articles 25 and 103 of the UN Charter to claim that obligations arising from Security Council resolutions prevailed over Libya's rights and duties under the Montreal Convention of 1971. In the *Lockerbie* cases, the ICJ accepted this argument 'prima facie' at the provisional measures stage in 1992,[79] and, as the case did not reach the Merits stage when the issue would have been addressed in full, this interpretation has been the one relied upon by the UK in subsequent cases brought against it before national and regional courts.

The UK government has extended its primacy argument to claim that obligations arising from Security Council decisions prevail over those duties it has under human rights treaties, both in defending itself against claims brought by targeted individuals and intervening in other key cases. It intervened in the *Kadi* case of 2008, brought against the European Community before the European Court of Justice, arguing that obligations arising under the Charter prevailed over fundamental rights.[80] However, the Court, in emphasising that the Community was based on the rule of law, held that the right to be heard as well as property rights of the plaintiff who had been listed by the Security Council's 1267 Committee were violated by the European regulation that gave force to Security Council Resolutions.[81]

Undeterred the UK has continued to argue for absolute primacy of security obligations derived from Security Council resolutions, in cases involving listing of suspected terrorists and other measures that restrict liberty. In the *Al-Jedda* case of 2007 brought against the UK, the government argued that the right to be free from arbitrary detention, guaranteed by Article 5 of the European Convention on Human Rights, was overridden by the obligation to detain contained in

[77] UN Doc S/RES/748 (1992).

[78] Arts 6 and 7 Convention for the Suppression of Unlawful Acts Against the Safety of Civil Aviation (Montreal Convention) 1971.

[79] *Questions of Interpretation and Application of the 1971 Montreal Convention Arising from the Aerial Incident at Lockerbie (Libya v United States, Libya v United Kingdom* (1992) ICJ Rep 3 (UK), 114 (US) at para 42.

[80] *Yassin Abdullah Kadi and Al Barakaat International Foundation v Council and Commission*, Joined Cases. C-402/05 P and C-415/05 P, European Court of Justice, Judgment, 3 September 2008, paras 262, 275–78.

[81] ibid at paras 281, 334.

a Security Council resolution authorising the US and UK forces in Iraq to take necessary measures, including detention, for imperative reasons of security.[82] The House of Lords upheld this argument, with Lord Bingham stating that obligations arising from the UN Charter must be respected above all else: 'emphasis has often been laid on the special character of the European Convention as a human rights instrument. But the reference in article 103 [of the UN Charter] to "any other international agreement" leaves no room for any excepted category …'[83] The European Court of Human Rights disagreed in 2011, but primarily on the basis that the Resolution in question did not expressly impose any obligation on states to detain, thereby leaving open the possibility that the Security Council could override human rights obligations of states simply by using express language to that effect.[84]

The UK has persisted in its contention about the overriding effect of obligations arising under the Charter as a result of Security Council resolutions, notably in cases where an individual has been listed at Security Council level. In the *Nada* case in 2012 brought against Switzerland before the Grand Chamber of the European Court of Human Rights, the UK intervened claiming that in the case in question the Security Council had used 'clear and explicit language' in Resolution 1267 of 1999 to impose obligations on states that would prevail over conflicting obligations under human rights treaties.[85] However, even though the Court accepted that this was a case of clearly conflicting obligations, it explored the latitude the Swiss government had in implementing its obligations arising under the Resolution to make its actions as human rights compliant as possible.[86] The UK intervened in the *Al-Dulimi* case of 2013 brought against Switzerland before a chamber of the European Court of Human Rights, repeating its argument about the prevailing effect of obligations arising under the Charter over conflicting human rights obligations.[87] The Court found that targeted measures, directed at individuals and non-state actors in Saddam Hussein's regime in Iraq,[88] violated the right of access to a court under Articles 6 and 13 of the European Convention, despite there being a direct conflict in obligations for a state between those arising from the UN Charter and those arising from Security Council resolutions.[89]

It would appear that the UK government has gradually lost the argument that the Security Council can create a form of security law that is automatically

[82] UN Doc S/RES/1546 (2004).

[83] *R (on the application of Al-Jedda)(FC) (Appellant) v Secretary of State for Defence (Respondent)* [2007] UKHL 58, paras 34–35.

[84] *Case of Al-Jedda v The* United *Kingdom* (Application no 27021/08) Grand Chamber Judgment, 7 July 2011, para 109.

[85] *Case of Nada v Switzerland* (Application No 10593/08) Grand Chamber judgment, 12 September 2012, para 111.

[86] ibid paras 186, 195, 197–98, 213.

[87] *Case of Al-Dulimi and Montana Management Inc v Switzerland* (Application no 5809/08) Second Chamber judgment, 26 November 2013, para 85.

[88] UN Doc S/RES/1483 (2003).

[89] *Al-Dulimi* above n 87 at paras 113–14.

constitutionally superior even to human rights norms. At the very least the European courts will rigorously test those claims and will not simply give precedence to security obligations. However, the following analysis will show that these judgments at the European level have not yet been accepted by the UK government, nor has the UK Supreme Court adjusted its jurisprudence to accept a human rights challenge to wrongful listing claims. The UK government, as a permanent member of the UN's executive body, supports a form of absolute primacy or supremacy for obligations arising from Security Council resolutions, as it enables it to use domestic executive orders to introduce immediately binding, unscrutinised and superior laws into UK domestic law. In purely pragmatic terms the UK's reluctance to give up, or substantially qualify, this form of UN-level federal law-making is understandable, particularly as it gives the government a very effective way of tackling suspected terrorists that is operated largely without hindrance from political and judicial forms of accountability.

IX. Supranational Measures within the Domestic Legal and Political Order

The impact of obligations arising under Security Council resolutions imposing non-forcible measures targeted at individuals, necessitating enforcement of such measures within domestic legal orders of Member States, has given rise to jurisprudence in domestic courts,[90] regional courts,[91] and under the individual complaint mechanism to the Human Rights Committee.[92] Before UK courts the key judgment is the *Ahmed* case decided by the UK Supreme Court in 2010, in which the Court was at the same time highly critical of the targeted sanctions regime and, as it proved, very limited in changing the effects of such measures on the lives of individuals. Lord Hope described the impact of the executive orders in the following terms:

> [P]ersons who have been designated … are effectively prisoners of the state … moreover, the way the system is administered affects not just those who have been designated. It affects third parties too, including the spouses and other family members of those who have been designated. For them too it is intrusive to a high degree.[93]

[90] For example, *Abdelrazik v Canada (Minister of Foreign Affairs* [2010] 1 FCR 267.

[91] *Kadi* above n 80, *Al-Jedda* above n 84, *Nada* above n 85, *Al-Dulimi* above n 87.

[92] *Nabil Sayadi and Patricia Vinck v Belgium*, Communication No 1472/2006, 29 December 2008, 16 IHHR 427.

[93] *Ahmed* above n 54 at para 4 (Lord Hope). Discussing the Terrorism (United Nations Measures) Order 2006 (SI 2006/2657) giving force to UK obligations arising from Security Council Resolution 1373 (2001); and the Al-Qaida and Taliban (United Nations Measures) Order 2006 (SI 2006/2952) giving force to obligations arising from Security Council Resolution 1267 (1999).

Lord Hope went on to state that:

> The consequences of the Orders ... are so drastic and so oppressive that we must be just as alert to see that the coercive action that the Treasury [has] taken really is within the powers that the 1946 Act has given them. Even in the face of the threat of international terrorism, the safety of the people is not the supreme law. We must be just as careful to guard against unrestrained encroachments on personal liberty.[94]

Nonetheless, the approach of the Supreme Court in 2010 in the *Ahmed* case was limited by its previous decision in *Al Jedda* of 2007,[95] which was only reversed by the European Court of Human Rights in 2011.[96] The UK Supreme Court may revisit its decision in the light of that 2011 judgment when given the opportunity.[97] However, in 2010 the Supreme Court felt bound by its previous decision in *Al Jedda* to the effect that obligations arising as a result of Security Council decisions must prevail over obligations to protect and uphold human rights under the European Convention on Human Rights, to deny the applicants any remedies under the Human Rights Act 1998 that implemented Convention rights in UK law.[98] By viewing the human rights avenue as blocked, the Supreme Court turned to domestic law, stating that the primacy clause in Article 103 was only applicable to conflicting obligations arising under international treaties,[99] to find that the Al-Qaida and Taliban Order violated the complainants' right to the enjoyment of their property, 'which could only be interfered with by clear legislative words',[100] and their right to 'unimpeded access to a court', which 'is not be to be excluded except by clear words';[101] while the Terrorism Order violated the fundamental rights of the citizen by introducing a reasonable suspicion test without the authority of Parliament.[102] Both Orders were therefore *ultra vires* the United Nations Act 1946.

Lord Hope's statements warn about the dangers of leaving such measures to the 'uncontrolled judgment of the executive', but also address the argument that the UK should honour its obligations under the Charter arising from Security Council resolutions:

> But these resolutions are the product of a body of which the executive is a member as the United Kingdom's representative. Conferring an unlimited discretion on the executive as

[94] *Ahmed* above n 54 at para 6 (Lord Hope).

[95] Above n 83.

[96] Above n 84.

[97] But see *Youssef v Secretary of State for Foreign and Commonwealth Affairs* [2016] UKSC 3, when, despite expectations, neither the Human Rights Act nor Art 103 of the UN Charter, were argued before the Court.

[98] *Ahmed* above n 54 at paras 71–74 (Lord Hope).

[99] ibid at para 11 (Lord Hope).

[100] ibid at para 75 (Lord Hope), relying inter alia on *Entick v Carrington* (1765) 19 Howell's State Trials 1029, 1066.

[101] ibid at para 75 (Lord Hope), relying inter alia on *Pyx Granite Co Ltd v Ministry of Housing and Local Government* [1960] AC 260 at 286.

[102] ibid at para 61 (Lord Hope). But see *Youssef v Secretary of State for Foreign and Commonwealth Affairs* above n 97.

to how those resolutions, which it had a hand in making, are to be implemented seems to me to be wholly unacceptable. It conflicts with the basic rules that lie at the heart of our democracy.[103]

Despite these ringing words in *Ahmed*, the Supreme Court's reliance on rights under domestic law to declare that the executive orders promulgated without Parliamentary scrutiny under the United Nations Act 1946 were *ultra vires* the 1946 Act on the basis that it did not expressly permit the infringement of individual rights, proved to be a brief victory for civil liberties and the rule of law.[104]

The *Ahmed* judgment led to the government curing the 'defects' of the executive orders by tabling primary legislation in the form of the Terrorism Asset-Freezing (Temporary Provisions) Act 2010. In the debates about the Terrorism Asset-Freezing Bill of 2010, which was to replace the temporary Act, some reference was made to the Supreme Court's judgment, with one MP referring to Lord Brown's statement that 'the draconian nature of the regime imposed under these asset-freezing Orders can hardly be over-stated'.[105] This was understood to mean 'not that these were draconian because they were orders, but that they were draconian because of their content. So we need to be careful before reintroducing measures that are very similar to those orders'.[106] The point that measures could be the same whether made directly by executive order pursuant to the 1946 Act or by executive order pursuant to a 2010 Act of Parliament seemed to be lost on the House. The reality was better reflected by a statement by one MP that during his 23 years in the House he found that 'whenever the word "terrorism" appears in any order or other legislation, there tends to be cross-party support'.[107]

X. Conclusion

Law-making that is a combination of international and national executive decision-making offends the rule of law in the sense used in this chapter because the executive has been allowed by Parliament and the Courts to by-pass human rights guarantees. The international and national executives have harnessed the supranational potential of the UN so that UK law is subject to the decision-making of the Security Council which, though located within a treaty and therefore a legal instrument, is almost wholly uncontrolled by that instrument or by the judicial

[103] ibid at para 45 (Lord Hope).

[104] See also *Bank Mellat v HM Treasury (No 2)* [2013] UKSC 39, in which the Supreme Court quashed an executive order (SI 2009/2725) made under the Counter-Terrorism Act 2008 against an Iranian Bank pursuant to Security Council Resolutions (UN Doc S/RES/1747 (2006), UN Doc S/RES/1747 (2007) and UN Doc S/RES/1803 (2008)) on the basis, inter alia, it they violated notions of common law fairness.

[105] *Ahmed* above n 54 at para 192.

[106] Hansard HC Debates, cols 691–92, 15 November 2010.

[107] ibid at cols 688–89 (Vaz).

mechanisms created by it, as evidenced by the International Court's judgments in the *Lockerbie* cases. Plato warned that 'where the law is subject to some other authority and has none of its own, the collapse of the state … is not far off'.[108]

Thus far the UK Supreme Court has failed to adopt a strong presumption that human rights obligations should not be overridden by obligations arising under Security Council resolutions, in contrast to European judgments discussed above.[109] Those judgments leave a number of questions unanswered, including the relationship between international, regional and national legal orders, but they do invite the UK to look more closely at ways of upholding its human rights obligations while respecting security duties arising out of Security Council decisions.

The analysis in this chapter has shown that the UN was not simply an improvement on the cooperative model of international organisation embodied in the League of Nations. The UN Charter contained elements of centralisation and supranationality that had the potential, when the geopolitical context allowed, to unleash a federalising international order. In discussing processes of federalisation Livingston warns that centralised instruments created to solve problems become part of the governmental architecture and, furthermore, can easily become outdated and difficult to remove. The idea of a federation of 'Great Powers' in the core membership of the Security Council, including the UK and France, is no longer valid, and the idea of a world government in matters of peace and security in the hands of five states, formed out of the alliance forged in the Second World War, bears little resemblance to the multipolar and changing world in which we live. Livingston states further:

> As the nature of society changes, demands for new kinds of instrumentalities are created and these demands are met by changing or abolishing old instrumentalities and substituting new ones in their place. But it can scarcely be hoped that the new instrumentalities will keep pace with the changing pattern of social relationships, and as a result the pattern of instrumentalities tends to lag behind the changes in society itself … This is complicated further by the fact that the instrumentalities, once put into operation, become rigidified and acquire status of their own.[110]

Hence, what started in 1945 as a new kind of instrumentality, namely an executive instrument for action on matters of international peace and security, has become a centralised governing and law-making body and the pivotal component of a federalising international legal and political order, increasingly encroaching on national legal and political orders, but only possessing the most rudimentary elements of accountability to those national orders. There are examples of states refusing to comply with Security Council sanctions, for example African states with regard to the measures imposed on Libya in 1992 for its alleged support

[108] Plato, *The Laws* (trans TJ Saunders, London, Penguin, 1970) 174.
[109] *Kadi* above n 80, *Al-Jedda* above n 84, *Nada* above n 85, *Al-Dulimi* above n 87.
[110] Livingston above n 2 at 93–94.

of terrorism,[111] but such non-compliance is unlikely in the case of the UK as it is part of the UN executive.

Tushnet, in considering national federal systems, makes the following point:

> Federal systems in the modern world drift towards centralization because of globalization and the dominance of a legal realist legal culture. The rate of drift, however, is affected by elements in the design of federal institutions. A constitutional specification of powers to be exercised solely by national units, *a priori* judicial review, a dual judiciary, and judges trained in formalist traditions all retard the drift towards centralization.[112]

At the international level there is a drift towards centralisation in the Security Council for certain security matters, which can only be countered by states asserting their sovereignty, not to exclude human rights criticism as has occurred in the past, but to protect the human rights they have agreed to uphold. National judiciaries, as well as regional courts, will have to compensate for the International Court of Justice's inherent weaknesses as a court of review, and reliance by courts on agreed human rights norms as opposed to accepting realist arguments based on security, will further limit the drift towards a federalising international order.

In order to nudge security obligations towards rule of law compliance at both international and national levels, UK courts will need to develop a more critical and coherent approach to the obligations arising under the Charter in order to reconcile those obligations with ones arising from human rights and other treaties. Article 103 was not intended, and in any case should not be seen, as a constitutional supremacy clause to be relied upon to make it easier for the Security Council and governments (ie executive powers) to take unconstrained and open-ended security measures; it was intended as a conflicts clause drafted to ensure that states could not refuse to carry out their obligations arising under the Charter by dint of pre-existing and directly conflicting treaty obligations, for example under trade agreements.[113] Furthermore, national Parliaments have to bear a greater burden of scrutiny of processes and legislation that implement these obligations and potentially undermine human rights and civil liberties, since it will only be by a combination of national political and judicial scrutiny that the executive encroachment on basic rights on the grounds of security will be checked.

A largely unchecked amalgam of international and national executives has utilised powers granted in the UN Charter to develop an extremely strong and overriding coercive regime of targeted sanctions, but an extremely weak one in terms of rule of law compliance. In straightforward terms, these 'sanctions' are not imposed in response to breaches of national or international law, but on the

[111] E de Wet, *The Chapter VII Powers of the United Nations Security Council* (Oxford, Hart, 2004) 382.

[112] M Tushnet, 'Federalism and Liberalism' (1996) 4 *Cardozo Journal of International and Comparative Law* 329 at 340.

[113] R Liivoja, 'The Scope of the Supremacy Clause of the United Nations Charter' (2008) 57 *International and Comparative Law Quarterly* 583 at 612.

basis of suspicion of involvement in terrorism. The origins of this regime in the political discretion of the Security Council, where decisions on sanctions are taken largely behind closed doors,[114] signifies that when decisions impact directly and significantly on domestic legal orders and the rights of individuals therein, the result is the creation of federalised security measures that have been permitted by weaknesses in the national constitutional order to erode the rule of law in the UK. The current consensus in the Security Council that has driven this development is, so far, confined to non-forcible measures, but there is always a possibility of its extension to forcible measures. In August 2015, the UK government authorised a drone strike in Syria against an individual belonging to Islamic state, as an act of self-defence of the UK as well as Iraq.[115] Although not authorised by the Security Council, that body took a step in the direction of sanctioning targeted killings when, following terrorist attacks in Paris in November 2015, it adopted what appeared to be a non-binding resolution that called upon states to take 'necessary measures' (Security Council code for the use of force) against Islamic State in Syria and Iraq.[116] This falls short of authorising targeted killings of suspected terrorists, particularly those within the UK, but the fact that it is a step towards the centralised sanctioning of such uses of force illustrates the dangers of an unchecked creeping federalising international order.

[114] D Hovell, 'The Deliberative Deficit: Transparency, Access to Information and UN Sanctions' in J Farrall and K Rubenstein (eds), *Sanctions, Accountability and Governance in a Globalised World* (Cambridge, Cambridge University Press, 2009) 95.

[115] Letter of the UK letter to President of the Security Council, 7 September 2015, UN Doc S/2015/688.

[116] UN Doc S/RES/2249 (2015) op para 5. The Council expressly referred to members of Islamic State listed by the Security Council under its targeted sanctions regime.

Conclusion: We Have Always been Federal

DAVID ARMITAGE

We are all federalists now—or so one might conclude from reading the rich and wide-ranging chapters in this timely volume. Not federalists in the strong sense that every one of the authors, let alone a broad range of publics in Britain, would defend a division of powers and authority between a strong central government and various subsidiary bodies. And not federalists even in the weaker sense of promoting more flexible conceptions of 'self-rule plus shared rule' for the United Kingdom, whether internally or externally.[1] However, we—the contributors to this book, as well as an expanding range of political actors, legal scholars and interested historians—are finally overcoming a very British aversion to imagining federalism as applicable to Britain's past, its present or its future. What had seemed unthinkable is now being widely thought: the book's authors all show that, for Britain at least, federalism is very good to think with. In light of the scholarship on display here, this renewed 'faith in federalism' can hardly be called 'faith without knowledge', as AV Dicey described an earlier moment of British interest in the topic in the 1880s.[2] If even scholars of Britain can embrace federalism in this way, then there is hope for questioning more persistent but historically quite recent conceptions of unitary sovereignty. We might also reimagine sovereignty's presumptive homology with territoriality and question the ingrained teleology of statehood assumed not just by English lawyers but by much of the modern human sciences in the twentieth century. In this sense, we may all be federalists yet.

One great strength of the volume is its remarkable breadth in both space and time. For example, Robert Schütze's chapter takes us back to the eighteenth century, Alvin Jackson and Peter Oliver's essays illuminate colonial and imperial contexts in the nineteenth century and Nigel White traces developments in the international realm to the mid-twentieth century.[3] These and other contributions

[1] Daniel Elazar, *Exploring Federalism* (Tuscaloosa, University of Alabama Press, 1987) 12, quoted in Adam Tomkins, 'Shared Rule: What the UK Could Learn from Federalism', 75 above.

[2] AV Dicey, 'Federal Government' (1885) 1 *Law Quarterly Review* 80. On the broader context of that earlier federal moment, see especially Duncan Bell, *The Idea of Greater Britain: Empire and the Future of World Order, 1860–1900* (Princeton NJ, Princeton University Press, 2007).

[3] Robert Schütze, 'The United Kingdom and the Federal Principle: An Overview', the Introduction above; Alvin Jackson, 'The Failure of British and Irish Federalism, c. 1800–1950', ch 1 above; Peter Oliver, 'Parliamentary Sovereignty, Federalism and the Commonwealth', ch 2 above; Nigel White, 'A Willing International Federalist? The UK's Pivotal Role within the United Nations', ch 10 above.

also link British discussions to a global history of federalism within the English-speaking world, from Canada to Australia, and from the United States to the United Nations, as well as to debates on federalism in Italy and Spain.[4] At its core, any conception of federalism grapples with the problem of shared recognition and authority between large and small communities, in situations of diversity and often combining distinct but overlapping conceptions of political and cultural space. Any treatment of federalism imperatively demands the wide-angle view: this volume amply fulfils that need.

And yet a *longue-durée* view also requires admitting that our contemporary grasp of federalism and its forms barely compares with the historical knowledge possessed by past actors. Earlier students of the subject, such as the eighteenth-century Swiss jurist Emer de Vattel, David Hume or his follower James Madison could conjure with examples of federalism over across almost two millennia, from the Achaean and Amphictyonic Leagues of ancient Greece to the federal and quasi-federal arrangements of early modernity, in Switzerland and the Netherlands.[5] As Vattel wrote in 1758,

> [S]everal sovereign and independent states may unite themselves together by a perpetual confederacy, without ceasing to be, each individually, a perfect state. … Such were formerly the cities of Greece; such are at present the Seven United Provinces of the Netherlands and such the members of the Helvetic body.[6]

Later commentators like Gladstone could add the United States to this roster, along with contemporary states like Austria-Hungary and Canada, which presented more successful models for late nineteenth-century observers after US federalism had survived a near-death experience in 1861–65.[7] Even a thorough-going sceptic about federalism's relevance for Britain such as Dicey drew on this repertoire of past and current examples to inform his own lack of faith in federalism. We are perhaps not as fortunate as these mighty forebears to consider federalism over such great sweeps of time, but this volume will better equip readers to enter present debates with an appropriate arsenal of historical and contemporary instances and counter-examples.

The deep and wide view of federalism reveals it to be less a single concept or unique political or legal structure than a family of ideas and practices that developed and diverged across history and in multiple contexts. Etymology is not destiny but it is salutary to recall that the terms 'federal' and 'federalism'

[4] Barbara Guastaferro and Lucía Payero, 'Devolution and Secession in Comparative Perspective: The Case of Spain and Italy', ch 5 above.

[5] James Madison, 'Notes on Ancient and Modern Confederacies' (1786), in *The Papers of James Madison*, ed Robert A Rutland and William ME Rachal, 17 vols (Chicago, University of Chicago Press, 1962–91) IX 3–23.

[6] Emer de Vattel, *The Law of Nations* or, *Principles of the Law of Nature, Applied to the Conduct and Affairs of Nations and Sovereigns* (1758), ed Béla Kapossy and Richard Whatmore (Indianapolis, Liberty Fund, 2008) 85 (I. i. 10).

[7] On Gladstone, see Jackson, 'The Failure of British and Irish Federalism, c. 1800–1950' 38–39 above.

both derive from the Latin word *foedus*—that is, a covenant, pact or treaty.[8] In English, at least, the word 'federal', or 'foederal[l]', began its lexical career in the early seventeenth century as a theological term denoting the covenantal relations between believers and God; slightly later, it came to cover any relationship based on a formal agreement such as a treaty. The Articles of Confederation for the newly independent United States were just such a 'federal' arrangement; so, too, was the US Constitution designed to replace the Articles, in so far as it was a contractual agreement among states (or their representatives). Only in the closing decades of the eighteenth century, did the adjective 'federal' spawn the nouns 'federalism' and 'federalist' in the context of debates on the ratification of that Constitution.[9]

The concept and practice of federalism long preceded the modern neologism used to describe it.[10] However, in common with many parallel ideas in what the German conceptual historian Reinhart Koselleck called the *Sattelzeit*—the 'saddle-time'—of the late eighteenth and early nineteenth centuries, federalism as a concept became politicised and ideologised and singularised in that moment.[11] What had for centuries been a set of disparate but related practices for dividing and distributing authority now became an identifiably political phenomenon. It also became a subject of ideological contestation. And it emerged as an essentially contestable concept, with distinct and sometimes incompatible meanings that could be deployed strategically in political debate, as it was during the arguments over the ratification of the US Constitution. From this time onwards, federalism had a name but no agreed or stable identity. It could connote either the strength of central government, based on a compact or treaty relationship among sovereign entities (as it did in the US ratification debate), or imply a pluralistic distribution of authority and functions (as it would do mostly outside the United States). With these divergent forms in mind, we should think of federalism not in rigorously normative terms—as a critic like Dicey evidently did—but instead as a suite of ideas or a bundle of overlapping and related concepts that may be recombined but also deconstructed.

Modern federalism emerged in an environment where sovereignties were layered and divided more often than they were exclusive and hard-edged. Early modern Europe and its overseas extensions comprised a congeries of composite monarchies rather than a club of 'Weberian' states, of polities held together by rulers over multiple domains that had been combined through inheritance, conquest,

[8] JGA Pocock, 'States, Republics, and Empires: The American Founding in Early Modern Perspective' in T Ball and JGA Pocock (eds), *Conceptual Change and the Constitution* (Lawrence, Kansas, University Press of Kansas, 1988) 67–72.

[9] David C Hendrickson, *Peace Pact: The Lost World of the American Founding* (Lawrence, University Press of Kansas, 2003); *Oxford English Dictionary*, s.vv. 'federal', 'federalism', 'federalist'.

[10] Murray Forsyth, *Unions of States: The Theory and Practice of Confederation* (London, Leicester University Press, 1981).

[11] On Koselleck, the *Sattelzeit* and its development in his thought, see Niklas Olsen, *History in the Plural: An Introduction to the Work of Reinhart Koselleck* (New York, Berghahn Books, 2012) 171–78.

cession or treaty.[12] Britain itself was a classic example of such a composite state. England's monarchs first conquered Ireland and later incorporated Wales into an Anglo-Welsh union that supplied the Tudor dynasty in the sixteenth century. The royal line passed by inheritance to a Scottish king, leading to a British union of the crowns in 1603 whose destabilising effects would only be settled by a union of parliaments in 1707. This fundamental union was achieved both by act of Parliament within municipal law—formally dissolving both the English and Scottish Parliaments in order to create a British legislature where the English one had formerly stood—and by a treaty between the English sovereign (Queen Anne) and the Scots sovereign (also Queen Anne) under the law of nations. This was both a parliamentary union and, in contemporary terms, a 'federal' union, based on a *foedus*.[13] That federal union endures to this day: even the most hard-nosed Diceyan would have to admit that Britain has been federal in one very basic sense, for more than three centuries under public international law, as a unitary state (or, rather, succession of states) containing a plurality of nations, each with historic or more recently devolved institutions.

Legal pluralism rather than legal uniformity was the norm in the early modern world that gave birth to the British state. Distinct bodies of local, regional and transnational law encouraged eclecticism, forum-shopping and the collision as well as the cross-fertilisation of legal systems. This was especially the case in the extra-European inter-cultural encounters created by the expansion and competition of empires but was not confined to them.[14] Such legal pluralism fed off the division of sovereignty and the distribution of powers among distinct and overlapping agencies, whether within states or among states, trading companies and bodies of indigenous people with whom colonial powers made engagements by treaty. Until well into the nineteenth century, legal theorists from Hugo Grotius to Henry Maine had assumed that sovereignty was divisible not unitary: as Maine argued in 1864,

> [s]overeignty is a term which, in international law, indicates a well-ascertained assemblage of separate powers or privileges ... there is not, nor has there ever been, anything in international law to prevent some of those rights being lodged with one possessor and some with another. Sovereignty has always been regarded as divisible.[15]

[12] HG Koenigsberger, 'Composite States, Representative Institutions and the American Revolution' (1989) 62 *Historical Research* 135–53; JH Elliott, 'A Europe of Composite Monarchies' (1992) 137 *Past and Present* 48–71.

[13] [James Hodges,] *The Rights and Interests of the Two British Monarchies: With a Special Respect to an United or Separate State* (London, 1703) 2–4; TB Smith, 'The Union of 1707 as Fundamental Law' in TB Smith, *Studies Critical and Comparative* (Edinburgh, W Green, 1960) 1–27.

[14] Lauren Benton, *A Search for Sovereignty: Law and Geography in European Empires, 1400–1900* (Cambridge, Cambridge University Press, 2010); Lauren Benton and Richard J Ross (eds), *Legal Pluralism and Empires, 1500–1850* (New York, New York University Press, 2013).

[15] Henry Maine, quoted in Edward Keene, *Beyond the Anarchical Society: Grotius, Colonialism and Order in World Politics* (Cambridge, Cambridge University Press, 2002) 77.

'The powers of sovereigns,' he reaffirmed in 1887, 'are a bundle or collection of powers, and they may be separated one from another.'[16] Maine referred specifically to international law and to forms of sovereignty in North America and South Asia but his generalisations could have been applied illuminatingly across the world, within and between sovereign communities and their neighbours, until at least the age of Dicey. Indeed, by juxtaposing Maine and Dicey on either side of a *debate* over the divisibility of sovereignty we can see it was just that—a debate, not a doctrine, an ideological argument in which it could not be taken for granted that sovereignty was unitary and indivisible. That understanding of sovereignty had to be argued *for*, as Dicey did against more immediate opponents like the Imperial federalists and Irish Home Rulers.[17]

Federalism was merely one species of divisible sovereignty: the question, then, is how did a dogma of *indivisible* sovereignty come to triumph ideologically over alternative conceptions of the distribution of functions, powers and authorities in Britain? Answering that question is beyond the scope of this volume, or this afterword. However, it should alert us to the contingency of assuming that federalism is somehow un-British, or that the aversion to it is a 'neurosis', as David Marquand pungently put it.[18] Barely 50 years ago, to imagine Britain as in any way federal aroused at most a question-mark, as in JC Banks's *Federal Britain?*.[19] Within a quarter of a century, scholars were more confident in excavating a 'British tradition of federalism' and in telling the history of 'federal Britain'.[20] In light of their researches, we can see that we are currently in far from the first federal moment in British history. Our period of debating anew the implications and limitations, the morphology and the genealogy of federalism, is not only not unprecedented; it is but one such moment in a succession of British federal moments, stretching back at least to the Union of 1707 and erupting with some regularity, for example in the 1760s (and the first crises of Atlantic sovereignty), the 1780s (and the federalist moment in the United States), the 1860s (and Irish Home Rule), the 1880s (and the Imperial Federation movement) and onwards to the Second World War with the abortive plan, taken seriously even by Winston Churchill, for a federal union between Britain and France in June 1940, and thence to the era of decolonisation.[21]

[16] Henry Maine, quoted in ibid, 108.

[17] Alvin Jackson, 'The Failure of British and Irish Federalism, c. 1800–1950' ch 1 above; Peter C Oliver, *The Constitution of Independence: The Development of Constitutional Theory in Australia, Canada, and New Zealand* (Oxford, Oxford University Press, 2005) 54–75; Dylan Lino, 'Albert Venn Dicey and the Constitutional Theory of Empire' (2016) 36 *Oxford Journal of Legal Studies* 751–80.

[18] David Marquand, 'Federalism and the British: Anatomy of a Neurosis' (2006) 77 *Political Quarterly* 175–83.

[19] JC Banks, *Federal Britain?* (London, George G Harrap, 1971).

[20] Michael Burgess, *The British Tradition of Federalism* (London, Leicester University Press, 1995); John Kendle, *Federal Britain: A History* (London, Routledge, 1997).

[21] Andrea Bosco, *June 1940, Great Britain and the First Attempt to Build a European Union* (Newcastle upon Tyne, Cambridge Scholars Publishing, 2016); Kendle, above n 20, 123–49.

All these earlier moments showed that federalism was both a flexible means for combining, without dissolving, distinct sovereignties and a feasible alternative to unitary statehood, particularly in the context of decolonisation. Federalism provided an alternative to nationalism and a creative answer to the minority problem of the inter-War period; it offered a potential solution to the problem of protecting the identities of both Jews and Palestinians; it could strengthen smaller states emerging from empire in regions from the West Indies to Southeast Asia; and it could redistribute rather than rupture sovereignty in the transition from empire in French West Africa and the Caribbean.[22] Sovereign statehood was not the necessary endpoint of anti-colonial nationalism.[23] The process of unwinding empire showed that, despite the assumed antipathy to federalism at home, Britain was a willing and enthusiastic promoter of federalism abroad. The presence of monarchy had long facilitated this manoeuvre: from Thomas Jefferson's 'plan for a federal union' of legislatures under the Crown in 1774 via the promise of Dominion status to Canada and Australia through to the looser association of the Commonwealth, allegiance to the Crown offered a guarantee of equality within hierarchy and independence with association.[24] In this regard, federalism was rather like written constitutionalism—good for foreign export, especially to Britain's colonies, but apparently not fit for domestic consumption.[25]

Federalism could thus be the answer to many different questions. Within the context of the British Empire, it could be the solution to the problem of diversity within unity but often within a hierarchical structure under monarchy. After empire, it could offer political and economic cover for newly independent states potentially too small to pull their weight in regional and international orders, or the means to suspend difference in contexts where anti-colonialism empowered multiple communities who could not agree on a single nationalist destiny. And in the context of the British—or, at times, British-and-Irish—state, it presented a third way between domination and subordination on the one hand and absorption and uniformity on the other.

Just how federalism offered solutions to these problems depended on the means of entry into federal arrangements—what kind of negotiations took place, what

[22] Frederick Cooper, *Citizenship Between Empire and Nation: Remaking France and French Africa, 1945–1960* (Princeton NJ, Princeton University Press, 2014); Gary Wilder, *Freedom Time: Negritude, Decolonization, and the Future of the World* (Durham NC, Duke University Press, 2014); Gil Rubin, 'From Federalism to Binationalism: Hannah Arendt's Shifting Zionism' (2015) 24 *Contemporary European History* 393–414; William Selinger, 'The Politics of Arendtian Historiography: European Federation and *The Origins of Totalitarianism*' (2016) 13 *Modern Intellectual History* 417–46.

[23] Manu Goswami, 'Imaginary Futures and Colonial Internationalisms' (2012) 117 *American Historical Review* 1461–85.

[24] Anthony M Lewis, 'Jefferson's *Summary View* as a Chart of Political Union' (1945) 5 *William and Mary Quarterly* 34–51; Alison LaCroix, *The Ideological Origins of American Federalism* (Cambridge MA, Harvard University Press, 2011); Oliver, 'Parliamentary Sovereignty, Federalism and the Commonwealth' ch 2 above; Philip Murphy, *Monarchy and the End of Empire: The House of Windsor, the British Government, and the Post-War Commonwealth* (Oxford, Oxford University Press, 2013).

[25] On the British export of constitutions, see Linda Colley, 'Empires of Writing: Britain, America and Constitutions, 1776–1848' (2014) 32 *Law and History Review* 237–66.

sort of agreements settled which competences. It could also arise from the means of exit from prior structures of power, whether through revolt, secession or act of Parliament, for example. And it would be determined by the relative sizes of the parties entering into federal arrangements: massive inequities, in population, resources or economic power, can stifle federalism, whether as a plan for combining independent sovereignties or as a prospect for redistributing existing authority when one of the parties (for example, a devolved England within a federalised United Kingdom) would greatly outweigh the others (Wales, Scotland, Northern Ireland). Now, at a time when, as Stephen Tierney puts it, 'the internal territorial constitution of the UK is rapidly changing' under the pressures of devolution, 'the federal question can no longer be avoided.'[26] What the answer to that question will be remains uncertain and contested. History can at least give some guidance, by showing how it has been answered in the past.

At the heart of the federal question is the problem of keeping various forms of diversity in suspension. The forms of that diversity have, of course, changed over time. In the nineteenth century, race set the limits of imperial federation: it was only imaginable for 'Anglo-Saxons' within a global community of settler colonial states. Within some, but not all, of those states, federal relations by means of treaties between the settler state and Indigenous peoples cross-cut the demands of shared rule between provinces and central administrations, and between the Dominions and metropolitan Britain. Federal relations determine the dimensions of multiculturalism as well as multinationalism and are, in turn, shaped by the demands of political economy, between the regions of federal states and in their relations with other economies. These latter federal questions are beyond the immediate scope of this volume but they do suggest the range of pressures that federalism has both relieved and exerted, over time and across the British world.

Britain's place in the world is likely to change quite radically in the coming years, with the prospect of its exit from the European Union in March 2019. This moment, concluding the two-year period mandated by Article 50 of the Lisbon Treaty, marks a 'foederal' cure (in the eyes of supporters of Brexit) for a 'federal' disease—the invocation of treaty rights against any further sharing of sovereignty. At the time of writing, none of the authors can foresee what form Brexit will take, what new relationships—with the EU or other international actors—Britain will forge after that moment, or what effect this will have on the composition of the United Kingdom. For the moment, at least, the shock of Brexit seems to have halted moves towards Scottish independence, whether temporarily or in the longer term it is not yet possible to say. The prospect of reconstructing a land border between the Republic of Ireland and Northern Ireland is the thorniest territorial problem arising from Brexit, with implications not just for Anglo-Irish trade but also for the Good Friday Agreement and the possibilities of reunification

[26] Stephen Tierney, 'Drifting Towards Federalism? Appraising the Constitution in Light of the Scotland Act 2016' 101 above.

on the island of Ireland. What supporters of Brexit termed 'taking back control'—allegedly from institutions outside Britain, presumably in favour of the legislative supremacy of Parliament and the primacy of British courts—has, so far, led only to fears of executive overreach and an unresolved collision between the will of the people (expressed in a non-binding, advisory referendum) and Parliamentary sovereignty. How this tangle of Gordian knots will be cut, and what might be the unintended consequences arising from such perilous procedures, we will discover in the coming years.

What seems clear, nonetheless, is that we need to be forearmed with creative solutions to the problems exposed by the 2016 referendum and those already evident in the aftermath of triggering Article 50. How will the British union state resist the pressure to devolve power in more radical ways after Brexit, perhaps with a solution to the 'West Lothian question' leading to greater autonomy for England, the heartland of support for Brexit, with or without London, one of the democratic bulwarks against it? Does the return of a hard border in Ireland make more elaborate sharing of functions more plausible, or does the reversion of part of the island to third-country status vis-à-vis the European Union foreclose that option? Will gradual disengagement from the European Court of Justice lead to greater judicial independence or the likelihood of more vigorous judicial review, that great mark of federalism for Dicey and other critics? And where will all this leave the European Court of Human Rights, the product 'not of a national constitution' but of a concordat long prior to the European Union and spearheaded by Britain?[27] It is too soon to tell. Federalism would certainly 'institutionalise power-sharing across the board', as Jo Murkens notes, particularly within what Nigel White calls 'a federalising international order'.[28] With the variety of deep and wide perspectives presented in this collection, there is much less danger of simply 'drifting towards federalism', as Stephen Tierney puts it. With our eyes open to the possibilities, we may become federalists again—as, indeed, we have long been.

[27] Roger Masterman, 'Federal Dynamics of the UK/Strasbourg Relationship' 211 above; Marco Duranti, *The Conservative Human Rights Revolution: European Identity, Transnational Politics, and the Origins of the European Convention* (Oxford, Oxford University Press, 2017).

[28] Jo Eric Khushal Murkens, 'The UK's Reluctant Relationship with the EU: Integration, Equivocation, or Disintegration?' 172 above; Nigel D White, 'A Willing International Federalist: The UK's Pivotal Role in the United Nations' 252 above.

SELECT BIBLIOGRAPHY

Adams, RG, *Political Ideas of the American Revolution: Britannic-American Contribution to the Problem of Imperial Organisation* (Dublin, Trinity College Press, 1922)

Adler Nissen, R, *Opting Out of the European Union: Diplomacy, Sovereignty and European Integration* (Cambridge, Cambridge University Press, 2015)

Agranoff, R and Ramos-Gallarín, JA, 'Toward Federal Democracy in Spain: An Examination of Intergovernmental Relations' (1997) 27 *Publius* 1

Antonetti, N and De Siervo, U (eds), *Ambrosini e Sturzo. La nascita delle regioni* (Bologna, Il Mulino, 1998)

Aroney, N, *The Constitution of a Federal Commonwealth: The Making and Meaning of the Australian Constitution* (Cambridge, Cambridge University Press, 2009)

Banks, JC, *Federal Britain?* (London, George G Harrap, 1971)

Barnes, J, *Federal Britain: no longer unthinkable?* (London, Centre for Policy Studies, 1998)

Bates, E, *The Evolution of the European Convention on Human Rights: From its Inception to the Creation of a Permanent Court of Human Rights* (Oxford, Oxford University Press, 2010)

Beaud, O, *Théorie de la Fédération* (Paris, PUF, 2007)

Bell, D, *The Idea of Greater Britain: Empire and the Future of World Order, 1860–1900* (Princeton NJ, Princeton University Press, 2007)

Benton, L and Ross, RJ (eds), *Legal Pluralism and Empires, 1500–1850* (New York, New York University Press, 2013)

Bogdanor, V, *Devolution in the UK* (Oxford, Oxford University Press, 2001)

—— *The New British Constitution* (Oxford, Hart Publishing, 2009)

Brazier, R, 'The Constitution of the United Kingdom' (1999) 58 *Cambridge Law Journal* 96

Brown, J, 'The Australian Commonwealth Bill' (1900) 61 *LQR* 24

Bryce, J, 'The Action of Centripetal and Centrifugal Forces on Political Constitutions' in J Bryce, *Studies in History and Jurisprudence*, vol 1 (Oxford, Clarendon Press, 1901)

—— *The American Commonwealth* (London, Macmillan, 1888)

Bühler, K, *State Succession and Membership in International Organizations* (The Hague, Kluwer, 2001)

Burgess, M, *Comparative Federalism: Theory and Practice* (London, Routledge, 2006)

—— *Federalism and the European Union: the Building of Europe, 1950–2000* (London, Routledge, 2000)

—— *The British Tradition of Federalism* (London, Leicester University Press, 1995)

Burrows, N, *Devolution* (London, Sweet & Maxwell, 2000)

Butt, I, *Home Government for Ireland: Irish federalism! Its meaning, its objects and its hopes* (Dublin, Falconer, 1870)

Camps, M, *Britain and the European Community: 1955–1963* (Princeton, Princeton University Press, 1964)

Colino, C, 'Constitutional Change without Constitutional Reform: Spanish Federalism and the Revision of Catalonia's Statute of Autonomy' (2009) 39 *Publius: The Journal of Federalism* 262

Craig, P, 'Constitutionalising Constitutional Law: HS2' (2014) *Public Law* 373

—— 'Sovereignty of the United Kingdom Parliament after Factortame' (1991) 11 *Yearbook of European Law* 221

Curtin, D, 'The Constitutional Structure of the Union: A Europe of Bits and Pieces' (1993) 30 (1) *Common Market Law Review* 17

Davis, SR, *The Federal Principle: A Journey through Time in Quest of a Meaning* (Berkeley, University of California Press, 1978)

Defoe, D, *History of the Union between England and Scotland* (London, Stockdale, 1786)

Dicey, AV, 'Federal Government' (1885) 1 *Law Quarterly Review* 80

—— *England's case against Home Rule*, 3rd edn (London, 1887)

—— *An Introduction to the Study of the Law of the Constitution* 8th edn reprint (Indianapolis, Liberty Fund, 1982)

Dicey, AV and Rait, RS, *Thoughts on the Union between England & Scotland* (London, Macmillan, 1920)

Douglas-Scott, S, 'Brexit, Article 50 and the Contested British Constitution' (2016) 79 *MLR* 1019

Duncan Hall, H, *Commonwealth: A History of the British Commonwealth of Nations* (New York, Von Nostrand Reinhold, 1971)

Elazar, D, *Exploring Federalism* (Tuscaloose, University of Alabama Press, 1987)

—— *Federal Systems of the World: A Handbook of Federal, Confederal and Autonomy Arrangements* (Harlow, Longman, 1994)

Ferguson, W, *Scotland's Relations with England: A Survey to 1707* (Edinburgh, Donald Publishers, 1977)

Fletcher of Saltoun, A 'State of the Controversy betwixt United and Separate Parliaments' (1706—reprinted for the Saltire Society by Blackwood Publishing, 1982)

Garside, P and Hebbert, M (eds), *British Regionalism 1900–2000* (London, Mansell Publishing 1989)

George, S, *An Awkward Partner: Britain in the European Community* (Oxford, Oxford University Press, 1994)

Goldsworthy, J, *Sovereignty of Parliament: History and Philosophy* (Oxford, Oxford University Press, 2001)

Goodwin, GL, *Britain and the United Nations* (Oxford, Oxford University Press, 1957)

Greer, S, *The European Convention on Human Rights: Achievements, Problems and Prospects* (Cambridge, Cambridge University Press, 2006)

Hadfield, B, 'Devolution, Westminster and the English Question' (2005) *Public Law* 286

Hallstein, W, *Der unvollendete Bundesstaat* (Dusseldorf/Wien, Econ, 1969)

Hazel, R (ed), *The English Question* (Manchester, Manchester University Press, 2006)

Hicks, U, *Federalism, Failure and Success: A Comparative Study* (London, Palgrave Macmillan, 1978)

Howe, G, 'Sovereignty and Interdependence: Britain's Place in the World' (1990) 66(4) *International Affairs* 675

Hudson, WJ and Sharp, MP, *Australian Independence: Colony to Reluctant Kingdom* (Melbourne, Melbourne University Press, 1988)

Jackson, A, *Home Rule: An Irish History* (Oxford, Oxford University Press, 2004)

—— *The Two Unions: Ireland, Scotland and the Survival of the United Kingdom, 1707–2007* (Oxford, Oxford University Press, 2012)
Jennings, I, *Constitutional Laws of the Commonwealth* (Oxford, Clarendon Press, 1952)
—— *The British Constitution* (Cambridge, Cambridge University Press, 1966)
Kant, I, 'Perpetual Peace: A Philosophical Sketch' in H Reiss (ed) *Kant's Political Writings* (Cambridge, Cambridge University Press, 1970), 93
Keith, AB, *Responsible Government in the Dominions* (Oxford, Oxford University Press, 1928)
—— *The Governments of the British Empire* (London, Macmillan, 1936)
Kendle, J, *Federal Britain: A History* (London, Routledge, 1997)
—— *Ireland and the Federal Solution: the Debate over the United Kingdom Constitution, 1870–1921* (Kingston and Montreal, McGill-Queen's University Press, 1989)
Kennedy, P, *The Parliament of Man: The Past, Present and Future of the United Nations* (London, HarperCollins, 2006)
Lefroy, HF, 'The Commonwealth of Australia Bill' (1st Article) (1899) 58 *LQR* 155; and (Second Article) (1899) 59 *LQR* 281
—— *Canada's Federal System* (Toronto, Carswell, 1913)
Lenaerts, K, 'Constitutionalism and The Many Faces of Federalism' (1990) 38 *American Journal of Comparative Law* 205
Liivoja, R, 'The Scope of the Supremacy Clause of the United Nations Charter' (2008) 57 *ICLQ* 583
Livingston Schuyler, R, *Parliament and the British Empire* (New York, Columbia University Press, 1929)
Livingston, WS, *Federalism and Constitutional Change* (Oxford, Clarendon Press, 1956)
MacCormick, N, 'Beyond the Sovereign State' (1993) 56 *MLR* 1
—— *Questioning Sovereignty. Law, State and Nation in the European Commonwealth* (Oxford, Oxford University Press, 1999)
Madden, F and Fieldhouse, D, *The Classic Period of the First British Empire, 1689–1783* (Westport CT, Greenwood Press, 1985)
Madison, J (et al), *The Federalist* (Cambridge, Cambridge University Press, 2003)
Maitland, FM, *The Constitutional History of England* (Cambridge University Press, 1908)
Marquand, D, 'Federalism and the British: Anatomy of a Neurosis' (2006) 77 *The Political Quarterly* 175
Masterman, R and Murkens, JEK, 'Skirting Supremacy and Subordination: the constitutional authority of the United Kingdom Supreme Court' (2013) *Public Law* 800
Masterman, R, 'Taking the Strasbourg Jurisprudence into Account: Developing a "Municipal Law of Human Rights" under the Human Rights Act' (2005) 54 *International and Comparative Law Quarterly* 907
Mazower, M, *No Enchanted Palace: The End of Empire and the Ideological Origins of the United Nations* (Princeton University Press 2009)
McCrudden, C, 'Northern Ireland' in J Jowell and D Oliver (eds), *The Changing Constitution* (Oxford, Oxford University Press, 2004), 195
Michelmann, H, Soldatos, P (eds), *Federalism and International Relations, the Role of Subnational Units* (Oxford, Oxford University Press, 1990)
Mitchell, JDB, 'Sovereignty of Parliament—Yet Again' (1963) 79 *Law Quarterly Review* 196

—— 'The Westminster Model and the State of Unions' (2010) 63(1) *Parliamentary Affairs* 85

Moore, HW, *Constitution of the Commonwealth of Australia* (London, John Murray, 1902)

Murray, F, *Unions of States: The Theory and Practice of Confederation* (London, Leicester University Press, 1981)

Nicol, D, 'Lessons from Luxembourg: Federalisation and the Court of Human Rights' (2001) 26 *EL Rev HR* 3

O'Day, A, *Irish Home Rule 1867–1921* (Manchester, Manchester University Press, 1998)

Oliver, PC, *The Constitution of Independence: The Development of Constitutional Theory in Australia, Canada, and New Zealand* (Oxford, Oxford University Press, 2005)

Peatling, GK, *British Opinion and Irish Self-government, 1865–1921: from Unionism to Liberal Commonwealth* (Dublin, Irish Academic Press, 2001)

Pescatore, P, *The Law of Integration: Emergence of a new Phenomenon in International Relations, based on the Experience of the European Communities* (Sijthoff, Springer, 1974)

Riker, W, *Federalism: Origin, Operation, Significance* (Oxford, Oxford University Press, 1964)

Robertson, J (ed), *A Union for Empire: Political thought and the British Union of 1707* (Cambridge, Cambridge University Press, 1995)

Saul, M, 'The European Court of Human Rights' Margin of Appreciation and the Processes of National Parliaments' (2015) *Human Rights Law Review* 1

Schütze, R, *European Constitutional Law* (Cambridge, Cambridge University Press, 2015)

—— *From Dual to Cooperative Federalism: The Changing Structure of European Law* (Oxford, Oxford University Press, 2009)

Scott, PP, *1707: The Union of Scotland and England* (Edinburgh, Saltire Society, 1979)

Seeley, JR, *The Expansion of England* (London, 1883)

Smith, TB, 'The Union of 1707 as Fundamental Law' in TB Smith, *Studies Critical and Comparative* (Edinburgh, W Green, 1960)

St J Barclay, G, *Commonwealth or Europe* (Brisbane, University of Queensland Press, 1970)

Tierney, S, *Constitutional Law and National Pluralism* (Oxford, Oxford University Press, 2006)

—— 'Federalism in a Unitary State: A Paradox too Far?' (2009) *Regional and Federal Studies* 237

Tomkins, A, *Public Law* (Oxford, Oxford University Press, 2003)

Tully, J, *Strange Multiplicity: Constitutionalism in an Age of Diversity* (Cambridge, Cambridge University Press, 1995)

Tuytschaever, F, *Differentiation in European Law* (Oxford, Hart, 1999)

Von Bogdandy, A and Venzke, I, 'In whose Name? An Investigation of International Courts' Public Authority and its Democratic Justification' (2012) *European Journal of International Law* 7

Wade, HWR, 'Sovereignty—Revolution or Evolution?' (1996) 112 *Law Quarterly Review* 568

Walker, N, 'Beyond the Unitary Conception of the United Kingdom Constitution' (2000) *Public Law* 384

—— 'Sovereignty and Differentiated Integration of the European Union' in Z Bankowski and A Scott (eds), *The European Union and its Legal Order* (Oxford, Blackwell, 2000), 31

Warbrick, C, '"Federal" Aspects of the European Convention on Human Rights' (1989) 10 *Michigan Journal of International Law* 698

Watts, RL, *Comparing Federal Systems in the 1990s* (Montreal and Kingston, McGill-Queen's University Press, 1999)

Wheare, KC, *Federal Government* (Oxford, Oxford University Press, 1963)

White, ND, *Keeping the Peace: The United Nations and the Maintenance of International Peace and Security* (Manchester, Manchester University Press, 1997)

Wicks, E, 'A New Constitution for a New State? The 1707 Union of England and Scotland' (2001) 117 *Law Quarterly Review* 109

INDEX

www.ingramcontent.com/pod-product-compliance
Ingram Content Group UK Ltd.
Pitfield, Milton Keynes, MK11 3LW, UK
UKHW020219041026
15470UKWH00012B/642

9 781509 907175